# Because of Our Success

# Because of Our Success

## The Changing Racial and Ethnic Ancestry of Blacks on Affirmative Action

### Kevin D. Brown

RICHARD S. MELVIN PROFESSOR OF LAW
INDIANA UNIVERSITY MAURER SCHOOL OF LAW

Carolina Academic Press
Durham, North Carolina

Copyright © 2014
Kevin D. Brown
All Rights Reserved

Brown, Kevin Dion.
  Because of our success : the changing racial and ethnic ancestry of Blacks on affirmative action / Kevin Brown.
      pages cm
  Includes bibliographical references and index.
  ISBN 978-1-61163-444-0 (alk. paper)
  1. Affirmative action programs in education--United States. 2. Racially mixed people--United States. 3. United States--Race relations. 4. Social justice--United States. I. Title.

LC213.52.B76 2014
379.2'6--dc23

2014024226

Carolina Academic Press
700 Kent Street
Durham, North Carolina 27701
Telephone (919) 489-7486
Fax (919) 493-5668
www.cap-press.com

Printed in the United States of America

# Contents

| | |
|---|---|
| Foreword by Theodore M. Shaw | xiii |
| Foreword by Dennis J. Shields | xix |
| Preface | xxv |
| Acknowledgments | xxix |

| | | |
|---|---|---|
| Introduction | | 3 |
| I. | Changes in the Racial and Ethnic Ancestry of Blacks Since the Origin of Affirmative Action Admissions Policies | 3 |
| II. | Disproportionate Numbers of Black Multiracials and Black Immigrants Attending Selective Higher Education Institutions | 7 |
| III. | What Stands to Be Lost by the Ethnic Cleansing of Ascendant Blacks from the Campuses of Selective Higher Education Programs | 10 |
| IV. | Discussing the Virtual Elimination of Ascendant Blacks Demonstrates the Weakening Power of Racism | 17 |
| V. | Suggested Changes in the Admissions Process | 19 |
| VI. | Limitations on the Scope of This Book | 26 |
| VII. | Chapter Summaries | 27 |
| | Chapter One | 27 |
| | Chapter Two | 28 |
| | Chapter Three | 29 |
| | Chapter Four | 30 |
| | Chapter Five | 31 |
| Chapter One · Historical Development of Federal Racial and Ethnic Classifications in Education | | 33 |
| I. | History of the Federal Government's Use of Racial and Ethnic Classifications Until the 1970s | 37 |
| | A. Use of Racial Classifications for Census Purposes from 1790 to 1840 | 38 |
| | B. Efforts to Separate Mixed-Race Blacks: 1850 to 1920 | 39 |

v

|  | C. One-Drop Rule Becomes Official and Census Moves to Self-Reporting Forms: 1930 to 1970 | 40 |
|---|---|---|
|  | D. Hispanics/Latinos and the Census | 41 |
| II. | Efforts to Standardize the Collection of Data on Race and Ethnicity in the 1970s: Adoption of Directive 15 | 43 |
| III. | Adoption of the 1997 Revisions | 48 |
|  | A. Need to Revise Directive 15 | 48 |
|  | B. 1997 Revisions | 50 |
|  |    1. Hispanic/Latino Ethnicity Question and the Two-Question Format | 50 |
|  |    2. How to Collect Data on Individuals of Multiple Racial Heritage | 51 |
|  |    3. Modifications for the Racial Categories | 52 |
|  | C. Results of the 2000 and 2010 Censuses | 53 |
| IV. | The Final Guidance | 55 |
|  | A. Adoption of the EEOC Revisions | 56 |
|  | B. The Final Guidance Procedures for Collecting and Reporting Racial and Ethnic Data to the Department of Education | 58 |
|  | C. Impact of the Final Guidance on Admissions Prospects of Black Hispanics and Blacks with Two or More Races | 60 |
|  | D. The Final Guidance Was Not Meant to Address Black Immigrants | 62 |
| Conclusion | | 63 |

| **Chapter Two · The Two Aspects of the History of the Black Experience** | | **65** |
|---|---|---|
| I. | The Traditional View of the African American Experience of Being Raced | 68 |
|  | A. Treatment of Blacks during the Colonial and Antebellum Eras | 70 |
|  |    1. Origins of Slavery | 70 |
|  |    2. Slavery in the South | 71 |
|  |    3. Conditions of Blacks in the North during the Antebellum Period | 73 |
|  | B. From the Civil War until the Disenfranchisement of Black Males | 76 |
|  | C. The Rise of Segregation | 80 |
|  | D. Desegregation Era | 83 |
|  |    1. Rationales Justifying the Oppression of Blacks | 83 |

|  |  |  |
|---|---|---|
|  | 2. Emergence of Expert Opinion that Racial Differences Result Primarily from Socioenvironmental Conditions | 86 |
|  | 3. Desegregation of American Society | 88 |
|  | E. Post-Racial/Colorblind Era | 90 |
| II. | Race as the Characteristic that Bound Black People Together in a Collective Struggle Against Their Oppression | 96 |
|  | A. Resistance to Slavery During the Colonial and Antebellum Eras | 98 |
|  | 1. Violent Resistance to Captivity by Black Freedom Fighters | 99 |
|  | 2. Self-Liberation | 102 |
|  | 3. Involvement in Abolition Movements | 104 |
|  | 4. Day-to-Day Resistance to Slavery | 106 |
|  | B. Liberation Efforts During the Civil War and Reconstruction | 108 |
|  | 1. Black Liberation Efforts During the Civil War | 108 |
|  | 2. Advocating for Civil and Political Rights | 111 |
|  | 3. Failure to Receive Land | 113 |
|  | C. Struggle against Racial Oppression in the Form of Segregation | 114 |
|  | 1. The Black Church | 115 |
|  | 2. Education | 116 |
|  | 3. Emigration Movements | 120 |
|  | 4. Business, Professional, and Civil Rights Organizations | 121 |
|  | 5. Involvement in Civil Rights Organizations and Protest Movements | 124 |
|  | 6. Conclusion | 127 |
|  | D. Liberation Efforts during the Desegregation Era | 127 |
|  | E. Continued Struggle in the Post-Racial/Colorblind Era | 132 |
|  | Conclusion | 139 |
| **Chapter Three · Black Multiracials: Why They Should Not Be Preferred over Ascendant Blacks** |  | **141** |
| I. | Increasing Interracial Sexual Relationships and Black Multiracials since the Institution of Affirmative Action | 147 |
|  | A. Increasing Acceptance and Number of Interracial Sexual Relationships | 148 |
|  | B. Increasing Numbers of Black Multiracials | 150 |

|     |     |     |
| --- | --- | --- |
|     | C. Evidence of Overrepresentation of Black Multiracials Attending Selective Higher Education Institutions | 150 |
|     | D. Parental Educational Levels and Higher Family Incomes Explain Part of the Overrepresentation of Black Multiracials | 153 |
|     |    1. Black Multiracials Tend to Have Parents with Higher Levels of Academic Achievement | 154 |
|     |    2. Black Multiracials Tend to Come from Families with More Income | 155 |
| II. | History of Antimiscegenation Measures and the Treatment of Mixed-Race Blacks during the Colonial and Antebellum Eras | 156 |
|     | A. Antimiscegenation Measures and the Treatment of Mixed-Race Blacks in the Upper South and North | 157 |
|     | B. Status of Mulattoes in the Lower South during the Antebellum Era | 161 |
|     |    1. Charleston, South Carolina | 161 |
|     |    2. New Orleans, Louisiana | 163 |
|     |    3. Mobile, Alabama | 164 |
| III. | The Rise of the One-Drop Rule | 165 |
|     | A. The Rise of Scientific Concerns about the Nature of Mulattoes | 166 |
|     | B. The Validity of Antimiscegenation Measures in Light of Major Legal Changes during Reconstruction | 169 |
|     | C. The Rise of the One-Drop Rule: Scientific Concerns about Miscegenation after Abolition and the Civil War | 171 |
|     | D. The Marginal Man Hypothesis: Mixed-Race Blacks Encouraged to Identify with Only Their African Ancestry | 176 |
| IV. | The Demise of the One-Drop Rule and the Rise of Black Multiracials | 177 |
|     | A. The Supreme Court Strikes Down Antimiscegenation Statutes | 178 |
|     | B. The Rise of the Multiracial Movement | 180 |
|     | C. The Federal Government's Move to Self-Identification of Race | 183 |
|     | D. Immigration Has Changed the Face and Complexion of American Society | 184 |
| V. | Why Ascendant Blacks Should Receive More Positive Consideration in the Admissions Process | 185 |

    A. The Ancestry of Black Multiracials Means That They
       Have Fewer Experiences Than Ascendant Blacks     186
    B. Research on the Racial Identity Formation of
       Black Multiracials Suggests They Are Less Likely
       to Identify Only as Black     186
    C. Many Black Multiracials Grow Up in Households
       without any Blacks     188
    D. Black Multiracials May Also Have Divided Loyalties     189
    E. Conclusion     189
Conclusion     190

**Chapter Four · Black Immigrants: Why They Should Not Be Preferred over Ascendant Blacks**     193

I. Increasing Numbers of Black Immigrants since the Institution of Affirmative Action     195
    A. Increasing Numbers of Foreign-Born Blacks     196
    B. Evidence of Overrepresentation of Black Immigrants Attending Selective Higher Education Institutions     197
    C. Why Black Immigrants Perform Better Academically than Ascendant Blacks     199
       1. Black Immigrants Tend to Have Parents with Higher Levels of Academic Attainment     200
       2. Black Immigrants Tend to Come from Families with More Income     201
       3. Children of Foreign-Born Blacks Are More Likely to Grow up with Two Parents     201
II. History of Black Migration Before the Adoption of Affirmative Action Policies     202
    A. Black Migration Before the Abolition of Slavery     202
    B. Black Immigration from the Abolition of Slavery to the Immigration Reforms of the 1920s     203
    C. Restrictive Immigration Reforms and Black Immigration after the 1920s     205
III. Modern Wave of Black Migration     207
    A. International Conditions that Contributed to the Modern Wave of Black Immigration into the United States     208
       1. Restrictive Immigration Measures Enacted in Europe, Especially in the United Kingdom     208
       2. Causes of Caribbean Immigration to the United States     212

      3. Causes of African Immigration to the United States    213
   B. Changes in U.S. Immigration Law Starting with the
      Passage of the Hart-Cellar Act    214
   C. Specific Changes to U.S. Immigration Law that
      Benefitted Black Immigration    215
 IV. Why Ascendant Blacks Should Receive More Positive
    Consideration in the Admissions Process of Selective
    Higher Education Institutions    216
   A. Sociocultural Differences Between Adult Black Immigrants
      and Ascendant Blacks    217
     1. Adult Black Immigrants Occupy a Unique
        Sociocultural Status    219
     2. Foreign-Born Blacks Tend to Have a More
        Optimistic Outlook    221
     3. Foreign-Born Blacks Have a Less Oppositional
        Culture than Native-Born Blacks    224
     4. Race Is Not as Salient a Feature of the Experience
        of Foreign-Born Blacks as It Is for Native-Born Blacks    225
     5. Foreign-Born Blacks are Used to Seeing Blacks Occupy
        All Positions in the Socioeconomic Order    226
     6. The Reasons Foreign-Born Blacks Come to the
        United States Militates against Experiences
        Related to the History of Discrimination    227
   B. Differences between Next-Generation Black Immigrants
      and Ascendant Blacks    228
 Conclusion    232

**Chapter Five · Proposal for Changes in the Admissions Process**    233
  I. Changes to Admissions Forms    235
 II. The Proposal's Hybrid Approach to Positive Consideration
    in the Admissions Process    239
III. How the Proposal Applies to Various
    Black Racial/Ethnic Groups    241
   A. Implications for the Admissions Prospects of
      Black Hispanic Applicants    242
   B. Implications for the Admissions Prospects of
      Blacks with Two or More Races    243
   C. Implications for the Admissions Prospects of
      Black Immigrant Applicants    246

    D. Implications for the Admissions Prospects of
        Ascendant Black Applicants                      247
    Conclusion: Limitations of the Proposal            248

**Conclusion**                                                                    251
**Endnotes**                                                                       255
**Bibliography**                                                              317
**Index**                                                                               351

# Foreword by Theodore M. Shaw

In recent years some observers have come to a growing awareness that the demographics of black enrollment in higher education have changed. Always modest in numbers, increasingly, black students at selective institutions of higher education, including graduate and professional schools, now come from first or second-generation immigrant families from the Caribbean or from Africa. Harvard's Lani Guinier and Henry Louis Gates are two of the better known members of the academy to publically acknowledge this phenomenon, but others have began to research and write about it. Now Professor Kevin Brown, of Indiana University's Maurer School of Law, has written the most densely and comprehensively researched analysis of this phenomenon. In the course of doing so Prof. Brown, who has extensively and insightfully researched and written about race and law for many years, unpacks the complex, sometimes absurd, and yet undeniably and powerfully real and continuing significance of race we have collectively inherited and constructed.

Black America has always been internally diverse, even though this internal diversity was obscured and eclipsed by our Nation's preoccupation with race and the subordination of people of color in the service of white supremacy. Indeed, differences have long existed between "West Indians" and descendants of the U.S. intergenerational slavery to Jim Crow experience. The former, in spite of their own histories of slavery, racism and subordination, have often occupied different places on the ladder to educational and economic success. African Americans, in turn, sometimes perceived "West Indians" to be condescending as a consequence of their relative educational and economic success. Yet the two communities never maintained complete separation. Socialization, intermarriage, a shared understanding of their place in the African diaspora and their common struggle bound and blended these communities over time. Yet newer generations of Caribbean immigrants continue to stand apart to some degree, and, as is generally true for immigrant communities, some achieve elevated levels of success. Ideologically and politically progressive African Americans have welcomed ties with other members of the African diaspora, and may be uncertain and hesitant to talk about this phenomenon. But these difficulties disappear if one is clear about what is at issue. I, for one, am pleased to see the sons and daughters of Caribbean and African immigrants enrolled in selective American institutions of higher education. The concern is not about who is enrolled at these institutions; the concern is about who, increasingly, is not enrolled. African Americans who are descended from the intergenerational slavery-to-Jim Crow continuum are increasingly absent, especially black males.

Similarly, in recent decades African immigrants have come to the United States in greater numbers, and African students have pursued higher education at American universities in much the same way as have other foreign nationals. Immigrant black families may, and do, bring much to American colleges and universities, including their own perspectives as individuals, sometimes from communities and countries that have been impacted by racism, colonization, and other experiences, collective and individual. These experiences and perspectives may be considered in admissions under prevailing Supreme Court precedent. Or it may be that these students are being admitted much as any others, without race as a factor. Colleges and universities are effectively prohibited, however, from considering the most powerful and the original rationale for consciously engaging in efforts to admit African Americans from the U.S. slavery-to-Jim Crow continuum: remedial efforts to undo entrenched and systemic inequality of opportunity traceable to our Nation's long history of subordination of black Americans in the service of white supremacy.

The great irony is that affirmative action began as a remedial imperative, in the 1960s, in the wake of the Civil Rights and Black Power Movements. Yet in 1978, barely a decade after this imperative began in earnest, the U.S. Supreme Court decided *Regents of the University of California v. Bakke*. In *Bakke*, Justice Lewis Powell wrote an opinion bridging a Court deeply divided on the issue of whether the Constitution allowed public institutions of higher education to consider race in admissions to selective colleges and universities. Alan Bakke, an unsuccessful thirty-seven year old white applicant to the University of California at Davis Medical School, sued the Regents alleging discrimination on the basis of race, arguing that an affirmative action program designed to produce more minority doctors violated his rights under the Fourteenth Amendment. Four justices would have allowed the Medical School to consider race by applying a more lenient equal protection standard based upon its benign intent, i.e., the laudable goal of integrating the medical school and the medical profession. Four other justices believed that "benign discrimination" should be judged under the same standard as invidious discrimination motivated by the belief that individuals were inferior or superior on the basis of race. By a narrow majority the Court declined to apply a different standard of review to challenges to race conscious affirmative action aimed at opening opportunities to African Americans, Latinos, and others who historically had been excluded from, and who remained underrepresented at, selective institutions of higher education. For civil rights advocates this and other aspects of the *Bakke* decision was a crushing blow. The silver lining in *Bakke* was Justice Powell's opinion, which found that colleges and universities had a First Amendment based academic freedom interest in diverse student enrollment, which justified limited consideration of race as one factor among many in admissions. While at the time it was unclear how much water *Bakke* could carry in the effort to enroll minority students, it became clear over time that colleges and universities could admit modestly significant numbers of students of color to their incoming classes under the banner of diversity.

Efforts to increase the number of black students, and by extension, other students of color, at selective institutions of higher education began as a remedial, not a diversity, imperative. The driving rationale was rooted in the need to address the exclusion from opportunity experienced by black Americans as a consequence of the slavery-to-Jim Crow continuum. The remedial imperative was attacked as soon as it was initiated, and whatever its merits, *Bakke* narrowly limited its reach and applicability, and thereby signaled its demise. The diversity rationale, however, had far reaching potential, theoretically touching all aspects of a student's identity and experiences. By grounding affirmative action efforts in universities' interest in enrolling students of different backgrounds because of the educational value of diversity, the *Bakke* Court theoretically circumvented the still smoldering issues of America's history of racial discrimination, and substituted universal interests for remedial claims on behalf of the Nation's most disfavored minority group. Past discrimination and contemporary inequality was arguably no longer the touchstone for consideration of race in college admissions. If *Bakke* sanctioned diversity as a compelling state interest, allowing consideration of race as one factor among others, diversity-writ-large extends far beyond race or the interests and experiences of members of minority groups once excluded from higher education. In other words, after *Bakke*, diversity transcended but included race. Still, diversity remained a lightening rod for conservatives who equated affirmative action with "reverse discrimination." To be sure, the focus has not been on diversity writ large; to counter the effects of underperformance of males that leads to more qualified women applicants for admissions to many colleges and universities, gender based affirmative action on behalf of (white) males has been quietly implemented without so much as a peep, and a growing chorus is now pushing, appropriately, for conscious efforts to admit students from poor and working class families to elite selective colleges and universities. The heat, manifested in a series of cases in federal courts over the last four decades, has almost exclusively concerned efforts to admit African American students. The growing irony, emerging in recent years, is that in spite of the continuing assault on affirmative action/diversity, the original intended beneficiaries of affirmative action are increasingly missing at the most selective institutions. Black students are being admitted, but increasingly they are not the descendants of the U.S. intergenerational experience of slavery and Jim Crow.

It's complicated.

Professor Brown's thoughtful and scholarly study comprehensively analyzes a complex subject with variables that are widely misunderstood or ignored. It sets out to navigate sensitive and difficult terrain, noting distinctions between "Ascendant Blacks," "Black Multiracials," and "Black Immigrants." These categories provide imperfect but useful groupings that reflect varying experiences which usually fall under the umbrella of "black"-ness or African American identification. Race has always been a social construct, and its meaning in the early twenty-first century is shifting and changing as members of American society continue to redefine their identities. The intergenerational experiences of African American families descended from slavery and Jim Crow (Brown's "Ascendant Blacks") have been part of a long struggle to overcome the effects of racial subordination with contemporary reach, making it America's unfinished business. Yet waves of new immigrants, including many who are black and brown, are redefining the stage on which this unfinished business must be played out. Moreover, in recent decades intermarriage among racial groups has created multi-racial families that may eschew traditional categorization defined by the "one drop" rule, pursuant to which any visible black ancestry assigned blackness no matter how physical appearance manifested. In the face of this complex and ever-changing America, Brown engages in a historically based analysis of race and its meaning, past and present. He flies in the face of popular wisdom and jurisprudence, which counsel us to give a quick and cursory acknowledgment to our long and terrible history of racism and subordination before antiquing its reach and effects, all the while drawing the improbable conclusion that any massive racial inequality we find is not connected to that long history, which temporally dwarfs modern era of formal legal equality. The easiest way out of this mess, contemporary wisdom tells us, is to declare victory—i.e., color blindness and post-racialism—and get out of the business of race. Brown resists this temptation, even while he explicitly declines to reargue the justifications for affirmative action. He takes Justice O'Connor's opinion in Grutter as a closed debate, but nonetheless demonstrates why the diversity rationale as applied to African American applicants will often require consideration of the effects of their historical experiences., which, of course, define who and what they are, and what they bring to the table.

The core of Professor Brown's thesis is that "Ascendant Blacks," i.e., descendants of the intergenerational U.S. slavery to Jim Crow experience, should be granted more preference in admission to selective colleges and universities because, even compared to Black Immigrants, and to multi-racial applicants, they are disadvantaged. They are less likely to come from two-parent households and they are more likely to carry the burdens and effects of discrimination. Brown prescribes even deeper dives on what race should mean in admission processes, which will no doubt drive diversity opponents even further into frenzy. His is not the step toward the color-blind society. It is Powell's diversity rationale's chickens coming home to roost. You may disagree, but you will think.

If you care about these issues, this book forces you to rethink some of your assumptions, or at least to re-examine the path that Justice Powell's opinion in *Bakke* charted almost four decades ago, when the Court effectively blocked deliberate and focused efforts to openly remedy the effects of our long racial supremacy nightmare. We remain confused about race, and Kevin Brown tells us about the consequences.

*Theodore M. Shaw is the Former Director-Counsel and President of the NAACP Legal Defense and Educational Fund, Inc. and Julius L. Chambers Distinguished Professor of Law and Director of the Center for Civil Rights at the University of North Carolina School of Law.*

# Foreword by Dennis J. Shields

We are in a different place with regard to race relations in this country than we were even as recently as the early 1980s when I first became an admissions officer at the University of Iowa College of Law. Inside this frame, Professor Brown's book, *Because of Our Success*, raises important questions: What is the purpose of "affirmative action"? Can it and should it be seen as a part of reparations for Ascendant Blacks? Is it based on the experience of being a member of a historically discriminated group in the United States? Is affirmative action something different from the broader descriptor of "diversity"? This book stimulates discussion about these questions, makes the case for considering the impact of current and future policies on the Ascendant Blacks, and proposes a method by which admissions officials might incorporate Ascendant Blacks into their student bodies.

I approach the issues raised by *Because of Our Success* from two vantage points. First, 28 years of experience in legal education—twenty-five as the lead admissions officer at three different law schools. And second, from several years of university related international travel as the president of a medium sized public university. My university is a point of access and affordability for many first generation college students. So, access to higher education and the impact success at that level can have for my students is consistently in the forefront of my thoughts about higher education.

As the dean of law admissions at the University of Michigan and then at Duke University, I made the overwhelming majority of decisions on admission applicants.[1] This work required me to make comparative assessments of candidates for admission while keeping in mind the school's educational mission, admissions policies and the law. My recent international travels have given me the opportunity to see the alternative ways that other countries (and their educational institutions) have thought about and reacted to issues caused by the oppression of minority populations.

I have had the opportunity to travel twice to Europe, twice to Brazil, and three times to China. My university has a relationship with South Central University for Nationalities (SCUN) in Wuhan, China. SCUN is one of eight universities in China set up to address the educational needs of ethnic minorities in China. China has 57 different ethnic minority groups (3% of 1.3 billion Chinese). During my visits to Brazil, I had occasion to learn about recent efforts there to improve the educational opportunities for African-Brazilians who are the descendants of slaves in that country.[2] Brazil was the last country in the Western Hemisphere to outlaw slavery. China and Brazil possess very different histories with regard to minority groups. The history of race in the United States is very different from that of Brazil and China. I have been struck however by the somewhat more forthright way these societies have begun to address the disparate treatment of minority groups than we seem to be able to do in this country. I am not arguing that these countries have more positive histories (in some ways their historical treatment of minority groups is worse than ours). Rather that, at least to me, they have been more direct in acknowledging the need to redress at least some of the wrongs visited upon their ethnic minorities if their societies are to advance.

Since the establishment of affirmative action policies in the 1960s to expand the number of black Americans into institutions of higher learning in the United States, the programs themselves and selection criteria have been hotly disputed. In that era it was pretty clear that blacks were the primary group considered who were underrepresented at predominantly white selective colleges and universities as a result of discrimination. The purpose of affirmative action was both backward looking and forward looking. As to the former, taking affirmative steps to increase black participation in higher education was to redress the impact of wide-spread discriminatory practices that had limited access for blacks to the selective institutions. As to the latter, affirmative action was intended to increase the wider participation in society and to improve the education of all students by diversifying the makeup of student bodies and thereby broadening the nature and context of interactions in the educational environment.

During the early days of affirmative diversity efforts the focus was primarily directed at blacks, but since, a more robust inclusive regime has developed. Women, Hispanics, Native Americans, Asians and Foreign students have come into the mix. In addition, the representation of women and underrepresented minorities in applicant pools has grown substantially. The competition for seats at the selective institutions has become fiercer. Particularly in law school admissions, ranking has had an outsized influence on the behavior of law schools in their decision making. Thus admission decision making has become an even more high stakes process fraught with more contentiousness by disappointed denied applicants.

As early as 1978, the Supreme Court issued a decision in the *University of California v. Bakke* case.[3] In that case the court upheld affirmative action in admissions but ruled against specific quotas for minority students. But that was not the end of the discussion. Challenges to college and professional school admissions programs have continued unabated, by students concerned that the admission of minorities, specifically black minorities have prevented them from earning a "deserved" seat at institutions of higher education.

When I was Dean of Admissions at the University of Michigan law school, I was personally sued by Barbara Grutter. She challenged our admissions policy which she claimed discriminated against her based on race in violation of the Fourteenth Amendment, Title VI of the Civil Rights Act of 1964 and 42 U.S.C. Section 1981, by giving black or minority applicants what appeared to be a greater chance of admission than white students. At Michigan, we determined that a diverse student body was critically important to our educational mission. The Michigan law school after careful deliberation by a committee composed of a representative cross section of the faculty, students and administrators at the school developed a policy that took account of the mission of the school and described how the admission policy was to be used to further that mission. The Supreme Court held that the policy and its implementation had been narrowly tailored to promote diversity in the law school student body. The diversity we contemplated included ethnic minorities that had historically been underrepresented in law schools and the legal profession. But it was also broader than those groups. We sought to attract students that came from across the United States and the world. We sought diversity in academic disciplines and socio-economic status. We sought diversity in life experience and political perspectives, understanding that admissions decision making was not a science, rather a matter of looking closely at what each candidate had to offer and making our best judgment about those who had the talent and potential to succeed in law school and the profession.

Professor Brown's work takes up an important issue, the fate of Ascendant Black students under the affirmative action/diversity policy regime. Brown's argument, that Ascendant Blacks, those descended from blacks who were formerly underrepresented and discriminated against in the United States, are being passed over for professional school admissions in favor of multi-racial and foreign blacks is an argument worthy of consideration. What is the impact of current policies on Ascendant Blacks and should it matter? Is there justification for making sure access to higher education, especially at our selective institutions, includes a critical mass of Ascendant Blacks? Is there room in the current diversity regime for this nuanced consideration?

Brown's argument is about what the purpose of at least some portion of the affirmative diversity efforts should be. Here I must acknowledge my discomfort about this kind of granular parsing of ethnicity in making admission decisions. I acknowledge the appeal of addressing past discrimination to the descendants of slaves and the aftermath of slavery. But my years in making the decisions makes me leery of the ability to discern with clarity who "qualifies" for favorable consideration under this kind of policy. Having acknowledged the difficulty of determining Ascendant Black candidates, it is still worth considering the merits of concern about Ascendant Blacks access in the broader efforts to diversify opportunity if admission to selective institutions of higher education.

Support for the use of race in admissions decisions making is no longer justified by a single reason. A collection of policy considerations is in play in what is becoming an ever more multi-cultural/ethnic society. Some of the policy justification for considering Ascendant Blacks is to redress the past oppression of specific groups that limited prior opportunities. Some of it is justified by the systemic impact of past and current discrimination on the Ascendant Blacks. Some of it is justified by the educational benefits of a diverse student body that includes individuals impacted by their status as Ascendant Blacks. Some of it is justified by the need to look beyond traditional measures of merit (i.e., test scores and previous academic work) to discern other indicators of ability and potential for all candidates. Some of it is defensible because it is easily proved by past experience that academic achievement or the potential professional contributions to social good cannot be measured solely or accurately by the traditional measures of merit alone.

Certainly the merits of considering ascendant status needs to be discussed given the American experience of the descendants of slaves. When I worked in the trenches as an admissions person at Iowa, at Michigan and at Duke, reviewing applications meant looking beyond the traditional indicators of merit to the essays that were required of the candidates. I read the letters of reference. I spoke with the candidates and their advocates. Always, I looked to find something that warranted thinking about the candidate beyond test scores and grades to see potential for academic excellence, professional contributions, and contributions to the education of their classmates, etc. The goal was to assemble not some quantifiable best group to include in the class. Rather to assemble a cohort of superbly talented, interesting, and capable people who would learn from one another, contribute in meaningful ways to the discourse in and outside of class and that showed the potential to contribute in meaningful ways to the advancement of the profession and society in general. Obviously the experience of at least some Ascendant Blacks could be argued to possess knowledge and experience that would add positively to the afore mentioned goals.

Admissions officers and university administrators should consider the argument Professor Brown is making and the statistics he cites showing that Affirmative Action policies are not serving Ascendant Blacks. Colleges, universities and professional schools would do well to consider using the enhanced demographic information provided today by the Common Application to identify formerly disenfranchised students and should consider Brown's suggested changes in the admissions process to prevent the eradication of Ascendant Blacks from the campuses of our nation's selective higher education institutions. The incorporation of Professor Brown's ideas will aid professional schools in creating diverse student bodies that include underrepresented minorities with a history of discrimination as affirmative action was built to do. This will be in accordance with the law, promote diversity in the workforce and benefit society at large by remedying some of the past discrimination that has injured our nation and our law schools to date.

Dennis J. Shields<br>
Chancellor, University of Wisconsin-Platteville<br>
Former Director of Admissions,<br>
The University of Michigan Law School

# Preface

During the early part of my academic career, my scholarship focused on school desegregation and school desegregation termination litigation. As a product of *de jure* segregated schools in Indianapolis and integrated schools in the suburbs of Indianapolis during the 1960s and 1970s, I came to believe that the best possible educational situations for African-Americans were in schools with integrated student bodies, diverse faculties, and true multicultural educational philosophies. While my scholarship focused on K–12 education, I always viewed improving primary education as part of the process of increasing the numbers of African-Americans who would eventually attend selective higher education institutions. This was a necessary step in our society's process of eliminating the effects of its history of racial discrimination inflicted on black people in the United States root and branch. As a result, the true purpose of my putting forth legal theories that would preserve or allow for integrated schools was an effort to increase the number of African Americans who obtained highly valued educational credentials. This would significantly increase the numbers of African-Americans who were employed in prestigious jobs or elite occupations. Thus, while my scholarship focused on desegregating America's primary schools, the ultimate goal was to increase the numbers of African-Americans who came through the educational pipeline and landed in elite jobs and occupations in American society.

I have two Ascendant Black and two Black Multiracial (black/white) children. I have also spent a considerable amount of time in South Africa where I was the foreign-born black in a country with a history of racial discrimination. Up until the fiftieth anniversary of the Supreme Court's 1954 decision in *Brown v. Board of Education*, as most other Americans, I determined who should receive positive considerations for being black by admissions officials of selective higher education programs based on the idea that all blacks in the United States are alike, regardless of race or ethnicity. Thus, I accepted the one-drop rule and did not draw distinctions between foreign-born and native born blacks.

In the fall of 2004, I became the Director of the Hudson & Holland Scholars Programs (HHSP) at Indiana University Bloomington. HHSP is a scholarship program and its mission is to recruit, retain, and prepare students with outstanding records of academic achievement, strong leadership experiences, and a commitment to social justice for their futures after college. But, since HHSP was part of the campus' efforts to assure the benefits of diversity, HHSP gave substantial positive weight during the admissions process to applicants from underrepresented minority groups with a history of discrimination. HHSP was, therefore, a selective minority scholarship program that provided students with funds to cover approximately half the cost of in-state tuition.

When I resigned as Director in the fall of 2008, there were about 570 HHSP Scholars spread throughout the four undergraduate years. At that time, HHSP had approximately 25 percent of the black and one-third of the Latino undergraduate students on the campus. However, HHSP also produced nearly 50 percent of the campus' graduates from both of these minority groups and about 75 percent of those that graduated with a 3.5 cumulative grade point average or better. In other words, the overwhelming majority of black students from Indiana University-Bloomington who would go on to selective graduate programs like law schools, medical schools, dental schools, and other selective graduate programs were HHSP Scholars.

As the Director of HHSP, I reviewed over sixteen hundred applications from underrepresented minorities throughout the United States, but since about 80 percent of our HHSP Scholars were resident students, the overwhelming majority of applications came from the State of Indiana. The Associate Director for Recruiting, Anthony Scott, and I jointly made all the admissions decisions. While HHSP was not an affirmative action college admissions program, we encountered all of the issues that admissions committee members at selective colleges, universities, and graduate programs encounter when trying to decide which underrepresented minorities to admit. We also employed a holistic approach in making our admissions decisions, as dictated by the Supreme Court's opinion in *Grutter v. Bollinger*. Nevertheless, the applicants' academic record as determined or explained by ACT or SAT scores, strength of high school's academic reputation, number of advanced placement courses, high school grade point averages, and high school class ranks were the primary factors that we considered during our admissions process.

In my first year as Director, I noticed that a significant number of our black students were either Black Multiracials or Black Immigrants. So, we changed our application forms in order to accurately track both the race and ethnicity of our black students. While we tried to do the same with Hispanic/Latino students, we quickly came up against the reality that many of them do not view race in the same way that most blacks and whites in the U.S. view race. As a result of our revised application forms, Anthony and I discovered that thirty percent of our incoming black HHSP Scholars for the fall of 2006 were Black Multiracials and another five percent were Black Immigrants. Furthermore, after having then served as Director for two years, it was plain that many of the Black Multiracials and Black Immigrants in HHSP did not identify with the historic struggle of blacks against racial oppression like our Ascendant Black Scholars. Also, many of the Black Multiracial and Black Immigrant Scholars did not have the same experiences of and reactions to race, racism, and America's history of racial discrimination that were so common among their fellow Ascendant Black Scholars. Given that the percentage of Black Multiracials among blacks approaching college age in the State of Indiana would skyrocket in the next 15 years, as it would nationally, it was clear that, if nothing changed, Ascendant Blacks would virtually be eliminated from HHSP long before the expiration of the 25 year time-table for affirmative action that Justice O'Connor mentioned at the end of her opinion in *Grutter v. Bollinger*. Since the State of Indiana is in America's heartland, it was also obvious that the changing racial and ethnic ancestry of blacks that I was witnessing occurring on HHSP had to be happening at other selective higher education programs in the country.

Because of this knowledge, I was forced to ask, "which blacks should benefit from programs established by selective higher education institutions to benefit those underrepresented minorities with a history of discrimination?" In trying to answer that question, I had hundreds of discussions with others, blacks, whites, Asians, and Hispanic/Latinos about the racial and ethnic ancestry of blacks on HHSP. Many people had a hard time distinguishing blacks based on race or ethnicity. They were caught in the notion that I had previously believed, the experiences of blacks in the U.S. were similar regardless of race or ethnicity. What I began to notice, however, is that they viewed blacks primarily from the standpoint of people who had been victims of racism and racial discrimination. For them the experience of being black in the United States was limited to the experience of being a victim of discrimination. As a result, since Black Multiracials and Black Immigrants also encountered discrimination in the United States, they had the necessary experience of being a member of a historically discriminated group in the United States. But, this was an understanding of the black experience in the U.S. that only reflected one perspective. It failed to appreciate the counter-discourse of struggle against their oppression that the descendants of the soil of Africa created. The experience of being black in America involves not just being victimized by racism, but the struggle against it. Here then was the issue, many Black Multiracials and Black Immigrants do not identify with the struggle against racial oppression of blacks in the United States, nor do they, in general, have nearly the same amount of experience shaped by the history of discrimination suffered by blacks in the United States that Ascendant Blacks have.

Since the graduates of selective higher education programs come to dominate the boardrooms, the corner offices, the faculty lounges, the pressrooms, the courthouses, and the statehouses in the United States, the impact of the changing racial and ethnic ancestry of blacks on affirmative action would affect which "black" individuals come to dominate public life in the next generation. In addition, the blacks who attend selective higher education institutions also influence the educational experiences of all other students who are enrolled in these programs. Thus, the changing racial and ethnic ancestry of blacks benefiting from affirmative action will also impact the formal and informal education of all of those in the nation's selective higher education programs. It could lead to a systematic mis-education about the black experience in the United States by those who we are training to occupy our most important social positions. This understanding made me realize that much of the scholarship, theorizing, and political discussions about race and education, at least as it regards African-Americans, was already obsolete. This included my own scholarship that focused on improving the educational situation of public primary education for African-Americans. Such lines of reasoning were based on several assumptions that simply no longer held true: such as racial categories are stable, race is a socially ascribed characteristic not the product of self-identification, and all blacks' experiences with America's history of racial discrimination are similar regardless of their ancestry.

# Acknowledgments

The genesis for this book can be traced back to September 2007 when my colleague, Jeannine Bell, asked me to co-write a piece with her about the effect of the changing racial and ethnic ancestry of blacks on affirmative action. Jeannine was concerned that Black Multiracials and Black Immigrants did not share the same commitment to the historic struggle of blacks against the continuing effects of the history of race discrimination on blacks in the U.S. of Ascendant Blacks. She realized that these changes were significantly undermining not just the ability, but also the desire, of the more successful members of the "Black Community" to engage in racial upliftment. As a result, she suggested that we entitle the article we co-wrote, *Demise of the Talented Tenth: Affirmative Action and the Overrepresentation of Black Biracials and Black Immigrants*. We published that article in the 2008 Ohio State Law Review's symposium issue on "The School Desegregation Cases and the Uncertain Future of Racial Equality." I want to acknowledge the tremendous assistance and support that I received on this project from Jeannine and give her my special thanks for being such a wonderful and valuable longtime colleague and friend.

Over the past seven years, I have presented pieces of this work at numerous conferences, workshops, and to various law faculties, including at Annual American Association of Law Schools Conferences, Columbia University, Education Law Association Annual Conference, Emory University School of Law, Hamline University School of Law, Harvard Law School, Law & Society Annual Conferences, the University of Miami Law School, Ohio State University, Ohio State University Law School, Society of American Law Teachers Annual Conference, Southeast/Southwest People of Color Legal Scholarship Conference, Texas Southern University Thurgood Marshall School of Law, Texas Wesleyan University School of Law, and University of Washington Law School. I would like to thank the attendees and participants in those various conferences, workshops, and the law school faculties for their very helpful suggestions and thoughts about the subject of this book.

I would also like to thank several people from whose discussions this book has greatly benefited: Jennifer Allen, Mario Barnes, Hannah Buxbaum, Devon

Carbado, Ghangis Carter, Erica Cooper, Ken Dau-Schmidt, Don Gjerdingen, Linda Greene, Michael Higginbotham, Danielle R. Holley-Walker, Feisal Amin Istrabadi, Charles Lawrence, Jeremy Levitt, Caralee Jones, D. Marvin Jones, Eboni Nelson, Kimberly Jade Norwood, Kenneth Nunn, Michael Olivas, Angela Onwuachi-Willig, john powell, Susan Prager, Lauren Robel, Reginald Robinson, Anthony Scott, Jeffrey Stake, Kent Syverud, Mary Tourner, Vincene Verdun, Camille Walsh, Susan Williams, and Steven Winter. I would also like to provide my special thanks to several outstanding research assistances that have helped me with this book including, Jalil Dozier, Tamisha Evans, Dorianne Mason, Dominque McGee, Yoni Moise, Steven Reynolds, and Dominique Nicole Taylor. However, I want to specifically make note of the truly extraordinary research assistance I received from Renee Turner and Aminta Moses and the proofreading skills of Kristen Hansen.

I want to thank my loving wife, Dianne, who has had to endure far too many discussions about the changing racial and ethnic ancestries of blacks on affirmative action. Her patience and understanding were critical to my ability to complete this project. "Dianne, thank you for all of your love and support. It is deeply appreciated."

Finally, I want to dedicate this book to my four children, Nichole, Crystal, Shayla, and Devin. The four of you are always upmost in my thoughts, especially for a book like this. I love all of you very much, Dad.

# Because of Our Success

# Introduction

## I. Changes in the Racial and Ethnic Ancestry of Blacks Since the Origin of Affirmative Action Admissions Policies

In the introduction to their groundbreaking book, *The Shape of the River*, William Bowen and Derek Bok noted, "it is probably safe to say, ... that prior to 1960, no selective college or university was making determined efforts to seek out and admit substantial numbers of African Americans...."[1] However, once selective higher education institutions—institutions that only admit a subset of the students who apply, including selective undergraduate institutions, law schools, and medical schools—began to employ special efforts to recruit black students, their numbers immediately increased. For example, in 1965, law schools began employing affirmative action admissions practices.[2] Within ten years, the portion of black students enrolled in the nation's law schools jumped from about 1 percent to 4.5 percent.[3] The portion of blacks enrolled in Ivy League colleges increased from 2.3 to 6.3 percent between 1967 and 1976. The effect of affirmative action on the nation's medical schools was similar to that of law schools and the Ivy League colleges. In the 1968–69 academic year, only 2.2 percent of the nearly 36,000 medical school students were black, with almost 60 percent of them enrolled at the two historically black medical schools of Howard University College of Medicine and Meharry Medical College.[4] Seven years later, blacks constituted 6.2 percent of the nation's medical school students.[5]

When affirmative action policies were first instituted, the racial and ethnic makeup of the United States was very different from what it is today. According to the 1960 census, whites constituted 88.8 percent of all Americans, with an additional 10.6 percent classified as black.[6] The 1960 census categorized Hispanics/Latinos based on their race, not their ethnicity;[7] thus, blacks and whites comprised 99.4 percent of the American population.[8] Also, in 1960, interracial marriage between blacks and whites was still illegal in over twenty states.[9] Of the nearly twelve million blacks over the age of fifteen,[10] less than one half of one percent of them were married to whites.[11] With regard to determining a person's racial classification, the Census Bureau and American society used the one-drop rule. Thus, the instructions for the 1960 census form continued the change originally adopted in 1930: "A person of mixed white and Negro blood was to be returned as Negro, no matter how small the percentage of Negro blood."[12] In addition, census enumerators were still responsible for determining a person's racial classification based on phenotypical appearances.[13] Because a person's physical appearance may not reveal the fact that they had a very small quantum of black blood, it was possible for some blacks to pass as white, despite the one-drop rule.[14] Nevertheless, the use of the one-drop rule and the dual-race nature of American society meant that Americans, in the overwhelming majority of cases, could determine a person's race based on their physical appearance. Thus, as affirmative action commenced, race was not only a socially ascribed identity, but simply put, there was no such concept of a Black Multiracial person, only blacks who possessed lighter or darker complexions.

In addition to the dual-race nature of American society, dominant American cultural attitudes and social practices did not differentiate blacks who descended from those Africans brought to America in chains during the Transatlantic Slave Trade from those who were recent arrivals from the Caribbean or Africa. With some justification, Americans did not recognize the existence of "black ethnicity." In 1960, the 125,000 foreign-born blacks[15] in the United States comprised only 0.7 percent of the black population.[16]

Although the one-drop rule sought to support white privilege, the Black Community also appropriated this norm to promote community cohesion, strength, and pride, and readily accepted mixed-race blacks as members.[17] In 1957, Ghana became only the third independent nation in Africa, joining Liberia and Ethiopia. Over the next dozen years, however, thirty-five other sub-Saharan African countries gained their independence from European colonial rule.[18] This new source of pride in Africa contributed to the notion of the black civil rights movement of the late 1950s and 1960s, which also fostered a strong belief among black people in the United States that all black descendants of the soil of Africa shared a common culture and worldview, had a common destiny, and a common experience of slavery, colonialism, oppression, and exploitation.[19]

At the time of the institution of affirmative action admissions policies by selective higher education programs, from the perspectives of both dominant

American cultural attitudes and the Black Community, in terms of race, distinctions were not drawn between single-race blacks and Black Multiracials[20] (for this book the term "Black Multiracial" refers to those blacks with a non-black parent). In other words, the concept of Black Multiracials did not exist. Nor did dominant American cultural attitudes or the Black Community draw significant distinctions between native blacks and Black Immigrants (for this book the term "Black Immigrants" refers to those with at least one foreign-born black parent). And the reason ethnic distinctions were not drawn among blacks is because the numbers and percentages of blacks who were Black Immigrants were too small to think about. As a result, the most important assumption upon which selective higher education institutions developed affirmative action admissions plans was that the predominant beneficiaries of affirmative action would be those blacks whose ancestors were victims of the history of discrimination in the United States. These were the sons and daughters of two American-born black parents (as determined by the application of the one-drop rule). Others have referred to this racial/ethnic group of blacks as "third-generation" or "legacy" blacks.[21] This book will refer to them as "Ascendant Blacks"[22] to denote the historical connection between this racial/ethnic group of blacks and the history of the ascendancy of blacks out of slavery and segregation. The ascendancy of this racial/ethnic group of blacks not only helped to bring about affirmative action, but also made possible the dramatic increases in interracial cohabitation, Black Multiracials, foreign-born blacks, and Black Immigrants that have occurred over the past fifty years.

Since the origination of affirmative action admissions policies, much has changed with regard to the racial and ethnic ancestry of American society, including that of blacks. As time passed, the objections to interracial dating and marriage between blacks and whites began to wane. In 1958, for example, only 4 percent of whites approved of interracial marriage with blacks.[23] However, in its 1967 decision of *Loving v. Virginia*,[24] the Supreme Court struck down antimiscegenation marriage statutes throughout the country. This decision and other societal changes led to more acceptance by Americans of interracial sexual relationships. By 2003, the Gallup poll showed that 70 percent of whites and 80 percent of blacks approved of such unions.[25] The portion of those who accept interracial marriage continues to increase during the twenty-first century.[26] This is especially true among younger adults, the ones in their prime reproductive years. According to a 2010 Pew Research Center report, almost all Millennials (18- to 29-year-olds in 2010) accept interracial dating and marriage. The Report notes that 92 percent of white and 88 percent of African American Millennials say that they would be fine with a family member marrying someone outside of their group.[27]

The greater societal acceptance of interracial dating and marriage also increased its frequency. Figures from 2010 show that about 9.0 percent of married blacks were married outside of the race.[28] The percentage of black males who marry outside of the race continued to be significantly higher than black females, 12.5 compared to 5.5 percent. Interracial marriages also made up a much larger percentage of new marriages by blacks than existing marriages. Thus, among 2010 newlyweds, 23.6 percent of black males and 9.3 percent of black females married outside of their race.[29]

Increased interracial dating, cohabitation, and marriage have also increased the percentage of blacks with interracial parents. According to the 2010 census, 7.4 percent of blacks[30] (up from 4.8 percent in 2000[31]) indicated another racial category, over two and a half times the 2.9 percent of the American population as a whole.[32] As one might expect, the younger blacks are, the more likely they are to be multiracial. Census figures from 2012 show that the portion of mixed-race blacks between the ages of 20 and 24 was only 7.9 percent.[33] However, the portion of mixed-race blacks among blacks between the ages of 15 and 19 was 8.9 percent, between 10 and 14 years it increased to 10.9 percent, between 5 and 9 years to 15.0 percent, and for those under the age of 5 it was 19.1 percent.[34]

In addition to the increase in Black Multiracials, the ethnic ancestry of blacks has also changed significantly since the advent of affirmative action. The emergence of independent predominately black nations in the Caribbean and Africa, globalization, and changes in American immigration law, starting with the landmark Hart-Cellar Act of 1965, led to substantial increases in the percentages and numbers of foreign-born blacks in the United States. The percentage of blacks who were foreign-born increased from 1.1 percent in 1970,[35] to 4.9 percent in 1990,[36] to almost 10 percent in 2012.[37] Since 1960, the number of foreign-born blacks in the United States has also increased over thirty-fold to over 3,900,000.[38] As a result, the percentage of younger blacks in the United States who are Black Immigrants is also on the rise. Whereas only 2 percent of black children are foreign-born, approximately 12.7 percent of black children under the age of 18 are Black Immigrants.[39] However, this percentage is on the rise because of the significant increase in foreign-born blacks in the country and the possibility that foreign-born black women will continue to have more children than native black women. For example, foreign-born black women bore approximately one out of every six black children in 2004, and in Massachusetts, where one out of every three blacks is currently foreign-born, since 2008 a majority of black babies born there have been to the immigrant mothers.[40]

## II. Disproportionate Numbers of Black Multiracials and Black Immigrants Attending Selective Higher Education Institutions

The Supreme Court has recently addressed the issue of affirmative action in *Fisher v. University of Texas*[41] and *Schuette v. Coalition to Defend Affirmative Action*.[42] However, these Court opinions have left intact its 2003 holding in *Grutter v. Bollinger*,[43] which upheld the affirmative action admissions policy of the University of Michigan Law School. At the conclusion of Justice O'Connor's opinion for the five-person majority in *Grutter*, she indicated, "We expect that twenty-five years from now, the use of racial preferences will no longer be necessary to further the interest approved today."[44] The precise implications of O'Connor's twenty-five-year period are debatable. At one extreme, it is an essential part of the holding of *Grutter*. As a result, affirmative action policies must end in twenty-five years.[45] At the other extreme, it is a time to reflect upon where higher education and American society are with respect to the continued need for affirmative action.[46] Regardless of how the federal courts ultimately resolve the 2028 deadline, two things are clear: both supporters and critics of the Supreme Court's opinion in *Grutter* must have envisioned that a substantial percentage of the black beneficiaries of affirmative action would continue to be Ascendant Blacks; and the twenty-five-year period has created an inevitable date with destiny for affirmative action programs. The closer American society gets to 2028, the greater the impetus will be for a renewed examination and discussion about it and its continued beneficial effects. However, this book is an effort to accelerate that discussion because of growing evidence regarding the virtual elimination of Ascendant Blacks from the campuses of many selective higher education institutions.[47]

Until recently, selective higher education institutions have generally treated all black applicants alike, grouping them into a unified "Black/African/African American" category regardless of their racial or ethnic ancestries.[48] As Lee Stetson, the former Dean of Admissions of the University of Pennsylvania, stated a few years ago, "we do not focus specifically on whether students are Caribbean American, African American or African. We do not involve ourselves with exact roots."[49] However, of late, commentators have identified growing changes in the racial and ethnic ancestries of blacks[50] enrolled in America's selective higher education programs.[51] Increasing percentages of blacks benefitting from affirmative action are Black Multiracials and Black Immigrants.

At about the same time that the Supreme Court announced its decision in *Grutter v. Bollinger*,[52] Harvard professors Lani Guiner and Henry Louis Gates pointed out the racial and ethnic changes in the black undergraduate student body of their university. At a gathering of the Harvard Black Alumni in the summer of 2003, they noted that Black Multiracials and Black Immigrants comprised two-thirds of Harvard's black undergraduate population.[53] Following this Harvard revelation, a 2005 article in *Diverse Issues in Higher Education* pointed to the findings in a study of the black presence that included twenty-eight selective colleges and universities in 1999.[54] The study revealed that Black Multiracials made up 17 percent of those black freshmen and that 41 percent were either Black Multiracials or Black Immigrants.[55]

Specifically with regard to the increasing percentage of Black Multiracials among the black college population at selective higher education institutions, a published study tallied the 2007 reports from the Consortium on Financing Higher Education (COFHE) Enrolled Student Survey.[56] COFHE is an institutionally supported organization of thirty-one selective private colleges and universities, including many of the most elite ones in the country.[57] According to this study, 19 percent of the black students indicated that they had a parent of another race, and additional 4 percent answered "yes" to the Hispanic/Latino ethnicity question.[58] As further evidence of the widespread nature of the increase in Black Multiracials at selective higher education institutions, statistics from the Vice President of Enrollment Services of Indiana University Bloomington, who also heads the admissions office, showed that Black Multiracials comprised 18.4 percent of the black students on campus in the fall of 2013.[59]

With regard specifically to the increasing portion of Black Immigrants among black students, a follow-up to the study mentioned above in *Diverse Issues of Higher Education* focused solely on the presence of Black Immigrants. The follow-up study noted that whereas only 13 percent of black 18- and 19-year-olds in the country in 1999 were Black Immigrants, they made up 27 percent of black freshmen at these institutions.[60] The portion of Black Immigrants was actually higher at the ten most selective schools in the study, constituting 35.6 percent of their black students. It was even higher at the four Ivy League schools (Columbia, Princeton, University of Pennsylvania, and Yale) in the survey, where they made up 40.6 percent of the black students enrolled. In addition, a 2006 article discussed the results of a 2004 study, which showed that Black Immigrants comprised 20.9 percent of the nation's black undergraduates and 27.4 percent of enrolled black graduate students.[61] Another study by Pamela R. Bennett of Johns Hopkins University and Amy Lutz of Syracuse University found that Black Immigrant high school graduates were almost four times more likely to attend selective colleges and universities than other blacks.[62] Moreover, according to Dr. Michael T. Nettles, Vice President for Policy Evaluation and Research at the Educational Testing Service, "If Blacks are typically

5 percent and 6 percent of the population at elite colleges, then the representation of native United States born African-Americans might be closer to 3 percent."63

What is striking about the evidence above is the magnitude of the overrepresentation of Black Multiracials and Black Immigrants among black students in selective higher education programs. Yet the overrepresentation of Black Multiracials should come as no surprise. Studies have pointed out that "black/white intermarriages tend to occur when the white spouse trades the privilege of racial status for the higher status of a better-educated black partner."64 U.S. Census Bureau statistics indicate that Black Multiracials tend to come from parents with more education and live in families with higher incomes than single-race blacks.65 Black Multiracial students are also more likely to live with both parents and live in families that own their own home.66 Black Multiracials, especially if their nonblack parent is white or Asian, may also have less cultural discontinuities with educational institutions and school officials than other black students. This could also aid their academic performance.67 Like Black Multiracials, the overrepresentation of Black Immigrants among black students at selective higher education institutions should not come as a surprise either. The same differences exist between the family characteristics of the children of foreign-born blacks and native-born blacks that exists between the families of Black Multiracial children and the families of single-race black children. Like Black Multiracials, Black Immigrants tend to come from families with more parental education and higher family incomes than other blacks. Black Immigrants also have at least one parent whose ancestral line does not include that of a native born black. This could also aid their academic performance.

The socioeconomic advantages that Black Multiracials and Black Immigrants have over Ascendant Blacks likely explain the overrepresentation of those groups among black students attending selective higher education programs. Yet, these explanations point to a couple of other issues relevant to affirmative action. They suggest that, absent substantial changes in the admissions processes of selective higher education institutions, these overrepresentations will likely persist. And this is because Black Multiracials and Black Immigrants, compared to Ascendant Blacks, generally have fewer experiences derived from the historical discrimination suffered by blacks in the United States.

Beyond the evidence of the current overrepresentation of both Black Multiracials and Black Immigrants among black students in selective higher education programs, the percentages of both groups among the blacks who are approaching college age are rapidly increasing. Thus, no matter how overrepresented Black Multiracials and Black Immigrants are now, given their increasing percentage among blacks who are approaching college age, the negative impact of these overrepresentations on the admissions prospects of Ascendant Blacks is likely to increase significantly over the next fifteen years. As a result, America's selective higher education institutions appear set on a path toward the virtual elimination of Ascendant Blacks[68] from the campuses of most of these institutions well before the expiration of the Supreme Court's 25-year deadline in 2028. Thus, in an ironic twist of fate, selective higher education institutions, in the near future, could very well eliminate from their campuses the very group for whom they created affirmative action to benefit.

## III. What Stands to Be Lost by the Ethnic Cleansing of Ascendant Blacks from the Campuses of Selective Higher Education Programs

In order to raise concerns about the changing racial and ethnic ancestry of blacks on affirmative action, we need a vision in place that indicates which blacks deserve special considerations in the admissions process. Although scholars and commentators have offered various suggestions for why selective higher education institutions should employ affirmative action admissions policies,[69] the approach in this book is to begin from the proposition that this debate is closed. As our society moves closer to the end of the 25-year time limit set by Justice O'Connor in *Grutter*, the rationale for affirmative action is a *fait accompli*. Thus, the starting point has to be the Supreme Court's opinion in *Grutter v. Bollinger*,[70] since this opinion provides the rationale for the use of racial classifications in the admissions process. The University of Michigan Law School admissions policy sought to achieve the diversity among its student body that had the potential to enrich everyone's education.[71] However, that policy also sought to enroll a critical mass of students from groups that have historically been the object of discrimination to ensure their ability to make their unique contributions to the character of the Law School.[72]

Testimony from officials of the Michigan Law School revealed why they took race into account. Professor Richard Lempert chaired the faculty committee of the Law School that drafted the affirmative action policy. In his testimony during the District Court trial, Lempert noted that the affirmative action policy "did not purport to remedy past discrimination, but rather to include students who may bring to the Law School a perspective different from that of members of groups which have not been the victims of such discrimination."[73] Lempert also noted that some groups have suffered a history of discrimination in the United States, such as Asians and Jews, but were not included in the policy because the Law School already admitted members of these groups in significant numbers.[74] The then-Director of Admissions of the Law School, Erica Munzel, indicated during her testimony that "critical mass" means "meaningful numbers" or "meaningful representation." By this, she meant that the numbers of underrepresented minority students were sufficient to encourage these students to participate in the classroom and not feel isolated.[75] Dennis Shields, the Director of Admissions for Michigan Law School at the time that Barbara Grutter applied, testified that he sought to ensure that a critical mass of underrepresented minority students were included in order to realize the educational benefits of a diverse student body.

Justice O'Connor's opinion for the Court agreed that the benefits derived from this diversity were substantial.[76] With respect to the educational benefits, she noted that the Law School's admissions policy promotes cross-racial understanding, helps to break down racial stereotypes, and enables students to understand people of different races better. As O'Connor stated, "these benefits are important and laudable, because classroom discussion is livelier, more spirited, and simply more enlightening and interesting when the students have the greatest possible variety of backgrounds."[77] Justice O'Connor also noted that Michigan Law School did not premise the need for a critical mass of underrepresented minority students on any belief that minority students always (or even consistently) express some characteristic minority viewpoint on any issue. O'Connor further stated:

> Just as growing up in a particular region or having particular professional experiences is likely to affect an individual's views, so too is one's own, unique experience of being a racial minority in a society, like our own, in which race unfortunately still matters.... By virtue of our Nation's struggle with racial inequality, such students are both likely to have *experiences* of particular importance to the Law School's mission, *and less likely to be admitted in meaningful numbers on criteria that ignore those experiences.*[78]

Thus, Justice O'Connor's opinion authorizes the use of racial classifications for the inclusion of *underrepresented* racial minorities who have *experiences* derived from our nation's struggle with racial inequality. These *experiences* are important to include in the student body because of their educational benefits. They also explain why these *underrepresented* minorities are likely not to be admitted in meaningful numbers without the consideration of their racial/

ethnic backgrounds. In short, the benefits of diversity represent the compelling state interest for the ability of selective higher education programs to employ racial classifications in the admissions process of those applicants who come from minority groups that are underrepresented and who have experiences of being a member of a historically discriminated against group.

The history of discrimination that justifies the use of racial classifications in admissions, to which O'Connor referred in her opinion, was that which took place in the United States, not the treatment of blacks in the Caribbean, Africa, or the rest of the world. This seems obvious. After all, no one seriously contends that selective higher education programs could justify affirmative action in the United States to target the effects of oppression in other parts of the world, including, for example, the exploitation of Koreans in Japan, the negative effects of untouchability on Dalits in India, French Colonialism in the Caribbean, or British Imperialism in Africa or the New World. The legacy of North American and European slavery and American foreign policy over the years has had negative consequences for a number of countries where a majority of the population is black, including countries of origin of most Black Immigrants.[79] However, the rational solution for those harms is not to create a brain drain by inviting the best and brightest from those affected countries to come and remain in the United States for the purpose of contributing to the economic development of this country. To do so simply does further damage, rather, it would be some form of economic or educational development assistance in those countries.

To determine which black applicants have experiences of being a member of a historically discriminated group in the United States, it is necessary to understand the historical experience of discrimination of the Black Community. The central feature in that experience is race; however, there are two different aspects. One aspect involves blacks being discriminated against and victimized because of their race. For much of America's history, dominant American society viewed blacks as inferior in some important way to whites. This attitude helped to make the oppression of, and discrimination against, blacks appear to be part of the natural order of things. Thus, this aspect of the experience of historical discrimination for blacks is the experience of what it means to be "raced" or branded as inferior.[80] This aspect of the black experience is readily recognized within mainstream American culture. However, against the background of racial domination in the United States, the descendants of the sons and daughters of the soil of Africa developed a counterdiscourse to how mainstream American society normally viewed and treated them. From the point of view of this counterdiscourse, race was also the central characteristic that united blacks, but this counter historical view of the experience of being black understood them as oppressed, not inferior. As a result, it involved the active engagement in a collective struggle against white supremacy and black subjugation. So the experience of the history of discrimination against black people in the United States is like a two-sided coin. On one side, race was, and is, the immutable characteristic that formed the basis of the belief that blacks were inferior. On the other side was the Black Community's (and others') resistance to their oppression. Race was, and is, the immutable characteristic that bound blacks together as a people in a constant struggle against their subjugation. Thus, black applicants who should receive the maximum positive consideration in the admissions process of selective higher education programs because of their race should be those with sufficient experiences of both aspects of the experience of discrimination of blacks in the United States.

Since the inception of affirmative action, one of the consequences of the attenuation of racism in American society is that not all people with some African ancestry have sufficient experiences of *both* aspects of being black in the United States. For example, as this book will discuss in detail in Chapter One, the U.S. Department of Education (DOE) issued the "Final Guidance on Maintaining, Collecting, and Reporting Racial and Ethnic Data to the United States Department of Education" (hereinafter, the Final Guidance), which had an implementation date of the reporting school year of 2010–11.[81] The Final Guidance has changed the way that all educational institutions, including selective higher education institutions, collect and report racial and ethnic information to the DOE. One of the primary motivations for the adoption of the Final Guidance was the advocacy by multiracial groups that wanted to add a separate multiracial category to all local, state, and federal government forms that sought to collect racial and ethnic data, but especially the forms for the 2000 census.[82] During those discussions, multiracial advocates generally argued that mixed-race individuals, including mixed-race blacks, viewed themselves as multiracial rather than belonging to a single racial or ethnic group. A "multiracial" designation was, therefore, a better reflection of the true understanding of the multiracial person's racial identity. They noted that the one-drop rule, used for so long to classify any person with any black blood as black, was inherently racist.[83] These advocates also noted the psychological problems created for multiracial children who were forced to identify with one parent more than the other. Thus, as these arguments imply, many Black Multiracials may not see their racial identity as black, but as multiracial. As a result, they may view their racial identity as distinct from that of single-race blacks.

Many Black Immigrants do not identify with the historical experience of discrimination encountered by blacks in the United States. Many of them may not see either of the aspects of that experience as part of their experience.

Speaking with the knowledge of one who travelled extensively through South Africa after majority rule was established,[84] I understand these sentiments. Even though many native South Africans (black, white, Asian, and colored) mistook me for a black South African, and I was subjected to many forms of discriminatory treatment that black South Africans encounter, those experiences never altered my self-identified racial/ethnic identity. I was an African American, not a black South African, Ndebele, Xhosa, or Zulu. When I was victimized by racism, I attributed it to the lack of knowledge on the part of the perpetrator about my background and not as an attack on me or my heritage. Nor did my encounters with South African racism move me to embrace the collective fight against racial oppression of black South Africans as my own. Simply put, the history of racism that black South Africans suffered was different from that of my racial/ethnic group, those who victimized them were different, and the ways in which they were victimized were different. Many Black Immigrants will have similar feelings in the United States to those I had while in South Africa and, thus, will not identify with the historical experience of blacks in the United States.

Even if Black Multiracials and Black Immigrants identify with both aspects of the history of discrimination of blacks in the United States, in general, their experiences will not be nearly as numerous or abiding as they are for Ascendant Blacks. What differentiates Ascendant Blacks from Black Multiracials and Black Immigrants is that both of their parents are descendants of the ancestral lines of blacks that endured the experience of a historically discriminated group in the United States. The vast majority of Ascendant Blacks come from ancestral lines that extend to the time of chattel slavery in the United States. In addition, the ancestors of Ascendant Blacks, on both sides, lived through the period of time when segregation and conscious racial discrimination formed part of customary American business, educational, political, and social practices. Thus, when discussions about the victimization of blacks throughout America's history of racial discrimination occur in the classroom, for Ascendant Blacks these are not abstract discussions about disconnected individuals from a long ago past. Rather, they are discussions about their mother and father, as well as their aunts, uncles, grandparents, great grandparents, great aunts, great uncles, and their earlier ancestors on both sides. Therefore, for Ascendant Blacks, the history of discrimination in the United States suffered by blacks is the history of their family tree.

The ability of individuals to self-identify their racial classification means that many Black Multiracials may simply view themselves as multiracial and not as black. Experiences of what it means to be a member of a historically underrepresented group with a history of discrimination requires an identification with that group. Thus, many Black Multiracials do not encounter nearly as many experiences of being raced as Ascendant Blacks. As for Black Immigrants, the ones who came to the United States as adults do not have the same extensive experience of being raced in the United States that is so common to Ascendant Blacks. Some foreign-born blacks will attribute their encounters with racism in the United States to the fact that they are foreigners or to a reflection of the lack of knowledge of discriminators operating on the misperception that all blacks are alike, rather than as an attack upon their racial identity. Thus, many Black Immigrants may not have the same psychological, sociological, or philosophical reactions to racist encounters that Ascendant Blacks have. Although the foreign-born blacks who come to the United States as children and the U.S.-born sons and daughters of foreign-born blacks are likely to have more encounters with what it means to be raced than their parent(s), their parent(s)' influence will also reduce the number and impact of their perceptions of these encounters, thereby reducing their experiences of being raced.

Beyond the historical aspect of the black experience that deals with being raced, many Black Multiracials and Black Immigrants may not experience the need to engage in the collective historical struggle against the racial oppression of black people in the United States. Viewing themselves as multiracial and not black, many Black Multiracials may not view this historic struggle as one that involves them. They, rightly so, will also be concerned about their family and friends on both sides of their family tree, including their nonblack relatives. Thus, the acculturated affinities of family will mean that many Black Multiracials will have less experience with the need to struggle against racial oppression of blacks to the same extent as Ascendant Blacks. As for Black Immigrants, the ones who come to the United States as adults will clearly have less experience fighting against the racial oppression of blacks in the United States than Ascendant Blacks brought up here. Understandably, many of these foreign-born blacks are more concerned about the conditions of their relatives, friends, and other people in the countries that they left. Thus, they may be more interested in assisting those they care about in their countries of origin, rather than participating in the collective historic struggle waged by blacks against racial oppression in the United States.[85] There is ample proof of this concern on the part of foreign-born blacks. Remittances received by relatives and friends from natives living abroad are a major source of income for many developing nations in Africa and the Caribbean.[86] The attitudes of the foreign-born parents are also likely to influence their children who immigrate to the United States while young, as well as their American-born children. Thus, like many Black Multiracials, Black Immigrants are also less likely than Ascendant Blacks to have as many experiences with the aspect of the history of racial discrimination against blacks that deals with the collective historical struggle against racial oppression.

The impact of the virtual elimination of Ascendant Blacks from the campuses of selective higher education programs cannot be overstated. Graduates of selective higher education programs tend to command an economic premium in the labor market and have elevated career ambitions as a result of access to exceptional alumni and peers. They also have increased civic engagement and more social capital. The reach of affirmative action decisions, therefore, affects public life for all Americans, because graduates of selective higher education institutions come to hold important positions in America. Also, affirmative action admissions decisions influence the educational experiences of all students that attend these programs. As the then-President of Princeton, William Bowen, noted in the *Princeton Alumni Weekly* that Justice Powell quoted in a footnote in his opinion in *Bakke*,

> a great deal of learning occurs informally.... In the nature of things, it is hard to know how, and when, and even if, this informal "learning through diversity" actually occurs. It does not occur for everyone. For many, however, the unplanned, casual encounters with roommates, fellow sufferers in an organic chemistry class, student workers in the library, teammates on a basketball squad, or other participants in class affairs or student government can be subtle and yet powerful sources of improved understanding and personal growth.[87]

The impact of the virtual elimination of Ascendant Blacks from the formal and informal education of those in the nation's selective higher education programs will have dramatic effects on the educational environment in those institutions. The voice of blacks steeped in the experiences of our society's history of racial discrimination may fade away from the campuses of selective higher education programs. What may be even more important is that the nonblack faculty and students may not sufficiently appreciate the loss of this voice. The dominant American ethos continues to view all blacks alike, regardless of racial or ethnic differences. This is particularly true during these times where the President of the United States is the son of a Kenyan immigrant and a white mother, but clearly identifies with Ascendant Blacks.[88] However, Barack Obama grew up during a time when all blacks were viewed as the same regardless of their race and ethnicity. Thus, because of the massive demographic changes in the United States over the past fifty years, many Black Multiracials and Black Immigrants do not share his identification. As a result, many nonblack faculty and students will presume that the experiences and opinions expressed by Black Multiracials and Black Immigrants represent those of the vast majority of blacks. Yet, since Ascendant Blacks still constitute the overwhelming majority of blacks in the United States, this is likely to lead to a systematic miseducation of how race is understood by blacks in the United States, by those whom American society is training to occupy its most important economic, academic, media, legal, and political positions. Thus, the virtual elimination of Ascendant Blacks from the campuses of selective higher education institutions will not only impact which black individuals come to shape business, education, the media, the law, and politics for the next generation, but also the education of the vast majority of the future leaders of American society.

## IV. Discussing the Virtual Elimination of Ascendant Blacks Demonstrates the Weakening Power of Racism

Despite the ominous implications of the virtual elimination of Ascendant Blacks from the campuses of selective higher education institutions, the need to call attention to this development must stand as an undeniable testament to the fading hold of racial discrimination since these institutions first introduced affirmative action admissions policies. Blacks, as a group, continue to lag far behind non-Hispanic whites on virtually every important socioeconomic measure, including attainment of college degrees, scores on standardized tests, median family income, family wealth, poverty rates, life expectancy, and incarceration rates. However, without a weakening of the influence of racism in American society, the conditions that have allowed for the growth of interracial sexual relationships involving blacks, the increase in Black Multiracials, the immigration of blacks from the rest of the world, and the increase in Black Immigrants would not have occurred. All Americans also confront further evidence of the weakening hold of racial discrimination against blacks, because they encounter very successful black individuals on a daily basis. In *Disintegration: The Splintering of Black America*, noted black journalist Eugene Robinson pointed to several recent divisions that now exist within the Black Community.[89] Robinson not only pointed to emergent groups of mixed-race blacks and foreign-born blacks, he also noted a small elite group of blacks with enormous wealth, power, and influence. He called them "Transcendents."[90] Thus, Americans live with the reality that Oprah Winfrey is on the list of the wealthiest Americans[91] and that a number of blacks, including

Robert Johnson, Michael Jordan, Magic Johnson, and Bill Cosby, have amassed substantial fortunes.[92] Blacks have run or run some of the most powerful corporations in the world including: Rosalind Brewer, President and CEO of Sam's Club; Ursula Burns, President of Xerox Corporation; Stanley O'Neal, former Chairman/CEO of Merrill Lynch & Co. Inc.; Richard Parsons, Chairman of Citigroup and former Chairman/CEO of AOL Time Warner; Don Thompson, President of McDonald's USA; and Ronald Williams, Chairman/CEO of Aetna, Inc.[93] Black athletes like Tiger Woods, Kobe Bryant, and LeBron James are among the most highly paid marketing personalities in America.[94] More than one hundred blacks are presidents of traditionally white universities.[95] A black Miss America or Miss USA is no longer a major news item.[96] There are currently forty-three black members of the House of Representatives[97] and three served in the Senate in 2013,[98] the most in any given year in the history of the United States. When David Patterson succeeded Eliot Spitzer as Governor of the State of New York in March of 2007, for the first time in American history, two blacks were serving as the chief executive officers of their respective states. Patterson joined Deval Patrick, whom the voters of Massachusetts elected in 2006 and again in 2010.[99] Most notable of all, Barack Obama now sits on the seat of power in the White House as the popularly elected 44th President of the United States. The cover of the March 2008 issue of *Ebony Magazine* captured the sentiments of many Americans at the time of his first campaign when it displayed a picture of Barack Obama with the simple caption, "IN OUR LIFETIME—Are we really witnessing the election of the nation's First Black President?"[100]

Only the most obstinate observers of America's racial history would argue that American society has not made remarkable progress since the institution of affirmative action admissions policies in the 1960s. However, despite the declaration of many pundits that America has already become a post-racial society,[101] there are still racial hurdles and obstacles that American society has to overcome or remove before all of the effects of our history of racial discrimination have been eliminated root and branch. The words of Justice Anthony Kennedy's deciding opinion in the 2007 school desegregation case, *Parents Involved in Community Schools v. Seattle School Dist. No. 1*, provides an excellent summary of the American struggle to assure that opportunity is not denied on account of race.

> Our Nation from the inception has sought to preserve and expand the promise of liberty and equality on which it was founded. Today we enjoy a society that is remarkable in its openness and opportunity. Yet our tradition is to go beyond present achievements, however significant, and to recognize and confront the flaws and injustices that re-

main. This is especially true when we seek assurance that opportunity is not denied on account of race. The enduring hope is that race should not matter; the reality is that too often it does.[102]

It takes time to end racial oppression that has existed for almost four centuries, since the first Africans walked off a ship in Jamestown, Virginia, in 1619.[103] In conceptualizing the process of the elimination of the effects of this history, instead of a metaphor of a track, a road, or a journey, the metaphor of a light dimmer switch is more useful. Ending racial oppression is not like turning on a light switch that instantly lights a dark room. Rather, it is more like slowly increasing the light in the room by gradually turning up a dimmer switch. Little by little and over an extended time, increasing the light illuminates more and more features of the room that the darkness previously obscured. And like the room, as American society shines the light of more and more understanding on the effects of racial oppression, it confronts different facets that were previously hidden by the darkness. The need to tackle these new aspects of racism is not in spite of, but *because of our success* in this ongoing struggle. For example, when selective higher education programs initiated affirmative action policies, American society was unfamiliar with concepts like "unconscious racism,"[104] "spirit murdering,"[105] or "white privilege."[106] Conscious expressions of racial hatred and inferiority that black Americans encountered on a daily basis overshadowed these more obscure facets of racial oppression. However, as American society eliminated public expressions of explicit racism, these other aspects were illuminated and those struggling against racial oppression recognized the need to address these new challenges.

## V. Suggested Changes in the Admissions Process

It is in the spirit of optimism and with the recognition of notable successes in the effort of American society to eliminate the negative consequences of our history of racial oppression that I want to propose a way to address the ethnic cleansing of Ascendant Blacks from the campuses of our nation's selective higher education institutions. Thus, I make this proposal with the acknowledgment of the tremendous progress that has occurred in American society in eradicating barriers of racial and ethnic oppression since the inception of affirmative action admissions policies. Yet I also write this proposal in the hope that selective higher education institutions in American society will recognize this trend and, in the spirit of the words of Justice Kennedy's reflection upon our traditions, that they take up the challenge to commit themselves and their institutions to go beyond their present achievements in diversity to assure that opportunity is not denied to Ascendant Blacks on account of their race and ethnicity.

As noted earlier, the DOE adopted new regulations on the collection and reporting of racial and ethnic data that all educational institutions must follow. These new regulations, which I call the "Final Guidance," went into effect for students enrolling in the fall of 2010. Under the Final Guidance, forms used by educational institutions to collect racial and ethnic data to report to the DOE must ask respondents whether they are Hispanic/Latino and must allow them to select one or more of the following racial groups: (1) American Indian or Alaska Native, (2) Asian American, (3) Black or African American, (4) Native Hawaiian or Other Pacific Islander, and (5) White. In this way, those who fill out these forms are asked to self-identify their racial and ethnic groups.

For purposes of reporting racial and ethnic information to the DOE, under the Final Guidance, educational institutions must include individuals who answer "yes" to the Hispanic/Latino question in their counts of Hispanic/Latinos, regardless of the racial categories they indicate. Educational institutions must include non-Hispanic/Latinos who indicate more than one racial category in a new "Two or More Races" category. Thus, non-Hispanic/Latino individuals who indicate that they are Black/African American and at least one other racial category are included in counts in the Two or More Races category, not in the Black/African American. The DOE also concluded that it was too administratively burdensome to have educational institutions throughout the country report the separate racial identities of those in the Hispanic/Latino or the Two or More Races categories. As a result, the Final Guidance has rejected the view of treating all blacks alike, regardless of racial or ethnic ancestry. The Final Guidance effectively divides those with some black ancestry into three categories: Black/African American, "Black Hispanics" (who are reported as Hispanics/Latinos), and "Blacks with Two or More Races" (who are reported as Two or More Races).

The Final Guidance, effectively, separates Black Multiracials into those that are Black Hispanics and those that are Blacks with Two or More Races. Thus, when addressing the impact of the Final Guidance, including the Proposal laid out in Chapter Five that takes into account the unfolding impact of the Final Guidance and the changing racial and ethnic ancestry of blacks benefitting from affirmative action, it is necessary to maintain the separation of Black Multiracials into Black Hispanics and Blacks with Two or More Races. Also, since the central concern of this book is the virtual elimination of Ascendant Blacks from selective higher education, the terms Black Multiracials, Black Immigrants, and Ascendant Blacks are based on parentage. This creates some inevitable confusion because for purposes of complying with federal regulations regarding the collecting and reporting of racial and ethnic data, the forms used must allow individuals the right to self-identify their racial and ethnic categories. Thus, the terms used for Ascendant Blacks, Black Multiracials, and Black Immigrants will not completely mesh with data generated by forms used to collect racial and ethnic information for purposes of complying with federal regulations. This is a problem that unfortunately cannot be resolved, only brought to the attention of the reader.

By instituting the changes in their application forms required by the Final Guidance, selective higher education institutions can, generally, distinguish Black Multiracials from Black/African American applicants. However, in trying to determine which blacks have a nonblack parent, relying on self-identification will be far from perfect. While normally self-identification is the appropriate way to determine race/ethnicity, the problem with self-identification in the context of applying to selective higher education institutions is the possibility that individuals will indicate their identification on application forms primarily for the strategic purpose of improving their admission prospects.[107] Thus, the statistics reported by selective higher education institutions that they gather from forms used by their admissions offices are likely to understate the number and percentages of Black Multiracials among blacks from what actual parentage would reveal.

In addition to the difficulty of determining which individuals with black ancestry have a nonblack parent, given the requirements of the Final Guidance, it is not possible to differentiate Ascendant Blacks from Black Immigrants among those counted as Black/African Americans. However, the Final Guidance allows educational institutions to include ethnic subcategories within these broad racial categories. Selective higher education programs should, therefore, change their application forms so that they can separate Ascendant Blacks from Black Immigrants. If they want a short-form way for black applicants to indicate their ethnic ancestry, then they should alter the Black/African American category to look something like this:

> Black or African American (country or countries of family's origin _____)

Another way that educational institutions could change their admissions form to provide more clarity and detail for applicants would be to change the Black/African American category to look something like this:[108]

> \_\_\_\_\_ Black or African American (Which best describes your Black or African American background?

U.S./African American    \_\_\_
Africa                   \_\_\_
Caribbean                \_\_\_
Other (Specify other Black or African American background) _____)

The reason for dividing the Black/African American category into these four subcategories is because approximately a third of foreign-born blacks are from Africa and about 52 percent are from the Caribbean,[109] so this list should be adequate for purposes of distinguishing Black Immigrants from Ascendant Blacks. By following what the Final Guidance requires, with the addition of subcategories within the Black/African American category, selective educational institutions can distinguish between self-identified Black Multiracials, Black Immigrants, and Ascendant Blacks.

I do not object to Black Multiracials or Black Immigrants benefitting from affirmative action. Over the centuries of struggle against racial oppression, many of the prominent figures in the Black Community in the United States were mixed-race individuals, including Crispus Attucks, Josephine Baker, Frederick Douglass, Lani Guinier, Prince Hall, P. B. S. Pinchback, Robert Smalls, Bishop Henry McNeal Turner, Booker T. Washington, Walter White, and of course, Barack Obama. Also, many prominent figures of the Black Community were foreign-born or had at least one foreign-born black parent, including Stokley Carmichael (Kwame Ture), Shirley Chisholm, Marcus Garvey, James Weldon Johnson, Colin Powell, Sidney Poitier, Malcolm X, and of course, Barack Obama. These individuals experienced the impact of being raced. They also added their voice, commitment, and talent to the collective struggle of blacks against racial subjugation in the United States. The primary concern that motivates and animates this book is that the overrepresentation of Black Multiracials and Black Immigrants is leading to the elimination of Ascendant Blacks from campuses. But any suggestion on how admissions committees should use the race and ethnicity of those of African descent to determine how to award positive consideration in the admissions process must be sensitive to the large contributions of blacks of mixed-race heritage and those with foreign-born parent(s) to the historical experiences of the Black Community, as well as to the need to assure that a significant number of Ascendant Blacks are in the student body.

Beyond the addition of ethnic subcategories under the Black/African American category, I urge selective higher education institutions not to rely solely on a purely biological box-checking approach. The first weakness of this box-checking approach is that it is too easy for applicants with some black ancestry to game the system. For example, one website that provides valuable advice to students applying for law school specifically states in its section for multiracial applicants, "If a school lets you identify only one racial category, check the box that indicates the most disadvantaged group: Native American or Black first...."[110] More importantly, however, since the justification for the use of racial categories in the admissions process is to ensure the inclusion of underrepresented minorities with experiences of our country's history of discrimination, it is necessary to provide black applicants with the opportunity to submit a supplemental statement that discusses the experiences they have had. How else can selective higher education programs be certain that they are using race in the admissions process in an appropriate way? In the allowance for these supplemental statements, the admissions form should encourage individuals to discuss their experiences of being raced and what they have done to struggle against the racial subjugation of blacks in the United States. The application form could add a statement that goes something like this for all of those who select the Black/African American category:

> **For those who have indicated Black/African American:** We believe that it is important to include in our student body meaningful numbers of blacks who have had substantial experiences derived from the historic experience of the Black Community in the United States with race discrimination and the struggle by blacks seeking to attenuate the effects of that history of discrimination. Thus, we invite you, at your option, to submit a supplemental statement that discusses both your experiences of being negatively impacted by the legacy of discrimination in the United States suffered by blacks and your efforts to assist our society in overcoming that legacy. Among the experiences that are relevant would be your participation in activities or organizations dedicated to attenuation of the continuing effects of history of discrimination in the United States, experiences in your life where race made a huge difference, and experiences that you have had with individuals you met because of race.

The Proposal, laid out in detail in Chapter Five, offers a hybrid approach to determine which blacks should receive positive consideration in the admissions process and how much they should receive. Admissions officials should take account both of the ancestry of blacks and of their experiences of both aspects of the historical experience of discrimination against blacks in the United States. First, admissions officials should give positive consideration in their holistic evaluation to those who appear to be Ascendant Blacks based on their applications. This is because of the ancestral connection that Ascendant

Blacks have to the historical experience of discrimination against blacks in the United States, which, in general, provides them with more experiences of that history than other racial/ethnic groups of blacks. Selective higher education programs should also allow any individual who checks the Black/African American box—including Black Multiracials, Black Immigrants, and Ascendant Blacks—the option of writing a supplemental statement that discusses their experiences of both aspects of the historical experience of discrimination against blacks. To further assess a black person's experiences of historical discrimination, admissions committees can also look at the various extracurricular activities that the applicant includes on their admissions forms. The more substantial an individual's experiences of being black in the United States, the more positive consideration admissions committees should award. Ascendant Blacks that supply these supplemental statements should receive what amounts to double-positive consideration: one amount based on their racial/ethnic ancestry and a second based on their supplemental statement.

If an admissions committee cannot conclude from the supplemental statement and extracurricular activities that the application of a Black Multiracial or Black Immigrant submits has sufficient experiences with both aspects of the historical experiences of blacks, then the admissions officials should not award such a person any positive consideration based on their being a member of an under represented minority group with a history of discrimination. This does not mean that these individuals would not be admitted, only that the admissions decisions should be based on judgments that do not award any positive consideration for them being a member of the black underrepresented minority group.

The general goals of the revised admissions process are to assure a substantial presence of Ascendent Blacks in the student body and to make certain that a critical mass of individuals sufficiently experienced with the history of racial oppression of blacks in the United States are included in the student body. I recognize that the terms "substantial presence" and "sufficiently experienced" are vague. The Supreme Court, however, has emphatically rejected quotas, so it is inadvisable to assign a percentage to the concept of substantial presence. And, as with any holistic evaluation, it is not possible to quantify the amount of positive consideration applicants should receive because of their racial/ethnic ancestry.[111] The important thrust of this book is to sensitize readers about the need to abandon the concept of treating all blacks alike for admissions purposes, because doing so obscures the declining proportions of Ascendant Blacks who are actually in their student bodies. Thus, the term substantial presence should be understood in light of the need to ensure that there are enough Ascendant Blacks so that the student body can appreciate their experiences. With regard to determining which applicants with some black ancestry have had sufficient experiences of the history of racial oppression of blacks in the U.S., admissions officials should seek to ensure that these are individuals who have had enough experiences that they are knowledgeable about and have a substantial appreciation of the history of racial oppression that blacks have encountered in the U.S. Admissions officials must determine that as they grapple with each individual black applicant.

Admittedly, the above proposal is still open to the possibility that individuals with some black ancestry will only reveal the portion of their racial/ethnic identity that maximizes their admissions prospects. Also, applicants might falsify or manufacture evidence indicating that they have had substantial experience with both aspects of the history of discrimination that blacks have encountered. To eliminate these weaknesses in the proposal, however, would require selective higher education institutions to adopt intrusive measures requiring the applicant to supply independent verification or documentation regarding their racial ancestry and their experiences of being black that many applicants, as well as admissions officials, would find abhorrent. The burden of composing a supplemental statement, however, will function as a disincentive for those who otherwise merely have to check a box to receive positive consideration based on African ancestry. In addition, selective higher educational programs would have the right to sanction applicants for misrepresentation under the general prohibition against falsifying the application.

It is also important to keep in mind that this book and these changes in the admissions process are concentrating on current applicants to selective higher education programs. As such, I am addressing the huge racial and ethnic changes that have occurred within the black population in the past two generations. Thus, the focus is on the racial and ethnic ancestry of blacks who are approaching college age, not on earlier generations of blacks. However, I agree wholeheartedly with President Obama's decision to indicate that he was Black/African American on his census form, despite the fact that he is the son of a Kenyan immigrant and a white mother.[112] In 1961, when the President was born, neither dominant American society nor the Black Community drew distinctions based on the race or ethnicity of blacks. Thus, he grew up at a time when American society and the Black Community considered someone like him to be the same as single-race, native-born blacks. Although Sasha and Malia will not need positive consideration based on their racial/ethnic ancestry in order to be admitted to a selective higher education institution, the definition of the term Ascendant Blacks (a person with two American-born black parents as determined by the one-drop rule) includes them even though their father's parents were a foreign-born black and a white person.

## VI. Limitations on the Scope of This Book

This book resists the impulse to further divide blacks by socioeconomic class.[113] The history of affirmative action admissions policies and the Supreme Court cases addressing these policies have been about the use of race and ethnicity in the admissions process, not socioeconomic class. In addition, admissions to selective higher education programs have always disproportionately involved members of the higher economic classes of American Society. For example, one report that looked at 146 selective colleges and universities in the United States noted that approximately 74 percent of all students hail from top quarter of the socioeconomic status scale (as measured by combining family income and the education and occupations of the parents), compared with only 3 percent from the lowest quartile, and only 10 percent are from the bottom half.[114] Thus, for discussing affirmative action, the economic divide within the Black Community is not nearly as salient as the racial/ethnic divide.

Like blacks, various ethnic groups within the broad racial/ethnic categories of American Indian or Alaska Native, Asian American, Hispanic/Latino, and Native Hawaiian or Other Pacific Islander are also lumped together. The failure to draw ethnic distinctions within these groups negatively affects the admissions prospects of those ethnic subgroups with relatively lower standardized tests scores and grade point averages. Oftentimes these ethnic differences in objective academic credentials within broad racial/ethnic groups are also based on the fact that the academically privileged ethnic subgroups have far less of a history of discrimination in the United States than the other ethnic subgroups. For example, Cubans tend to come from more privileged backgrounds than Puerto Ricans and Mexican Americans. In addition, Cubans do not have nearly as negative a history of discrimination in the United States as the other two groups.[115] Although it is beyond the scope of this book to address the impact of taking account of ethnic subcategories for the other broad racial/ethnic categories, I want to note in passing that many of the standardized testing agencies do report the test results for various Hispanic/Latino ethnic groups. For example, the College Board reports SAT scores for Mexican Americans, Puerto Ricans, and Other Hispanics.[116] In addition, the Association of American Medical Colleges reports MCAT scores for Mexican Americans, Puerto Ricans, Cubans, and Other Latinos.[117] Through the 2008–2009 testing years, the Law School Admissions Council reported LSAT scores for Mexican Americans, Puerto Ricans, and Other Hispanics.[118] There is an argument that the history of discrimination in the United States for those from Mexico and Puerto Rico is both quantitatively and qualitatively different than that of other Hispanic/Latino ethnicity groups.[119] Thus, the divisions that I am suggesting for blacks have some precedence in how various institutions involved in the higher education admissions process have recognized distinctions among Hispanic/Latinos.

## VII. Chapter Summaries

### Chapter One
### Historical Development of Federal Racial and Ethnic Classifications in Education

The promulgation of the Final Guidance is part of a much longer history of the federal government's use of racial classifications to collect racial and ethnic data. This chapter will briefly discuss that history. However, the federal government did not have any standards for the collection of data on race and ethnicity that applied to all of its agencies before 1970. Until the 1960s, Americans primarily employed racial classifications and racial data for the purposes of exclusion and segregation. With opinions by the Supreme Court in the 1950s, 1960s, and early 1970s, passage by Congress of civil rights legislation, and institution of President Johnson's Great Society programs, the nature of the use of racial classifications and racial data changed. Governmental entities and private institutions began to employ racial and ethnic classifications not to exclude, but to include individuals from previously discriminated minority groups. By the early 1970s, several different federal agencies employed racial and ethnic classifications and generated racial and ethnic statistics in their efforts to combat discrimination against individuals from minority groups. The federal government's need for consistent racial and ethnic data led to its first effort to standardize the collection and reporting of this information. In 1977, the federal government promulgated Statistical Policy Directive No. 15, Race and Ethnic Standards for Federal Statistics and Administrative Reporting (hereinafter, Directive 15). This chapter will discuss the process that led to the adoption of Directive 15.

For the next twenty years, Directive 15 was the principal document used for determining how the federal government would collect and report racial and ethnic statistics. It also significantly influenced the collection and reporting of this data by state and local governments and private industry. After its adoption, however, Directive 15 was subjected to much criticism and debate. From 1993 to 1997, the federal government conducted a review of Directive 15 that culminated with the Office of Management and Budget (OMB) publishing revisions in 1997 (the 1997 Revisions). This chapter also discusses the process that led to the issuance by OMB of the 1997 Revisions.

The 1997 Revisions provided that after reviewing the results of the 2000 census, all federal programs adopt the changes it proposed. Since educational institutions not only have to report the race and ethnicity of their students to the DOE, but also the race and ethnicity of their employees to the Equal Employment Opportunity Commission (EEOC), the DOE decided to wait until the EEOC enacted regulations before it proposed its own. After the EEOC finalized its regulations in 2005, the DOE issued proposed and then final regulations. The final regulations were promulgated by the DOE on October 19, 2007, with an implementation date for the school year of 2010–11. The Final Guidance changes the way that all educational institutions, including selective higher education programs, collect and report racial and ethnic data. These changes redefine those categories, including the definition of who is black. Therefore, this chapter will conclude by discussing the Final Guidance's impact on the admissions prospects of various racial and ethnic groups of black applicants that will unfold for years to come.

## *Chapter Two*
## *The Two Aspects of the History of the Black Experience*

As O'Connor indicated in *Grutter*, it is the experience of being a member of an underrepresented minority group with a history of discrimination that justified the consideration of race in the admissions process. The central feature in the historical experience of discrimination of the Black Community in the United States is race. However, there are two different aspects of that experience. One aspect involves blacks being discriminated against and victimized because of their race. This view of blacks as inferior to whites helped to make the oppression of blacks appear to be part of the natural order of things. Thus, one aspect is the experience of what it means to be "raced" or branded as inferior. Against the background of racial domination in the United States, however, the descendants of the sons and daughters of Africa developed a counterdiscourse, also based on race, in which blacks came together in a collective struggle for their liberation from white supremacy, not in the acquiescence to their racial inferiority. Consequently, the second aspect is the use of race as the characteristic that bound them together in a collective struggle for their racial liberation.

The first part of this chapter focuses on the aspect of the historical experience of blacks that resulted from the use of race as the characteristic to subjugate them based on their presumed inferiority. This chapter considers five periods of American history. The first period covers the arrival of blacks in British North America through the abolition of slavery. The second period covers the end of the Civil War through the rise of segregation. The third period deals with the Segregation Era and ends, roughly, with the Supreme Court's decision in *Brown v. Board of Education*, which heralds the end of legally enforced segregation. The fourth period is the Desegregation Era, which starts with the Court's opinion in *Brown v. Board of Education* and lasts into the 1990s. The fifth period discusses the modern era of race relations, the Post-Racial/Colorblind Era. This chapter will discuss both the principal mechanisms of oppression of blacks during each of these five eras and the dominant forms of justification for the belief in the inferiority of blacks that obscured the realization of the oppression of blacks.

The second part of this chapter focuses on the other aspect of the historical experience of discrimination of the Black Community in the United States, which involved its struggle against its racial oppression. Like the first part, it is also divided into five time periods. The first section discusses the ways in which blacks resisted slavery. The second section discusses the efforts engaged in by blacks to liberate themselves from their racial oppression during the Civil War and Reconstruction. The third section discusses the resistance of blacks to their racial oppression during the Segregation Era. The fourth section discusses efforts of blacks to work for the achievement of full equality during the Desegregation Era. The fifth section discusses the continuing struggle of blacks against their racial oppression by pointing out the various ways in which colorblindness tends to obscure their continued racial oppression.

## *Chapter Three*
## *Black Multiracials: Why They Should Not Be Preferred over Ascendant Blacks*

It took European colonists in the land that would come to constitute the United States some time to work out the relationship of mixed-race blacks to both whites and blacks. As a race-based system of slavery developed in colonial North America, interracial unions created a problem because they blurred the boundary lines between the races and raised questions about the justifications for slavery. Virtually every one of the American colonies banned interracial marriage during the colonial period. Also, whereas some colonies drew distinctions between blacks and mixed-race blacks, whom they referred to as "mulattoes," with the exception of the urban areas of the lower South like New Orleans, Charleston, and Mobile, early dominant American culture recognized little difference between mixed-raced blacks and single-race blacks. Scientific concerns about the products of interracial relationships, which began to be expressed in the 1840s, helped to lead to the acceptance of the one-drop rule throughout American society by the dawn of the twentieth century. Thus, from that time through the advent of affirmative action, there were no mixed-race blacks, only blacks with more or less African blood.

With the civil rights movement and the Supreme Court's 1967 decision in *Loving v. Virginia*, objections to intimate interracial relationships with blacks began to wane. The greater acceptance of interracial relationships led both to an increase in their numbers and to an increase in Black Multiracials. These larger numbers helped to spark the multiracial movement in the 1990s that led to changes in the 2000 census, which allowed individuals to self-identify with multiple racial categories. During this process, multiracial groups argued for an identity for Black Multiracials that distinguished them from the larger Black Community.

This chapter will discuss the history of the treatment of miscegenation and mixed-race blacks, the recent increases in interracial relationships and Black Multiracials, and the emergence of the multiracial movement. It will then discuss the evidence of the increasing percentages of Black Multiracials among black students on college campuses, in general, and in selective higher education programs, in particular. Black Multiracials tend to have several socioeconomic advantages over Ascendant Blacks in the pursuit of highly valued admissions seats in selective higher education programs. These advantages help to explain the overrepresentation of Black Multiracials among black students in selective higher education programs. There are also sociocultural differences between Black Multiracials and Ascendant Blacks, which suggests that Black Multiracials, in general, have less experiences consistent with the historical experience of blacks in the United States than Ascendant Blacks. This chapter will conclude by discussing these differences, because they justify providing more positive consideration in the admissions process of selective higher education institutions for Ascendant Blacks than Black Multiracials.

## *Chapter Four*
## *Black Immigrants: Why They Should Not Be Preferred over Ascendant Blacks*

Although the United States is a land of voluntary immigrants, before the origination of affirmative action very few blacks chose to immigrate into the United States. Until the institution of affirmative action, mainstream American society did not typically draw distinctions between descendants of blacks who arrived in chains and those who were recent voluntary arrivals. The Black

Community also embraced foreign-born blacks and their children as part of its community. However, at the same time that selective higher education programs were instituting affirmative action admissions policies, Congress was enacting new immigration legislation. In 1965, Congress enacted the Hart-Cellar Act, which became effective on July 1, 1968. This Act, other changes in American immigration law, and various international developments combined to create the conditions for a dramatic increase in immigration to the United States, including immigration by blacks. In 2012, the over 3.9 million foreign-born blacks, primarily from the Caribbean and Africa, constituted 9.9 percent of the black population. These foreign-born blacks and their one million American-born children are transforming the experience and meaning of being black in the United States. One of the places where this transformation is most apparent is in higher education, particularly at selective colleges, universities, and graduate programs.

This chapter will discuss the history of black migration to the United States from the colonial period to the present, including the explosion of voluntary black immigration that has occurred in the last fifty years. It will then discuss the evidence of the increasing percentages of Black Immigrants among black students on college campuses, in general, and in selective higher education programs, in particular. Like Black Multiracials, Black Immigrants tend to have several socioeconomic advantages over Ascendant Blacks in the pursuit of highly valued admissions seats in selective higher education programs. These advantages help to explain the overrepresentation of Black Immigrants among black students in selective higher education programs. There are also sociocultural differences between Black Immigrants and Ascendant Blacks, which suggests that Black Immigrants, in general, have less experiences consistent with the historical experience of blacks in the United States than Ascendant Blacks. This chapter will conclude by discussing the differences between Black Immigrants and Ascendant Blacks that justify providing more positive considerations in the admissions process of selective higher education institutions for Ascendant Blacks than for Black Immigrants.

## *Chapter Five*
## *Proposal for Changes in the Admissions Process*

This chapter offers a Proposal to take account both of the changing racial and ethnic ancestry of blacks and of the impact of the Final Guidance on admissions to selective higher education programs. This Proposal suggests a hybrid approach to the awarding of positive consideration to those of black ancestry in the admissions process. Selective higher education admissions officials should take account both of the racial and ethnic ancestry of blacks and of their experiences of both aspects of the historical experience of discrimination of blacks in the United States. First, admissions officials should give positive consideration to Ascendant Blacks as part of their holistic evaluation. In addition, selective higher education programs should also allow any individual who checks the Black/African American box—including Black Multiracials, Black Immigrants, and Ascendant Blacks—the option of writing a separate supplemental statement that discusses their experience of both aspects of the historical experience of discrimination of blacks. This, along with evidence of their experiences that is revealed in the other parts of their admissions materials, including their extracurricular activities, should be analyzed to determine how much experience they have of that history. The greater their experience of both aspects of the historical experience of blacks in the United States, the more positive consideration admissions committees should award. Ascendant Blacks that supply a supplemental statement would be eligible for what amounts to double-positive consideration: one amount based on their racial/ethnic ancestry and a second based on their supplemental statement.

As with any holistic evaluation, it is not possible to quantify the amount of positive consideration candidates should receive because of their racial/ethnic ancestry and their supplemental statement. However, selective higher education programs should seek to assure a substantial presence of Ascendant Blacks in their student body and to obtain a critical mass of individuals that have sufficient experience of both aspects of the history of racial oppression of blacks in the United States. The latter number is larger than the former and would include all Ascendant Blacks regardless of whether they submit a supplemental statement.

# Chapter One

# Historical Development of Federal Racial and Ethnic Classifications in Education

Before the founding of the Republic, race was used to determine legal rights. Because legal rights often turned on a person's race, there is a long history of legal disputes resolved in various state courts that centered on this issue.[1] However, since we are addressing affirmative action in higher education, the racial classifications that are most relevant for our purposes are those of the federal Department of Education (DOE). Thus, this chapter will address the history of federal racial classifications that culminated in the adoption by the DOE on October 19, 2007, of the "Final Guidance on Maintaining, Collecting, and Reporting Racial an Ethnic Data to the U.S. Department of Education" (hereinafter, the Final Guidance). The Final Guidance lays out the DOE's requirements for collecting and reporting data on race and ethnicity that all educational institutions must follow. The implementation date for the Final Guidance was the school year of 2010–11.[2]

From the time that predominately white colleges and universities started to admit blacks in significant numbers in the 1960s until the effective date of the Final Guidance, their admissions officials treated all blacks alike. They normally did not distinguish between black applicants based on racial or ethnic ancestry, but grouped them into a unified "Black/African/African American" category.[3] This changed with the implementation of the Final Guidance, which also marks the first time that the federal government dictated the procedures for collecting data on the race and ethnicity of students by educational institutions, including higher education programs.[4] Previous federal regulations, such as Title IV of the Higher Education Act, required colleges and universities to report data about the race and ethnicity of their students to the DOE, but the Department did not specify how to collect that data.[5] The DOE left higher education programs free to gather information using different methods from those employed by the federal government. This flexibility was important because it allowed higher education programs to respond more efficiently to their various local needs for the racial and ethnic data about their students.

The purpose of the Final Guidance is to "obtain more accurate information about the increasing number of students who identify with more than one race."[6] It requires educational institutions to collect racial and ethnic data that are reported to the DOE using a two-question format. Educational institutions must raise an initial question about the individuals' ethnicity that requires them to respond to whether they are Hispanic/Latino.[7] Then educational institutions are required to allow respondents to "mark one or more" categories of the following racial groups that apply to them: (1) American Indian or Alaska Native, (2) Asian American, (3) Black or African American, (4) Native Hawaiian or Other Pacific Islander, and (5) White.

When it comes to reporting racial and ethnic data to the DOE, the Final Guidance makes the Hispanic/Latino ethnic category the privileged category; therefore, it trumps all the racial categories. Thus, higher education programs must report to the DOE as Hispanic/Latino any individual who answers "yes" to the Hispanic/Latino question, regardless of what racial group(s) they designate. However, the Final Guidance requires that educational institutions report non-Hispanics/Latinos who identify with more than one racial category in a new racial category, Two or More Races. The specific racial designations of those in the Hispanic/Latino or the Two or More Races category are not reported. Thus, in the tallies of racial and ethnic data that educational institutions report to the DOE, it is impossible to tell the racial makeup of Hispanics/Latinos or the specific racial makeup of those reported in the Two or More Races category. As a result, Hispanics/Latinos who also check the black racial box (Black Hispanics) are not distinguishable from Hispanics/Latinos who check any other racial box(es). Similarly, non-Hispanic/Latino individuals who check the black racial box and another racial box (Blacks with Two or More Races) are not tallied separately from other individuals included in the Two or More Races category. The Final Guidance effectively, divides Black Multiracials into Black Hispanics and Blacks with Two or More Races.

Prior to the Final Guidance, most colleges and universities did not use the two-question approach to obtain information on the race and ethnicity of their students, nor allow them to mark more than one racial/ethnic box on their admissions forms.[8] An applicant had to identify him- or herself as only one of the following: American Indian or Alaska Native; Asian or Pacific Islander; Black, not of Hispanic origin; Hispanic; or White, not of Hispanic origin. As a result, admissions officials did not have to decide how to handle those who identified multiple racial/ethnic categories. With the implementation of the Final Guidance, however, colleges and universities will have to address how to treat Black Hispanics and Blacks with Two or More Races in the admissions process. Should they be treated like Black/African Americans? Should Black Hispanics be treated like Hispanics/Latinos? Should Blacks with Two or More Races be treated like others in the Two or More Races category? No matter how selective higher education institutions initially resolve these issues, the longer the Final Guidance is in effect, the greater the impetus will be to no longer treat Black Hispanics or Blacks with Two or More Races as Black/African American during the admissions process. Thus, the unfolding of the implication of the Final Guidance will most likely negatively impact the admissions prospects of self-identified Black Hispanics and Blacks with Two or More Races.

Since the adoption of the Final Guidance was motivated by the concern about the growing multiracial population in the United States, and not by immigration, it does not require colleges and universities to collect or report information about the ethnic background of blacks applying or attending their institutions. Black Immigrants, who are U.S. citizens or at least permanent residents, are included in counts of Black/African Americans that educational institutions report to the DOE. As Black Multiracials, who may score higher on standardized tests than Black/African Americans, are reclassified out of the Black/African American category, this will have the concomitant effect of increasing the competitiveness of applications from Black Immigrants, who will remain in the Black/African American category. Thus, while the implementation of the Final Guidance is likely to negatively impact the admissions prospects at selective higher education institutions of Black Multiracials, Black Immigrants are likely to benefit from the implementation of the Final Guidance.

This chapter will discuss the historical development of the federal government's effort to standardize the use of racial and ethnic classifications that, for purposes of educational institutions, culminates with the implementation of the Final Guidance. It will conclude with a discussion of the Final Guidance and its potential impact on the admissions prospects of Black Hispanics, Blacks with Two or More Races, and Black Immigrants.

The promulgation of the Final Guidance is part of a very long history of the federal government's efforts to gather and report racial and ethnic information about the American people that began with the adoption of the Constitution in 1787. To understand the adoption and impact of the implementation of the Final Guidance, it is helpful to discuss the history of the federal government's use of racial and ethnic classifications. Prior to the 1970s, there were no standards used by all federal agencies to collect data on race and ethnicity. However, the first and primary place where the federal government encountered the need to define racial and ethnic categories was the decennial census.

Part I will discuss the history of the use of racial and ethnic categories for descendants of Africa and for Hispanics/Latinos from the first decennial census in 1790 to the 1970s.

Up to the 1960s, the primary uses of racial/ethnic data and racial/ethnic classifications were the basis of exclusion, segregation, and discrimination directed at individuals from minority groups. With opinions by the Supreme Court in the 1950s, 1960s, and 1970s, passage by Congress of civil rights legislation, and the institution of President Johnson's Great Society programs, however, the nature of the use of racial/ethnic classifications and racial/ethnic statistics changed. As the 1960s and 1970s unfolded, government, private institutions, and advocacy groups began to employ racial and ethnic statistics to benefit disadvantaged populations and to use racial and ethnic classifications to determine beneficiaries of policies and programs to dismantle the effects of discrimination. Thus, by the early 1970s, several different federal agencies were also collecting, reporting, and using racial and ethnic data. This generated the first effort by the federal government to standardize the collection and reporting of such information. Part II will discuss the federal government's adoption in 1977 of its first document that standardized the racial and ethnic categories and their definitions, "Statistical Policy Directive No. 15: Race and Ethnic Standards for Federal Statistics and Administrative Reporting" (hereinafter, Directive 15). The driving force behind the adoption of Directive 15 was the need for comparable data to monitor the socioeconomic status of population groups that historically had experienced discrimination and differential treatment because of race and ethnicity.[9]

After its adoption, Directive 15 was subjected to much controversy and criticism. By the late 1980s, multiracial advocates were also pushing for the inclusion of a separate "multiracial" category on all governmental forms that asked for racial and ethnic information. From 1993 to 1997, the federal government conducted a review of Directive 15 that culminated with the Office of Management and Budget (OMB) publishing on October 30, 1997, its revisions to Directive 15 (hereinafter, the 1997 Revisions). Part III will discuss the process that led to the issuing of the 1997 Revisions and the differences between those revisions and Directive 15.

The 1997 Revisions provided that after the 2000 census, all federal programs adopt standards of reporting racial and ethnic data consistent with it. Since educational institutions not only have to report the race and ethnicities of their students to the DOE, but also the race and ethnicities of their employees to the Equal Employment Opportunity Commission (EEOC), the DOE decided to wait until the EEOC enacted regulations before it proposed its own. Part IV will discuss the process that led the DOE to issue the Final Guidance and its implications for the use of race and ethnicity of those with black ancestry for admissions to selective higher education programs.

# I. History of the Federal Government's Use of Racial and Ethnic Classifications Until the 1970s

The original mandate of the federal government to collect and report racial data derives from Article I, Section 2, Paragraph 3 of the U.S. Constitution. This provision specified the population formula for representation of the various states in the House of Representatives and the apportionment of direct taxes. The formula required the federal government to generate population counts for each state that excluded Native Americans, but included the whole number of free persons and three-fifths of all other persons (black slaves). It effectively required that individuals be broken down into three categories: free persons, slaves (all of whom were black), and Native Americans, who were generally not included in the counts. The first section below discusses the history of the federal government's efforts to collect and report racial data on the American population from the first census in 1790 to 1840. It was not until 1850 that the census added a "mulatto" category to distinguish mixed-race blacks from other blacks.[10] Every census conducted from 1850 to 1920, except for 1900, included at least one census category for mixed-race individuals. The second section below discusses the various census categories used to count mixed-race individuals during this period. The 1930 census abandoned the effort to separate mixed-race blacks from other blacks. Instead, the instructions for this census included the requirement that the census form of "a person of mixed White and Negro blood was to be returned as Negro, no matter how small the percentage of Negro blood." Concerns about the undercounting of blacks by census enumerators led to the development of census forms that respondents filled out in 1960. The third section discusses the adoption by the Census Bureau of the one-drop rule to determine who is black for the 1930 census. It also discusses the Census Bureau decision to switch from using census enumerators, who determined an individual's racial classification while filling out the census form, to self-reporting forms for the 1960 and 1970 censuses. The efforts of the Census Bureau to count Hispanics/Latinos began with the addition of "Mexican" as a separate racial category on the 1930 census form. In subsequent censuses, the Bureau reported those who identified Spanish as their mother tongue or people with Spanish surnames. The 1970 census form, however, was the first to list

"Hispanic" as a separate census category. The fourth section discusses the methods the Census Bureau employed to count or estimate the Hispanic/Latino population from the 1930 to the 1970 census forms.

## A. Use of Racial Classifications for Census Purposes from 1790 to 1840

The U.S. Constitution is the source of the original requirement for the federal government to classify individuals based on their race. Article I, Section 2, Paragraph 3 of the U.S. Constitution states:

> the House of Representatives and direct Taxes shall be apportioned among the several States which may be included within this Union, according to their respective Numbers, which shall be determined by adding to the whole Number of free persons, including those bound to Service for a Term of Years, and excluding Indians not taxed, three fifths of all other Persons.[11]

Since the Constitution also specifies that the number of electors in the Electoral College allowed for each state is determined by its representation in Congress, the above section also dictates state representation in the Electoral College.[12] The above paragraph later states that an actual enumeration of the U.S. population be made within three years after the first meeting of Congress and every ten years thereafter.

The Constitution thus recognized race as a fundamental element of political administration. Effectively, it required the federal government to count all whites, who would then be included in the counts of free persons. For blacks, two separate counts were needed: one count for those blacks who were free and, thus, part of the free person category, and another for black slaves who constituted the "all other Persons." Native Americans were divided into those who were taxed and those who were not.

The federal government conducted its first census in 1790. From 1790 to 1840, the census only reported counts for whites and blacks. The black counts were designated as either free or slave.[13] During this time, the census did not report counts for Native Americans. Nor is it certain how census enumerators treated those who were neither black nor white, but their numbers were probably small.

Through the 1810 census, the census forms generally sought only to determine the number of people and did not include questions for information beyond age, race, gender, and whether the person was slave or free.[14] The 1820 census form added questions to determine the number of foreign residents and categories to determine who was employed in agriculture, manufacturing, or commerce. The 1830 census added questions to determine which persons were deaf, dumb, or blind.

The 1840 census was the first to include data on those suffering from mental illnesses. This data showed that higher rates of mental illness existed among the black population than the white.[15] According to the data, the rate of insanity of free blacks in the North was ten times higher than among slaves.[16] This information quickly found its way into the debates about slavery. For pro-slavery advocates, this was strong evidence that freedom drove black people insane, and they argued that slavery was the natural state for blacks. However, closer examination of some of the census results by Dr. Edward Jarvis, a physician and founding member of the American Statistical Association, revealed significant errors. Jarvis' work showed that on returns from several towns, the number of insane black people equaled the number in the town, and on other returns, insane black people were counted in towns that did not have any blacks at all.[17]

From the first census until the one in 1840, the Secretary of State supervised the federal marshals who conducted the census.[18] Before the controversy regarding the counts of blacks who suffered from mental illness could be addressed, Secretary of State Abel Upshur died in an accidental explosion aboard the battleship *Princeton* on the Potomac River.[19] John C. Calhoun was appointed to replace him. Calhoun, a former Vice President of the United States and Senator from South Carolina, was the country's leading advocate for slavery. He had headed the pro-slavery faction in the Senate for many years.[20] Even though Calhoun served as Secretary of State for only one year, he had no desire to correct any errors in the 1840 census. Calhoun was among those who argued that the census and other documents demonstrated that changing the condition of the blacks from slave to free made things worse for them. He also asserted that the errors in the census were so numerous that they balanced out.[21] Yet despite Calhoun's position, confidence in the census-taking process was badly damaged by these controversies.

## B. Efforts to Separate Mixed-Race Blacks: 1850 to 1920

In response to the problems generated by the 1840 census, Congress created a special board composed of the Secretaries of State and the Interior and the Postmaster General to oversee the census. The board granted considerable authority to its new Superintendent of the Census, Joseph C.G. Kennedy. Kennedy implemented a number of changes in the way the census was conducted and sought advice from the leaders of the American Statistical Association and the

American Geographical and Statistical Society.[22] Thus, the 1850 census was the first to benefit from scientific advice. The census questionnaire was considerably more extensive than its predecessors and the first one to add a "mulatto" category.[23]

By 1850, a significant scientific debate about the nature of racial differences was raging in the United States. The scope of this debate is extensively discussed in Chapter Three. Southern physician Josiah C. Nott (his textbook *Types of Mankind*, written with G.R. Gliddon in 1854, was the contemporary best seller in the field of anthropology) led a group of scientists who argued that blacks and whites were separate species. Nott theorized that because of this, the products of interracial unions would be frailer and thus live shorter lives.[24] One of the justifications for adding the mulatto category was the desire to test Nott's theories.

The 1860 census was the first one that reported counts of groups other than blacks and whites. The War with Mexico ended in 1848, and much of the newly acquired western region was enumerated in the census for the first time in 1860. This census provided counts for American Indians (excluding those not taxed) and Chinese (in California only).[25] Only about 79,000, or 0.25 percent of the total U.S. population, fell into these categories.[26]

With the exception of the year 1900, a mulatto category was included among the questions about race or color on the census form from 1850 through 1920.[27] In 1890, the census actually subdivided the categories of mixed-race blacks to include one for mulattoes, quadroons, and octoroons.[28] However, the 1900 census abandoned the effort to divide mixed-race blacks from other blacks. There were two reasons for this change: the census had no clear mandate to collect information on subdivisions of mixed-race blacks; and the spread of Jim Crow legislation and greater reliance on the one-drop rule made distinctions among blacks unnecessary.[29] Nevertheless, the mulatto category made a return for both the 1910 and 1920 censuses.

## C. One-Drop Rule Becomes Official and Census Moves to Self-Reporting Forms: 1930 to 1970

The Census Bureau finally ended its efforts to divide blacks based on racial ancestry with the 1930 census. The instructions for filling out the census form stated that "a person of mixed White and Negro blood was to be returned as Negro, no matter how small the percentage of Negro blood."[30] This essentially made the one-drop rule a part of the compilation of census statistics.

The 1940 census produced a number of undercounting controversies. One study of that census demonstrated an undercounting of 2.8 percent of men aged 21 to 35. The Census Bureau's undercount of black men in this age range, however, was 13 percent.[31] The highly regarded demographer Ansley Coale studied the 1950 census and concluded that there was an undercount of nonwhites by 12 to 13 percent.[32] The problem of undercounting blacks was traced to mistakes by census enumerators. To remedy this problem for the 1960 census, the Bureau decided to adopt the practice of sending forms to homes, where the head of the household would fill them out before the enumerator arrived. Over 80 percent of American households received an advanced copy of the 1960 form.[33] If needed, the enumerators would correct forms improperly completed. The 1970 census form was the first designed to be completed by respondents without any assistance from census enumerators.[34] The Census Bureau viewed these changes as improving the accuracy of racial statistics it generated. However, having enumerators determine a person's racial classification based mainly on phenotypical appearances and the enumerator's visual acuity was consistent with the view of race as a socially ascribed characteristic. The number of blacks, for example, represented the number of individuals in our society who appeared to be black. As a result, the census tallies with regard to racial data provided information that allowed our society to map the effects of racial social practices, casual racial identification, and the structure of racial hierarchies.

Although there is little evidence indicating that the Census Bureau was aware of it at the time,[35] the change from enumerators filling out the forms to heads of households doing it, initiated a process that has increasingly produced a fundamental redefinition in the meaning of racial identification. This process will be discussed in greater detail in Chapter Three. However, with individuals preparing their families' census forms and selecting their family members' racial/ethnic categories (along with other developments), racial identity shifted from a socially ascribed characteristic to self-perception.[36] As a result, the number of individuals now counted in a given racial/ethnic category is more a manifestation of cultural affiliation and personal belief than a reflection of who constitutes the socially ascribed members of a given racial/ethnic category.

## D. Hispanics/Latinos and the Census

The 1930 census was the first major effort by the Census Bureau to count the Latin American population. The rationale for including a Mexican category was the significant and recent increase in immigration of Mexicans during and after the Mexican Revolution. The 1930 census actually listed "Mexican" as a separate racial category. The Census Bureau used the "Mexican" identifier even though many of the individuals counted were U.S. citizens. The instructions indicated that "practically all Mexican laborers are of a racial mixture difficult to classify."[37] Mexicans were defined as all persons born in Mexico or having Mexican parents, but who were "not definitely white, Negro, Indian, Chinese, or Japanese."[38] The 1930 census reported 1,422,533 Mexicans, which was 1.2 percent of the population.[39]

The 1940 census instructions rejected the characteristic of Mexicans as a separate racial group. That census classified "persons of Mexican birth or ancestry who were not definitely Indian or of other nonwhite race ... as white."[40] Mexican Americans had lobbied against maintenance of the Mexican category with the assistance of the Mexican government. They perceived a connection between the designation and the forced repatriation of 400,000 Mexicans and Mexican Americans in the Southwest to Mexico in the 1930s.[41] Thus, the Census Bureau did not report Mexicans in 1940; rather, it reported the number for those who identified Spanish as their "mother tongue."[42] In 1950 and 1960, the Census Bureau compared the last names of respondents in the five southwestern states that had originally been part of Mexico (Colorado, California, Arizona, New Mexico, and Texas) to a list of Spanish surnames in order to generate a compilation of Hispanics/Latinos.[43] The Census Bureau limited the collection of Spanish surnames to those five states because people who migrated from European countries like Spain, Italy, and Portugal also had Spanish surnames.[44] Europeans with Spanish surnames, however, were more likely located outside of the Southwest.

Coming into the 1960s, several terms were in use for those referred to as Hispanics/Latinos today. The terms "Chicano," "Mexican American," "Spanish surname," and "Spanish-speaking," among others, were usually used interchangeably by government officials. Individuals used these ambiguous terms to refer to Mexican Americans, Puerto Ricans, and, increasingly, Cubans.[45] Those in the Southwest primarily spoke of Mexican Americans, whereas those in the Northeast almost always had Puerto Ricans in mind. This confusion also reflected confusion with regard to government data collection. The situation was accurately reflected in comments read into the Congressional Record on June 15, 1967, by Congressman Henry González:

> In the first place, there is the problem of definition. There is not even a generally accepted name for this minority group. Americans of Spanish surname are called Mexicans, Mexicanos, Latins, Latinos, Latin Americans, Mexican Americans, and Hispanic Americans.... This group of people is so scattered about the land and so disparate in its origins that it has problems defining itself, just as the government has problems in defining it.[46]

Advocates for the Hispanic/Latino population lobbied for inclusion as a separate census designation in the late 1960s. The Census Bureau resisted these efforts because it was late in their planning process. However, the Nixon Administration supported the idea as an outgrowth of the Republican "Southern Strategy." Since Nixon appealed to disaffected white voters, he viewed the black vote as lost to the GOP, but Hispanics were a minority group that Republicans could potentially cultivate. However, because of the lateness of the request from the Nixon Administration, the parties reached a compromise. The Census Bureau sent out two separate long-form questionnaires in addition to the standard questionnaire. The long-form questionnaire sent to a 15-percent sample asked respondents to indicate household members who spoke the Spanish language and had Spanish as their mother tongue. The Census Bureau counted all members in the household as having a Spanish-speaking background if either the head of household or the spouse of the household spoke Spanish as a child.[47] The Bureau also sent out a different long-form questionnaire to a 5-percent sample of the population, in which it asked, "Is this person of Spanish/Hispanic origin?" This form included five different responses: Mexican, Puerto Rican, Cuban, Central or South American, or other Spanish.[48] (The remaining 80 percent of the general population received the standard questionnaire.) From these results, the Census Bureau estimated 9.7 million Hispanics/Latinos, making up 4.7 percent of the U.S. population.[49] However, many scholars and activists criticized the 1970 census and suspected that it seriously undercounted the Hispanic population.[50]

## II. Efforts to Standardize the Collection of Data on Race and Ethnicity in the 1970s: Adoption of Directive 15

Until the 1960s, the primary uses of racial classifications were for the purposes of exclusion, segregation, and discrimination of members of minority groups. For example, public school officials identified black or colored schoolchildren and assigned them to separate and inferior schools. As late as 1960, interracial marriage between blacks and whites was illegal in over twenty states.[51] Thus, it was necessary to determine who was black to prevent miscegenation. Employers and labor unions often denied skilled employment to those determined to be black. Discriminatory practices by the real estate industry restricted the residential choices of blacks to certain substandard neighborhoods. Many business operators of merchandise stores, hotels, and restaurants refused to serve black customers. The proponents of these discriminatory practices used racial statistics to justify their actions. As a result, many civil rights leaders opposed the collection and production of racial statistics.[52] Not surprisingly, minority groups did not participate in the decision-making process for determining how to collect national statistics on race and ethnicity.[53]

Supreme Court rulings in the 1950s and 1960s outlawed racial and ethnic discrimination by governmental entities. Congress passed civil rights legislation in the 1960s, including the 1964 Civil Rights Act, the 1965 Voting Rights Act, and the 1968 Fair Housing Act. Many of the social welfare programs enacted as part of President Johnson's Great Society initiative sought to distribute federal funds based on population to improve living conditions in the cities and address the problems of disadvantaged groups. Because of these and other developments, the need and the purpose of employing racial classifications and collecting racial and ethnic data changed. Governmental entities and private institutions began to use racial and ethnic classifications not to exclude but to include individuals from previously oppressed minority groups. Enforcement of federal, state, and local civil rights statutes required accurate racial and ethnic statistics to demonstrate the existence of legally recognized discrimination. In addition, the motivating logic of civil rights activists was that racism was not simply a product of isolated actions and decisions by individuals, but part of a much larger system of discrimination and oppression. To demonstrate the systematic nature of racial oppression, statistics of various social and economic differences based on race were crucial. Civil rights activists also used racial and ethnic statistics as the basis for generating support for new laws and policies to address the impact of discrimination. Thus, as the 1960s unfolded, government, private institutions, and advocacy groups increasingly employed racial and ethnic classifications and used racial and ethnic statistics to benefit disadvantaged minority populations.

Even though the federal government had collected racial data for 200 years, before the 1970s no federal standards existed for the collection of data on race and ethnicity that applied to all federal agencies.[54] Largely because of court decisions and civil rights laws noted above, many more federal agencies beyond the Census Bureau and the Immigration and Naturalization Service were collecting racial and ethnic information. In 1976, Congress passed Public Law 94-311 in response to criticisms that Hispanics/Latinos were undercounted during the 1970 census. That law required federal agencies to provide separate counts for the Hispanic population to remedy discrimination against those of Hispanic origin.[55]

> The driving force for the development of the federal standards on racial and ethnic classifications in the 1970s was the need for comparable data to monitor equal access, in areas such as housing, education, mortgage lending, health care services, and employment opportunities,

DEVELOPMENT OF RACIAL CLASSIFICATIONS IN EDUCATION    45

for population groups that historically had experienced discrimination and differential treatment because of race and ethnicity.[56]

The origin of the effort to standardize the collection and reporting of racial and ethnic data by the federal government lies with President Johnson's Executive Order 11185 issued in October of 1964. The order created the Federal Interagency Committee on Education (FICE).[57] The Commissioner of Education chaired the Committee and reported to the Secretary of the Department of Health, Education, and Welfare (HEW). The FICE Subcommittee on Minority Education completed a report in April 1973 on higher education for Chicanos, Puerto Ricans, and American Indians. HEW Secretary Caspar Weinberger was particularly interested in the part of the report pointing to the lack of useful data on racial and ethnic groups. Weinberger encouraged the implementation of the recommendations of the Subcommittee's report that stated: "... (1) coordinate development of common definitions for racial and ethnic groups; [and] (2) instruct the Federal agencies to collect racial and ethnic enrollment and other educational data on a compatible and nonduplicative basis."[58]

In June 1974, FICE created the Ad Hoc Committee on Racial and Ethnic Definitions to implement the above recommendations. The Ad Hoc Committee came up with terms and definitions to cover the major categories of race and ethnicity that all federal agencies could use to meet their particular data requirements. The Committee recommended the following categories and definitions:

1. **American Indian or Alaskan Native**—A person having origins in any of the original peoples of North America;
2. **Asian or Pacific Islander**—A person having origins in any of the original peoples of the Far East, Southeast Asia, or the Pacific Islands. This area includes, for example, China, Japan, Korea, the Philippine Islands, and Samoa;
3. **Black/Negro**—A person having origins in any of the black racial groups of Africa;
4. **Caucasian/White**—A person having origins in any of the original peoples of Europe, North Africa, the Middle East, or the Indian subcontinent; and
5. **Hispanic**—A person of Mexican, Puerto Rican, Cuban, Central or South American, or other Spanish culture or origin, regardless of race.[59]

Even though Supreme Court cases had previously rejected arguments by those from the Indian subcontinent who wanted the government to classify them as white,[60] the Ad Hoc Committee included those from the Indian subcontinent in its definition of Caucasians as opposed to Asians. The Committee expressed its belief that the term "Asian" should refer more to East Asians. In addition, the Committee noted that although individuals from the Indian subcontinent were from Asia, and some were victims of discrimination, the discrimination they faced appeared to be concentrated in specific geographical and occupational areas.[61]

The Ad Hoc Committee considered creating an Other category for use principally by individuals of mixed racial backgrounds.[62] However, a majority of the Committee members opposed this because it would complicate the process of collecting data and add to the cost.[63] The Committee did recognize that the use of an Other category might be appropriate when entities were collecting racial and ethnic data using a self-identification approach. If an Other category was used, however, the respondent should also be required to specify the group with which they identify. Thus, the Ad Hoc Committee sought to provide the means to edit the responses of those who chose the Other category. This would help to keep the number of responses in the Other category to as few as possible. When an entity used an observer identification method to gather data, however, the Ad Hoc Committee viewed the Other category as undesirable.

In the spring of 1975, OMB, HEW, EEOC, and the General Accounting Office all agreed to use the racial and ethnic categories developed by the Ad Hoc Committee on a trial basis for at least a year.[64] After the trial period, representatives from a very broad range of federal agencies—all of the above, plus the Department of Justice, the Department of Labor, the Department of Housing and Urban Development, and the Bureau of the Census—discussed the experiences of the trial period. After the meeting, OMB agreed to prepare a final draft of the definitions for comment by the various federal agencies.

In addition to slight revisions to the categories and definitions initially adopted by the Ad Hoc Committee, OMB made two major changes.[65] First, they moved individuals with Indian subcontinent ancestry from the Caucasian/White category to the Asian category. Second, OMB made it clear that individuals who were in the American Indian or Alaskan Native category were those who maintained a cultural identification through tribal affiliation or community recognition. OMB made no provision for an Other category.

On May 12, 1977, the "Race and Ethnic Standards for Federal Statistics and Administrative Reporting" became effective for all federal government agencies and required that all existing data collections comply with its terms and definitions by January 1, 1980.[66] In 1978, the standards were renamed "Statistical Policy Directive No. 15, Race and Ethnic Standards for Federal Statistics and Administrative Reporting," or Directive 15.[67] Directive 15 listed the following five racial/ethnic categories and definitions:

## DEVELOPMENT OF RACIAL CLASSIFICATIONS IN EDUCATION    47

a. **American Indian or Alaskan Native**—A person having origins in any of the original peoples of North America, and who maintains cultural identification through tribal affiliation or community recognition;
b. **Asian or Pacific Islander**—A person having origins in any of the original peoples of the Far East, Southeast Asia, the Indian subcontinent, or the Pacific Islands. This area includes, for example, China, India, Japan, Korea, the Philippine Islands, and Samoa;
c. **Black**—A person having origins in any of the black racial groups of Africa;
d. **Hispanic**—A person of Mexican, Puerto Rican, Cuban, Central or South American or other Spanish culture or origin, regardless of race; and
e. **White**—A person having origins in any of the original peoples of Europe, North Africa, or the Middle East.

Directive 15 noted that those who sought to comply with it should not construe it to limit the collection of data to the categories described above. It permitted the use of subcategories within any of the basic racial/ethnic categories. However, those who used subcategories had to organize their use in a way that allowed for the aggregation of the information in the subcategories into the basic racial/ethnic categories.[68] Directive 15 also concluded that it was preferable to collect data on race separately from ethnicity in a two-question format, but it provided for a way to collect this information in a combined one-question format. If collected separately, then the minimum designations were:

a. <u>Race</u>:
   American Indian or Alaskan Native
   Asian or Pacific Islander
   Black
   White
b. <u>Ethnicity</u>:
   Hispanic origin
   Not of Hispanic origin

If collected in a one-question format, then the minimum acceptable categories were:

   American Indian or Alaskan Native
   Asian or Pacific Islander
   Black, not of Hispanic origin
   Hispanic
   White, not of Hispanic origin.[69]

From this brief history, it is apparent that the Census Bureau's use of racial and ethnic categories to gather data serves a different purpose from the federal racial and ethnic categories standardized in the 1970s.[70] The goal of the Census Bureau is to collect as much demographic information about the U.S. population as possible. However, the primary purpose of the federal race and ethnic categories standardized in the 1970s was to track discrimination against specific racial and ethnic groups—not all possible racial and ethnic groups—in the United States. The link between the racial and ethnic categories in Directive 15 and those used by the Census Bureau comes from the requirement that all federal agencies use the Directive 15 categories and definitions. Thus, when the Census Bureau uses subcategories, it must arrange their use in such a way that the data gathered are capable of being condensed into the federal racial/ethnic categories specified in Directive 15.

## III. Adoption of the 1997 Revisions

Directive 15 became the foundation of the process for collecting and reporting racial and ethnic data over the next twenty years. It not only altered the way the federal government collected and reported this data, but also affected the collecting and administrative record keeping of such data for state and local governments as well as the private sector. However, intense debates existed about the categories and definitions of Directive 15. These debates eventually caused the federal government to undertake a review of Directive 15 from 1993 to 1997. The review culminated in the issuance on October 30, 1997, by OMB of the "Revisions to the Standards for the Classification of Federal Data on Race and Ethnicity" (hereinafter, the 1997 Revisions).[71] The 1997 Revisions also provided that other federal programs adopt its standards. The first section of this part will briefly discuss the need to revise Directive 15. The second section will discuss the changes to the federal standards contained in the 1997 Revisions, which were implemented in the 2000 and 2010 censuses. The third section includes the racial/ethnic counts of the American population for the 2000 and 2010 censuses.

### A. Need to Revise Directive 15

After the adoption of Directive 15, intense debate commenced about its categories and definitions. The criticisms were the result of logical flaws in the categories and definitions, the rapidly changing nature of the American population, and the growing recognition that racial and ethnic categories were social constructs.[72] Those who pointed to the logical flaws noted that some of the categories were racial, some were geographic, and some were cultural.[73]

For example, according to the definitions, whites, Asians, Pacific Islanders, and American Indians had origins in original peoples, but blacks had origins only in black racial groups of Africa. Also, who were the original people of North Africa or the Middle East? For Hispanics, they could be of Spanish culture or origin, regardless of race. Of all of the racial groups, only those who were American Indians and Alaskan Natives had to maintain tribal affiliations or community recognition. Some individuals also complained that they could not locate themselves within any of the racial and ethnic categories. Among these were the parents of multiracial children who protested against the requirement to select only one race for their children.[74] The 1990 census generated considerable evidence of the latter compliant. The instructions for designating race on the 1990 census forms required individuals to check the one box that best described their race. Despite these instructions, however, more than 500,000 people selected more than one racial category.[75]

From 1993 to 1997, the federal government conducted an extensive review of the categories specified in Directive 15.[76] The various federal agencies created an Interagency Committee for the Review of Racial and Ethnic Standards to make recommendations to OMB. The Interagency Committee included representation from thirty federal agencies.[77] Numerous opportunities for public comment and public hearings were provided around the nation at various stages of the process. The public comments helped to identify several areas of concern for the Interagency Committee to address, including the following:

- Should "Hispanic" be a response option to the race question?
- Should data on race and ethnicity be gathered via two separate questions? If yes, then what should be the sequence of these questions? Or should data on race and ethnicity be gathered in a single question?
- How should data on individuals of multiple racial heritages be classified?
- Should the Asian or Pacific Islander category continue to include data collected on Native Hawaiians?
- Should the minimum number of racial and ethnic categories be expanded to include other population groups?[78]

The Interagency Committee examined various criticisms of and suggestions for improving the Directive 15 categories and developed a research agenda for some of the more significant issues. After the Interagency Committee conducted an extensive evaluation of the Directive 15 categories, it presented its report to OMB on July 9, 1997. With a few modifications, OMB adopted the Interagency Committee's recommendations and issued the 1997 Revisions.[79]

## B. 1997 Revisions

OMB agreed that self-identification is the preferred means of obtaining information about an individual's race and ethnicity. However, in some situations observer identification is more practical (e.g., completing a death certificate). The 1997 Revisions also provided that after a review of the 2000 census all federal programs adopt the standards it proposed.[80]

### 1. Hispanic/Latino Ethnicity Question and the Two-Question Format

OMB decided to use the term "Hispanic or Latino" as opposed to "Hispanic." OMB indicated regional differences in the terms used: "Hispanic" was the commonly used term in the eastern United States, "Latino" in the west. OMB also changed the definition to the following:

> "Hispanic or Latino": the term "Hispanic/Latino" refers to persons who trace their origin or descent to Mexico, Puerto Rico, Cuba, Central or South American or some other Spanish culture.

The research conducted under the auspices of the Interagency Committee found that the best way to produce the most complete and accurate data on Hispanics/Latinos was to separate the Hispanic/Latino origin question from the question about race. When respondents are asked both questions, the research indicated that it was best to ask the Hispanic/Latino origin question first.[81] The 1997 Revisions were guided by the conclusions of this research.[82]

The research suggested that the main reason to gather data on Hispanics/Latinos the way that OMB agreed to do it was because they do not always identify with the American racial categories. There was plenty of evidence of this on the 2000 census. Although 1997 Revisions did not allow for the use of a "Some Other Race" category, the Census Bureau obtained an exemption to permit its use for the 2000 (and later 2010) census primarily because it believed that many Hispanics/Latinos would mark it.[83] Slightly more than 35 million people indicated on their 2000 census forms that they were Hispanic/Latino. About 47.9 percent checked only the white racial box, and an additional 42.2 percent checked only the Some Other Race category. In addition, of those who checked the Some Other Race box, over 95 percent also identified themselves as Hispanic/Latino.[84] "Thus it is clear that reporting of [Some Other Race] is highly related to how Hispanics report race."[85] In 2010 census, the portion of Hispanics/Latinos selecting only Some Other Race dropped to 36.7 percent, with an additional 53.0 percent selecting white only.[86]

## 2. How to Collect Data on Individuals of Multiple Racial Heritage

According to OMB, the most controversial and sensitive issue during discussions about revising Directive 15 dealt with how to address the classifications of individuals with parents of different races.[87] Individuals in black-white marriages[88] and multiracial advocacy groups spearheaded efforts to add a "multiracial" option to the collection of data for the 2000 census.[89] These proponents generally argued that mixed-race individuals viewed themselves as multiracial rather than belonging to a single racial or ethnic group. A multiracial designation was, therefore, a better reflection of the true understanding of the multiracial person's racial identity. These groups pointed to the psychological problems created for biracial children who are forced to identify with one parent more than the other. In addition, they noted that the one-drop rule, used so long to classify any person with any black blood as black, was inherently racist.[90]

Opponents of the inclusion of a multiracial category on federal forms pointed to several difficulties that its addition would create.[91] A multiracial category could confuse many respondents. Many Americans are of mixed ancestry, including most blacks. Because of centuries of interracial mixing in the United States, experts estimated that between 75 and 90 percent of America's black population have some white genes. Researchers place the overall white gene proportion of American blacks at somewhere between one-fifth and one-fourth.[92] Presumably, the multiracial category relates to individuals who have parents of different races or ethnicities as determined by existing cultural practices at the time the parents were born, which included the one-drop rule for determining who is black. If respondents abandoned the one-drop rule when thinking about their parents' race and identified their ancestries going back many generations, then the multiracial category could prove to be very large and destabilizing for blacks. Beyond blacks, as Maria Root noted, "virtually all Latinos and Filipinos are multiracial, as are the majority of American Indians and Native Hawaiians. Even a significant proportion of White-identified persons are of multiracial origin."[93]

Another problem with including a multiracial category on federal forms was the potential variability of a person's racial identity over time. Individuals who identify themselves as multiracial at one stage in life may identify themselves in a single race or ethnic category later on. Thus, the individuals included in a multiracial category will fluctuate from time to time.

Yet another problem stems from the primary reason the federal government adopted the definitions for the standard racial and ethnic classifications in Directive 15. Since the driving force behind Directive 15 was the need to combat discrimination and differential treatment experienced by historically oppressed population groups, how should current civil rights legislation treat multiracial individuals? A key decision was whether the multiracial category would be a protected class with the same legal rights to representation as the current minority categories, or whether all multiracial individuals would be reclassified into the existing five categories. If they were reallocated, then other objections arose related to the potential controversies and difficulties associated with their reallocation. What method of reallocation should institutions employ? For example, the Tabulation Working Group of the Interagency Committee, which recommended the changes eventually adopted as the 1997 Revisions, came up with eleven different ways to reallocate multiracials.[94] Also, if the reason to allow individuals the option of selecting a multiracial category was respect for individual self-identification, then reallocation would violate that principle. A solution to this reallocation objection would reject the multiracial category in favor of allowing individuals to check all the racial categories that applied to them. However, if individuals were allowed to check multiple boxes and no reallocation occurred, then there would be a very large number of categories that reflected all of the different multiracial combinations, many of which would have very few individuals. This would not only create a large administrative burden, it would also create very difficult sampling issues. Categories with small numbers are far more vulnerable to inaccuracies from sampling errors than are categories with large numbers.

In the end, OMB rejected the addition of a multiracial category for individuals to select. After the 1990 census, experts generally placed estimates of the U.S. multiracial population at between 4 and 6 percent, with highest estimate at 6.6 percent.[95] OMB's research, however, showed that less than 2 percent of the population selected two or more races, but the percentage of multiracials was growing.[96] Even though OMB rejected the multiracial category, it decided that when self-identification, which is the preferred method, is used, forms to gather racial and ethnic data must employ a method that allows individuals to check more than one race category from the given list of races. Thus, with the adoption of the 1997 Revisions, the federal government—for the first time ever—allowed individuals to designate more than one racial category.

### 3. Modifications for the Racial Categories

The 1997 Revisions included five racial categories and the Hispanic/Latino ethnic category, to replace the previous five included in Directive 15. A number of witnesses and groups sought to extend the categories beyond those included in Directive 15. Categories suggested included Middle Easterners/Arabs, Cape Verdeans, Europeans Americans, German Americans, and Creoles. However, OMB agreed only to alter the Asian and Pacific Islanders category of Directive 15 by removing the Pacific Islanders and combining them into a new category with Native Hawaiians. During Congressional testimony in 1993, Senator Daniel Akaka of Hawaii asserted on behalf of the entire Hawaii congressional delegation, Hawaii's Governor John Waihee, Native Hawaiian organizations, and the National Coalition for an Accurate Count of Asians and Pacific Islanders that they sought a separate classification for Native Hawaiians. Akaka argued that Native Hawaiians fell through the cracks between being defined as Native Americans in many federal laws and classified as Asians or Pacific Islanders on federal forms. OMB removed Pacific Islanders from the Asian category and placed them in a new combined category, Native Hawaiian or Other Pacific Islanders. The other significant change from Directive 15 in the definitions of the categories adopted by OMB was to change the definition of American Indian or Alaska Native by including the "original peoples from South and Central America" to those from North America. Thus, the five racial categories and their definitions contained in the 1997 Revisions were as follows:

a. **American Indian or Alaska Native**—A person having origins in any of the original peoples of North and South America (including Central America), and who maintains tribal affiliation or community attachment.
b. **Asian**—A person having origins in any of the original peoples of the Far East, Southeast Asia, or the Indian subcontinent including, for example, Cambodia, China, India, Japan, Korea, Malaysia, Pakistan, the Philippine Islands, Thailand, and Vietnam.
c. **Black or African American**—A person having origins in any of the black racial groups of Africa.
d. **Native Hawaiian or Other Pacific Islander**—A person having origins in any of the original peoples of Hawaii, Guam, Samoa, or other Pacific Islands.
e. **White**—A person having origins in any of the original peoples of Europe, the Middle East, or North Africa.[97]

## C. Results of the 2000 and 2010 Censuses

The 2000 census form generally followed the 1997 Revisions. It separated the Hispanic/Latino ethnicity question from the question about race. However, it added to the five racial categories a "Some Other Race" category. As noted above, although the 1997 Revisions did not allow for the use of such a category, the Census Bureau obtained an exemption from OMB to permit its use.[98]

The Census Bureau compiled data in two different ways: based solely on the Hispanic/Latino ethnicity question and based on the question of race. Thus, the 2000 census reported:

### HISPANIC OR LATINO

| | | |
|---|---:|---:|
| Total population | 281,421,906 | (100.0) |
| Hispanic or Latino | 35,305,818 | (12.5) |
| Not Hispanic or Latino | 246,116,088 | (87.5) |
| White alone | 194,552,774 | (69.1) |

### RACE

| | | |
|---|---:|---:|
| Total population | 281,421,906 | (100.0) |
| One race | 274,595,678 | (97.6) |
|   White | 211,460,626 | (75.1) |
|   Black or African American | 34,658,190 | (12.3) |
|   American Indian and Alaska Native | 2,475,956 | (0.9) |
|   Asian | 10,242,998 | (3.6) |
|   Native Hawaiian and Other Pacific Islander | 398,835 | (0.1) |
|   Some other race | 15,359,073 | (5.5) |
| Two or more races | 6,826,228 | (2.4)[99] |

Since individuals were allowed to mark one or more of the races that apply to them, the Census Bureau also published counts for the separate racial groups that comprised the total for the Two or More Races category. With the five racial categories and the Some Other Race category, the Census Bureau reported population figures in 57 different multiracial categories.[100] There were 15 unique biracial combinations, 20 three-race combinations, 15 four-race combinations, 6 five-race combinations, and 1 combination with all six races. The largest groups numerically were

1. White and Some Other Race: 2,206,251 (32.32% of those who checked more than one race);
2. White and American Indian and Alaska Native: 1,082,683 (15.86%);
3. White and Asian: 868,395 (12.72%);
4. White and Black: 784,764 (11.50%); and
5. Black and Some Other Race: 417,249 (6.11%).[101]

Fifteen of the subcategories of those who checked more than one racial box contained less than a thousand people.[102] In addition, approximately 2.8 million, or 4 percent, of those under the age of 18 were included in the Two or More Races category.[103]

For the 2010 census, the comparable counts were as follows:

### HISPANIC OR LATINO

| | | |
|---|---:|---:|
| Total population | 308,745,538 | (100.0) |
| Hispanic or Latino | 50,477,594 | (16.3) |
| Not Hispanic or Latino | 258,267,944 | (83.7) |
| White alone | 196,817,552 | (63.7) |

### RACE

| | | |
|---|---:|---:|
| Total population | 308,745,538 | (100.0) |
| One race | 299,736,465 | (97.1) |
|   White | 223,553,265 | (72.4) |
|   Black or African American | 38,929,319 | (12.6) |
|   American Indian and Alaska Native | 2,932,248 | (0.9) |
|   Asian | 14,674,252 | (4.8) |
|   Native Hawaiian and Other Pacific Islander | 540,013 | (0.2) |
|   Some other race | 19,107,368 | (6.2) |
| Two or More Races | 9,009,073 | (2.9)[104] |

Of those in the Two or More Races category, 91.7 percent reported only two races, with an additional 7.5 percent reporting three. The largest groups numerically reported in the Two or More Races category were:

1. White and Black: 1,834,212 (20.4%);
2. White and Some Other Race: 1,740,924 (19.32% of those who checked more than one race);
3. White and Asian: 1,623,234 (18%);
4. White and American Indian and Alaska Native: 1,432,309 (15.9%); and
5. Black and Some Other Race: 314,571 (3.5%).[105]

## IV. The Final Guidance

The 1997 Revisions included a provision that required other federal programs to adopt its standards. However, not only do educational institutions have to report the race and ethnicity of their student bodies to the DOE, they also have to report the race and ethnicities of their employees to the EEOC on the EEO-1 Report.[106] As a result, the DOE chose to wait until after the EEOC adopted its revisions to the EEO-1 Report before proposing those that would apply to educational institutions. The EEOC submitted its revisions to OMB for approval in November 2005.[107] Following their acceptance by OMB, the DOE published its "Proposed Guidance, on Maintaining, Collecting, and Reporting Data on Racial and Ethnicity to the U.S. Department of Education" (hereinafter, the "Proposed Guidance") for comment on July 31, 2006.[108] After reviewing comments, the DOE issued the Final Guidance.

The DOE chose to follow the determinations made by the EEOC in the regulations contained in the Final Guidance. Thus, the first section of this part will discuss the adoption by the EEOC of its revisions to EEO-1 Report. The second section will discuss the procedures outlined in the Final Guidance that educational institutions must follow when collecting and reporting data on the race and ethnicity of its students to the DOE. The third section will discuss the impact of these changes in reporting requirements on the admissions prospects of Black Hispanics and Blacks with Two or More Races. The final section will discuss the ability to gather data on black ethnicity consistent with the Final Guidance so that educational institutions can separate those in the Black/African American category into Black Immigrants and Ascendent Blacks.

## A. Adoption of the EEOC Revisions

The DOE repeatedly received comments from educational institutions stating they preferred that the "various Federal agencies involved in data collection all use the same aggregate categories so that the burden of implementing changes is minimized and educational institutions are not forced to provide different and/or inconsistent data on race and ethnicity to federal agencies."[109] Therefore, the DOE decided to wait for the EEOC to announce its final implementation plan before publishing its proposed changes.[110]

The EEOC and the Office of Federal Contract Compliance Programs (OFCCP) jointly adopted the EEO-1 Report in 1966.[111] Private employers subject to Title VII with at least one hundred employees and federal government contractors with at least fifty employees and a contract of at least $50,000 are required to submit an EEO-1 Report to the Joint Reporting Committee, consisting of the EEOC and OFCCP, by September 30th of each year.[112] Data requested on the EEO-1 Report tracks employees by race, ethnicity, sex, and job classification.[113] The EEOC uses the data to support enforcement of federal antidiscrimination laws and to analyze employment patterns.[114]

The EEOC published its draft revisions to the EEO-1 Report for comment on June 11, 2003.[115] The EEOC adopted the same definitions for racial and ethnic categories and required the use of the two-question format as contained in the 1997 Revisions. In addition, the EEOC made some decisions that will have tremendous repercussions over the coming years. EEOC made the Hispanic/Latino category the privileged one for purposes of reporting data. When a person answers "yes" to the Hispanic/Latino question, they are reported by employers as Hispanic/Latino, regardless of any racial boxes they check. Although employers report Hispanic/Latino totals on their forms filed with the EEOC, the proposed revisions did not require employers to report the separate of races for Hispanics/Latinos.[116] Thus, the information that the EEOC required employers to provide does not allow for the breaking down of the aggregate numbers in the Hispanic/Latino totals by their race. That information is simply not generated. In addition, the EEOC proposed reporting non-Hispanic/Latino individuals who checked multiple racial boxes in a new Two or More Races category. As with Hispanic/Latino totals, employers were not required to report the separate races of those in the Two or More Races category.

During the comment period, civil rights groups, including the Mexican American Legal Defense and Education Fund (MALDEF), the Rainbow PUSH Coalition, and the National Asian Pacific American Legal Consortium, urged the EEOC to change its initial position and require employers to report the races of Hispanic/Latino employees.[117] Rainbow PUSH asserted that Hispanics/Latinos of mixed heritage with African ancestry were more likely to face discrimination than Hispanics/Latinos not of mixed heritage and without African ancestry.[118] Other groups pointed out that because the EEOC's procedure privileges the Hispanic/Latino category, this will artificially inflate the number of Hispanic/Latino employees since none of them are included in the Two or More Races category, and deflate the number in the other racial groups.[119] The EEOC rejected these concerns, noting that only a small percentage of those over the age of 18 indicated that they were Hispanic/Latino and a racial minority group on the 2000 census form. The EEOC also noted that it was not clear whether Hispanics/Latinos willingly or accurately self-identify using American racial categories when asked to do so.[120] Thus, requiring employers to report the race of Hispanic/Latino employees would provide little benefit. Such reporting would also create problems for OFCCP's system for targeting contractors for compliance review.[121] Since the OFCCP's statistical model for selecting contractors for compliance reviews uses aggregated minority and nonminority categories,[122] the OFCCP could simply incorporate the counts of those in the Hispanic/Latino category into its minority counts and continue using its current methodology with minor adjustments.[123]

Civil rights groups also urged the EEOC to adopt more detailed racial reporting for the Two or More Races category due to civil rights enforcement concerns and to be consistent with full compliance with the 1997 Revisions.[124] Reverend Jesse L. Jackson Jr.'s written testimony noted that the Two or More Races category would not be meaningful for affirmative action purposes.[125] But in response to these concerns, the EEOC concluded that requiring employers to report the separate races of those in the Two or More Races category would result in only a marginal improvement in the utility of the data. Such marginal improvement did not justify the added burden to employers and the government.[126] The administrative burden of reporting the various subcategories would be substantial. As noted earlier, 57 subcategories in the Two or More Races category were reported in the 2000 census, but that number was inflated because it reflected additional categories that resulted from the Census Bureau obtaining permission to use a Some Other Race category. Without the Some Other Race category, however, there would still be 26 separate combinations under the Two or More Races category, and the national counts on the 2000 census in 11 of those categories was less than 10,000 people.[127] The EEOC also pointed out that only 2.4 percent of the respondents selected the Two or More Races category on the 2000 census.[128] Additionally, as with reporting of Hispanics/Latinos, the EEOC indicated that adopting the Two or More Races category supported the OFCCP's use of the EEO-1 Report data.

## B. The Final Guidance Procedures for Collecting and Reporting Racial and Ethnic Data to the Department of Education

In November 2005, the EEOC submitted its revised EEO-1 Report to OMB. After a thirty-day period for public comment, OMB approved the revisions.[129] In July 2006, the DOE published the Proposed Guidance for comment.[130] After reviewing comments, the DOE issued the Final Guidance in October 2007.[131]

Following the 1997 Revisions and the EEOC, the Proposed Guidance used the same racial and ethnic definitions and required that educational institutions use the two-question format when they sought information about race and ethnicity from individuals. For the reporting requirements, the DOE also proposed to follow the EEOC. The Proposed Guidance made the Hispanic/Latino category the privileged category. The DOE noted that this approach would result in more accurate reporting of data on individuals who are Hispanic/Latino.[132] The Proposed Guidance also required that educational institutions report non-Hispanic/Latino students who check more than one race category in a new Two or More Races category. The DOE did not require the reporting of the specific races of those in either the Hispanic/Latino or Two or More Races categories.[133]

During the comment period a number of commentators expressed concern about these decisions. The DOE's response to these concerns, however, sounded as if the matters were *faits accomplis*.[134] At least one commentator noted that the DOE should not follow the same approach as the EEOC, because their objectives for collecting data were different.[135] In response, the DOE noted that educational institutions and other recipients repeatedly indicated their preference that the various federal agencies use the same aggregate categories to minimize the administrative burden.[136] The DOE also stated that it was too administratively burdensome to have educational institutions throughout the country report the separate racial identities of those in the Hispanic/Latino category.[137] The DOE noted that if it required the reporting of racial data for the Hispanic/Latino category, then the report would require six additional categories.[138] Racial categories are often cross-tabulated with other relevant information such as an individual's sex, disability category, or educational placement, thereby increasing the categories of information even more.[139] The DOE followed similar reasoning when it rejected a suggestion that educational institutions should report all or some of the separate racial identities of those in the Two or More Races category.[140]

The DOE received criticism from commentators that the reporting requirements of the Proposed Guidance with regard to the Two or More Races category could lead to a significant reduction in the black student population. The DOE responded by stating that "in most instances, the Department anticipates that the size of the Two or More Races category will not be large enough to cause significant shifts in students demographics."[141] The DOE noted in its background information that "in the 2000 census, 2.4 percent of the total population (or 6.8 million people) identified themselves as belonging to two or more racial groups. For the population under 18 years old, 4.0 percent (or 2.8 million children) selected two or more races."[142]

The problem with the DOE's response was that using national statistics obscured the much larger potential impact of the Two or More Races category on the counting of minority students, including black students. On the 2000 census, 4.8 percent of those who checked the black category also checked another category, twice the percentage of the American population as a whole. The younger the blacks were, the greater the percentage of those who reported black and another race. According to data from the 2000 census, for blacks between the ages of 15 and 19, those who reported that they were black in combination with another category constituted only 5.3 percent. However, for blacks between the ages of 10 and 14, it increased to 6.3 percent; for those between the ages of 5 and 9, to 8.1 percent; and for those under the age of 5, it was 11.4 percent.[143] Thus, although only 2.4 percent of Americans identified with more than one racial category on the 2000 census, by the time that the Final Guidance went into effect a decade later, a minimum of 8.1 percent of blacks under the age of 18 identified with more than one race.

The DOE's treatment of non-Hispanic Two or More Races students also represented a partial victory for the advocates of the inclusion of a multiracial category on governmental forms used to collect data on race and ethnicity. Although a multiracial category was not included, the DOE, effectively, required that educational institutions report all non-Hispanic multiracial students in the combined Two or More Races category. Also, the DOE's approach meant that the issue of multiracials did not affect Hispanic/Latino counts. As a senior spokesperson for MALDEF put it, "When [the multiracial category proposal] came up, we could have said 'it's not our issue.' But because we work in coalition with [other civil rights organizations] we took the position that would preserve the need of our coalition partners."[144] In fact, the Latino enrollment in U.S. Colleges actually increased by nearly a quarter for 2010, when the Final Guidance went into effect.[145]

## C. Impact of the Final Guidance on Admissions Prospects of Black Hispanics and Blacks with Two or More Races

Under the one-question format, individuals had to select one racial/ethnic category. Therefore, the problem of classifying individuals with black ancestry as Hispanic/Latino who identify more with their race than with their ethnicity did not exist. In addition, the issue of what to do with Blacks with Two or More Races never arose. Given the Final Guidance, however, selective higher education programs are going to have to report Black Hispanics in their counts of Hispanics/Latinos, and Blacks with Two or More Races in their counts of Two or More Races. However, since admissions officials will also be aware that individuals in both of these groups have black ancestry as well, they will have to decide how to treat their ancestry for purposes of admissions.

In *Grutter v. Bollinger*, the Supreme Court specified that when selective higher education programs use race and ethnic classifications for determining admissions, they must employ an individualized admissions process.[145] Nevertheless, there is little doubt that admissions officials—at least in their minds—compare the standardized tests scores and grade point averages of a particular applicant from a given racial/ethnic group to those of other applicants of the same racial/ethnic group.[146] The Final Guidance's new categorization requirements raise the question, should admissions officials compare Black Hispanics and Blacks with Two or More Races with Black/African Americans? Alternatively, should admissions officials compare Black Hispanics to other applicants in the Hispanic/Latino category, and Blacks with Two or More Races to others in the Two or More Races category? Or should admissions officials at selective higher education programs employ a completely different method?

How admissions officials resolve the questions of how to treat Black Hispanics and Blacks with Two or More Races will have a tremendous impact on their admissions prospects. Focusing on the racial/ethnic standardized test score gaps on tests used for admissions purposes by higher education programs reveals the precarious situation the Final Guidance creates for Black Hispanics and, especially, for Blacks with Two or More Races. The average combined SAT math, critical reading, and writing scores of blacks in 2013 was 1278. In contrast, the combined SAT scores for the various Hispanic/Latino groups ranged between 1354 and 1355; and the average combined SAT scores were 1427 for American Indians and Alaskan Natives, 1576 for whites, and 1645 for Asian Americans.[147] Significant racial/ethnic gaps also exist on standardized tests used to determine admissions to selective graduate programs like the GMAT, the GRE, the LSAT and the MCAT. For example, the average LSAT score for African Americans who took the test during the 2011–12 academic year was 141.8, for Latinos generally 146.3, for Puerto Ricans 138.1, for Asians 152.7, and for whites 152.8.[148] Thus, changes in the comparison group could harm the admissions prospects of many Black Hispanics. However, a change in the comparison group of Blacks with Two or More Races may have a devastating impact on their admissions prospects to selective higher education institutions. White/Asian multiracials are likely to constitute a significant proportion of those in the Two or More Races category. Thus, the Two or More Races applicants' average standardized test scores will be much higher than those of the Black/African American category.

For admissions officials to continue to treat Black Hispanics and Blacks with Two or More Races applicants as if they were Black/African Americans would constitute a blatant application of the one-drop rule. Admissions officials would treat individuals as black even though they have expressed a different racial/ethnic identity in the admissions process. Doing this would also invoke a certain irony. One of the principal motivations for the adoption of the 1997 Revisions, which prompted the issuance of the Final Guidance, was the desire of multiracial groups to avoid classifying Black Multiracials as black. Thus, if admissions officials treat Black Multiracials as Black/African American, this practice would run counter to one of the main reasons for adopting the Final Guidance.

Also, if admissions officials chose to treat Black Hispanics as if they were Black/African American, they will have to decide whether that is fair because the Black Hispanic's admission could come at the expense of another Hispanic/Latino who may have higher standardized test scores. The same holds true—but to a far greater extent—for Blacks with Two or More Races. Their admission could come at the expense of other multiracials reported in the Two or More Races category, who could very well have standardized tests scores that are significantly higher than those of Blacks with Two or More Races applicants admitted.

Regardless of how admissions decisions for Black Hispanics and Black with Two or More Races are treated over the next several years, as time passes from the effective date of the Final Guidance, the tendency of admissions officials to compare Black Hispanics to others in the Hispanic/Latino category will likely increase, as will the tendency to compare Blacks with Two or More Races to others in the Two or More Races category. Scholars understand the concept that race is socially constructed. Having changed the definitions of so many of the major racial/ethnic categories, the Final Guidance will provide an unfolding example of the workings of this concept in the field of education. As the years pass, educational institutions will become increasingly familiar with addressing the racial/ethnic reporting categories of the Final Guidance. Those who came of age when the one-drop rule was the common way to determine who was black will grow old and retire. In addition, the national statistics about the educational situation of various racial/ethnic groups, including high school graduation rates and college attendance rates, will be compiled from data reported to the DOE, which places Black Hispanics in the Hispanic/Latino counts and Blacks with Two or More Races in the Two or More Races counts. As admissions officials come to understand that Black Hispanics and Blacks with Two or More Races no longer increase the numbers of Black/African American students, the educational institutions may come to look at them in a different light.

## D. *The Final Guidance Was Not Meant to Address Black Immigrants*

The Final Guidance will allow selective higher education programs to collect data on Black Multiracials. However, it does not mandate the collection or reporting of data regarding the ethnicity of blacks. This is not surprising since the DOE promulgated the Final Guidance out of a concern for the growing multiracial population in the United States, not increasing immigration into the United States. Some commentators on the Final Guidance urged the addition of other racial/ethnic reporting categories, including Middle Eastern, Southeast Asian, and African (as a different category from African American), Indian/Pakistani (as a different category from Asian), Filipino, and Cape Verdean (as a different category from African American), but the DOE rejected these additions.[149] The discussion about this topic in the Final Guidance noted that these categories were rejected during the discussions that lead to the 1997 Revisions.[150] Based on the comments discussing the adoption of the 1997 Revisions, there does not appear to have been much additional discussion about separating Africans from African Americans or separating those from the Caribbean from African Americans.[151]

By complying with the Final Guidance, selective higher education institutions will only generate data that allow them to separate Black Multiracials from Black/African Americans. They will not be able to determine the ethnic breakdown of blacks in the Black/African American category. Since educational institutions will continue to include Black Immigrants in their counts of the Black/African American category, admissions officials of selective higher education programs will most likely continue to compare the academic credentials of Black Immigrants to those in the Black/African American category. As Black Multiracials, who may score higher on standardized tests than Black/African Americans, are reclassified out of the Black/African American category, this will have the concomitant effect of increasing the competitiveness of applications from Black Immigrants, who will remain in the Black/African American category. As a result, the unfolding of the Final Guidance will likely reduce the admissions prospects of Black Multiracials while improving the admissions prospects of Black Immigrants.

## Conclusion

Predominately white colleges and universities have generally grouped all blacks into a unified category regardless of their racial or ethnic ancestries since they first started to admit them in significant numbers in the 1960s. The Final Guidance, which went into effect for the 2010–11 academic year, has changed the definitions of racial and ethnic categories that selective higher education institutions must use when they report this data to the DOE. The promulgation of the Final Guidance is part of a very long history of the federal government's efforts to gather and report racial and ethnic information about Americans that dates back to the first census conducted in 1790.

The Final Guidance breaks Black Multiracials into two different groups, Black Hispanics and Blacks with Two or More Races. The Guidance also requires that educational institutions now report Black Hispanics in counts of Hispanics/Latinos and Blacks with Two or More Races in their counts of Two or More Races students. However, the Final Guidance does not mandate the collection or reporting of data regarding the ethnicity of blacks. This is because it was not adopted to respond to the increasing immigration in the United States. Rather the purpose of the Final Guidance is to "obtain more accurate information about the increasing number of students who identify with more than one race."[152] The likely effect of the Final Guidance, however, will be to increase the admissions prospects of Black Immigrants while reducing those of Black Multiracials.

Chapter Two

# The Two Aspects of the History of the Black Experience

Although scholars and commentators have put forth various suggestions of why selective higher education institutions should employ affirmative action admissions policies,[1] the approach in this book is to begin from the proposition that this debate is closed. Thus, the starting place for determining why selective higher education programs can take account of race and ethnicity in their admissions process is the opinion of Justice O'Connor for the Court in *Grutter v. Bollinger*.[2] O'Connor notes that the benefits from diversity are substantial: promoting cross-racial understanding, breaking down stereotypes, and enabling students to better understand people from different racial backgrounds. Thus, classroom discussions become more lively and spirited. O'Connor goes on to point out that the consideration of race is not based upon some notion that a minority student will express a characteristic minority point of view. Instead she writes,

> Just as growing up in a particular region or having particular professional experiences is likely to affect an individual's views, so too is one's own, unique experience of being a racial minority in a society, like our own, in which race unfortunately still matters.... By virtue of our Nation's struggle with racial inequality, such students are both likely to have experiences of particular importance to the Law School's mission, and less likely to be admitted in meaningful numbers on criteria that ignore those experiences.[3]

Thus, O'Connor's opinion authorizes the use of racial classifications for the inclusion of *underrepresented* racial minorities who have *experiences* derived from our nation's struggle with racial inequality. These experiences are not only important to include in the student body for the purpose of the benefits of diversity, but they also explain why *underrepresented* minorities are not likely to be admitted in meaningful numbers in the first place. Thus, the benefits of diversity represent the compelling state interest for the ability of selective higher education programs to employ racial classifications in the admissions process of those applicants who come from minority groups that are underrepresented and who have experiences of being a member of a historically discriminated against group.

The American motto *E Pluribus Unum* is an apt description of the historical black experience in the United States. The best estimates suggest that about four percent of the ten to twelve million Africans brought to the New World landed in what would become the United States.[4] Scholars estimated that 72 percent of the African base of U.S. slave population arrived during the colonial period. The Chesapeake Bay area had received all of its Africans by then and the states in the North had received 98 percent of their total.[5] Although some Africans came from the east coast of that continent, most came from a region in West Africa between the Senegal River in the north and the Congo in the south.[6] They came from coastal areas, inland forests, villages in the shadows of mountains, and riverside towns. Some were from advanced nations with long traditions of kings, courts, and well-defined civil societies. Others were from small clans composed primarily of family members. Some were farmers or herders, others were fisherman, craftsmen, and soldiers, and some were even slaves. These Africans came from different ethnic and kinship groups that had different cultural and religious traditions, but in the United States they were melded into one people.

The process by which a people define themselves and are defined by others is dynamic. Cultural identity is not fixed or static; rather it ebbs and flows as history unfolds.[7] As time passed those brought directly from Africa died off. Hampered by misconceptions about their mother country, faulty information, incorrect conjectures, omissions of historical facts, and inaccurate oral traditions, the ability of North American-born descendants of those Africans to identify with various African identities weakened. As they weakened, a collective African American identity emerged.[8]

Without question, the central feature of the African American experience in the United States was the treatment of an individual as an involuntary member of a historically oppressed racial group. Until the institution of affirmative action programs, blacks in America came face-to-face with laws, customs, and social practices designed to restrict or confine their social, political, economic, and educational rights and opportunities. As noted black scholar W. E. B. DuBois summarized it, "[t]he so called Negro group ... while it is in no sense absolutely set off physically from its fellow Americans, has nevertheless a strong, hereditary cultural unity born of slavery, common suffering, prolonged proscription, and curtailment of political and civil rights.... Prolonged policies of segregation and discrimination have involuntarily welded the mass almost into a nation within a nation."[9]

Race was the dominant feature of the historical experience of African Americans, but it will help to recognize two different aspects of that experience. One aspect involved what it meant to be a victim of racial discrimination. With regard to the descendants of the soil of Africa, for much of America's history, dominant American culture was deeply invested in notions of white (or at least Anglo-Saxon and Teutonic) superiority. Thus, dominant American cultural attitudes had clear concepts of what it meant to be black and imposed those notions on dark-skinned people. From this perspective, African Americans were viewed as passive objects that were moved around by whites for their purposes rather than as people with their own wills, hopes, and desires, who influenced their own destiny. This aspect also presupposed that blacks were inferior or substandard in some important way to whites. This belief obscured the injustice of the discriminatory treatment that blacks experienced and made their subjection appear as the natural order of things. By imposing upon black people a system that required their servitude and treated them as menials, their actual condition made them inferior. Thus, one aspect of the experience of historical discrimination is the experience of what it means to be "raced" or branded as inferior.[10]

Against the background of racial domination, the descendants of the sons and daughters of the soil of Africa were melded into one people, and out of the uniting factor of race they shaped a counterdiscourse to how mainstream American society viewed and treated them. They actively engaged in a collective struggle that resisted white supremacy. Commenting on this, Mari Matsuda noted that "Black Americans, the paradigmatic victim group of our history, have turned the Bible and the Constitution into texts of liberation."[11] From the perspective of the counterdiscourse, blacks are not viewed as inferior, but as oppressed. Thus, in contrast to the "raced" aspect of the historical experience of blacks was the active experience of a group who did not control the visible reins of power, but still served as the architects of their own struggles against the conditions of their oppression. This counterhistorical experience was limited by and responsive to the racial oppression imposed on the Black Community. Nevertheless, it is as much a part of the historical experience of blacks in the United States as the experience of being victims of racial oppression.

In sum, the experience of the history of discrimination against black people in the United States is like a two-sided coin. On one side, race was, and is, the immutable characteristic that formed the basis of the oppression of blacks. On the other side was the Black Community's collective effort to struggle against its oppression. This chapter discusses these two aspects. Because this chapter seeks to reveal the chorus of the black experience, and not the individual voices of the soloists, it is not intended to be an exhaustive and complete account of that experience. The basic point of this chapter is to establish that the historical experiences of blacks in the United States has been both about being victims of racial subordination and about actively engaging in the collective effort to liberate themselves from that subordination. As a result, any consideration of which blacks should benefit from affirmative action must focus on whether those individuals have had significant experiences involving both aspects of this history. Part I will discuss the experience of blacks being victimized because of race. Part II will discuss the history of the struggle by blacks against their racial domination.

## I. The Traditional View of the African American Experience of Being Raced

Prior to the road that led to the institution of affirmative action, there was a long history of discrimination against blacks in this country. The central feature of that discrimination was the belief that black people in some important way were inferior. It was this belief that made the oppression of blacks in the form of slavery and segregation seem as if these legally enshrined institutions were rational responses to the natural order of things. Even many of the policies and programs instituted to dismantle the effects of the history of racial oppression during the Desegregation Era were based on this belief. However, unlike the view of blacks during the periods of slavery and segregation that understood black inferiority as more or less immutable, the view of their substandard nature was more optimistic during the Desegregation Era. During this time, the basis of many of America's progressive policies was that although black people were inferior, they could be improved by enriching their social environment and assisting them in overcoming their deficit culture.

Since the English did not have much contact with sub-Saharan Africans before colonization of North America, it took some time for their colonists to learn to equate slavery with blacks. Once they did, the overwhelming majority of blacks in the English colonies of North America were held as slaves throughout the colonial period. As a result of the Revolutionary War, however, a wave of liberal sentiment swept through the northern part of the new nation. This more liberal sentiment, coupled with less of an economic incentive for slavery, led most Northern states to abolish slavery during or shortly after the Revolutionary War. But abolition did not equate to black equality. As a result, free blacks in the North found themselves locked into the bottom of a racial caste system. The first section of this part discusses the treatment of blacks during the colonial and antebellum periods in both the South and the North.

The victory of the North in the Civil War preserved the Union. With its conclusion, the condition and status of blacks throughout the country underwent dramatic changes. Slavery was abolished, and the country made blacks citizens of the United States and the states in which they resided, granted them new civil rights, and enfranchised black males. Yet despite these new legal rights, by the turn of the century almost all black males in the South had lost the right to vote. The second section discusses the period of time after the Civil War until disenfranchisement of black males.

Whereas segregation had existed as a matter of custom in many areas of Northern and Southern life, with the disenfranchisement of black males, Southern legislators began to enact segregation statutes starting in the late 1880s. Over the next six decades, segregation and conscious racial discrimination became the explicit law of the land in many areas of the country. The third section discusses the rise of segregation.

For centuries, American society attributed the substandard nature of blacks to causes that were essentially immutable to human engineering, such as God's divine will or deficient black biology. As long as that was the case, it did not make logical sense to pursue racial equality or to integrate society. Starting in the 1930s, leading social scientific opinion increasingly attributed the source of racial differences to the deficient cultural and social environment of blacks. This more optimistic social scientific view suggested that America could improve black people by enhancing their social environment and assisting them in abandoning their deviant culture. The Supreme Court embraced this rationale in its opinion in *Brown v. Board of Education*. The decision also initiated a fifteen-year period in which the Court, Congress, and the President all worked to dismantle segregation and alleviate the consequences that the legacy of discrimination had inflicted upon blacks and other minorities. Yet even during this effort, the dominant beliefs in the inferiority of blacks remained. The fourth section discusses the historical justifications for the inferiority of blacks before World War I, the change that started to occur in those beliefs in the 1930s, and how those changes helped to lead to the policies and programs that were instituted as part of the desegregation of American society.

By the middle of the 1970s, the Supreme Court had begun a long march toward reshaping its antidiscrimination jurisprudence to view race discrimination as a failure of government and private entities to embrace colorblindness and treat everyone as an individual. A majority of the Court has not yet embraced a completely colorblind interpretation of the Court's antidiscrimination jurisprudence; after all, race can still be used in the admissions process of selective higher education institutions. Nevertheless, the progression of the Court's antidiscrimination jurisprudence toward the colorblind ideal has drastically limited legal and political avenues for racial minorities to challenge the governmental policies and practices that produce disparate racial outcomes and the ability of government to institute policies and programs that take account of race to dismantle the continuing effects of America's history of racial oppression. While significant racial gaps continue to exist in all major socioeconomic indicators, because colorblind thinking discourages attributing these differences to race and ethnicity, nonracial explanations are often used to minimize the differences. To the extent the differences cannot be explained by nonracial factors, justifications for what remains continue to focus on notions of the deficit social environment and culture of blacks. The fifth section discusses the continuing notions of black inferiority in the Post-Racial/Colorblind Era.

## A. Treatment of Blacks during the Colonial and Antebellum Eras

Due to a lack of contact with sub-Saharan Africans, the English had to learn to equate slavery with black people. This section will first discuss the embrace by the English colonists of black slavery. Throughout the colonial and antebellum eras, the overwhelming majority of blacks resided in the South because slavery was more profitable there. The second subsection will discuss the experiences of blacks in the slaveholding South before the Civil War. Most Northern states abolished slavery during or shortly after the Revolutionary War. Nevertheless, blacks still experienced what it was like to be viewed as second class citizens on the free soil in the North. The third subsection will discuss the abolition of slavery in the North and the experiences of Northern blacks after the Revolutionary War.

### 1. Origins of Slavery

Although Muslim Moors from North Africa had controlled much of the Iberian Peninsula for seven centuries before Columbus sailed to the New World, Africans were not well known in northern European countries like England before the seventeenth century. Due to feudalism in Europe, however, the English were familiar with a form of bondage. But they had to learn to equate slavery with black people.

The first record of Africans in English North America occurs in a 1619 letter that John Rolfe, the husband of Pocahontas, wrote to Sir Edwin Sandys.[12] The Norfolk-born first recorder of the Virginia Colony wrote, "About the last of August, came in a dutch man of warre that sold us twenty Negars...."[13] Historians tend to believe that these first twenty blacks were traded for supplies. By 1640, there were only about 170 blacks and 2,300 white Virginians in the colony, but these first Africans were treated as indentured servants rather than slaves.[14]

Throughout much of the seventeenth century, England primarily sought to supply its North American colonial labor needs by importing white indentured servants from the mother country, most of whom were poor, convicted of crimes, or unable to obtain land at home. Newcomers to these English colonies only had a fifty-fifty chance of surviving five years. As a result, an investment in a person for life as opposed to a term of years was not always economically profitable, especially since a slave cost twice as much as an indentured servant.[15] The English discovered, however, that the demand for labor to develop their colonies in the New World outstripped the available supply of people they could send. As life expectancies increased, slavery began to make more economic sense; what a person paid to purchase the labor of a white indentured servant for a period of ten years, a black slave could be bought for life.[16] And after Bacon's Rebellion in 1676, Virginia's ruling elite realized they had another reason to prefer slavery to the continued use of indentured servants. Bacon's Rebellion revealed that Virginia was creating a crisis with white indentured servitude because these former servants would eventually become a class of property-less and mostly unmarried men who could become a dangerous revolutionary force.

By the early part of the eighteenth century, the British dominated the Transatlantic Slave Trade and slavery had become the lifeblood of their Empire. The British came to use slave labor for the cultivation of a large portion of their agricultural exports for world trade such as indigo, sugar, tobacco, and rice. As one contemporary British economist put it, "The daily bread of the most-considerable part of our British manufacturers, are owing primarily to the labor of the Negroes."[17] With these changes in views about slavery, the number of black slaves in North America exploded. For example, the population of blacks increased from 13,000 in Virginia and Maryland in 1700 to 200,000 seven decades later.[18]

## 2. Slavery in the South

At the time of the Declaration of Independence, the new nation inherited a race-based system of slavery. When the Founding Fathers met in Philadelphia for the Constitutional Convention, over 93 percent of the slaves resided in the five southernmost states of Virginia, North Carolina, South Carolina, Georgia, and Maryland.[19] Because of the institution's importance for the southern states, the acceptance of slavery in the Constitution was a foregone conclusion. At the heart of the Constitution was the protection of property and wealth. Nearly 20 percent of the population, almost one out of every five persons, was owned by another. Thus, ownership of slaves constituted an important form of property, a tremendous amount of wealth, and generated a significant portion of the income for many citizens of the new nation. Not one of the fifty-five delegates present at the Convention seriously advocated for the abolition of slavery.[20] Chief Justice Taney would later describe the Founding Father's view of blacks in his infamous *Dred Scott* opinion:

> It is difficult at this day to realize the state of public opinion in relation to that unfortunate race, which prevailed in the civilized and enlightened portions of the world at the time of the Declaration of Independence, and when the Constitution of the United States was framed and adopted. But the public history of every European nation displays it in a manner too plain to be mistaken.
>
> [Blacks] had for more than a century before [the Declaration of Independence] been regarded as beings of an inferior order, and altogether unfit to associate with the white race, either in social or political relations; and so far inferior, that they had no rights which the white man was bound to respect; and that the negro might justly and lawfully be reduced to slavery for his benefit. He was bought and sold, and treated as an ordinary article of merchandise and traffic, whenever a profit could be made by it. This opinion was at that time fixed and universal in the civilized portion of the white race. It was regarded as an axiom in morals as well as in politics, which no one thought of disputing, or supposed to be open to dispute; and men in every grade and position in society daily and habitually acted upon it in their private pursuits, as well as in matters of public concern, without doubting for a moment the correctness of this opinion.[21]

After independence, the black population continued to largely reside in the South. On the eve of the Civil War, 92.3 percent of blacks resided in the states that legalized slavery,[22] and 93.7 percent of them there were slaves.[23] As slaves, blacks were denied the status of a legal person.[24] Thus, laws in slaveholding states reflected the legal conclusion that they were property, not persons. Killing a slave was not considered murder, but destruction of property. Rape of a female slave was only considered trespassing against her owner's property interest. As a result, by legal definition, a slave master could not be said to have raped his slave. Slaves could not enter into contracts or buy, sell, rent, or lease property. They could not sue or be sued in court, provide testimony as witnesses in legal proceedings, vote, or hold public office. They were even forbidden the right to marry or leave the plantation without their master's consent.

Free blacks presented special problems in slaveholding states. Special laws were adopted to restrict their rights and their numbers. Laws were enacted to make manumission difficult. To ensure that free blacks were denied the ability to elevate their social standing, states passed laws to prevent them from owning arms, participating in militia exercises, and having sexual relations with whites.[25] Needless to say, free blacks were denied the franchise and the right to hold political office.

Supporters of slavery would often defend the institution by pointing to the benefits that it provided for blacks. Although the so-called positive good argument for slavery wasn't firmly stated until the 1830s, its antecedents were well established. As John C. Calhoun put it, "[n]ever before has the black race of Central Africa, from the dawn of history to the present day, attained a condition so civilized and so improved, not only physically, but morally and intellectually.... [T]he relation now existing in the slaveholding States between the two [races], is, instead of an evil, a good—a positive good."[26]

## 3. Conditions of Blacks in the North during the Antebellum Period

The Revolutionary War helped to unleash abolition sentiments in the Northern states. As John Jay, who would later become the first Chief Justice of the United States Supreme Court, put it, "to contend for liberty and to deny that blessing to others involves an inconsistency not to be excused."[27] This sentiment, when combined with the lack of a powerful economic incentive for the need of slaves, led the Northern states to adopt measures to abolish slavery. After breaking away from New York, Vermont existed as a republic for fourteen years and abolished slavery in its 1777 constitution. Pennsylvania adopted a gradual emancipation law three years later. In 1783, the decision by the Massachusetts Supreme Judicial Court in *Commonwealth v. Jennison* (one of the Quock Walker Cases) struck down slavery there.[28] New Hampshire's constitution, adopted the same year, declared that "all men are born equally free and independent." The following year both Connecticut and Rhode Island also enacted gradual emancipation statutes. In 1787, Congress passed the Northwest Ordinance, which included the first provision adopted by Congress to ban slavery. Article Six of the Ordinance stated, "There shall be neither slavery nor involuntary servitude in the said territory otherwise than for punishment of crimes."[29]

The New York legislature passed a gradual emancipation law in 1799. When New Jersey, the last Northern state to abolish slavery, did so in 1804, every northern state had enacted legislation to at least put slavery on the path to extinction. As late as 1810, however, 30,000 blacks, a quarter of their population in the North, were still held in captivity.[30] But black freedom was so complete in the North by 1830 that less than 4,000 were held in bondage, and two-thirds of this number resided in New Jersey.[31]

Even though blacks were free people in the North during much of the antebellum period, that did not mean that Northerners believed in racial equality. Although the extent of discrimination blacks encountered varied from state to state, generally they were locked into the bottom of the racial caste system by custom, if not by explicit law. Blacks were systematically separated from whites or excluded from railway cars, omnibuses, stagecoaches, and steamboats.[32] They were segregated into secluded and remote corners of theaters and lecture halls; they could not enter most hotels, restaurants, and resorts except as servants; and they prayed in separate pews and partook of the sacrament of the Eucharist after whites. Blacks were segregated in schools, hospitals, and cemeteries. Free blacks could not testify as witnesses against whites in court, were excluded from jury service, and could not become government officials. Indiana, Illinois, and Oregon incorporated in their respective state constitutions provisions restricting the admittance of Negroes into the states. By the eve of the Civil War, only 6 percent of blacks in the North lived in the five New England states—Massachusetts, New Hampshire, Vermont, Maine, and Rhode Island—which allowed them to vote on equal terms with whites.[33]

Many, if not most, of the whites who worked for abolition viewed the institution of slavery more in terms of its detriment to the interest of whites than to blacks.[34] They asserted that the domination of one person over another is fundamentally uncivilized, and such arbitrary power intoxicates the mind and corrupts the spirit of the slave master, tending to bring out the baser elements of the slave master's nature. Another argument against slavery was that it associated the concept of hard work with black slaves. As a result, slavery degraded work and deprived whites of the enterprising spirit necessary to become hard working and productive. Slavery also proved to be inconsistent with free white labor. White immigrants to the country would avoid the areas where slavery existed; they felt that their best chance for an improved life was in going to parts of the country not populated by blacks. Slavery also negatively impacted the procreation rate of whites and positively contributed to those of blacks. Daniel Raymond noted in his 1819 pamphlet entitled *Race, Slavery and Fertility* that the slave population increased faster by procreation than the white population of a slave state, and the white population of a non-slaveholding state increased faster than the white population in a slaveholding state.[35] Over time, slavery led to a reduction in the percentage of whites and an increase in the percentage of blacks. As a result, residents of a given state had a choice to make: either they were going to allow slavery and watch their state become blacker and blacker, or they would abolish slavery and make their state a safe haven for whites.

Given the harms that slavery visited upon whites, many white abolitionists believed that the emancipation of slaves should be accompanied by their emigration. Most of America's presidents from Jefferson to Lincoln supported the notion of establishing colonies outside of the United States to which blacks could be sent.[36] Several abolition groups advocated for colonization of free blacks as one of their principal goals. The best known of such organizations was the American Colonization Society, which was established in Washington, D.C., in 1816. Its members included John Marshall, Chief Justice of the Supreme Court, Henry Clay, Speaker of the House (who was its long-time presiding officer), Daniel Webster, and Patrick Henry.[37] By 1832, more than a dozen state legislatures, including the upper South slaveholding states of Maryland, Kentucky, and Virginia, gave their approval to the Society. At first the Society transported only free blacks to Liberia, on the west coast of Africa. But after 1827, some slaves were freed for the purpose of exporting them to Liberia. By 1830, over 1,400 blacks had resettled in this African colony. Over the life of the organization, the Society "repatriated" about 12,000 blacks.[38]

President Lincoln was one of the biggest supporters of the idea of emigration of blacks. Lincoln signed treaties in the spring of 1862 which recognized both Haiti and Liberia, motivated in part by his desire to pursue colonization. Once it became clear to Lincoln that blacks who were willing to leave favored staying on this side of the Atlantic, he sent his Secretary of State William Henry Seward to consult with the European governments that owned land in Latin America, including England, France, the Netherlands, and Denmark.[39] Shortly before announcing his intention to issue the Emancipation Proclamation in September of 1862, Lincoln invited a group of prominent free blacks to the White House and urged them to support colonization. In the first-ever meeting of an American president with black people in the White House to discuss a matter of great public significance, Lincoln told them, "Your race suffers greatly, many of them, by living among us, while ours suffer from your presence. In a word we suffer on each side. If this is admitted, it affords a reason why we should be separated."[40] Lincoln went so far as to sign a contract on December 3, 1862, with a dubious promoter who claimed to have an appropriate place for colonizing blacks in Haiti. Just weeks before signing the Emancipation Proclamation, Lincoln proposed three constitutional amendments that called for gradual voluntary emancipation, with compensation to slaveholders, which would culminate no later than the year 1900. In addition, the federal government would provide funds to help colonize any freed slave willing to leave. Finally, shortly before his assassination, Lincoln consulted with one of his army generals, General Benjamin F. Butler, about the feasibility of shipping blacks out of the country.[41]

## B. From the Civil War until the Disenfranchisement of Black Males

As armed conflict began in the Civil War, the dominant view in the North about blacks was accurately stated by W. E. B. DuBois:

> To the Northern masses the Negro was a curiosity, a sub-human minstrel, willingly and naturally a slave, and treated as well as he deserved to be. He had not sense enough to revolt and help Northern armies, even if Northern armies were trying to emancipate him, which they were not ... Negroes on the whole were considered cowards and inferior beings whose very presence in America was unfortunate.[42]

Although the North prevailed on the battlefield, that victory did not immediately translate into Southern acceptance of blacks as civil, political, or social equals. As Southern governments in the states that participated in the rebellion were reconstituted in the summer and fall of 1865, the first order of legislative business was to address the status of the newly freed people. These Southern legislators passed a series of laws that came to be known as the Black Codes. The Black Codes were first adopted by the state of Mississippi in November of 1865, just one month before the Thirteenth Amendment abolishing slavery was added to the Constitution. The goal of the Black Codes was to introduce a system to ensure that the whites could continue to extract the labor of blacks as was done during slavery, but grant them as few legal rights as possible. Among the provisions in various Black Codes were those that prevented blacks from owning land to farm. Thus, without a plot of land to produce crops for their own consumption, blacks would be compelled to work for others. Other provisions required the former slaves to sign labor contracts by the beginning of the year that could not be broken during that year. The contracts were normally executed with whites who owned agricultural land that needed cultivation. Any black person not gainfully employed was considered a vagrant and, upon conviction, these individuals were fined and imprisoned. But if their fines were paid by others, they were released into that person's custody, normally a former slave master, and forced to work for that person until they paid off their fine. Probate courts apprenticed orphaned black children to a suitable person (often a former master) until they reached the age of maturity. Blacks were prohibited from owning firearms. And none of the reconstituted state legislatures granted blacks the right to vote or hold public office.

Against the backdrop of the adoption of the Black Codes and violence in the South, Congress assembled in December of 1865. Despite President Johnson's proclamation that the Southern states had met his requirements for readmittance, Congress began by excluding any representatives from the states of the former Confederacy. It also established a Joint Committee on Reconstruction by concurrent resolution of the House and the Senate. This fifteen-member committee was charged with investigating the conditions in the Southern states to determine whether those states were entitled to representation in Congress.

As the new session started, Congress began to debate a major civil rights bill, the Civil Rights Act of 1866, and the Fourteenth Amendment. The Act and the Fourteenth Amendment conferred upon the former slaves citizenship of the United States and the state where they resided. They also removed many legal disabilities of blacks that existed because they were slaves and provided for the civil equality of blacks.

In February, President Johnson vetoed the Civil Rights Act of 1866, but Congress overrode his veto two months later. It was the first time in American history that Congress overrode a Presidential veto on a major piece of legislation.[43] Both houses of Congress passed the Fourteenth Amendment and sent it to the states for ratification in June of 1866. The Amendment, however, left to the states the question of granting the franchise to the freedmen. As an inducement to encourage the states to do so, Section 2 of the Amendment changed the formula for determining a given state's population for the purpose of calculating their representation at the federal level. Article 1, Section 2, Clause 3 of the Constitution laid out the original formula for determining a state's population count. According to that formula, black slaves only counted as three-fifths of a person. With the ratification of the Thirteenth Amendment and the abolition of slavery, however, under the original formula the former black slave now counted as a full person. Section 2 of the Fourteenth Amendment provided a state with a choice.[44] If a given state granted black males the franchise, then each would count as a full person in the population count of that state, but if a state chose not to enfranchise black males, then blacks would not be included in that state's population count. Thus, the choice presented to Southern states by Section 2 was to enfranchise black males and gain representation at the federal level or not to enfranchise them and lose representation.

For the Fourteenth Amendment to be ratified, at least four of the former Confederate states had to support it. By the end of 1866, of the eleven former Confederate states, only Tennessee adopted the Amendment. It was readmitted to the Union. Republicans swept to victory in the fall elections of 1866, winning every Northern state legislature, every gubernatorial seat, and more than two-thirds of the seats in both houses of Congress. Between December 1866 and February 1867, Republicans in Congress were able to enact legislation that granted blacks the franchise in the District of Columbia, removed the color qualifications for suffrage from unorganized federal territories, and made black suffrage a condition for the admission of Nebraska and Colorado. Thus, as Congress reassembled after the fall 1866 elections, the issue of black suffrage was at the top of the political agenda.

In March of 1867, Congress dissolved the state governments of the ten remaining former Confederate states and put them under military rule controlled by Congress. As part of the requirement for readmittance to the Union, the former Confederate states had to ratify the Fourteenth Amendment and hold a state constitutional convention with electors chosen by universal male suffrage. This ensured that the new state constitution would confer the franchise on blacks. Thus, black males were granted the franchise. The protection of black male voting rights was further secured by the ratification of the Fifteenth Amendment, which proscribed depriving citizens of the United States of the right to vote because of race, color, or previous condition of servitude.

In the ten years after the Civil War, the United States had added the Reconstruction Amendments to the Constitution, the Thirteenth, Fourteenth, and Fifteenth. To further delineate and protect the rights granted in the Reconstruction Amendments, Congress also passed five major civil rights measures, including the Civil Rights Act of 1866, the Enforcement Act of May 31, 1870, the Enforcement Act of February 28, 1871, the Enforcement Act of April 20, 1871, and the Civil Rights Act of 1875.[45] The last Civil Rights Act included provisions that granted blacks full and equal enjoyment to inns, public conveyances on land or water, theaters, and other places of public amusement. America had thereby put in place the legal structure to provide for civil, political, and social equality for blacks.

From the moment that black males were granted the right to vote, however, their political power was undermined. "The wave of counterrevolutionary terror that swept over large parts of the South between 1868 and 1871 lacks a counterpart in the American experience."[46] Blacks and whites sympathetic to their cause were shot and families terrorized to prevent blacks from voting. What made disenfranchisement of African Americans such an urgent matter for Southern whites was the large percentage of potential black voters in most states. According to the 1870 census figures, blacks constituted a majority of the population in three Southern states, South Carolina (59%), Mississippi (54%), and Louisiana (50.1%); and they were over 40 percent of the population in four others, Florida (49%), Alabama (48%), Georgia (46%), and Virginia (42%).[47] Thus, if whites were to reassert effective political control, it was necessary for them to contain the political strength of blacks.

By 1877, the party of Lincoln had lost its political control of the South. Most of the states there were under the control of the Democratic Party and dedicated to white supremacy.[48] As long as the federal government maintained troops in the South, blacks were not completely defenseless, but federal troops were pulled out of the South as a result of the Hayes-Tilden Compromise of 1877, which resolved the disputed presidential election the previous year. Although Southern politicians pledged to protect the new legal rights of the freedmen, with federal troops no longer in the South, whites used violence and intimidation to prevent blacks from going to the polls. When violence and intimidation were not enough, elections were rigged, ballot boxes stuffed, perjury committed, and votes stolen through fraud to prevent candidates sympathetic to the African Americans from getting elected.[49] As Senator Ben Tillman of South Carolina boasted on the floor of the Senate in 1900, "We have done our best. We have scratched our heads to find out how we could eliminate the last one of them. We stuffed ballot boxes. We shot them. We are not ashamed of it."[50] The removal of black voters in the South was so complete and effective when Tillman spoke that after Representative George White of North Carolina left Congress in 1901, another black would not be elected to Congress from one of the former Confederate states until the 1972 elections of Andrew Young and Barbara Jordan.

As conservative white Southerners regained control of state legislatures, they began to pass laws to further prevent black males from exercising the franchise. Because of the Fifteenth Amendment's prohibitions on state's restricting the franchise based on race, states had to adopt "racially neutral" approaches to eliminate black voters from the political process. Among the measures enacted were lengthy residency requirements (because young black males tended to move frequently) and permanent disenfranchisement of those who committed bigamy and petty theft (crimes associated with blacks, even though murder, rape, and grand larceny were not offenses that led to disenfranchisement). Since blacks left slavery as landless and penniless peasants, many Southern states conditioned voting on meeting certain property requirements and/or required payment of a poll tax as a prerequisite to obtaining a ballot.

The most ingenious provisions used to eliminate black male voters were the literacy and understanding requirements. These provisions mandated that a prospective voter demonstrate his ability to read or understand the Constitution or some other written text to the satisfaction of the voting registrar. This requirement granted sole discretion to white registrars, who routinely concluded that a potential white voter with few literary skills was qualified to vote, but excluded well-educated prospective black voters. In its 1898 opinion in *Williams v. Mississippi*, the Supreme Court upheld these "racially neutral measures" by concluding that a state does not violate the equal protection clause when it requires eligible voters to be able to read, write, interpret, or understand any part of the Constitution or other text.[51] Since these provisions could also operate to disenfranchise white voters as well, however, some states added a grandfather clause. Louisiana was the first state to do so in 1898. Under Louisiana's grandfather clause, if a man's father or grandfather was on the voter rolls as of January 1, 1867, a time before black males received the franchise, then such a male's right to vote was grandfathered without the need to pass a test. Although the Supreme Court would eventually strike down grandfather clauses in 1915, by then the disenfranchisement of black male voters was complete.[52]

One final method employed by some states to disenfranchise blacks was the institution of the white primary. Republicans, the party of Lincoln, lost their voting appeal in the South after Reconstruction. Since the result of the general election between the Republican and Democratic candidates was a foregone conclusion, in states that instituted the primary system the Democratic primary was far more important than the general election. In some states, with Texas leading the way, the Democratic Party limited voting in its primary to only whites. It argued that since the Party was not a state actor, this limitation did not violate the prohibitions against racial discrimination by the state in the Fourteenth or Fifteenth Amendment. It was not until World War II that the Supreme Court finally put an end to the white primary system by definitively ruling it unconstitutional.[53]

## C. The Rise of Segregation

The success of white supremacists in negating black political participation produced all sorts of collateral consequences burdensome for blacks. The elimination of black voters freed white politicians to ignore or attack the concerns of black constituents at little or no political cost. As blacks were eliminated as an effective voting force in the South, state legislatures enacted segregation policies into law. Commenting on this, Yale law professor and former attorney with the NAACP Legal Defense and Education Fund (LDF),

Charles Black, wrote, "Segregation in the South comes down in apostolic succession from slavery and the *Dred Scott* case. The South fought to keep slavery, and lost. Then it tried the Black Codes, and lost. Then it looked around for something else and found segregation."[54]

Despite all of the resistance that blacks encountered from whites, the period from 1865 to 1890 could be described as the springtime of race relations. By the 1890s, however, the cold, harsh winter of legal segregation started to settle into the country.[55] Prior to the last decade of the nineteenth century, segregation existed in many aspects of Southern society, but it generally was not part of the legal code. In 1883, the Supreme Court rendered its decisions in the *Civil Rights Cases*.[56] In those cases, the Court quashed indictments of private individuals who had denied admission to persons of color to hotels and theaters in violation of the Civil Rights Act of 1875. The Court concluded that legislating against discrimination by private parties in these situations went beyond the powers granted to Congress under the Thirteenth and Fourteenth Amendments. The denial to blacks of equal access by the owners of public accommodations did not violate the Thirteenth Amendment since it was not a badge or an incident of slavery, and the Fourteenth Amendment only applied to state action, not private parties.

Segregation statutes made their first appearances in the field of transportation. Through the mid-1880s, no state required segregation on railways. Florida passed the first such statute in 1887, separating passengers in first class. Mississippi followed suit the next year. Until the late 1890s, railroad car segregation was the only form of segregation required by law in a majority of the southern states.[57] Whatever constitutional concerns that existed about *de jure* segregation, however, were resolved by the Supreme Court in its 1896 opinion in *Plessy v. Ferguson*.[58] In denying an equal protection challenge to a statute that required separate-but-equal accommodations on railroad cars, Justice Brown's opinion for the Court stated that "in the nature of things [the Fourteenth Amendment] could not have been intended to abolish distinctions based upon color or to enforce social, as distinguished from political equality."[59] Brown went on to note, "If one race be inferior to the other socially, the Constitution of the United States cannot put them upon the same plane."[60] Thus, segregation was justified based on the notion that blacks were socially inferior to whites. According to the highest court of the land, this was a reality that even the Constitution could not overcome.

Three years after its decision in *Plessy*, the Court in *Cumming v. Richmond County Board of Education*[61] signaled that the requirement of equality did not have to be taken literally.[62] In the case, the Court sanctioned a situation in which the Richmond County Board of Education used taxpayer funds to defer a portion of the cost of the high school education for white students, but provided no financial assistance for black students seeking high school education.

Over the next six decades, segregation and conscious racial discrimination would become the explicit law of the land in many areas of the country, and where not explicit, still formed part of customary American business, educational, political, and social practices. Discrimination based on race in employment, merchandising stores, eating establishments, places of entertainment, and hotels and motels was generally accepted as a fact of life. Blacks seldom occupied positions above the most menial levels in American businesses and corporations. Even lower-level management positions were, for the most part, unobtainable. Blacks attended separate public primary schools and were excluded from white colleges and universities. At the national level, white supremacists in Congress stymied federal legislation aimed at relieving the oppression of the Southern Negro. On scores of occasions between 1920 and 1950, the Southern bloc in Congress even succeeded in stonewalling federal antilynching legislation. As for electoral politics, no man of color was elected mayor of a major U.S. city until after the middle of the twentieth century. And no more than two blacks served at one same time in the House of Representatives before 1955. In terms of social practices, many places in the country maintained separate water fountains, waiting rooms, transportation facilities, rest rooms, hospitals, and cemeteries for whites and coloreds. Blacks were generally required to enter the homes of whites through the back door, never to shake the hand of a white person, and grown black men were constantly referred to as "boy" or by their first name.

Despite the promises of freedom and economic opportunities during the Civil War and Reconstruction, blacks largely found themselves landless, penniless, and disenfranchised laborers by the latter decades of the nineteenth century through much of the first half of the twentieth century. During the last two decades of the nineteenth century, almost three-fourths of blacks lived in rural areas where most of them were tenant sharecroppers or agricultural laborers.[63] They were left at the mercy of unscrupulous property owners who often failed to pay them what they were due and merchants who charged them outrageous prices for goods that they had to purchase. It was virtually impossible for them to get ahead financially. Having enough resources to feed their families and provide adequate housing and clothing were constant problems. The black men and women in the urban areas were confined to manual jobs or personal service employment. They were mostly employed as bricklayers, stonemasons, janitors, public service workers, house servants, maids, porters, and hotel help. In 1940, for example, the poverty rate for blacks stood at 87 percent.[64] Thus, by the end of the nineteenth century through more than half of the twentieth century, blacks found themselves victims of a new form of oppression: segregation.

## D. Desegregation Era

For centuries, scientists, politicians, commentators, and most Americans attributed the substandard nature of blacks to explanations that humans could not alter. Until the twentieth century, these notions of black inferiority were grounded in either the divine will of God or the defective biology of blacks. When American society attributed the substandard nature of blacks to causes that were essentially immutable to human engineering, it did not make logical sense to pursue racial equality or to integrate society on an equal basis. The first subsection will discuss the type of beliefs about blacks which were dominant among scholarly experts and mainstream American society that justified the oppression of blacks through the first decades of the twentieth century. However, between World War I and World War II, a paradigm shift occurred regarding the nature of racial differences. Social scientists began to assert that these differences were not the result of biology, but of historical and environmental factors. To the extent that learned opinion viewed blacks as victims of both an impoverished social environment and a degenerate culture caused by their historical treatment as substandard humans, there was reason to be optimistic that blacks could be improved. The cure for the disease that afflicted black people was to enrich their social environment by increasing their contact with whites and assisting them in shedding their degenerate culture. The Supreme Court adopted this view of racial differences in its opinion in *Brown v. Board of Education*.[65] The second subsection discusses the emergence of this view of racial differences and its acceptance by the Court. The *Brown* opinion initiated a fifteen-year period in which the Court, the Congress, and the President all worked to dismantle segregation and alleviate the consequences of the legacy of discrimination. The third subsection discusses the desegregation of American society. But because American society followed the position of the Supreme Court about the causes of racial differences, the fundamental belief in the inferiority of blacks was not completely rejected. Thus, many of the desegregation efforts continued to embody the belief that there was something wrong with black people, only now their condition could be ameliorated.

### 1. Rationales Justifying the Oppression of Blacks

For centuries before the Desegregation Era, the dominant beliefs in American society regarding racial or ethnic members of minority groups were not the progressive individualist, liberal attitudes that began to emerge in the 1950s and 1960s. With respect to blacks those beliefs presupposed that they were ontologically inferior. Until the commencement of the efforts to desegregate American society, religious, scientific, and cultural reasons were put forth to justify confining blacks to a lowly status. In its legal decisions upholding slavery, segregation, or limitations on the rights of blacks, the Supreme court did not normally stress these religious or scientific rationales regarding racial differences. Nevertheless, the propounding of these rationales by experts and their acceptance by the general public helped strengthen the perception that the Court's decisions upholding slavery and segregation were rational given the nature of things.

From the perspective of morality, Europeans revered the divine word of the Almighty for centuries before significant contact with sub-Saharan Africans. Thus, Europeans turned to Biblical scripture to find the moral justifications for slavery. Abraham, the grand patriarch of Judaism, Christianity, and Islam, owned slaves. In Chapter 25 of Leviticus, God also sanctioned enslaving "the heathens among you," a description that applied to Africans.[66] Although Jesus was silent on the issue of slavery, the epistles clearly took it for granted.[67] With regard to enslaving blacks, two stories from Genesis were used, the curse of Noah and the story of Cain.

The primary religious justification for enslaving blacks, and blacks alone, was derived from the curse Noah placed on the descendants of Ham.[68] According to Genesis 9:21–27, Noah became drunk one day and was lying naked on the ground in his tent. He was discovered by his son, Ham, who saw Noah's nakedness. Ham told his brothers, Shem and Japheth. The other two brothers took a garment, laid it upon their shoulders, went backwards and covered their father. Unlike Ham, they never saw Noah's nakedness. When Noah awoke and discovered what had occurred, he blessed Shem and Japheth, but cursed the descendants of Ham to be servants to Shem and Japheth. Before the fifteenth century, both Christians and Muslims came to believe that the descendants of Ham had turned black.

A second story from Genesis was also used to justify the enslavement of blacks. This was the story of the murder of Abel by Cain, which brought human death into the world.[69] Cain was a tiller of the soil and Abel was a keeper of sheep. Both brothers made sacrifices to God: Cain offered the fruit of the ground, Abel offered a young sheep. God did not respect Cain's offer of a sacrifice, but did respect that of Abel. Angered by God's rejection, Cain slew his brother. In punishment, God placed a mark on Cain. As earlier Christian groups before them, some Christian groups in the United States, including the Southern Baptist and Mormons, believed that the mark God placed on Cain was black skin. But because the Cain story did not indicate that his descendants were to be enslaved, it lacked the justification for placing blacks in bondage. Thus these religious groups also asserted that a descendant of Cain married a descendant of Ham. Black people were, therefore, the descendants of the merging of these two cursed bloodlines. As a result, black people took their color from the mark of Cain and the curse of slavery by being the descendants of Ham.[70]

As the Scientific Revolution took hold in Europe and North America, racial scientists provided new forms of "scientific" evidence for the inferiority of blacks. Carolus Linnaeus (1707–78) developed a biological classification system in 1758 that included physical descriptions and personality traits for four major classifications of humans, Americans (i.e., American Indians), Europeans, Asiatics, and Africans. Linnaeus described African personality traits as phlegmatic, crafty, indolent, and negligent. Dutch anatomist Pieter Camper (1722–89) argued that facial angles proved that blacks were inferior.[71] Physician, professor of medical theory, founder of Dickinson College in Pennsylvania, and signer of the Declaration of Independence, Benjamin Rush (1746–1813) contended that the black hue of the negro was the result of leprosy.[72] However, the rationale most often cited by racial experts was that black skin was an aberrant development caused by extensive exposure of blacks to the sun in hot climates.[73] German anatomist and anthropologist Johann Blumenbach (1752–1840) also worked out an influential racial classification system that placed Caucasians at the top of the human ladder with Asians, Africans, Native Americans, and Polynesians at the lower rungs.[74]

Later scientists argued that their measurements of physical traits demonstrated the intellectual inferiority of blacks. For example, America's first great anthropologist, Samuel Morton (1799–1851),[75] in the 1830s and 1840s found that Caucasians had the largest skulls, followed by Mongolians, American Indians, and then Africans.[76] With the presumption that big-headed people were smarter, this meant that blacks had the least intelligence of any racial group. Morton also claimed to have human skulls of blacks and whites that dated back to Ancient Egypt. He indicated that the same differences he found in modern day skulls existed thousands of years ago as well and concluded that the differences were therefore permanent. His conclusion of this permanence was made in light of the pre-Darwinian belief still shared by many American and European scientists that the earth was created only four thousand years before the birth of Christ.[77] Paul Broca (1824–80), the founder of the Society of Anthropology of Paris, also demonstrated that variations in the shape of human heads were linked to significant differences in the mental capacities of the races.[78] Measuring brains of dead Civil War soldiers, Stanford Hunt would find that blacks had smaller brains than whites and declared that therefore, they were not as intelligent.[79]

Social Darwinists emerged in the latter decades of the nineteenth century and produced new theories about racial differences based on the theory of evolution. The most optimistic Social Darwinists asserted that intelligence evolves over time. Thus, in hundreds of thousands of years, blacks might evolve to the same intellectual level as whites. Other Darwinists argued that while blacks were evolving, so were whites, and that whites were evolving at a faster rate than blacks. Thus, no matter how large the racial differences were now, they would increase in the future. A third group of Social Darwinists argued that in the battle of the "survival of the fittest," blacks were destined to wither away and eventually become extinct.[80]

In the early part of the twentieth century, Alfred Binet's concept of I.Q. testing was brought to the United States by H.H. Goddard. Although Binet did not assert that he was measuring an innate, genetically inherited capacity, Goddard did.[81] Lewis Terman, a Stanford University professor, agreed with the position that an I.Q. test could measure innate abilities. In 1916, he revised Binet's scale, increased the number of tasks to be performed, and gave his revision the name Stanford-Binet. R.M. Yerkes, a Harvard University professor, convinced the U.S. Army to allow him to administer intelligence tests to all of its World War I recruits. Yerkes, Terman, Goddard, and other colleagues developed the army's I.Q. tests in the summer of 1917. As an army colonel, Yerkes presided over the administration of these tests to 1.75 million World War I recruits. One of Yerkes' lieutenants, E.G. Boring, selected 160,000 case files and produced results from this sample. He argued that his results confirmed the long-standing belief that blacks were a mentally deficient race. He found that blacks were at the bottom of the intellectual scale, with a full 89 percent testing out at the level of morons or below.[82]

## 2. Emergence of Expert Opinion that Racial Differences Result Primarily from Socioenvironmental Conditions

Until World War I, racial scientists generally assumed that race and culture were fused. Thus, cultural traits were a product of biological racial traits and tendencies. Between World War I and World War II, a paradigm shift among scholars of race regarding the source of racial differences occurred. Franz Boas emerged as the leading voice in the academic movement to challenge the dominant biological basis of racial traits. Boas, his students, and like-minded anthropologists asserted that there was no proof that any racial group possessed hereditary differences in intelligence or temperament, but that historical and environmental factors produced behavioral performance differences among racial groups.[83] Boas pointed out that African Americans were not racially inferior nor mentally inept. Rather they, like all peoples, participate in a culture that is a product of historical development. In his writings and those of other anthropologists, they noted that the problems associated with blacks resulted from the deleterious environmental conditions, racial discrimination, and the heritage of slavery that continued to plague them. As this view gained legitimacy in the eyes of social scientists of the day, it became increasingly possible to envision ways to improve blacks by enhancing their social environment.

Accepting the arguments put forth by the NAACP and LDF,[84] the Supreme Court began to chip away at segregation in the late 1930s and 1940s.[85] With its 1954 unanimous decision in *Brown v. Board of Education*, the Court struck down statutes that permitted or required segregation of public school children. This was a watershed moment. Chief Justice Earl Warren's opinion for the Court assumed that the physical facilities and other tangible factors of the public schools attended by black and white students were equal. Given the objectively measurable equality of segregation in this context, for the first time the Court was forced to identify another harm resulting from segregation. Accepting the position put forth by the LDF and citing studies by social scientists,[86] in one of the most quoted phrases from *Brown*, the Court stated:

> To separate [African American youth] from others of similar age and qualifications solely because of their race generates a feeling of inferiority as to their status in the community that may affect their hearts and minds in a way unlikely ever to be undone.[87]

The Court went on to quote approvingly from the district court in Kansas:

> Segregation of white and colored children in public schools has a detrimental effect upon the colored children. The impact is greater when it has the sanction of law; [f]or the policy of separating the races is usually interpreted as denoting the inferiority of the negro group. A sense of inferiority affects the motivation of a child to learn. Segregation with the sanction of law, therefore, has a tendency to [retard] the educational and mental development of negro children and to deprive them of some of the benefits they would receive in a racial[ly] integrated school.[88]

The Court quickly applied the holding in *Brown* to a number of other cases in which it struck down other segregation practices of government.[89]

With the cold reflection offered by sixty years' distance, what stands out in the justifications of the Supreme Court for striking down *de jure* segregation of public school students in *Brown* is the reality that the Court did not reject the fundamental belief in the inferiority of black people. *Brown* was a break from the historic, dominant racial attitudes about African Americans because the Court attributed black inferiority to differences in the deficit social environment available to them and their deviant culture, as opposed to unalterable causes. This change in the causes of the "less-than" nature of blacks was comparatively optimistic and hopeful when placed against the background of the dominant historical beliefs about the source of racial differences. Given these grounds of racial differences, then, it was possible to mitigate the race problem.

The Court's explanation led to the inevitable conclusion that the purpose of desegregating schools was to foster interracial contact for the sole benefit of blacks. Bringing black children into predominately white schools would help to enrich the black child's social environment. It increased their exposure to, presumably, more intelligent and better behaved white children and more qualified white teachers. White teachers and students with whom black children came into contact could function as role models and demonstrate to the black children the appropriate attitudes and forms of behavior they should emulate. Desegregation would also help black children repudiate their deficient and pathological culture and its associated ideas. In other words, desegregation would allow whites to provide blacks with social welfare benefits in the form of increased interracial contact. Although whites could expect little benefit for themselves or their children from such contact, hopefully, they would not suffer any harm because of it.

The Supreme Court never abandoned the view of the harm of segregation articulated in *Brown* as its justification for ordering the dismantling of racially identified school systems in every facet of operation, including students, faculty, staff, transportation, extracurricular activities, and facilities.[90] In fact, in the Court's second opinion that addressed when school desegregation decrees terminate in 1992, *Freeman v. Pitts*,[91] the Court restated the above passages from *Brown* when it discussed the harms generated by segregation that school desegregation orders were to remedy.[92]

## 3. Desegregation of American Society

After *Brown*, many school districts and states resisted the obligation to desegregate their schools. A full ten years after the Court's opinion, little actual integration had occurred, especially in the Deep South where resistance was the greatest. In 1964, only 2.14 percent of the black students in the eleven states of the former Confederacy attended desegregated schools.[93] However, the passage of the Civil Rights Act of 1964 and the Elementary and Secondary Education Act of 1965, along with the Court's opinions in *Green v. New Kent County School Board* and *Swann v. Charlotte-Mecklenburg Board of Education*[94] helped to spur the desegregation of public schools. The impact of these developments was dramatic and immediate. In 1968, 23.4 percent of black students attended majority-white schools nationwide; by 1972, this had increased to 36.4 percent, and it would reach its all-time high of 37.1 percent in 1980. Also in 1968–69 school year, 64.3 percent of black students went to schools where minorities comprised at least 90 percent of the student body; four years later, that had decreased to 38.7 percent, and it reached its all-time low of 32.5 percent in 1986. Desegregation was even more rapid and sizable in the South. In 1967, only 13.9 percent of black students attended majority-white schools; by 1972, that figure had jumped to 36.4 percent, and it reached its zenith of 43.5 percent in 1988.[95]

The Supreme Court's school desegregation jurisprudence also helped to set off a round of educational reforms. Taking the Court's opinion about the harms of segregation as gospel, educators generally perceived the underlying premises and structures of American education as basically sound and considered major reforms unnecessary.[96] Thus, the educational reform movement was based upon the same notion articulated by the Supreme Court, that racial isolation retarded the intellectual and psychological development of only black children. Educational reform was therefore dominated by a "cultural deprivation paradigm" with respect to minority groups. As Professor James Banks pointed out, educators expressed two major goals during this movement: "to raise the self-concepts of ethnic minority youths and to increase their racial pride."[97] Not only did this educational reform movement spark changes in the curriculum aimed at trying to improve the self-concept of blacks by portraying them as essentially "colored whites," but also cultural enrichment projects that took black students to concerts, art galleries, scientific laboratories, and museums were added to expose them to the artifacts and traditions of America's mainstream. Needless to say, no such programs were instituted to expose white children to the cultural aspects of the Black Community.

The Court's opinion in *Brown* also set off a remarkable fifteen-year period during which Congress, the President, and the Judiciary all sought to advance the cause of dismantling *de jure* segregation. The Court delivered several opinions that outlawed racial and ethnic discrimination by governmental entities. Congress passed several major pieces of civil rights legislation in the 1960s, including the 1964 Civil Rights Act, the 1965 Voting Rights Act, and the 1968 Fair Housing Act. Both Presidents Kennedy and Johnson made advancing civil rights part of their legislative agendas and took public stances against racial discrimination. Even a reluctant President Eisenhower sent federal troops to Little Rock in order to enforce the desegregation of Central High School.

As American society engaged in its efforts to dismantle segregation, the Court's view of blacks as the only group psychologically harmed by it was one of the common understandings used to justify such efforts. For example, in his landmark speech at the commencement ceremony at Howard University in June 1965, President Lyndon Johnson stated:

> You do not wipe away the scars of centuries by saying: Now you are free to go where you want, and do as you desire, and choose the leaders as you please. You do not take a person who, for years, has been hobbled by chains and liberate him, bring him up to the starting line of a race and then say, "you are free to compete with all the others," and still justly believe that you have been completely fair.[98]

Like the Supreme Court, Johnson was urging others to take account of race in an effort to assist a group that was not the equal of whites because it had been crippled by the scars from the chains of centuries of oppression.

Affirmative action policies adopted by selective higher education institutions also took on an explanation similar to that of school desegregation. In arguments that continue to reverberate today, the assumption was that the black students who benefitted from affirmative action were not as qualified as their white peers. Thus, many of these blacks students were placed in a situation where academic underperformance was all but inevitable because they were less academically prepared than the white students with whom they competed.[99] In addition, if they graduated, these blacks were still stamped with a badge of credential inferiority because their accomplishments were tainted since they were not worthy of the admission to their selective higher education institution in the first place.[100]

## E. Post-Racial/Colorblind Era

There were two different aspects of the desegregation movement's judicial decisions, legislation, and programs and policies. One aspect used race as a means for dismantling the effects of prior *de jure* segregation. As Justice Blackmun put it in his opinion in *Regents of the University of California v. Bakke*, "in order to get beyond racism, we must first take account of race."[101] The other aspect of the desegregation movement, however, involved the assertion of the need to transcend considerations of race. People should act as if they were colorblind and judge individuals based on the content of their character, not the color of their skin. Thus, the colorblind/individualist aspect of the desegregation movement sought to deemphasize the consideration of race in favor of treating people as individuals. As is obvious, the aspect of the desegregation movement that reinforced the importance of race was in considerable conflict with the colorblind/individualist aspect. Over time, this conflict became increasingly apparent. The second aspect would eventually become dominant and help lead to the Post-Racial/Colorblind Era.

By the middle of the 1970s, the Supreme Court began to limit the possible revolutionary changes from the rights granted to blacks and other minorities during the Desegregation Era.[102] Despite the Court's early willingness during the Desegregation Era to define race discrimination in terms of its discriminatory effect on blacks and other minorities[103] and to allow governmental entities to take account of race in order to remedy the effects of racial discrimination,[104] over the past four decades the Supreme Court has been marching toward a colorblind understanding of race discrimination under the Constitution and federal antidiscrimination law.[105] The Court increasingly came to view racially motivated decision making and the use of racial classifications as harms in and of themselves, regardless of the justifications for such use. For example, Justice Powell, in his 1978 opinion in *Regents of University of California v. Bakke*,[106] which rejected a set-aside of admissions seats for minorities in medical school, mentioned a number of potential harms generated by the use of racial classifications. He noted that racial classifications may compel innocent individuals to sacrifice their interest in order to redress the harm of others that they did not cause.[107] The use of racial classifications could place burdens upon individual members of beneficiary group in order to advance that particular group's general interest. Thus, the use of racial classifications could lead to the sacrifice of a black person's individual interest for the benefit of his or her race. Another harm that Powell noted was that the use of racial classifications could reinforce the common stereotype that certain groups cannot achieve success without special favors that have no bearing on individual ability.[108] This has been a common concern mentioned by a number of Supreme Court Justices. Justice Thomas, for example, in his concurring opinion in *Adarand Constructors, Inc. v. Pena*,[109] called this "racial paternalism." According to Thomas, "racial paternalism and its unintended consequences can be as poisonous and pernicious as any other form of discrimination.... [It] teaches many that because of chronic and apparently immutable handicaps, minorities cannot compete with them without their patronizing indulgence."[110] And Justice O'Connor's opinion in *City of Richmond v. J.A. Croson Co.* noted that racial classifications carry a potential danger of stigmatism that may promote notions of racial inferiority.[111] A number of Supreme Court justices also pointed to the harm of racial hostility that the use of racial classifications can generate.[112] The use of racial classifications can also create the abstract harm of a denial of individuality. In *Miller v. Johnson*,[113] the Court addressed a challenge to the racially motivated congressional redistricting plan adopted by the Georgia General Assembly. The Department of Justice had insisted that Georgia create a third majority-minority congressional legislative district in order to receive preclearance of its plan under Section 5 of the Voting Rights Act. Writing for the Court, Justice Kennedy responded to an argument made by the plan's defenders that the equal protection clause's general proscription on race-based decision making does not apply in the redistricting context because redistricting by definition involves racial considerations. Kennedy noted that underlying their arguments are the very stereotypical assumptions the equal protection clause forbids. Legislatures' consideration of race in redistricting decisions is "based on the demeaning notion that members of the defined racial groups ascribe to certain 'minority views' that must be different from those of other citizens," which is the precise use of race as a proxy the Constitution prohibits.[114]

In short, among the myriad of harms derived from racially motivated decision making and the use of racial classifications by government are: innocent persons may bear the burden of redressing grievances they did not cause; the interest of some minority individuals may be sacrificed for the benefit of their racial or ethnic group; racial paternalism; the generation of racial and ethnic hostility; and demeaning individuals because they are evaluated as a product of their race or ethnicity. It is apparent that all of the potential harms noted by the justices result from government's failure to be colorblind and, therefore, respect everyone's individuality.

A majority of the justices on the Court, however, have not yet fully embraced a colorblind interpretation of the equal protection clause or federal antidiscrimination law. For example, affirmative action admissions policies represent one such exception. Governmental units can also employ racial classifications in an effort to remedy identified acts of discrimination.[115] And Justice Kennedy's 2007 controlling opinion in *Parents Involved in Community Schools v. Seattle School District No. 1*[116] states that school officials are free to devise various race-conscious measures that do not employ individual racial classifications in order to pursue integrated schools. Yet, despite exceptions, including discriminatory impact legislation under Title VII, the evolution of the colorblind ideal has drastically limited avenues for racial minorities to challenge governmental policies and practices which produce disparate racial outcomes and the ability of government to institute policies and programs to take account of race.[117]

There are two different facets to the colorblind interpretation of federal antidiscrimination provisions that limit the ability of the government to address the effects of the history of racial oppression on blacks. The Court treats governmental entities as if they were individuals, presuming that their decisions to implement their policies and programs are motivated by their intent. Thus, the determination of whether government and private entities are engaged in race discrimination primarily depends upon their motivations, not the effects of their actions.[118] The actions of government and private entities that are not motivated by a desire to discriminate based on race may have a discriminatory effect on members of certain racial or ethnic groups, including blacks. Yet, the individuals whose interests are harmed by actions motivated by nonracial concerns are not viewed as victims of racial discrimination because it is not the *consequences* of an actor's actions that determine whether they are racially discriminatory, but the *intent* that motivated the actions. Thus, federal courts will view the negative disparate impact of racially neutral actions upon minority groups as an unfortunate byproduct. This facet of the Court's colorblind antidiscrimination jurisprudence has made it increasingly difficult for black plaintiffs to win discrimination challenges against public and private policies and programs. Often administrators can explain their decision to implement such plans by referring to racially neutral motives. Secondly, under the equal protection clause, government's ability to employ racial classifications, or require private actors to do so, is subject to strict scrutiny and, thus, severely limited. Only when government narrowly tailors its use of racial classifications to advance a compelling state interest will their use survive an equal protection challenge. The Supreme Court has rejected a number of rationales for governmental policies and programs that could attenuate the continuing effects of the history of race discrimination on blacks and other minority groups as not compelling, including curing societal discrimination,[119] creating set-asides for minority contractors,[120] providing black students with black teachers as role models of academic success,[121] creating majority-minority legislative districts,[122] and fostering racially balanced public schools.[123] Thus, this facet of the Court's colorblind equal protection jurisprudence has also made it relatively easy for white plaintiffs to establish a claim of reverse discrimination and, thereby, to invalidate good faith public and private efforts aimed at overcoming the continuing impact of discrimination on blacks and other minorities.[124]

Yet racial and ethnic disparities in important socioeconomic conditions remain widespread. For example, the median household income of blacks in 2012 was $33,321, which was only 58.4 percent of white family income and 48.4 percent of Asian family income.[125] With respect to per capita income, black earnings of $19,267 are only 57.6 percent of white and 60.4 percent of Asian per capita income.[126] The 2012 unemployment rates for blacks (13.8 percent) was significantly higher than they were for Asians (5.9 percent), whites (7.2 percent), and Hispanics (10.3 percent).[127] A much larger percentage of blacks are also more likely to live in poverty. The poverty rate in the Black Community stands at 27.2 percent, in contrast to Hispanics/Latinos at 25.6 percent,

Asians at 11.7 percent, and whites at 9.9 percent.[128] The disparities in poverty rates are even higher for blacks under the age of 18. Over a third of them, 36.7 percent, live below the poverty line, in contrast to Hispanics/Latinos at 33.8 percent, whites at 18.5 percent, and Asians at 13.8 percent.[129] According to an April 2013 report issued by the Urban Institute, in 2010 the average white family possessed $632,000 in wealth, compared to $98,000 for the average black family.[130] In other words, the average white family was more than six times wealthier than the average black family.

Substantial racial and ethnic gaps can also be seen in educational achievement statistics. The recent report by the National Center on Education Statistics noted that, for freshmen entering high school in 2005 and due to graduate in 2009, the number of students able to graduate in four years varied substantially for the different racial groups. Only 66.1 percent of blacks graduated in four years, compared with 69.1 percent for Native Americans, 71.4 percent for Hispanic/Latinos, 83.0 percent for whites, and 93.5 percent for Asians.[131] Also, the percentage of those with college degrees in 2010 varies substantially among the racial/ethnic groups. Thus, whereas 19.8 percent of blacks over the age of 25 have a college degree, 30.3 percent of whites and 52.4 percent of Asians have obtained such a degree.[132]

The over-inclusion of blacks within the criminal justice system is another place where huge disparities exist. In a thirty-year period, the U.S. prison population increased from 300,000 to almost two million.[133] According to statistics from the U.S. Bureau of Justice, in July 2009, about 840,000 black men in U.S. prisons made up approximately 40 percent of all inmates.[134] Whereas white men were incarcerated at a rate of 708 per 100,000, for black men the rate was 4,749 per 100,000.[135] In other words, the rate of incarceration of black men was more than six times higher than for white men. The likely imprisonment rate for white men is 1 in 17 and for white women it is 1 in 111, but the correspondingly rate for black men is 1 in 3 and for black women 1 in 18, respectively.[136] Also, the life expectancy of blacks is only 74.6 years, in contrast to whites at 78.9 years, Hispanics/Latinos at 82.8 years, and Asians at 86.5 years.[137]

Led by the rationale of Supreme Court decisions tending to discount race discrimination as an explanation for racial socioeconomic differences, dominant American discourse about race has also gradually embraced colorblindness.[138] The public, politicians, scholars, and commentators increasingly seek to explain such racial socioeconomic differences by attributing them to nonracial causes. Thus, for example, the gross racial differences in family income should be reduced to reflect nonracial factors such as the larger percentages of single-parent families among blacks, unwed black mothers living on welfare, and the higher percentage of blacks who live in the South where incomes are less than in the rest of the country.[139] In addition, since black people on average are younger than whites and have less formal education, taking account of these factors will further reduce the gaps in family or per capita incomes. With regard to educational achievement, for example, scholars have long focused on the persistent black/white test score gaps. In doing so, normally they attempt to control for such "nonracial" variables as family structure, socioeconomic factors, measures of school quality, parental levels of education, and neighborhood characteristics that reduce the disparities that they are addressing. Thus, despite the large observable racial differences revealed by socioeconomic statistics, focusing on nonracial factors seems to reduce the differences.

Even after many nonracial factors are controlled for, however, substantial racial socioeconomic gaps usually remain. Harkening back to earlier explanations of racial differences, in 1994, Richard Hernstein and Charles Murray pointed to biological differences to explain much of the racial disparities in socioeconomic statistics.[140] However, the overwhelming majority of commentators, politicians, and experts continue to follow the Supreme Court's lead in *Brown v. Board of Education* and believe that persistent socioeconomic gaps result from some kind of deficit social environment or culture that still negatively affects blacks. Thus, often educational achievement gaps not attributed to nonracial factors are instead attributed to differences in family structure or differences in culture, socialization, or behavior[141] that reflect negatively on the cultural practices of blacks. For example, the oppositional cultural theory has been one of the most popular cultural explanations for the low academic achievement of black youth in American schools for the past two decades.[142] According to this theory, in order to live with subordination, blacks in the U.S. developed coping mechanisms, which are often perceived as oppositional to those of the dominant group. This oppositional tendency inhibits the academic performance of urban black school children.[143] Others have argued that part of the educational achievement gap observed in elementary and secondary schools is because the black children lose more ground over the summer when compared to whites because their home and neighborhood environments are worse.[144] Roland Fryer and Steven Levitt found substantial racial achievement gaps in the test scores of blacks entering kindergarten. They asserted that by controlling for the children's age (the black children were on average about 20 days younger), child's birth weight (black children were 10 ounces lighter), mother's age at first birth (black mothers were on average 4 years younger), participation in the Women's Infant and Children program (black women are more likely to receive welfare assistance), the number of books in the home (blacks have fewer books in their homes), and measures of socioeconomic status, the gaps were largely eliminated. Thus, inadequate neonatal and parental practices of blacks explain a good portion of the poor academic performance of black kindergarteners.[145]

In discussing persistent socioeconomic racial disparities in his book *Losing the Race*, James McWhorter notes that things in America have improved greatly. McWhorter goes on to assert that the problem of blacks stems from the fact that many have adopted a "Cult of Victimology ... [an] unfocused brand of resentment and sense of alienation from the mainstream."[146] For him, those blacks who continue to talk about the lack of racial progress are deeply entrenched in a view based on outright myths or vast exaggerations and distortions born out of a filtering of reality that views it through the prism of aimless indignation over the unwillingness of America to solve its racial problem. McWhorter goes on to state that the reason that blacks do so poorly academically "decade after decade [is] not because of racism, funding, class, parental education, etc., but because of a virus of Anti-intellectualism that infects the black community."[147]

The important point of this section is that in the Post-Racial/Colorblind Era, when thoughts or discussions turn to racial differences, the source of the blame continues to be some form of deficit black culture or social environment. Even in today's more enlightened Post-Racial/Colorblind society, blacks still experience the impact of what it means to be raced.

## II. Race as the Characteristic that Bound Black People Together in a Collective Struggle Against Their Oppression

The preceding part discussed the experiences of blacks as victims of racial discrimination; this part will view the black experience from the perspective of the struggle by blacks against their oppression. Consistent with a group that felt its treatment in America was unjust, blacks formulated a counterdiscourse that provided an alternative understanding of their experiences different from that of the dominant American society. This counterdiscourse represents the other aspect of the historical experience of blacks. It also helped to forge a unifying and collective identity that Martin Delany described in 1852 as "a nation within a nation."[148] The central feature of this counterdiscourse was the collective struggle dedicated to the liberation of black people from their racial oppression. As James Forman stated about the African American experience, "our basic history is one of resistance."[149]

Like Part I, this part is also not intended to be a complete history of the black struggle against racial oppression. Its purpose is to establish the fact that throughout American history, blacks have waged a constant war against their racial oppression. Thus, when discussing the historical experience of the Black Community in the United States, it is necessary to acknowledge this history of struggle. This part is also broken into five sections, which reflects the mirror image of the previous part: resistance to slavery during the colonial and antebellum periods, liberation efforts during the Civil War and Reconstruction, resistance to racial oppression in the form of segregation, liberation efforts during the Desegregation Era, and the continued struggle in the Post-Racial/Colorblind Era.

Blacks began to resist their racial oppression on the very ships that brought them from the coast of Africa to the New World. Once they arrived in North America, they continued to resist their bondage in numerous ways. Although seldom able to attack their captivity directly, blacks did engage in several armed resistance movements. When possible, blacks engaged in acts of self-liberation from bondage by escaping from their slave masters. In the freer North, blacks participated in and created abolition movements to try and legally free their brethren held in captivity. Blacks also resisted their bondage in uncountable ways during their day-to-day activities. The first section discusses the ways in which blacks resisted slavery.

When armed hostilities broke out between the North and South, some blacks offered their services to the Union Army. These original offers were rejected. The North declared that its initial aim of going to battle with the Confederacy was to preserve the Union, not destroy slavery. Despite the North's initial reticence to allowing black males to enlist in the Union army, however, many blacks held in bondage seized this opportunity to liberate themselves. Impressive numbers of them also assisted the Union war effort in nonmilitary ways. And when given the chance to fight for their freedom, blacks enlisted in the Union Army in huge numbers. They were the Union's most courageous fighters, sustaining causality rates that were considerably higher than those of white troops. Lincoln would claim that the black soldiers were essential to the Union victory. After the Civil War, blacks took full advantage of the new civil and political rights their efforts on the battlefield helped them achieve. However, their tremendous desires to obtain land that would have allowed them true independence from their former slave masters were frustrated. The second section discusses their efforts to liberate themselves from their racial oppression during the Civil War and Reconstruction.

Despite their best efforts, blacks could not prevent whites from stripping black males of the franchise. After the loss of the right to vote in the South, Southern legislators began to enact segregation statutes. Although blacks found themselves segregated from the cradle to the grave, they did not accept defeat. Blacks used their segregation to create their own institutions within the Black Community. Some blacks, however, believed that true liberation from their racial oppression could only be obtained through emigration. Others fought against segregation by participating in civil rights and labor organizations determined to bring about its end. The third section discusses the resistance of blacks to their racial oppression during the Segregation Era.

With the Supreme Court's decision in *Brown v. Board of Education*, American society moved into the Desegregation Era. Blacks were very involved in forcing American society to grant them long overdue rights. Thus, blacks marched for jobs, civil rights, and the restoration of the franchise that most of them had been denied during the twentieth century. They also litigated for an end to racial oppression and segregation in the courts, and created, assisted, or joined grass roots organizations that worked to dismantle segregation. The fourth section discusses blacks' work to achieve full equality during the Desegregation Era.

The unprecedented changes in American society caused by the new legal rights won during the Desegregation Era helped to create tremendous opportunities for individual blacks. As a result of these changes, there are several highly visible, extremely successful, and very powerful blacks in the United States. However, despite the impressive successes of a small percentage of blacks, as the socioeconomic statistics discussed earlier in this chapter demonstrate, blacks as a group continued to lag far behind non-Hispanic whites (and Asians) on economic, educational, political, and other important measures. The belief that America is a Post-Racial/Colorblind society and that the best way to resolve existing racial issues is through colorblindness, obscures the persistent racial socioeconomic gaps as well as the continuing impact of America's history of racial discrimination on African Americans. The fifth section discusses the continuing struggle of blacks against their racial oppression by pointing out the various ways in which colorblindness tends to obscure the continued racial oppression of blacks.

## A. Resistance to Slavery During the Colonial and Antebellum Eras

The beginning of collective resistance by blacks to their enslavement started with the efforts of those captives to seize the very transport ships that took them from the coast of Africa. Shipping records from cargo ships with names like *The Liberty*, *The Freedom*, *The Gift of God*, *The Justice*, and *The Integrity* include plenty of references to efforts by the black captives to seize control and direct the ships back home.[150] However, for many of these slaves the only effective form of resistance they could choose on those ships was death.[151] Many Africans attempted to jump overboard even though there was no realistic chance of survival in the murky, shark-infested ocean waters, rather than submit to a life of bondage.[152] Other slaves sought to resist their oppression by starving themselves to death. However, since the remuneration of merchants who traded in human flesh depended upon freight delivered, these importers took measures to reduce "cargo losses," which included the placement of nets around the hulls of their ships to capture would-be escapees and methods to force feed defiant throats.

Once in North America, black detainees resisted their captivity in several different ways. Although the conditions of their captivity prevented major armed revolts, blacks did employ violent means to resist their enslavement when they could. Some detainees engaged in acts of self-liberation and simply escaped from their bondage. Blacks were also involved in abolition movements, especially in the North where they were freer to protest against the enslavement of their brethren in the South. They also resisted slavery while performing their everyday activities.

## 1. Violent Resistance to Captivity by Black Freedom Fighters

Blacks outnumbered whites by large numbers in many European colonies in the New World, but among the British North American mainland colonies, only in South Carolina did blacks make up a majority of the population for a significant period of time. This lack of numerical superiority limited the frequency, intensity, and size of armed black uprisings on the mainland compared to those that occurred in the Caribbean and South America.[153] Still, violent resistance occurred often enough to create a widespread fear among the white population in North America of servile rebellions.[154] Historian Herbert Aptheker catalogued some 250 slave revolts and conspiracies.[155] Because reports of black uprisings and conspiracies created anxiety and panic among the whites, the tendency in the antebellum South was to suppress news of insurrections. Thus, Aptheker's count might understate the number of attempted uprisings. However, as Eugene Genovese put it, "the significance of the slave revolts in the United States lies neither in their frequency nor in their extent, but in their very existence as the ultimate manifestation of class war under the most unfavorable of conditions."[156]

The earliest recorded revolt in which blacks participated occurred in Virginia in 1663 and involved both black and white indentured servants. This uprising ended with authorities executing several participants and displaying their heads on chimney tops as a warning to others.[157] In 1676, Virginia had to put down a rebellion, the largest one known in the English colonies before the American Revolution, led by Nathaniel Bacon.[158] Bacon's rebellion stemmed from complaints by the property-less white working class, most of whom were unmarried males, although 10 percent of Virginia's black population joined Bacon.[159] This rebellion helped to convince white elites in Virginia that by relying so heavily on white indentured servants to supply their labor needs, they were creating a dangerous situation. These indentured servants could one day become a disgruntled property-less class. White elites also recognized the need to prevent the formulation of class alliance between dissatisfied whites and blacks. On June 8, 1680, the General Assembly passed "[a]n act for preventing Negroes Insurrections." Among its provisions were ones that proscribed slaves from possessing any "club, staffe, gunn, sword or any other weapon of defense or offence," required that a slave could not leave his master's property without written permission, and prohibited slaves from lifting their hand up in opposition to any Christian.[160] Fears of black rebellions were heightened when Virginia colonists discovered the Negro Plot of 1687, the first conspiracy in British North America that did not involve white supporters or participants.[161]

The largest slave revolt until that time occurred in New York in 1712. By then New York had one of the largest black populations of all of the mainland colonies. As a result of the uprising, nine white men were killed before the militia could stop the assault. Subsequently, twenty-one rebels were executed. In response to this rebellion, New York adopted the most stringent race-control statute enacted in North America before independence.[162] Among the provisions included were ones that prohibited more than three black slaves meeting together, proscribed slaves from owning a gun, prohibited entertaining or harboring slaves or buying anything from them, prohibited free blacks or mulattoes from owning real property, and required slave masters to post a surety bond for any manumitted slave.[163]

Because black slaves were a large percentage of the population in South Carolina, it is not surprising that a number of rebel uprisings occurred there. Major black conspiracies were discovered in Carolina in 1713, 1720, 1729, and 1730.[164] The largest slave uprising during the colonial period in British North America was the Stono Rebellion of 1739. From the time the English established the Carolina Colony in 1670, conflict existed between their colony and the Spanish-held territories to the south. By the eighteenth century, Spain had adopted a policy of granting freedom to black captives escaping from British territories.[165] These freedom seekers were often put into the Spanish militia. A free black settlement grew up two miles north of St. Augustine around Fort Mose, which was established in 1738. The commander of the Fort was an escaped Carolinian slave known to the Spanish as Francisco Menendez.[166] In September 1739, an initial group of about twenty black slaves led by an African named Jeremy started an uprising at the Stono River. The rebels seized a store of firearms and began their march to what they hoped would be freedom once they reached Florida. Along the way other slaves joined them. However, they were overtaken by a much larger English colonial force. Before this rebellion was crushed, twenty whites and forty crusaders for freedom were dead.[167]

As the population of America exploded after the Revolutionary War, so did the number of black slaves in the South. The black population tripled between 1776 and 1820.[168] The possibility of black rebellions continued to be a concern in the Southern states. For example, a massive potential slave uprising under the leadership of Gabriel Prosser came to light in Virginia in the summer of 1800. Although no one knows how many blacks were involved in Prosser's attempted revolt, Vincent Harding noted that the estimates given ranged from dozens to more than a thousand.[169] The plot involved an effort by soldiers of liberty to seize control of the city of Richmond. But before its organizers could consummate the uprising, the plot was revealed to authorities, who informed the governor and future President, James Monroe. In addition, a massive downpour on the scheduled day of the rebellion flooded local roads and bridges, making them impassable. In the end, local courts tried more than seventy men, and twenty-five of them were executed for taking part in the potential rebellion.[170]

The largest confirmed slave revolt in the United States or the territories under its control occurred in 1811 in Louisiana, a year before it became a state. It involved between 200 and 500 captives.[171] Deciding that they would rather die than continue to work under the blazing Louisiana sun, this highly organized group of freedom fighters armed with guns, axes, and knives set out from Louisiana plantations with the intent of conquering the city of New Orleans. Under the leadership of Charles Deslondes, the rebels destroyed several plantations and killed at least two whites before authorities in New Orleans were alerted. A force of over 600 soldiers attacked the rebels, killing sixty-six of them. Another seventeen were captured, put on trial, and executed.[172]

In 1822, Denmark Vesey, a free black man who prospered as a carpenter, organized the most elaborate and well-planned potential black uprising in U.S. history.[173] Vesey recruited some nine thousand slaves to participate in a plot to seize Charleston, which at that time was the fifth largest city in the country. Among those recruited were trusted house servants of the governor of South Carolina and other high-ranking state officials. The freedom fighters planned on these recruits killing their masters when the uprising commenced. Vesey also prepared companies of armed slaves who would go through the streets of Charleston killing as many whites as possible. Vesey's plan called for the escapees to burn the city to the ground and board ships that would take them to Haiti or Africa. Vesey's plot, however, was discovered before it could commence.

In the summer of 1822, Vesey and seventy-seven of his followers were executed or imprisoned.[174]

In August of 1831, Nat Turner led the most famous slave revolt in U.S. history. This Baptist preacher was inspired by his religious zeal. While he started with just six other co-conspirators who were armed with only farm implements when they attacked the house of Nat's master, eventually his freedom fighters numbered sixty to eighty people.[175] Turner's revolutionaries moved between farms in Southampton County, Virginia, killing at least fifty-seven whites by the time they were stopped by authorities.[176] Turner eluded authorities for seventy days before he was caught, tried, and hung.

Arson was another violent means that blacks employed in resisting their bondage. Some fires blamed on slaves were of suspicious origin and may have had other causes, but authorities often suspected that black slaves set many fires. Kenneth Stampp argued that arson was the most common slave crime.[177] According to Vincent Harding, black slaves were accused of setting major fires in many American cities, including Charleston, Albany, Newark, New York, Savannah, and Baltimore.[178]

In the North, as free people, blacks were allowed more latitude in organizing themselves. Because of the threat of violence from whites that many free Black Communities encountered, some of them established militia groups for their common defense. For example, Brooklyn formed one in 1848, New Bedford Independent Blues was created in 1855, and that same year the Independent Village Guard was organized in New York. Other black militia groups were started in Detroit, Pittsburgh, Boston, Long Island, and Reading, Pennsylvania.[179]

## 2. Self-Liberation

Despite constant threats of punishment and retaliation for it, self-liberation was another form of resistance to bondage. Numerous records exist of individual blacks who escaped from captivity. Some outlier communities of runaways hid out in the woods for months or years, and other escapees established maroon camps in remote swamps and bayous.[180] These free communities of blacks lived on the outskirts of towns and villages.

When hostilities broke out between the American colonists and Great Britain, blacks were presented with an important opportunity to seize their own freedom. The British Governor of Virginia, Lord Dunmore, issued a proclamation on November 7, 1775, in which he offered freedom to those detainees who left their masters and joined "his Majesty's troops ... for the more speedily reducing the Colony to a proper sense of their duty."[181] In 1779, the British

Commander in Chief, Sir Henry Clinton, also offered freedom to every black who would desert the cause of the American colonist. And Lord Cornwallis refused to allow owners to recapture escapees once they reached his camp, regardless of whether the owners were rebels. Thus, during the Revolutionary War thousands of blacks seized upon the invitation from the British and took advantage of the opportunities created by the chaos of the war for their personal liberation. After the War, the British repatriated to Canada many of the former captives who sought them out. Other escapees went to free Black Communities in the United States where they assumed new identities.

There is no way to know how many blacks liberated themselves during the Revolutionary War, but some historians have put the numbers at between 80,000 and 100,000;[182] others have put the figure as low as about 20,000.[183] Thomas Jefferson, for example, estimated that in 1778 alone Virginia lost over 30,000 slaves.[184] One South Carolina historian put the number of slaves that ran away from that state during the War at over 25,000, and responsible citizens in Georgia estimated that they lost between 11,250 and 12,750 of their 15,000 slave population.[185] Whatever the number, the point remains: many blacks liberated themselves during the Revolutionary War.

The Underground Railroad was formed in the early 1800s and reached its peak in the 1850s. It was a series of escape routes for those in bondage and involved a vast network of individuals and associations that assisted blacks seeking to free themselves from captivity. In 1833, the British Parliament adopted the Slavery Abolition Act that abolished slavery throughout the colonies of the British Empire effective August 1, 1834.[186] After this, Canada became an important destination for blacks traveling on the Underground Railroad. Thomas Smallwood was directly involved in helping blacks along the way to freedom through the District of Columbia. In 1842, he and white abolitionist Charles T. Torrey helped 150 blacks escape to the North.[187] The Fugitive Slave Law of 1850, however, created additional problems for black liberty seekers by expanding the involvement of the federal government and the Northern states in the protection of the "property" of slaveholders. It also generated additional anger against and increased resistance to slavery by many Northern antislavery sympathizers. Thus they and others helped to provide more fuel for the Underground Railroad and aided even more fugitives who were seeking their freedom in the North or Canada.

Harriet Tubman was one of the most famous conductors of the Underground Railroad. She began to guide blacks to freedom in the 1850s and was called "Black Moses" because she led so many captives to freedom. During the Civil War, Tubman also took on a military role. She organized scouts and spies for the Union Army even as she continued to help other blacks gain their freedom. In the Combahee River Raid that Tubman commanded, along with Colonel James Montgomery, she led a group of 300 black soldiers on an operation in South Carolina in 1863, which freed over 800 slaves.[188]

### 3. Involvement in Abolition Movements

During slavery, the Black Community was involved in abolition movements in the comparatively free North. Blacks were aware that the institution of slavery was inconsistent with the self-evident truths declared in the Declaration of Independence "that all men are created equal, that they are endowed by their Creator with certain unalienable Rights, that among these are Life, Liberty and the pursuit of Happiness...." For example, Benjamin Banneker, a self-educated, free-born black who participated in the initial survey that mapped out the original boundaries of the District of Columbia, included a copy of the farmer's almanac he wrote with a letter that he sent to Thomas Jefferson in 1791. In the letter, Banneker pointed out the hypocrisy of Jefferson's statements in the Declaration of Independence while holding black people in bondage.[189] In 1799, under the leadership of Absalom Jones, some seventy members of the free Black Community of Philadelphia sent a petition to Congress calling for an end to the Transatlantic Slave Trade and the adoption of laws that would gradually abolish slavery.[190] Paraphrasing the Declaration of Independence, they stated, "We have with other men ... an unalienable right to life, liberty and the pursuit of happiness."[191] Congress normally referred such petitions from whites to a committee where they would languish. However, rather than encourage blacks to submit more petitions like this, Congress voted almost unanimously not to even accept the petition.[192]

The scattered resistance of blacks to slavery began to come together in organized movements in the 1800s as they united in opposition to the efforts of the American Colonization Society to export blacks to Africa. Richard Allen, one of the founders of the African Methodist Episcopal Church,[193] and James Forten presided over the organizational convention of the American Society of Free Persons of Color that met at Bethel Church in Philadelphia.[194] The group opposed the efforts of the American Colonization Society and others who wanted to send free blacks back to Africa. Among their objections were that the emigration of free blacks would make slavery more secure by removing a source of inspiration for the other captives and possible allies in a rebellion. The group vowed not to separate from their shackled brethren.

Most black leaders opposed emigration, but some saw this as the way for true freedom for blacks. Harkening back to those Africans who attempted to commandeer the very ships that were bringing them to the New World and sail back to Africa, many of these schemes sought black liberation by a return to the mother country. For example, Paul Cuffee, a black merchant and shipbuilder, petitioned Congress in 1814 to allow him to carry some black families to Sierra Leone. The bill passed the Senate but was defeated in the House. After the end of the War of 1812, however, Cuffee bore the cost of transporting thirty-eight blacks to Sierra Leone.[195] Alexander Crummell was an African American Episcopal priest who went to Liberia as a missionary and became a professor of philosophy and English at Liberia College. Crummell influenced Liberian intellectual and religious life as a preacher, prophet, social analyst, and educator. He taught that Africa had a special place because of its God-given moral and religious potential, and felt that African Americans had a special mission to return to the continent to help with its uplifting.[196] The passage of the Fugitive Slave Act of 1850 provided for much harsher treatment of black runaways in the North. It also motivated Martin Delany to publish his book on the condition of blacks. In it, Delany noted that the only self-respecting response of free blacks was to seek to emigrate from the United States as a temporary measure.[197] However, Delany came around to also supporting the permanent emigration of blacks as necessary for their political elevation. He also preached that blacks had a mission to help bring civilization to Africa.[198]

In 1829, David Walker's *Appeal to the Coloured Citizens of the World, But in Particular, and Very Expressly to Those of the United States of America* became the first major published work by an African American that openly criticized slavery.[199] Walker's appeal was an argument for the moral justification of resistance to slavery. He urged black people to seize every opportunity they could to throw off the shackles of this immoral institution.

White abolitionists were often extremely paternalistic in their dealings with blacks. They tended to want blacks to conform to white culture and assumed that black culture lacked civilization or value. As a result, blacks were underrepresented in white antislavery societies. Nevertheless, blacks played important roles in most of these organizations as writers and prominent abolition speakers, including Henry Bibb, William Wells Brown, Frederick Douglass, Charles Lenox Redman, Sarah Parker Remond, Samuel Ringgold, Barbara Steward, and Sojourner Truth.[200] Through public speaking and writing about their own experiences, these individuals rebutted the charges of black inferiority, proved the humanity of blacks, and demonstrated the intellectual potential of blacks if their development was not stunted by slavery. Beyond lending credence to the work of white antislavery societies, blacks were also avid consumers of their writings. In 1834, for example, blacks made up about three fourths of the subscribers to William Lloyd Garrison's publication, the *Liberator*.[201]

Many black abolitionists were frustrated by their experiences with white antislavery societies and believed that blacks needed to be in the forefront of the abolition movement. As a resolution adopted by a convention of blacks held in Hartford, Connecticut, stated, "we cannot delegate the protection of our rights to others in any sense as to relieve us of the measure."[202] Blacks began to form their own antislavery societies in the 1830s. The first women's antislavery society was the all-black Salem Female Anti-Slavery Society started in Massachusetts in 1832. Other early antislavery societies started by blacks were in Cleveland (1833), Philadelphia (1834), and Vermont (1834).

Frederick Douglass was the most outspoken of all black abolitionists. As with earlier black orators, Douglass would also point out the hypocrisy of a nation "dedicated to the proposition that all men are created equal" that also accepted slavery. In a memorable 1852 speech at a meeting sponsored by the Rochester Ladies' Anti-Slavery Society, Douglass addressed the question, "What, to the American slave, is your 4th of July?"

> I answer; a day that reveals to him, more than all other days in the year, the gross injustice and cruelty to which he is the constant victim. To him, your celebration is a sham; your boasted liberty, an unholy license; your national greatness, swelling vanity; your sounds of rejoicing are empty and heartless; your denunciation of tyrants, brass fronted impudence; your shouts of liberty and equality, hollow mockery; your prayers and hymns, your sermons and thanksgivings, with all your religious parade and solemnity, are, to Him, mere bombast, fraud, deception, impiety, and hypocrisy—a thin veil to cover up crimes which would disgrace a nation of savages. There is not a nation on the earth guilty of practices more shocking and bloody than are the people of the United States, at this very hour.[203]

## 4. Day-to-Day Resistance to Slavery

Adam Smith pointed out the difficulties of relying on slave labor in his classic book, *Wealth of Nations*. According to Smith,

> the experience of all ages and nations ... demonstrates that the work done by slaves, though it appears to cost only their maintenance, is in the end the dearest of any.... A person who can acquire no property can have no other interest but to eat as much and to labour as little as possible.[204]

Smith was pointing out one of the most common ways that ordinary blacks held in bondage engaged in what historians have called day-to-day resistance. The black detainees would do as little work as they could. They fought any increase in their work quotas, put rocks or dirt in the bottoms of their baskets to fatten loads, feigned illness or hid to avoid work, and even refused to do dangerous jobs. Their day-to-day resistance also included the following: breaking equipment and implements; mistreating horses, mules, and other livestock; damaging crops; appropriating poultry, pigs, money, watches, liquor, flour, tobacco, and food; and vandalizing wagons and fences.[205] Commentators on the behavior of slaves often noted that slave masters felt their black captives were shiftless, irresponsible, unfaithful, ungrateful, dishonest, drunk whenever possible, and worked neither hard nor regularly enough.[206] As W. E. B. DuBois pointed out:

> All observers spoke of the fact that the slaves were slow and churlish; that they wasted material and malingered at their work. Of course they did.... It was the answer of any group of laborers forced down to the last ditch. They might be made to work continuously but no power could make them work well.[207]

Often masters would hire black slaves out to others. In rural areas, planters and farmers needed extra bodies to harvest crops. Also, captives who were skilled artisans were hired out to those who needed carpenters, coopers, or mechanics. According to one estimate, on the eve of the Civil War, 31 percent of urban slaves and 6 percent of rural slaves were hired out.[208] For many of those hired out, this was a positive experience because it often allowed them to earn a small amount of extra cash. However, it could also mean that they might have to leave their families for up to a year at a time. Sometimes their new employers were harsh and ruthless. When these captives objected to being hired out, they might fail to show up to work, avoid work, or do as little as possible to spoil the benefit of the bargain that was to accrue to their temporary employer.

The Black Communities in some Northern cities also demonstrated their disdain for slavery by celebrating January 1st as both the day of Haitian independence and the end of the Transatlantic Slave Trade.[209] Many Black Communities also marked August 1st as a day of celebration with parades and picnics because on that day in 1834, Britain's Slavery Abolition Act went into effect.[210] Black abolitionists also traveled to Britain to lecture about, build support for, and raise funds to assist in the abolition efforts in the United States. One British reporter, impressed with what he witnessed, wrote, "if these are not men, where shall they be found?"[211]

## B. Liberation Efforts During the Civil War and Reconstruction

The Civil War presented blacks with an opportunity to take up arms for the liberation of their race. And they fought in impressive numbers. This section first discusses the participation of blacks in the Civil War. After the War, America had to decide what freedom for blacks would mean. Blacks did not simply want to be pawns in this process and actively engaged in advocating for their own versions of the rights they had earned on the battlefield. They also formed their own organizations and demanded the franchise until they received it. The second section discusses the advocacy of blacks during Reconstruction for their legal rights. As slaves, blacks were landless and penniless. They believed that true liberation from bondage required the ownership of land. With a plot of land, they could grow their own food for family consumption and sell additional crops. Thereby they could obtain an independence not based upon the whims of former slaveholders. Unfortunately, despite their advocacy for land redistribution and the reality that they had toiled for centuries to build wealth for others, the federal government never provided them with land. The third section will discuss the failure of blacks to receive land or any significant compensation for their prior labor for others. This failure left them primarily landless and penniless laborers as segregation was instituted across the South.

### 1. Black Liberation Efforts During the Civil War

When the rebels in South Carolina fired the first shots on Fort Sumter in April 1861, blacks in the North understood that this was an opportunity for them to take up arms in the struggle to free their enslaved brethren from bondage. As soon as hostilities broke out, they organized themselves into military units and offered their services to the Union government. Blacks in Providence, Rhode Island, prepared to leave for the war front with the First Rhode Island Regiment. The black Hannibal Guard in Pittsburgh quickly volunteered their services to defend the Union. A black scout, who had fought in the West with Kit Carson, wrote the Secretary of War and indicated that he knew of 300 reliable black citizens who wanted to help defend Washington, D.C.[212]

The initial appeals by blacks to fight for the northern cause were summarily rejected by the federal government. In the beginning of the conflict between the North and the South, the President and Congress made it clear that the preservation of the Union was their stated war objective. Fighting a war to end slavery was not popular with the white public in the North. And for the federal government to declare the abolition of slavery as a war objective created the risk that the slaveholding border states of Missouri, Kentucky, Maryland, and Delaware might join the Confederacy.

Even though the initial offers by black men to join the armed forces of the Union were rejected, blacks knew their time to fight would soon come. As Frederick Douglass put it, "The American people and the Government in Washington may refuse to recognize it for a time; but the inexorable logic of events will force it upon them in the end; that the war being waged in this land is a war for and against slavery...."[213]

Blacks held in bondage did not wait for the President or Congress to act against slavery. As soon as Union troops entered into the South, many blacks seized this opportunity for self-liberation. The North did not initially have a policy to address what to do with those seeking freedom by crossing Union army lines. However, as the number of blacks pursing self-liberation increased, the Northern generals were quickly forced to confront their status. Early in the War, the Union army returned the slaves to their masters. In May of 1861, General Benjamin Butler, whose command was stationed in Virginia, announced that the runaways would be treated as contraband or property taken during the war, so they could remain with the Union army. When other Union generals issued even more sweeping orders, however, President Lincoln overrode his commanders. Congress addressed this issue in August of 1861 when it passed the First Confiscation Act. The Act authorized court proceedings to strip rebels of their property, including slaves if they were being used to support the Confederates. Nevertheless, some Union soldiers continued to return slaves to their former masters. In March 1862, Congress passed a law proscribing any soldier from returning escaped slaves. Four months later, Congress passed the Second Confiscation Act that freed slaves of any master who was helping the Confederacy.[214]

As blacks came into Union army lines, they began to assist the war effort as drivers, cooks, blacksmiths, and construction workers. They helped to construct forts, loaded and discharged cargo, and built bridges. Since blacks knew the southern country better than the white northern invaders, blacks proved to be the best spies of the Union army. They could move in and out of the rebel encampments often without arousing suspicion and thereby obtain important intelligence information. By the end of the war, 300,000 blacks had joined the Union cause as laborers.[215]

By the summer of 1862, the Union viewed the use of black troops in a different light than when hostilities first broke out. The Union suffered a series of military defeats early in the War. When coupled with waning numbers of white volunteers willing to enlist and fight for the Union, and the need to curry favor among European nations, the concern about preserving slavery to reconstitute the Union was far less pressing. Congress enacted a law on July 17, 1862, allowing the enrollment of blacks for any military or naval service for which they may be found competent. On the 22nd of July, Lincoln told his cabinet that he was prepared to issue a proclamation that sought to free the slaves in the areas still in rebellion. One of the principal benefits of issuing the Emancipation Proclamation was that it paved the way for the aggressive recruitment of blacks troops. As Lincoln stated in early 1863,

> The colored population is the great *available* and yet *unavailed* of force for restoring the Union. The bare sight of fifty-thousand armed, and drilled black soldiers on the banks of the Mississippi, would end the rebellion at once. And who doubts that we can present that sight, if we but take hold in earnest?[216]

When it came time to fight for their freedom, black troops did so in huge numbers. Eighty-five percent of eligible black men in the North joined the armed struggle for the freedom of black people.[217] The recently freed slaves joined their black Northern brethren in the Union army, and by the end of the War, over 20 percent of blacks under the age of 45 had served.[218] Black troops fought in 449 engagements and 39 major battles.[219] By the end of the war, African Americans comprised 10 percent of the Union's armed forces. Official statistics show that almost 179,000 black soldiers served in the Union army, 7,122 of whom were officers.[220] An additional 29,000 served as sailors, comprising 25 percent of Union seamen.[221] The black troops also paid a heavy price for freedom: they suffered a disproportionately large number of casualties during the War. Approximately 37,300 blacks died during the conflict, accounting for over 10 percent of the Union war deaths.[222] This percentage is remarkably high given that the Union did not allow a significant number of blacks to engage in armed conflict until almost fifteen months into the war. Scholars have estimated that the mortality rate of black troops was actually 40 percent higher than that of white troops.[223]

As one Senator noted in 1864, the logical conclusion from the participation of black soldiers in the War meant that "the black man is henceforth to assume a new status among us."[224] As another put it, plenty of white soldiers had seen "colored men lying in columns on the field of battle with their faces upturned to Heaven mutely pleading ... for the rights of their race."[225] President Lincoln often emphasized the significance of the black soldiers to Union's war effort. Lincoln candidly noted that without the black troops, no administration could save the Union.[226]

The bravery and commitment of black troops helped to change the Republicans' vision of the black race. Not only did they come to understand the desire of blacks for freedom, but also, eventually, their potential as political allies. In what would be Lincoln's last public address on April 11, 1865, he supported granting the franchise to the black soldiers who fought for the Union cause and the intelligent of the black race.[227] Even the Supreme Court in its 1873 opinion in the *Slaughterhouse Cases* praised the contribution of the black troops to the war effort: "When hard pressed in the contest these men (for they proved themselves men in that terrible crisis) offered their services and were accepted by thousands to aid in suppressing the unlawful rebellion."[228]

## 2. Advocating for Civil and Political Rights

With the end of the Civil War, the Republican Party was firmly in control of the federal government. Blacks, however, did not want simply to be pawns or passive recipients of whatever measures the Republican Party deemed appropriate. For them, the destruction of slavery opened new possibilities. Blacks debated and discussed their own ideas about what freedom should mean. Northern blacks and urban freedmen argued in their 1865 and 1866 state conventions that America should live up to its professed ideals, and wrapped themselves in the statements of equality from the Declaration of Independence. Recognition of equal rights emerged as the driving force in their demands.[229] As the newspaper the *Black Republican*, which was started by former bondsmen Dr. S.W. Rogers in New Orleans, put it, "Let us be allies of the Republican Party, not their tools."[230]

Even though blacks had participated in the Civil War and helped save the Union, their efforts did not improve how Southern whites viewed them; if anything, it made it worse. Thus, after the War blacks found themselves fighting to prevent their former slave masters from reinstituting a new system of racial oppression to take the place of slavery. As Southern governments resumed operations, they enacted the Black Codes. Southern whites also resorted to violence once again to reassert control over their former slaves. However, in the summer of 1865, there were more than 120,000 black troops in the Union army, with most of them stationed in the South.[231] Shortly after the War ended, black troops seeking to protect black communities clashed with white policemen in Vicksburg and Memphis. They also clashed with white troops over the treatment of local black communities in Charleston, Atlanta, Danville, Chattanooga, and Jacksonville.[232] The successful response by black troops to the indignities inflicted upon their people caused Southern whites to appeal to President Johnson to have the black troops discharged as soon as possible—a request he granted.

Blacks had argued for the franchise during and immediately after the Civil War, but Congress failed to grant them that right in either the Civil Rights Act of 1866 or the Fourteenth Amendment. However, blacks did not give up their fight.

After Congress passed the First Reconstruction Act of 1867, which called for the ten unreconstructed former Confederate states to hold a constitutional convention based on universal male suffrage and draft new constitutions, blacks throughout the South began to participate in political rallies and meetings. As one Southern plantation manager put it, "You never saw a people more excited on the subject of politics than are the negroes of the south. They are perfectly wild."[233] The dramatic rise of the Union League in the South, one of the largest black social movements in American history, was a testament to the desire of the freedmen for the franchise.[234] Union Leagues had arisen among blacks in the South before 1867, but by the end of 1867, it seemed like virtually every adult black male in the South was a member of the League or another local political organization.[235] White Republicans provided some assistance, but wherever Leagues existed, black organizers were at work. The Leagues sought to secure the franchise for blacks as well as train them how to exercise the vote and to stimulate industry and education among them. Because of the inflammatory nature of the work of the Union Leagues, armed black sentinels often guarded their meetings. In addition to League meetings, blacks also organized state-wide conventions. Many of the basic themes at these convention meetings were the same. They noted that the military service of the black troops justified the franchise. They argued that they had won their citizenship and voting rights through the sacrifices of husbands, fathers, brothers, and sons on the battlefields. They argued that to reward the white Confederate traitors with full citizenship, privileges, and restoration of their lands, and at the same time deny blacks their essential rights, was unjust.[236]

In September of 1867, approximately 735,000 blacks, compared to 635,000 whites, were registered to vote in the ten unreconstructed states.[237] The turnout of black voters was impressive, ranging from 70 percent in Georgia to nearly 90 percent in Virginia. Blacks actually constituted a majority of the voters in South Carolina, Mississippi, Louisiana, Florida, and Alabama. This solid black voting strength secured the passage of the Fourteenth Amendment in enough Southern states to ensure its ratification.[238]

In the 1868 elections, blacks also revealed their national political muscle. Although Ulysses Grant won the Presidency with over 52 percent of the vote, he only received 300,000 votes more than his antiwar Democratic challenger. Blacks cast 500,000 votes, almost 9 percent of the total.[239] Grant's election margins were slim in several Southern states with large black voting populations, including Alabama, Arkansas, North Carolina, and South Carolina. After the election, Congress then adopted the Fifteenth Amendment, which provided: "The right of citizens of the United States to vote shall not be denied or abridged by the United States or by any State on account of race, color, or previous condition of servitude."[240] The Fifteenth Amendment was ratified in 1870.

Hiram Revels became the first African American to serve in Congress when he took the Senatorial seat that had formerly belonged to Jefferson Davis on February 25, 1870. Joseph Rainey of South Carolina was the first black person to serve in the House of Representatives, taking the oath of office on December 12, 1870. Before the end of the nineteenth century, twenty African Americans served in the House and two in the Senate, including Blanche Bruce from Mississippi. More than 600 African Americans also occupied seats in Southern legislatures before the withdrawal of federal troops as a result of the Hayes-Tilden Compromise of 1877.[241]

## 3. Failure to Receive Land

One of the principal demands of blacks during the Civil War and Reconstruction was for land. In the agrarian South, land was the source of wealth. With enough land and a little livestock, a black family could cultivate an adequate supply of crops that would provide them with true independence. It would also allow them finally to reap the fruits of their own labor.

In a few areas during the War, the Union army and the Freedmen's Bureau gave the former bondsmen property by dividing up plantations abandoned by slave owners as advancing Union troops approached, including in some parts of Georgia, off the coast of South Carolina, and in Davis Bend, Mississippi (which was part of the plantations owned by Confederate President Jefferson Davis and his brother).[242] In January of 1865, General William Tecumseh Sherman set aside land near the coast south of Charleston and on Sea Islands for blacks following his army. His Special Field Order No. 15 instructed the military to give each black family forty acres, and he encouraged the army to lend them a mule for plowing. Within six months, over 40,000 former captives had settled on nearly 400,000 acres.[243]

In 1865, the Freedmen's Bureau controlled over 850,000 acres of abandoned land. Commissioner of the Freedmen's Bureau, General Oliver Howard, issued instructions to Bureau agents to set aside forty-acre tracts of land for individual black families as rapidly as possible. However, President Johnson directed Howard to rescind his directive and ordered the restoration of land to all the owners that Johnson pardoned. Thus, virtually all the land controlled by the Bureau reverted back to its former owners.[244]

By the fall of 1865, most of the land still occupied by the former slaves was that which General Sherman had provided. It fell upon Commissioner Howard to take charge of evicting these black would-be landowners from the lands given to them. In some areas the process of dispossessing the former bondsmen of land was delayed for years. Ultimately, however, the amount of land that blacks came into possession of after the War was minuscule.[245]

## C. Struggle against Racial Oppression in the Form of Segregation

While segregation was an oppressive system, blacks continued to engage in their historic struggle against their racial oppression. They not only used this imposed separation to create and strengthen institutions within their own communities and to train and educate themselves, but they also continued to advocate for full equality. Blacks first encountered segregation during the antebellum period in the North. The demeaning treatment they received spawned the first and most important institution in the African American community, the Black Church. The first section discusses the origins of the Black Church. Blacks also recognized the importance of education. Even though their schools were seldom provided with the resources available for the education of whites, blacks did their best to obtain an education for themselves and their children. The second section will discuss the development of educational opportunities for blacks. Although some black leaders had supported emigration before the Civil War, such efforts waned with abolition and Reconstruction. However, as blacks saw their political, civil, and social rights being eroded in the latter decades of the nineteenth century, some black leaders began once again to call for emigration. The largest black emigration movement was that of Marcus Garvey. The third section will discuss black emigration movements. While segregation severely limited the business, professional, and employment opportunities of blacks, it also required them to produce their own newspapers to cover stories of interest for their communities, to establish businesses to serve black customers, and to become trained as their own professionals to serve their own communities. The fourth section discusses how blacks used segregation to develop their own talents and skills, even if they were used primarily for others in the Black Community. Blacks did not stand mute in the face of continuing oppression. As disenfranchisement and legal segregation became realities, they joined or created civil rights organizations and protest movements and continued to advocate for the rights that whites enjoyed. The fifth section will discuss the participation of blacks in these organizations and movements. In short, far from being passive victims of the imposition of segregation, blacks continued their historic struggle against their oppression during the Segregation Era.

## 1. The Black Church

When the Africans first arrived in the New World, they would have called upon their familial and tribal ancestors, whom they believed interceded on their behalf, to provide them with freedom, the restoration of their personal dignity, and communal belonging. Most historians assert that blacks did not embrace Christianity in large numbers until the first half of the eighteenth century.[246] Thus, the Black Church was an institution that developed on American soil and as a response to the racism that black parishioners encountered. The Church is also the largest institution established, led, and supported by black people. The church building served as a unifying edifice that was not only the sanctum sanctorum, but also the lyceum, the gymnasium, the community forum, the conservatory of music, and the place where the elocutionary, graphic, and literary arts were developed.[247] Historically, the Black Church was the driving force used to organize efforts to liberate the Black Community. Major social protest movements by African Americans tended to start in the Black Church. Historically, most of the Black Community's political leaders have been men of the cloth.

Those who held blacks in bondage believed that Christianity would foster greater acceptance of slavery by blacks.[248] Thus, although blacks were allowed to establish churches in the South in the late 1700s, their independence was limited. They were often required by custom or law to have white observers present during church services or to have those services led by white pastors. Nevertheless, blacks found time and space for their own religious services away from the prying eyes of white overseers. In these religious services, the captives transformed the Christian ideology intended to make them accept their subordinate status into a belief in equality.[249] They believed in a God who did not discriminate among persons, whether they were Jew or Gentile, black or white, slave or free. All were equal in the eyes of the Lord. They also worshipped a God who was on the side of the weak and exploited. Blacks saw themselves as the new children of Israel in the sense that God would deliver them from bondage as he had done for the Hebrews when they suffered under the yoke of Pharaoh. In the freer North during the antebellum period, the Church was a place where blacks could exercise real independence.[250] Once they were created, black churches helped to forge a network of connections and provided the black communities with a place for self-definition, a place where blacks could view themselves not as degraded and cursed descendants of Cain or Ham, but as a community on a spiritual quest. Thus, if black Christians were asked why they would embrace the religion of their oppressors, no doubt many would have echoed David Walker's response: "We didn't. We became Christians instead."[251]

The first African American Christian denomination resulted from a protest of black parishioners who attended St. George Methodist Church in Philadelphia. In 1793, church leaders forced the black parishioners to sit apart from the white ones in a newly built balcony at the rear of the sanctuary. During a prayer service one of the black members, Absalom Jones, was praying when one of the congregation's white officers tried to pull him to his feet and force him to the balcony. Rather than continue to endure such indignities, the black worshippers left the building and the church. In 1794, they formed two different churches, the Bethel Church led by Richard Allen, a formally licensed black Methodist minister,[252] and the St. Thomas African Episcopal Church with Jones as pastor. Jones would eventually become the first black ordained Episcopalian minister. Black Methodist parishioners in other cities also objected to the discriminatory treatment they received while worshiping. In 1816, representatives from several independent black churches in New Jersey, Philadelphia, and Baltimore came together and, led by Allen, established the African Methodist Episcopal (AME) Church.

Six years later the African Methodist Episcopal Zion (AME Zion) Church was established. Frederick Douglass, Sojourner Truth, and Harriet Tubman would all be members of this denomination.[253] Independent black churches were established in other Northern cites, including Indianapolis where the Bethel AME Church was established in 1836 along with at least five black Baptist churches between 1831 and 1846, and Detroit where two such churches were established in 1837–38.[254]

Once slavery ended, Southern blacks were free to organize into their own religious denominations. The AME and the AME Zion churches were joined by the Christian Methodist Episcopal Church (CME was founded as the Colored Methodist Episcopal), three major Baptist conventions (The National Baptist Convention, Inc., The National Baptist Convention of America, and the Progressive Baptist Convention), The Church of God in Christ, and dozens of smaller sects. Approximately 95 percent of the black Christians in the country today are members of black churches.[255]

## 2. Education

African Americans recognized that education was important for their liberation and self-definition. It was against the background of discrimination of black students in integrated schools in Boston that blacks made their first request for publicly funded separate education. Boston organized the first public school system in the nation.[256] The early Boston school law did not exclude blacks from attendance at these community schools.[257] Within one year, however, "vex and insult" had driven all but three or four black students from Boston's community schools.[258] Hosea Easton, a black who had been enrolled in the Boston community schools, recalled that his former school teachers sent bad youngsters, white and black, to the so-called nigger seat, telling them such things as they would be as poor or ignorant as a nigger, or have no more credit than a nigger.[259] The parents of Boston's black school children wanted to satisfy their desires that their children receive a quality education and shield them from the prejudice they were subjected to in integrated schools. Prince Hall delivered a petition from Boston's Black Community to the legislature of the Commonwealth of Massachusetts. The petition requested that the legislature order the Boston School Committee to establish a school for Boston's Black Community.[260] The petition was denied, but in 1798, a school for "colored children" was established in the home of Prince Hall.[261]

With regard to higher education in the North before the Civil War, in 1837, Cheyney State Training School in Philadelphia, Pennsylvania, was established as the first college in the nation for African Americans. Quaker Richard Humphrey provided a bequest of $10,000 for the school.[262] Avery College was established in 1849, Lincoln University in 1854, and Wilberforce University in 1856.[263]

Prior to the Civil War, with the exception of North Carolina, there was no general system of public education in the South. When freedom came, Christian missionaries flocked to the South. During slavery it was illegal to educate black slaves. The missionaries found that blacks had an intense desire for education. From very small beginnings, by 1865 some 575 schools, educating over 70,000 blacks, had been established in the Southern states.[264] Public education was one of the most important issues addressed by the 1867 and 1868 state constitutional conventions, which were called to comply with the requirements for readmission of the former Confederate states to the Union. When public education was discussed, the issue of school integration came up, but because of white resistance to integrated schools, the heated debates that occurred in nearly every state convention were, to a large degree, only theoretical. Most of the state conventions eventually avoided the issue by tabling these motions, whether they were to mandate or to prohibit segregated schools. Even though no state constitution required the schools be segregated, only two—Louisiana and South Carolina—forbade segregation in public schools. However, school integration in the South only prevailed for a short time in several Louisiana elementary schools, mostly in New Orleans, and at the University of South Carolina.[265]

Another impact of the loss of political power by blacks in the last decades of the nineteenth century was that state support for black public primary education declined drastically after 1890. For example, per-pupil expenditures in

Alabama and North Carolina were about the same for black and white students in 1890, and about twice as much per pupil was spent on the education of white children as compared to black children in Florida, Mississippi, and Louisiana. By 1910, however, Alabama was spending three times as much on the education of white children than it was spending on blacks, and North Carolina was spending twice as much. In Florida and Mississippi, the ratio increased to approximately four to one, and in Louisiana it was five to one.[266] In addition to fewer resources, the school year for black students was shorter, their teacher-pupil ratios higher, and black teachers were paid far less than their white counterparts. Disparities in per-pupil expenditures continued up to the eve of the Supreme Court's decision in the school segregation cases. For example, in 1930, South Carolina actually spent eight times more money on the education of white students than blacks, and the disparity was still three to one in 1945.[267] In 1929, Mississippi spent nine times more, and in 1945, four and one-half times more for the education of a white child than for a black child.[268]

Booker T. Washington was the most influential educational leader of the Black Community by the latter part of the nineteenth century. At the age of twenty-five, this former slave founded Tuskegee Institute in 1881. Twenty years later, Tuskegee had 109 full-time faculty members and 1,095 pupils. Washington was an excellent public orator and discovered that he could be an effective fundraiser for black education by parroting what white philanthropists wanted to hear. He was able to secure substantial financial contributions from wealthy white individuals, foundations, and corporations for his endeavors to uplift the black race.[269] Washington developed his educational philosophy for a people coming out of bondage in an extremely hostile environment. He understood that blacks gained their freedom in a condition that left them as poor, illiterate laborers without the necessary knowledge and skills to make a decent living. The educational philosophy he stressed was the acquisition of skills and knowledge that could be used to generate gainful employment and financial independence. However, Washington's educational philosophies were criticized by other blacks, especially W. E. B. DuBois, for accepting the notion that blacks should remain at the bottom of the social hierarchy. Washington also built the powerful Tuskegee Machine that financed black-owned newspapers, advised major philanthropic organizations about where to donate their funds to assist the Black Community, and influenced political appointments to and discharges from federal positions.

Beyond Tuskegee, blacks and the white supporters of their causes worked within the constraints of segregation to create a parallel higher education system for blacks, the remnants of which exist today. In 1862, Congress enacted the First Morrill Act, which provided states with funds to foster educational opportunities for all students, especially freed blacks. However, only Mississippi, Virginia, and South Carolina spent some of these funds on the education of black students.[270] Black churches, including the AMEs, the CMEs, the AME Zions, and the Baptist churches, also took the lead in founding educational institutions for African Americans.[271] Thus, by 1890, there were about a hundred colleges and universities for blacks, primarily in the South. The vast majority of these institutions, however, were controlled by white philanthropic agencies such as the American Missionary Association, the American Baptist Home Mission Society, and the Freedmen's Aid Society of the Methodist Episcopal Church.[272] Most of these colleges were offering coursework on the high school level, and the white missionaries that controlled these institutions tended to limit the type of education in these colleges to primarily vocational education. Howard University, which was established in 1866, however, was mainly for the purpose of catering to those who wanted to do collegiate and professional work.[273]

The Second Morrill Act, in 1890, required that states either allow blacks to enter existing colleges or provide separate educational facilities for them. A total of nineteen land-grant institutions for blacks were created as a result, but initially they were non-degree-granting agricultural, mechanical, and industrial schools.[274] Opportunities for African Americans to pursue higher education in the South remained grossly limited through the 1940s. Segregation practices generally banned them from white colleges and universities, and black ones were inferior in curricular offerings, library materials, qualifications of faculty, and physical accommodations. Discrimination was even greater at the graduate and professional school level. In 1940, only three of the seventeen segregationist states[275]—Virginia, Texas, and North Carolina—offered any graduate-level instruction at their public historically black colleges and universities (HBCUs). In addition, none of the approximately thirty public HBCUs in the segregationist states offered any doctoral programs, and only two had professional schools.[276] In contrast, all seventeen segregationist states had white public colleges with extensive graduate and professional school programs. The numbers of segregation states that offered different professional degrees at their white public colleges were as follows: 17 in graduate engineering, 16 in law, 15 in medicine, 15 in graduate commerce and business, 14 in pharmacy, 11 in library science, 9 in social service, and 4 in dentistry.[277]

Despite the lack of resources provided for black education, prior to the desegregation litigation, there were few occupational options for college-educated blacks other than public education. Thus, in the 1950s, half of all black professionals were public school teachers.[278] But, the centuries-old struggle by blacks for access and parity in education has been emblematic of their larger fight for equality. Black teachers and administrators labored long hours in these underresourced institutions to provide black students with the best education possible under difficult circumstances.

## 3. Emigration Movements

As Reconstruction waned and it became painfully apparent to blacks that American society did not plan on granting them true equality, many African Americans once again came to see the logic of emigration. Henry Adams and Benjamin Singleton led the push to convince African Americans to consider immigrating to West Africa. Bishop Henry McNeal Turner of the AME Church also championed the notion of mass black emigration to Africa in the closing decades of the nineteenth century.[279]

The largest black emigration movement in American history was the one led by Jamaican-born Marcus Garvey. In 1914, Garvey established a black nationalist self-help organization, the Universal Negro Improvement Association (UNIA). Garvey actually founded UNIA in Jamaica and had members in the other parts of the West Indies and Africa, but his largest influence was among blacks in the United States. Although Garvey made claims that he had at least two million members,[280] by the early 1920s, there were over 700 UNIA branches in North America and a membership of at least a half a million.[281] Garvey preached that African Americans were black first and American second. He believed that if the 400 million people of African descent united, they could free the continent from the yoke of colonial oppression. The goals of Garvey's organization were, after gaining economic and political control of black communities in the United States, to develop an independent black colony in Africa. The message that Garvey delivered was that "black skin was not a badge of shame but a rather glorious symbol of national greatness."[282] Garvey argued that blacks should create their own black republic because America was so irredeemably oppressive and fundamentally racist that blacks could not expect justice here. His organization developed its own flag, its own national anthem, and constantly repeated its motto, "One God! One Aim! One Destiny!"[283]

For most blacks, colonization was never a serious alternative. They were natives of the United States, not of Africa. However, leaving the South was another matter. During World War I, the United States introduced a military draft, and with declining European immigration as a result of restrictive immigration measures enacted by Congress in the 1920s, jobs with higher wages became available for hundreds of thousands of blacks in the North. The six-decades-long Great Migration of blacks out of the South to the cities of the North began around 1910. When it commenced, 89 percent of blacks lived in the South; by 1970, only 53 percent were there.[284] For each individual black who left, the move to the North represented a form of resistance to racial oppression. By moving North they were seeking to escape extreme poverty, disenfranchisement, lynching, lawlessness, and an oppressive plantation system of sharecropping, all of which were used to maintain white supremacy in the South.

## 4. Business, Professional, and Civil Rights Organizations

Segregation severely limited the business, professional, and employment opportunities of blacks. Nevertheless, this separation also provided distinct spaces for them to build and develop their own talents and skills, even if they were often limited to serving other blacks. Thus, segregation required blacks to create their own newspapers and businesses, and to train and provide continuing education for their own professionals who were serving their own communities as teachers, doctors, dentists, nurses, and lawyers.

Blacks produced newspapers and periodicals to cover events that were of particular interest to them. The first African American newspaper was the *Freedom Journal*, published by John B. Russwurm and S.E. Cornish between 1827 and 1829.[285] The *Journal* was published in New York City and contained stories that covered regional, national, and international current events. It also included editorials decrying slavery, lynching, and other injustices inflicted upon blacks. The paper circulated in eleven states, the District of Columbia, Canada, Haiti, and Europe. In 1829, the Journal was superseded by *The Rights of All*, published between 1829 and 1830 by Cornish.

In 1903, Robert S. Abbott, an attorney who could not obtain legal work because of his dark complexion, began publishing the *Chicago Defender*, Chicago's first African American newspaper. Within a decade, it was the best-selling black newspaper in the South[286] and one of the country's most influential African American newspapers.[287] The *Defender* played an important role in the migration of blacks from the South to the North by encouraging them to come to Chicago in search of a better of life. Other examples of black newspapers were the *Detroit Tribune*, the *Pittsburgh Courier*, the *Amsterdam News*,[288] and the *Indianapolis Recorder*. *Ebony*, a magazine that focused on African American life and achievements, was founded by John H. Johnson in 1945[289] and became an instant classic. It highlighted the achievement of African Americans and made them aware of their potential for both social and economic success in the United States. A large number of black newspapers and magazines are still in circulation today that continue to tell the stories of the day through the eyes of black people.

Because black businesses could not count on patronage from the white community, African American entrepreneurs sprung up to service a black clientele. Their large-scale business successes were in fields left open to them due to racism. Blacks established successful banks because white bankers often felt that their accounts would be too meager to manage. Madame C.J. Walker and Mrs. A.E. Malone became wealthy selling hair and skin care products for black people.[290] In 1898, the National Afro-American Council was founded with an emphasis on civil rights and suffrage. But in 1900, the Council's energies were diverted to economic advancement promoted by a group founded in Boston, the National Negro Business League.[291] Booker T. Washington was elected the first president.[292] The basic principal of the League was well stated by John Hope: "The salvation of Black America depends, to a great extent, on the development of a business class. We must take in some, if not all, of the wages, turn it into capital, hold it, increase it."[293] Thus, the League sought to create a national group to promote black commerce through a program of education, organization, encouragement, and inspiration. It effectively functioned as the black Chamber of Commerce.

One of the best known organizations for the advancement of black economic and employment interests formed during the Segregation Era was the National Urban League. This organization was established in 1911.[294] The Urban League did not seek charity, but opportunities for blacks. Initially, it assisted black Southerners who arrived in Northern communities in various ways, including helping them find jobs and suitable housing and providing them with advice about adapting to northern culture.[295] The Urban League also conducted scientific investigations of conditions among urban blacks to provide an evidentiary basis for effective social reforms. From its beginning, the Urban League advocated for cooperation between the races. Its stationary stated, "Let us work, not as colored people nor as white people for the narrow benefit of any group alone, but *together* as American citizens, for the common good of our common city, our common country."[296] By the end of World War I, the Urban League had eighty-one staff members in over thirty cities.

African American women were important and significant participants and leaders in various organizations established by blacks as a result of segregation. In 1896, the National Association of Colored Women (NACW) was founded with Mary Church Terrell as its first president. The NACW focused on sexual abuse, attacks on the moral character of black women, lynching, education, inadequate health care, lack of child care services, and poverty. By 1915, there were over a thousand clubs nationwide with 50,000 members.[297]

Because black professionals were excluded from membership in white professional associations, they formed their own. Black newspaper editors, for example, established the Colored Press Association in 1880, and black schoolteachers founded a national association in 1889.[298] African American doctors, who were excluded from the American Medical Association, formed the National Medical Association in 1895.[299] Today, the organization has a membership of over 30,000 African American physicians.[300] In 1900, a group of 200 black dental practitioners, who were excluded from membership in the American Dental Association, formed the Washington Society of Colored Dentists. The organization was renamed several times before 1932, when it settled on the National Dental Association.[301] Its membership currently consists of over 6,000 black dentists.[302] Similarly the National Association of Colored Graduate Nurses was formed in 1908[303] for the purpose of creating an avenue to keep abreast of medical advancements in nursing and to advance the standards of nursing among the group.[304] Although the organization merged with the American Nurses Association in 1951,[305] its roots stand as a testament to the resilience and resourcefulness of African American professionals in the face of segregation. Excluded from membership in the American Bar Association, a group of African American lawyers established the National Bar Association in 1925.[306] Since that time the organization has led the charge on many issues facing the Black Community from equal rights, to criminal justice, to education.[307] Today, the National Bar Association is a professional network of over 44,000 members, including lawyers, judges, law students, and educators.[308] The annual national convention is attended by nearly 1,800 members.[309] Among the many other professional organizations established by blacks during the Segregation Era are the National Technical Association in 1925,[310] the National Banker's Association in 1927,[311] and the National Newspaper Publishers Association in 1940.[312]

White fraternities and sororities excluded blacks and refused to establish chapters on the campuses of black colleges and universities. But in 1904, the first fraternity for black professionals was established, Sigma Pi Phi ("The Boulé").[313] Then in 1906, Alpha Phi Alpha, the first intercollegiate black fraternity, was founded at Cornell University.[314] Two years later, the first intercollegiate sorority for black women, Alpha Kappa Alpha, was founded at Howard University. These pioneers were joined in 1911 by the Kappa Alpha Psi fraternity founded at Indiana University. The next four black Greek originations were established at Howard University: Omega Psi Phi fraternity in 1911, Delta Sigma Theta sorority in 1913, Phi Beta Sigma fraternity in 1914, and Zeta Phi Beta sorority in 1920. Two years later, Sigma Gamma Rho sorority was founded at Butler University. The final two black Greek fraternities, Iota Phi Theta and Phi Eta Psi, were founded in the 1960s at Morgan State University[315] and in Flint, Michigan,[316] respectively. The importance of black Greek organizations to the African American community cannot be overestimated. Membership in these organizations symbolizes a commitment to academic excellence, service to the community, and a constant striving toward the betterment of the Black Community. There are currently over 2.5 million active members of black Greek organizations.[317]

## 5. Involvement in Civil Rights Organizations and Protest Movements

African Americans also helped to found and joined civil rights organizations to engage in struggles against their disenfranchisement, segregation, and racial oppression. Black leaders had long protested lynching. Ida B. Wells was the foremost antilynching advocate of her time. Her pamphlet *Southern Horrors*, published in 1892, was the first study of lynching. She noted that there were over 700 black victims of lynching between 1882 and 1891, mostly males, and 241 in 1892 alone.[318] Apologists for white lynch mobs typically justified hanging black men as a punishment for their raping white women. Wells showed that was not true because less than a third of black men lynched were even accused of rape. Instead, Wells showed that lynching was an attempt by whites to terrorize and subjugate the black population.[319] She took her message to Britain for four months in 1894.[320]

The most prominent civil rights organization during the Segregation Era was (and still is) the National Association for the Advancement of Colored People (NAACP). W. E. B. DuBois organized a meeting in 1905 for twenty-nine people from fourteen states at Fort Erie, Ontario. They created a militant civil rights organization known as the Niagara Movement, which advocated for universal manhood suffrage, abolition of all caste distinctions based on race or color, and recognition of the principles of a united human brotherhood.[321] At its second annual meeting, the Niagara Movement issued a manifesto in which it stated:

> We will not be satisfied to take one jot or tittle less than our full manhood rights. We claim for ourselves every single right that belongs to a freeborn American, political, civil and social and until we get these rights we will never cease to protest and assail the ears of America.[322]

During its short five-year tenure, the Niagara Movement had some successes, including the defeat of legislation that would have created racially segregated railroad cars in Massachusetts.[323]

The mission of the Niagara Movement was taken up by the NAACP. A terrible race riot occurred in 1908 in Springfield, Illinois, Abraham Lincoln's hometown. During the riot, over 2,000 blacks fled Springfield and authorities summoned nearly 5,000 militiamen to restore order.[324] In response to the riot,

Oswald Garrison Villard, the grandson of abolitionist William Lloyd Garrison, took the lead in issuing a call for national conference to address the rights of blacks in honor of Lincoln's 100th birthday.[325] Among those who signed the call were important figures in the Black Community, including DuBois, Monroe Trotter, Bishop Alexander Walters, and Wells. The NAACP grew out of that conference and was to become the major confrontational group that launched frontal attacks on "separate but equal."

The NAACP's national board was integrated—unusual for its time—but black board members always held significant roles. By 1914, most of the thirteen African American board members were former members of the Niagara Movement.[326] The Board chose DuBois to be the Director of Publications and Research. In that position, he launched the publication of *The Crisis*. Through the magazine, DuBois became the voice of unrelenting opposition to racial inequality. As DuBois put it in *The Crisis*, "The struggle for social equality was absolutely essential to erod[ing] the walls of racial segregation and to expand[ing] political and economic opportunities for black Americans."[327] Blacks also dominated membership in local chapters of the NAACP, which grew rapidly. Within ten years of its founding, there were over 300 local branches and 88,000 members, and 155 of these branches with 42,000 members were in the South.[328]

One of the major political victories of the NAACP occurred in 1930, when it led a successful campaign to defeat President Herbert Hoover's appointment of John J. Parker to the U.S. Supreme Court. Parker had stated during his unsuccessful run for governor of North Carolina in 1920 that he did not believe blacks were at a stage of development where they could share the burdens and responsibilities of government.[329] Mass meetings were called and representatives from the national office of the NAACP, including DuBois, Arthur Springarn, and Walter White, went on speaking tours to drum up support against the nomination. Parker's nomination was defeated in the Senate by a vote of 39 to 41.

The NAACP was particularly active in a number of litigation efforts attacking segregation, discrimination, and disenfranchisement of blacks. For example, the NAACP was able to convince the U.S. Supreme Court to strike down grandfather clauses in its 1915 decision in *Guinn v. United States*.[330] It won another major legal victory with the 1917 Supreme Court decision *Buchanan v. Warley*.[331] In that case, the NAACP convinced the Court to strike down a Louisville, Kentucky, ordinance that sought to impose residential segregation. In 1939 the NAACP established a separate organization, the NAACP Legal Defense and Educational Fund, Inc. (LDF) to carry on much of its litigation work.[332] These organizations successfully litigated against the white primaries, eventually convincing the Supreme Court to strike this practice down in the 1944 decision *Smith v. Allwright*.[333] The Court's decision in *Buchanan* applied only to government efforts to segregate housing. Housing segregation pursuant to the desires of private individuals and entities was considered to be an entirely different matter. Thus, to get around the Court's decision, housing discrimination was privatized. Private owners of residential property began to place restrictive covenants in the deeds of their property that limited resales to members of the same race. It was not until 1948 in *Shelley v. Kraemer*[334] that LDF lawyers convinced the Supreme Court to strike down these racially restrictive covenants because they violated the equal protection clause of the Constitution.

A. Phillip Randolph was the leader of the largest African American labor union, the Brotherhood of Sleeping Car Porters. This organization won significant concessions from the railroad industry for black porters in the 1930s. In 1936, Randolph was elected President of the short-lived National Negro Congress, which was created under the direction of John Davis and Ralph Bunche, who at the time chaired the Department of Political Sciences at Howard University. The purpose of the organization was to unite all African American organizations and press for the socioeconomic recovery of the African American community.[335] As America's rearmament program was pulling the country out of the Depression, Randolph noted that the "whole national defense set-up reeks and stinks with race prejudice, hatred and discrimination."[336] The expanding war-based economy was putting white workers back to work, while not employing black workers. Over half of the firms that responded to a governmental questionnaire stated that they would not hire any blacks.[337] Thus, Randolph issued a call for up to 100,000 blacks to come to the nation's capital for a march that would culminate with demonstrations at the Lincoln Memorial against segregation and discrimination. Fearing the consequences of such a march, President Roosevelt issued Executive Order 8802 on June 25, 1941, which proscribed discrimination based on race, creed, color, or national origin in the employment of workers in the defense industries. The Order also created the Fair Employment Practice Committee (FEPC) to receive and investigate complaints of discrimination in violation of the order.[338] Although the Executive Order and the FEPC were not enough to overcome entrenched racism, this was the first time that the federal government had made fair employment a national policy.

Lynching reached its peak from 1882 until 1927, when over 3,500 blacks were hanged.[339] However, it declined significantly by the mid-1930s, with only 44 people being murdered between 1937 and 1946, when the NAACP's anti-lynching campaign peaked and the Roosevelt Administration created the Civil Rights Section in the Justice Department.[340] Nevertheless, lynchings that occurred in 1946 led to a meeting between Walter White, the Executive Secretary of the NAACP, and President Truman. Truman expressed his dismay about the problem and vowed to act. He created the President's Committee on Civil

Rights and charged them with recommending more adequate and effective means to protect the civil rights of American people. Later that year, the Committee issued a report entitled *To Secure These Rights*.[341] Among the many progressive recommendations contained in the Report were calls for federal laws against lynching and police brutality, abolition of the poll tax, federal protection of voting rights, a federal fair employment law, the establishment of a permanent Civil Rights Commission, more vigorous action by the FBI to stop civil rights violations, and desegregation of the military.

Randolph and Grant Reynolds founded the League for Nonviolent Civil Disobedience to the Draft to protest segregation in the armed forces. Randolph testified in March 1948 before the Senate Armed Services Committee, as the Cold War was commencing. During his testimony, he stated that unless segregation and discrimination were banned, he would personally urge blacks to refuse to fight for a democracy that they could neither possess nor enjoy.[342] This pressure and the desire to win votes from blacks in key Northern industrial states in the upcoming 1948 election helped to motivate President Harry Truman to issue Executive Order 9981, which required the desegregation of the military. In the November presidential election, Truman received 70 percent of the black vote. Thus, Blacks provided Truman with his margin of victory in California, Ohio, and Illinois that allowed him to secure an additional seventy-eight electoral votes that were necessary for his election.[343]

### 6. Conclusion

Segregation imposed severe restraints on the political, social, economic, and educational opportunities for blacks. But blacks used the opportunity of this separation to develop their own talents and skills and to strengthen their own sense of community. Blacks developed their own religious organizations. They educated themselves in separate public primary schools and attended a separate black collegiate system. They published their own newspapers and magazines to keep abreast of issues that were of interest to their communities, created organizations to provide for the needs of black people, and developed business to serve the Black Community. Excluded from white professional organizations, blacks established their own. Thus, far from passively accepting the injustices of segregation, blacks continued to organize and struggle for their own liberation from racial oppression in response to segregation.

## D. Liberation Efforts during the Desegregation Era

The attorneys for the NAACP and LDF, along with courageous participation of black plaintiffs and communities willing to risk everything, orchestrated the legal strategy that would eventually lead to the fall of segregation. The litigation that resulted in the Supreme Court's *Brown v. Board of Education*[344] decision was the result of a long-term legal strategy to attack segregation initiated and carried out by the NAACP and LDF. Between 1938 and 1950, the NAACP and LDF successfully litigated four cases attacking segregation in graduate and professional schools in front of the Supreme Court.[345] Unlike in *Brown*, however, the Supreme Court could strike down segregation in those contexts without the need to discuss any intrinsic harm that resulted from segregation when physical facilities and other tangible factors of the education were arguably equal for the black and white students.

Chief Justice Warren's unanimous opinion for the Court in *Brown* based the decision to strike down segregation on its negative psychological impact only on African American school children. It is impossible to overstate the long-term consequences of this rationale which effectively limited the psychological damage of segregation to black people and presumed whites were unaffected. However, prominent social scientists who filed an *amicus* brief with the Court pointed out that segregation also harmed white children. Their brief noted that, whereas the impact of segregation on white children was more obscure, they "often develop patterns of guilt feelings, rationalizations and other mechanisms which they must use in an attempt to protect themselves from recognizing the essential injustice"[346] done to black people. In 1973, Justice Douglas echoed the dual harm of America's history of racial discrimination expressed by the social scientists in his dissenting opinion from the Supreme Court's decision to dismiss as moot the first challenge to an affirmative action admissions program in place at the University of Washington Law School in *DeFunis v. Odegaard*. "The years of slavery did more than retard the progress of blacks. Even a greater wrong was done the whites by creating arrogance instead of humility and by encouraging the growth of the fiction of a superior race."[347] If the Court had noted the existence of the dual harm of segregation, then Americans might have viewed remedies for it as benefitting all school children and all Americans. Such a decision could have provided us today with better tools to attack more difficult forms of racism such as unconscious bias and institutional racism. By attacking the legality of *de jure* segregation of public schools, African Americans were demanding respect and equality. They were asserting their own humanity as equal to whites and insisting that their humanity be recognized. However, given the Court's explanation of the harm of segregation, the Court converted those demands for respect and equality into a request for a social welfare program. African Americans asserting their constitutional rights were recast as beggars seeking an in-kind benefit from whites in the form of interracial contact. Thus, the Court never rejected the underlying premise of segregation—that whites were superior to blacks.

Regardless of the Supreme Court's explanation for school desegregation, blacks used the decision to spawn grassroots protests by community activists against segregation practices throughout the South. For example, when Rosa Parks refused to give up her seat on a Montgomery bus and was arrested, she ignited a one-day, city-wide boycott on December 5, 1955. A black women's civic organization, the Women's Political Council, took the lead in initiating the boycott among the Black Community, which made up 70 percent of the bus riders.[348] After the success of the local one-day boycott, organizers created the Montgomery Improvement Association to coordinate a longer one. The Association selected Reverend Martin Luther King Jr. as its President. Over 90 percent of Montgomery's 40,000 black population honored the boycott that lasted until December 21, 1956—382 days.[349] The Supreme Court eventually upheld the legal challenge of the Black Community to segregation of the buses in Montgomery in *Gayle v. Browder*.[350]

On February 1, 1960, four black college freshmen at North Carolina A&T State University sat down at the Woolworth Store's whites-only lunch counter located on South Elm Street in Greensboro, North Carolina. In so doing, they challenged the store's segregation policies. Their sit-in was followed five days later by a sympathy sit-in of a group of forty-five students in Nashville, Tennessee.[351] The sit-in movement spread throughout the South, and by August of 1961, over 70,000 people had participated in sit-in protests with over 3,000 arrests.[352]

Against the backdrop of the centennial anniversary of the outbreak of hostilities that started the Civil War, thirteen individuals—six blacks and seven whites—boarded two busses in Washington, D.C., and headed for New Orleans. These freedom riders, who were sponsored by the Congress of Racial Equality (CORE) and assisted by the Student Nonviolent Coordinating Committee (SNCC), were scheduled to arrive in New Orleans on May 17th, the seventh anniversary of the Supreme Court's decision in *Brown*.[353] The freedom riders were out to challenge the mores of the racially segregated South by the simple act of travelling together throughout the South in interracial groups. Their bus was attacked in Montgomery by white racists, but this attack did not deter the movement. Even though they frequently encountered hostility from supporters of segregation, eventually 400 people participated in the Freedom Rides in the summer of 1961.[354]

In August of 1963, over 250,000 people descended on the Nation's capitol in the March on Washington for Jobs and Freedom. The purpose of the March was to focus the nation's attention on the injustice and inequality that black Americans faced on a daily basis. The organizers produced ten demands for the

March, including: comprehensive civil rights legislation with provisions for full access to all public accommodations, decent housing, adequate and integrated education, and the right to vote; desegregation of all school districts; withholding of federal funds from programs in which discrimination existed; massive federal programs to train and place all unemployed workers in meaningful and dignified jobs with decent wages; authorizing the Attorney General to institute injunctive suits when any constitutional right is violated; and federal legislation in employment that bars discrimination by federal, state, and municipal governments, and by employers, contractors, employment agencies, and trade unions.[355] Reverend Martin Luther King Jr.'s memorable "I Have a Dream" speech capped the event. The march helped to generate public support for the enactment of the Civil Rights Act of 1964, the most sweeping civil rights legislation in the nation's history. With its passage, and that of subsequent legislation, almost all of the marchers' demands became federal law.

On "Bloody Sunday," March 7, 1965, 600 civil rights marchers started what was supposed to be a fifty-mile march for voting rights from Selma to Montgomery. The marchers got as far as the Edmund Pettus Bridge, only six blocks. There they were confronted by Alabama state troopers and local law enforcement officers with billy clubs, tear gas, and attack dogs. The brutal attacks were the leading story on the national television news programs and on the front page of major newspapers. Shortly after the ruthless attack, President Johnson sent to Congress the Voting Rights Act of 1965. After winning a cloture vote in the Senate only sixteen days after Bloody Sunday, the Act passed both houses and Johnson signed it into law on August 6.[356] The Voting Rights Act, together with other actions to increase the number of registered black voters in the South, had a dramatic impact on the number of blacks who exercised the franchise. In Alabama, for example, only 13.7 percent of blacks were registered to vote in 1960; that increased to 64 percent by 1970. Other impressive increases in the percentage of black registered voters over the 1960s were recorded in Mississippi, from less than 7 to over two-thirds; Virginia, from 23 to 60.7; Louisiana, from 30 to over 60; and Texas, from less than a third to almost 85.[357]

Black athletes also got involved in the civil rights struggle. For example, black football players of the American Football League decided not to play the 1965 All-Star game in New Orleans because a number of them were refused service in hotels and business establishments, and virtually all of them were subjected to verbal abuse while walking on Bourbon Street. The game was moved to Houston.[358] Noting that he didn't have any quarrel with the Viet Cong, in 1967, heavyweight boxing champion Muhammad Ali made national headlines for refusing induction into the military. The Supreme Court would later overturn his conviction for evading the draft.[359] Tommy Smith and John Carlos made their famous black fist salute on the medal stand after the 200-meter dash at the 1968 Mexico City Olympics.

The struggle against racial oppression took many forms during the 1960s and 1970s other than the nonviolence associated with Reverend King. With the help of LDF lawyers and the National Guard, James Meredith integrated the University of Mississippi in 1962. As the first black to attend Ole Miss, Meredith felt a special obligation to assist in the liberation struggle of blacks. Meredith decided to challenge the fear that continued to dominate the day-to-day lives of blacks in the South by walking from Memphis to Jackson, Mississippi. On June 6, 1966, the second day of his march, when he was just twenty-eight miles inside of Mississippi, he was shot. A few days later in Greenwood, Mississippi, a mass rally was held in support of a revised march by civil rights leaders to complete Meredith's March Against Fear. SNCC Chairman Stokley Carmichael (who later changed his name to Kwame Toure) told the crowd of 3,000, "We been saying freedom for six years and we ain't got nothing. What we gonna start saying now is Black Power."[360] Black Power symbolized a greater sense of militancy, a willingness to meet force with force, and the rejection of both nonviolence and the dream of a colorblind society. CORE and SNCC would go on to formally reject nonviolence and expel white members from their organizations. A year later, H. Rapp Brown would take over as the Chairman of SNCC. At his first news conference, he called President Johnson a "mad dog" and stated that "violence was as American as apple pie." A month later, Brown would go on to tell a crowd, "Don't be trying to love the honkey to death. Shoot him to death."[361]

The Black Nationalist movement of the 1960s echoed sentiments like those expressed by Martin Delany a century earlier. "Our elevation must be the result of self-efforts, and work of our own hands. No other human power can accomplish it. If we but determine it shall be so, it will be so."[362] One such nationalist organization was the Black Panther Party, founded in California by Bobby Seale and Huey Newton from Oakland. They burst onto the national scene in May of 1967, when Panther Party members went into the California State Capitol wearing black leather jackets, black berets, and carrying guns. They were there to protest legislative efforts to ban the public display of firearms. The Panthers also developed a ten-point platform for the promotion of the Black Community that included full employment, an end to police harassment, promotion of black history, adequate housing, and reparations.[363] Among the activities that the Panthers engaged in were feeding breakfast to the poor and shadowing the police to prevent them from harassing other blacks. Another nationalist organization was the Nation of Islam, whose primary spokesperson during the early 1960s was Malcolm X. The Nation preached separatism and self-help as the solution to the racism that blacks encountered in the United States. As Harold Cruse noted, the Nation's basic program called for black unity, economic self-help, hard work, maintenance of high morality standards, obeying the law, vocational training, and separation from whites.[364] The Nation of Islam also developed a program that called for the United States to provide land for a separate black homeland within its territorial boundaries.[365] And, when Martin Luther King Jr. was assassinated on April 4, 1968, riots broke out in 125 cities across the nation, the most widespread night of racial violence in American history.[366]

Blacks carried on the struggle for equality in the economic arena as well. For example, nepotism was rampant in the construction trades of Philadelphia, which led to several building trade unions being virtually all white. In 1969, in response to protests against discrimination in the construction industry, the Nixon Administration approved the Philadelphia Plan to increase the number of minorities working in that industry. The plan required contractor bids to produce minority group representation in all trades and in all phases of federally funded construction projects. Nixon's Secretary of Labor, George P. Shultz, strongly endorsed the policy. The Philadelphia Plan was subjected to several months of contentious legislative battles in Congress before it won a vote of confidence from both houses of Congress in December 1969. The requirement of goals and timetables to employ minorities was subsequently extended to most federal contractors with contracts over $50,000.[367]

## E. Continued Struggle in the Post-Racial/Colorblind Era

Over the past four decades, the Supreme Court's antidiscrimination jurisprudence has moved closer and closer to a colorblind interpretation of the equal protection clause and has carried much of American society with it. However, the evolution of the colorblind ideal drastically limited abilities for blacks to win legal challenges to public and private policies and practices that produce disparate racial outcomes and significantly constrained governmental efforts aimed at overcoming the continuing impact of discrimination.[368] For example, in a 1976 decision in *Washington v. Davis*, the Supreme Court rejected an argument that discriminatory effects of governmental policies could trigger a *prima facie* case of unconstitutional race discrimination. In arriving at that conclusion, the Court stated:

> A rule that a statute designed to serve neutral ends is nevertheless invalid, absent compelling justification, if in practice it benefits or burdens one race more than another would be far-reaching and would

raise serious questions about, and perhaps invalidate, a whole range of tax, welfare, public service, regulatory, and licensing statutes that may be more burdensome to the poor and to the average black than to the more affluent white.[369]

The Court went on to quote from a law review article that noted such a definition of discrimination could invalidate such things as "sales taxes, bail schedules, utility rates, bridge tolls, license fees, and other state-imposed charges."[370] Thus, in *Washington v. Davis*, the Court faced the specter that defining racial discrimination by its discriminatory effects would require radical changes in the socioeconomic structure of American society precisely because blacks had fewer material resources. When faced with such a substantial amount of disruption, the Court rejected the discriminatory effects approach to defining unconstitutional discrimination. In addition, the Court has severely limited the ability of governmental units to use racial classifications in policies and programs to mitigate the continuing effects on black people of America's history of racial discrimination.

Nevertheless, the unprecedented changes in American society caused by the legal rights won by blacks during the Desegregation Era helped to pave the way for significant progress in the historical struggle of the Black Community against its racial oppression. Because of those changes, today there are several highly visible, extremely successful, and very powerful blacks in the United States. Journalist Eugene Robinson coined the term "Transcendents" to describe a small elite group of blacks with enormous wealth, power, and influence.[371] This group includes individuals like Ursula Burns, Bill Cosby, Valerie Jarrett, Robert Johnson, Michael Jordan, Stanley O'Neal, Richard Parson, Susan Rice, and Oprah Winfrey. Thus, there are blacks who are among the wealthiest people in America and others who run or have run some of the most powerful corporations in the world. In addition, over a hundred blacks are presidents of traditionally white universities, a black Miss America or Miss USA is no longer a major news item, forty-three black members currently serve in the House of Representatives[372] and three served in the Senate in 2013.[373] These changes, along with the election in 2008 and 2012 of Barack Obama to the Presidency of the United States, are undeniable signs of racial progress.

After the election of Obama many commentators began to argue that America was on the verge of becoming a Post-Racial/Colorblind society.[374] This notion is based upon a desire or belief that we no longer need to worry about or talk about racial issues, including racial discrimination. Yet, despite the impressive performance by a number of black individuals, as the socioeconomic statistics discussed earlier in this chapter demonstrate,[375] blacks as a group continue to lag far behind non-Hispanic whites (and Asians) on these all important measures. However, post-racialism and colorblindness make it easier to ignore those persistent racial socioeconomic gaps as well as the continuing impact of America's history of racial discrimination on African Americans.[376] As Sherrilyn Ifill, President and Director-Counsel of LDF, said, "With colorblindness as a cynically deployed rhetorical cloak, lawmakers adopt policies that squeeze out opportunity for poor black and brown Americans—rejecting almost any legislation that would improve public services, support urban centers and aid those at the economic edge."[377] Thus, blacks continue their historic struggle against racial oppression.

One of the important ways in which this continuing struggle is carried out is by pointing out the inherent limits of the colorblind ideal. As noted earlier, the notion of colorblind thinking tends to lead commentators, politicians, and experts to try to equate the socioeconomic differences among racial groups to nonracial factors. For example, the gross racial differences in family income, noted earlier in this chapter, could be explained by asserting that the differences should be reduced to reflect such nonracial factors as that blacks have less formal education, that blacks are less likely to be in the labor force, that blacks have a larger percentage of single-parent families, and that a higher percentage of blacks continue to live in the South where income is lower than in the rest of the country.[378] Yet from the perspective of the long, historic struggle by blacks against racial oppression, these nonracial factors are very much a product of the history of discrimination. It is due in large measure to that history that blacks still have less formal education, are less likely to be in the labor force, have a larger percentage of single-parent families, and that a larger percentage of them live in the South. Thus, to try to reduce the racial socioeconomic gaps by adjusting for nonracial factors is simply another way of obscuring the continuing impact of the history of racial discrimination on the Black Community.

Another problem with colorblind thinking, which urges individuals not to consciously think about race, is that it tends to obscure more important forms of discrimination. Current theories in psychology, sociology, anthropology, and education strongly indicate that the most prevalent forms of racial discrimination today tend not to result from intentional or blatant racism.[379] Rather, disparate outcomes appear to be shaped by individuals within institutions, participating in habitual patterns of action. These patterns may be largely unconscious, but if left unchecked, they contribute to discriminatory outcomes that reproduce inequity and reduce opportunity for certain groups.

Charles Lawrence, for example, in his seminal 1987 article entitled "The Id, the Ego, and Unconscious Racism," pointed out the negative impact of unconscious racism, which cannot be adequately addressed when the concept of racial discrimination is limited to consciously motivated decision making, as suggested by the colorblind approach to defining race discrimination.[380] Lawrence noted that limiting the definition of racism to actions motivated by intentional racial decision making is misplaced because such actions are rare and represent only a small part of the racial oppression that continues to plague blacks. Blacks are far more victimized by unconscious racism and by institutional racism, which is racism derived from the standard operating procedures of an institution that are prejudiced against, derogatory to, or unresponsive to the needs of blacks.

Neil Gotanda also noted the limitations of the colorblind norm not only as a behavioral model for private citizens but also for promoting social change.[381] The colorblind ideal and protection of individual self-determination from the effects of intentional race discrimination is effective in fighting racial oppression in the form of conscious, racially motivated decision making such as segregation statutes, business owners' refusal to serve black customers, race-based limitations placed on voting rights, and employment decisions. However, limiting the concept of race discrimination to intentional discrimination provides no help for other forms of race discrimination, including unconscious discrimination, institutional discrimination, or cultural discrimination.

Perhaps the best place to note how colorblind thinking can obscure the continuing impact of the history of race discrimination in the United States is by focusing on the Supreme Court's opinion in *McCleskey v. Kemp*. In *McCleskey*, the Court followed colorblind thinking in rejecting a challenge to the Georgia death penalty scheme. If a society is prepared to obscure the existence of racism in determining who it is going to execute, then *a fortiori*, racial disparities in other matters will also be obscured—like the disparate impact of disciplinary proceedings on the educational opportunities of black school children,[382] the use of a curriculum culturally biased against blacks by public school districts,[383] or the underrepresentation of blacks in selective higher education programs.

McCleskey argued that the Georgia capital sentencing process was discriminatory against blacks in violation of both the equal protection clause and the Eighth Amendment's cruel and unusual punishment clause. According to McCleskey, the discrimination was of two different types. First, persons who kill whites were more likely to be sentenced to death. Second, black defendants were more likely to get the death penalty. Since McCleskey, a black, killed a white person, he fell into the group with the highest probability of receiving the death penalty. McCleskey cited a study conducted by Professors David Baldus, George Woodworth, and Charles Pulaski. The Baldus Study, which conducted a statistical analyses of over 2,000 murder cases in Georgia during the

1970s, including McCleskey's, was the most comprehensive statistical analysis of the racial demographics of a state's capital sentencing process ever done.[384] Among the findings of the Baldus Study was that the death penalty was assessed in the following combinations of defendant and victim race: 22 percent of the time with a black defendant and white victim; 8 percent with a white defendant and white victim; 3 percent with a black defendant and black victim; and 4.1 percent with a white defendant and black victim.[385] The Baldus Study also found that prosecutors sought the death penalty in the above combinations of defendant and victim race 70 percent, 32 percent, 15 percent, and 19 percent of the time, respectively.[386] While a black perpetrator of a capital crime was slightly more likely to receive the death penalty than a white perpetrator, the person who killed someone white was far more likely to receive the death penalty than the person who killed someone black. One model of the study took into account 39 nonracial variables. It revealed that "defendants charged with killing white victims were 4.3 times as likely to receive a death sentence as defendants charged with killing blacks ... [but], black defendants were 1.1 times as likely to receive a death sentence as other defendants."[387] The disparity was so great that in Justice Brennan's dissenting opinion, joined by three other justices, he stated:

> At some point in this case, Warren McCleskey doubtless asked his lawyer whether a jury was likely to sentence him to die. A candid reply to this question would have been disturbing.... The story could be told [by the attorney] in a variety of ways, but McCleskey could not fail to grasp its essential narrative line: there was a significant chance that race would play a prominent role in determining if he lived or died.[388]

In a 5–4 decision, the Court found no constitutional violation. Writing for the majority, Justice Powell assumed the validity of the Baldus Study and agreed that it showed a discrepancy that correlated with race. However, when addressing the equal protection challenge, Powell noted that McCleskey must do more than demonstrate that the State allowed its capital punishment statute to remain in force despite its allegedly discriminatory application. As Powell stated, "discriminatory purpose implies more than intent as volition or intent as awareness of consequences. It implies that the decision maker, in this case a state legislature, selected or reaffirmed a particular course of action at least in part because of, not merely in spite of, its adverse effect upon an identifiable group."[389] In discussing McCleskey's Eighth Amendment claim, Powell went on to note that the Baldus Study could not demonstrate that race was a factor in McCleskey receiving the death penalty. At most statistics can only show a likelihood that a particular factor entered into some decision.[390] Thus, despite the existence of racially discriminatory effects in the application of the death penalty in Georgia, the Court noted that this did not establish the intentional discriminatory decision making necessary to demonstrate that McCleskey's death sentence was the result of constitutionally recognized racism.

Tanya Hernandez and Randall Kennedy both wrote about how colorblindness obscures the functioning of racism in the death penalty. Hernandez noted that the Court's focus on the need for McCleskey to prove *intentional* discrimination obscured how racial stereotypes about blacks could influence actors involved in the capital sentencing process.[391] In other words, forms of unconscious bias against blacks, as opposed to intentional racial animus, could not be ascertained in the Court's view of the death penalty. In contrast, Kennedy noted that the Court's opinion was unfair to the Black Community for another reason. The Baldus Study made it clear that someone who killed a black person was far less likely to receive a death sentence than someone who killed a white person. Thus, the Court's opinion, effectively, did not treat those who killed blacks as committing as serious a crime as those who killed whites.[392]

Another example of how colorblindness obscures the impact of the effect of the history of racial discrimination on blacks can be seen when discussing the use of race and ethnicity in the admissions process of selective higher education institutions. The Supreme Court concluded that the primary justification for the ability of selective higher education institutions to consider the race and ethnicity of underrepresented minorities is to obtain the benefits of diversity in the education process. Among the harms that have been noted as deriving from affirmative action are the following: the harm suffered by innocent victims who would have been admitted had the admissions officials not taken into account the race and ethnicity of successful underrepresented minority candidates; the stigma imposed upon underrepresented minority candidates who were admitted without the help of the consideration of their race or ethnicity; and the violation of the simple justice notion that people should be judged based on the content of their character not the color of their skin. In fact, the very idea that we refer to people of color as "beneficiaries of affirmative action" suggests that they have received a positive good that they did not earn—thus making the whites not admitted innocent victims of racial discrimination.

There is a counterinterpretation for the rationale behind considering race in the admissions process of selective higher education institutions, however, that comes from the long struggle against racial oppression that blacks have suffered where the above harms do not exist. As Part II of this chapter has discussed, blacks have struggled against a plethora of presumably objective, neutral, rational, and nonbiased justifications for their oppression in the United States since the colonial era. For almost 400 years, general consensus, religious justifications, expert scientific opinion, and politicians have found ways to obscure the oppression of blacks and, at the same time, make it appear to be the natural order of things. The notion of viewing recipients of affirmative action as beneficiaries, as the Court's rationale for affirmative action and the harms associated with it do, derives from an assumption that the lower scores by blacks on standardized tests constitute a racially neutral and colorblind way to determine academic merit. Thus, the lower performance by blacks presupposes that, for the purpose of admission to selective higher education programs, academic qualifications can be determined without regard to race. Abigail Fisher captured this sentiment when she said, "There were people in my class with lower grades who weren't in all the activities I was in, who were being accepted into UT, and the only difference between us was the color of our skin."[393] The problem with this claim of simple calculation is that it has to be based on the assumption that race and ethnicity are irrelevant considerations in determining a person's merit. For this to be true in America, it would be necessary for race to have no more relevance in our society than, say, the length of a person's ring finger. But changing someone's race in America is not like changing the length of the ring finger. The tremendous achievement of some successful blacks should not blind our society to the reality of the continued existence of the effects of discrimination upon underrepresented minority groups. Changing a person's race from white to black would likely change the neighborhoods they would grow up in, the schools they would attend, the reaction of their teachers to them in their schools, the friends they would make, the television shows and movies they would watch, the foods they would eat, the sanctuaries in which they would worship, the music and radio stations they would prefer, and the places they would go for vacations, if they go any place at all. In short, changing their race would change their entire life. Part of that change would no doubt negatively affect their scores on standardized tests like the LSAT, the SAT, or the ACT. Simply put, because of the existence of the history of racial and ethnic oppression in our country, right now it may not be possible to develop a culturally neutral standardized test. But, I do not wish to overstate the case of the differences between blacks and whites. In the context of standardized tests, it is the differences among test takers that are important. If all test takers would answer 99 percent of the questions correctly, then these questions would be excluded from the test. What will matter for standardized tests are questions that evoke different responses. Thus, the differences between individuals are magnified because only differences matter. Thus, regarding standardized tests, negligible differences appear to be very large ones.

Perhaps the Supreme Court justice who captured this perspective best was Justice Douglas in his dissenting opinion in *Defunis* noted earlier. After noting that the LSAT reflects questions that touch on cultural backgrounds, Douglas noted that "Admissions Committees acted properly in setting minority applications apart for separate processing."[394] If this is not done, then race can become a subtle force in eliminating minorities based on their cultural differences. The reason for the separate treatment of minority applicants is so that certain racial factors do not militate against them in the admissions process. With this understanding and Douglas' understanding in mind, taking account of race and ethnicity in the admissions process is proper "not as a preference but an effective and efficient mechanism to counteract racial preferences"[395] that white applicants would otherwise receive. In other words, the ability to overcome the obstacles that race places in the path of black applicants is part of the meritocratic evaluation of the admissions process. Simply put, all things being equal, if a black applicant has the same test scores as a white applicant, then the black applicant is not equally qualified, but more qualified. Douglas went on to conclude that the case "should be remanded for a new trial to consider, inter alia, whether the established LSATs should be eliminated so far as racial minorities are concerned."[396]

# Conclusion

To argue that the race and ethnicity of blacks should matter for purposes of admission to selective higher education institutions, it is necessary to understand why racial classifications can be taken into account in the admissions process in the first place. The starting place for answering that question is Justice O'Connor's opinion for the Court in *Grutter v. Bollinger*. In that opinion, O'Connor authorizes the use of racial classifications for the inclusion of *underrepresented* racial minorities who have *experiences* derived from our nation's struggle with racial inequality. These *experiences* are not only important to include in the student body for the purpose of the benefits of diversity, they also explain why *underrepresented* minorities are not likely to be admitted in meaningful numbers in the first place.

Based on the Supreme Court's opinion in *Grutter*, to determine which black applicants have experiences of being a member of a historically discriminated group in the United States, it is necessary to understand the historical experience of discrimination of the Black Community. This chapter has discussed that experience. The central feature in that experience is race, of which two different aspects are in play. One aspect involves blacks being discriminated against and victimized because of their race. For much of America's history, dominant American society viewed blacks as inferior in some important way to whites. This attitude helped to make the oppression of, and discrimination against, blacks appear to be part of the natural order of things. Part I of this chapter dealt with that aspect of the historical experiences of the Black Community. However, against the background of racial domination in the United States, the descendants of the sons and daughters of the soil of Africa developed a counterdiscourse to how mainstream American society normally viewed and treated them. In this counterdiscourse, race was also the central characteristic that united blacks together, but it viewed blacks as oppressed, not inferior. As a result, it involved the active engagement in a collective struggle against white supremacy and black subjugation, not the acceptance of black racial inferiority. Consequently, the other aspect of the history of discrimination against black people in the United States is the struggle against their oppression.

In terms of determining which blacks should receive positive consideration in the admissions process of selective higher education institutions, it is necessary to determine whether they have had sufficient experience with both aspects of the history of discrimination that blacks have suffered in the United States. To determine how much of the experience a particular applicant with black ancestry has, it is necessary to give them the opportunity to address it in their application forms.

# Chapter Three

# Black Multiracials: Why They Should Not Be Preferred over Ascendant Blacks

Race is a socially constructed concept. Nowhere is this more obvious than when dealing with the historical treatment of mixed-race individuals with some African ancestry in the United States. For virtually the entire twentieth century, the one-drop rule determined who was black. Thomas F. Dixon Jr., author of *The Clansman* (the book that was turned into D. W. Griffith's epic movie *Birth of a Nation*), expressed the accepted view about one drop of black blood in his 1902 best-selling fictional novel, *The Leopard's Spots*. "One drop of Negro blood ... kinks the hair, flattens the nose, thickens the lip, puts out the light of intellect, and lights the fires of brutal passions."[1] Thus, the current recognition of Black Multiracials as distinct from other blacks is an emerging and relatively recent phenomenon. As a result, the issue of distinguishing Black Multiracials from single-race blacks for purposes of admissions considerations to selective higher education institutions has only now emerged.

As late as 1960, 99.4 percent of Americans were considered either black or white.[2] Even though a person's physical appearance may not reveal the fact that he or she possessed a very small quantum of black blood, the use of the one-drop rule and the dual-race nature of American society, nevertheless, meant that Americans could almost always tell a person's race based on their physical appearance. Thus race was a socially ascribed characteristic, not a matter of personal identification as it is increasingly becoming today. As long as American society socially constructed race based on the one-drop rule, simply put, there were no Black Multiracials. And the issue about how to treat them differently from other blacks for purposes of consideration in the admissions process of selective higher education institutions did not exist.

Since the adoption of the 1997 Revisions, the federal government started to allow individuals to designate all of their racial categories on forms used to gather and report this data. In so doing, the federal government abandoned the one-drop rule and forced many public and private institutions to do so as well. By doing so, it also contributed to the process of distinguishing Black Multiracials from single-race blacks.

The 1997 Revisions also firmly rejected the notion that race should be a socially ascribed characteristic. Rather it explicitly made self-identification the preferred means by which to determine a person's race. This change alone may not have been enough to allow individuals to self-identify their race. However, the substantial influx of immigrants of color from Asia, Latin America, the Middle East, and North Africa over the past fifty years altered the complexion and the facial features of American society. As a result, even those who wish to continue to apply the one-drop rule can no longer determine the race of increasing numbers of Americans based on their physical appearance alone. With regard to racial identity, as the twenty-first century unfolds, blacks with "racially ambiguous" (a term also of recent origin) features increasingly encounter the question "What are you?" It is more socially accepted for a person with some African ancestry to have a choice in how to respond to such a question. They could choose to say "I am black," "I am multiracial," "It depends," "I am \_\_\_\_\_ (fill in the blank)," or "I am just me." In other words, they are more able than ever to choose their racial identification. Thus, the recent massive immigration of people of color from the rest of the world helped to enhance the ability of Black Multiracials to choose their racial identification.

The 1997 Revisions also required that other federal agencies adopt new regulations for collecting and reporting the racial and ethnic data that they compiled. The DOE's corresponding regulations, the Final Guidance, went into effect in the fall of 2010. As we move beyond the Supreme Court's decisions in *Fisher v. University of Texas* and *Schuette v. Coalition to Defend Affirmative Action*, for purposes of affirmative action, it is not whether Black Multiracials self-identify as black or with all of their racial categories that is significant. What is important is the demise of the one-drop rule, coupled with the ability of individuals to self-identify their race. These developments have created the social reality that Black Multiracials now have the option of choosing a racial identity other than "Black or African American," especially on forms used by educational institutions. It is the fact that Black Multiracials can now make this choice, regardless of their individual choices, that has dramatically altered the admissions landscape. Because Black Multiracials can choose their racial identity, policies and procedures based on their inability to do so are outdated. Selective higher education institutions should, therefore, make adjustments in how race for those with black ancestry is treated in their admissions process to take into account this new reality.

There are different ways to determine who is a Black Multiracial. One can follow self-identification, as is required by federal regulations on forms used to collect and report this data to various federal agencies, or one can determine who is multiracial based on the race of their parents. Normally self-identification provides the appropriate method to determine a person's race. However, the problem with self-identification in the context of applying to selective higher education institutions is the possibility that individuals will indicate their racial identification on application forms primarily for the strategic purpose of improving their admissons prospects.[3] Also, the primary concern of this book is the virtual elimination of Ascendant Blacks, who are determined based on parentage, from the campuses of selective higher education institutions that is occurring now. Given the central concern of this book, Black Multiracials are understood to be those with one black and one nonblack parent, with the parent's race determined by application of the one-drop rule, a rule that was firmly in operation at the time that selective higher education programs initially adopted affirmative action policies.

This chapter will discuss the differences between Black Multiracials and Ascendant Blacks. In so doing, it will not argue that Black Multiracials should receive no positive consideration in the admissions process. Rather it will argue that Ascendants Blacks should be preferred over Black Multiracials to such an extent as to assure the inclusion of a substantial presence of Ascendant Blacks in the student bodies of selective higher education institutions. Following Justice O'Connor's rationale, there are two reasons that Ascendant Blacks should receive preference over Black Multiracials. First, Ascendant Blacks are far more likely to be underrepresented in many, if not most, of the nation's selective higher education institutions than Black Multiracials. Second, the history of discrimination suffered by blacks in the United States affected the ancestors of Ascendant Blacks, as well as Ascendant Blacks themselves, far more than it did Black Multiracials. As a result, in general, Ascendant Blacks will have far more experiences with both aspects of the history of discrimination suffered by blacks in the United States than Black Multiracials.

Black Multiracials are products of interracial sexual relationships involving blacks. Historically, Americans had strong objections to interracial marriages. As late as the 1950s, thirty states still banned marriages between blacks and whites.[4] One of American society's principal motivations behind the desire to prevent miscegenation was the goal of minimizing the number of mixed-race individuals. However, since the origination of affirmative action policies, American acceptance of interracial dating and marriage has increased significantly. This greater acceptance led to an increase in the numbers of blacks involved in interracial sexual relationships and corresponding increases in Black Multiracials of college age. Part I of this chapter will discuss the increasing acceptance by American society of interracial sexual relationships with blacks and the increasing numbers of these relationships since the establishment of affirmative action policies. It will also discuss the increasing numbers of Black Multiracials. As should be expected, the younger blacks are, the higher the percentage of Black Multiracials among them. Thus, the percentage of Black Multiracials among the population of blacks approaching the age at which most people attend college is on a steep upward trajectory. Although the Final Guidance did not go into effect until the fall of 2010, some evidence generated prior to this time strongly suggested that Black Multiracials were significantly overrepresented among black students at selective colleges and universities. Part I will also discuss the evidence that points to the overrepresentation of Black Multiracials among black students at selective higher education institutions. No matter how overrepresented Black Multiracials are now, given their increasing percentage among blacks that are approaching college age, the impact of this overrepresentation on the admissions prospects of Ascendant Blacks is likely to increase significantly over the next fifteen years. Given what educational research has long told us about family characteristics that aid in educational success, there are several reasons why Black Multiracials are likely to do better in American educational institutions than Ascendant Blacks. Black Multiracials tend to come from families with more income and better-educated parents than the children of single-race blacks. The final section of Part I will discuss these family characteristics. The educational performance of Black Multiracials, especially if one of their parents is white or Asian, may also benefit from certain sociocultural advantages as well.[5] However, these sociocultural differences are far more relevant for the discussion in Part V, which deals with why Ascendant Blacks should be preferred to Black Multiracials in the admissions process.

To understand why current Black Multiracials should be treated differently in the admissions process from how they were when affirmative action commenced, it is necessary to discuss the history of mixed-race blacks. As Carter G. Woodson described it, there was extensive miscegenation in the English colonies before the master race realized the apparent need for maintaining its racial integrity.[6] During the colonial period, the colonies not only fashioned a race-based system of slavery, but also used race to determine the legal rights of those not held in bondage. As a race-based system of slavery developed in colonial North America, interracial unions created a problem because they blurred the boundary lines between the races and raised questions about the justifications for slavery. Virtually every one of the American colonies banned interracial marriages during the colonial period. Also, whereas some colonies drew distinctions between blacks and mixed-race blacks, whom they referred to as "mulattoes," with the exception of South Carolina, this was a distinction without much difference. For the most part in the English mainland colonies, race was bimodal, black-white or white-colored (including mulattoes and blacks). However, before the 1850s, the situation for mulattoes was different in the major urban areas of the Lower South than in the Upper South and North. In addition to Charleston, in New Orleans and Mobile, places colonized by the Spanish or French before the founding of the American republic, many mulattoes were the offspring of wealthy white males who often supported and recognized their mixed-race children. As a result, there were many affluent free mulattoes in the Lower South. Elite whites tended to treat them more as a sort of third class, an intermediate class between black and white, slave and free. Part II of this chapter will discuss the history of antimiscegenation measures adopted during the colonial period and the treatment of mulattoes during this era in the Upper South and the North. It is during this time that the ideas were established about mixed-race blacks that would continue to exist during the antebellum period there. Part II will conclude with a discussion of the higher regard for mulattoes that existed in the major urban areas of the Lower South than in other parts of the country prior to the 1850s.

The rise of the one-drop rule can be traced back to the scientific debates that emerged in the 1840s about the dangers of miscegenation. In addition to long-standing religious objections to interracial sexual relationships, a new racial scientific theory emerged that rejected the dominant belief of the time that although blacks and whites were different, they were of the same species. Instead, this new polygenesis theory asserted that blacks and whites were not just different varieties of humans, but separate species altogether. As a result, miscegenation amounted to interspecies mating, so the products of miscegenation would be worse physically, and possibly mentally and morally, than their black or white parents. This controversy led to the inclusion of a "mulatto" category on the 1850 census and almost all subsequent censuses through 1920. Throughout the Civil War, agencies of the U.S. government conducted autopsies and anthropological studies that involved wide-scale measurements of soldiers. These were the first mass studies of physical differences of the races that presented evidence of mixed-race blacks as a group distinguished from single-race blacks. The scientists interpreted this evidence to affirm the notion that interracial breeding produced individuals with diminished physical capacities, and possibly diminished mental capacities, when compared to their black or white parents. The prevention of miscegenation provided the strongest justification for the institution of racial segregation after the Civil War. As succinctly summarized by the Pennsylvania Supreme Court in an 1867 opinion, which upheld racial segregation on a railroad car, "From social amalgamation it is but a step to illicit intercourse, and but another to intermarriage."[7] By the end of the nineteenth century, American society as a whole had adopted the one-drop rule as the primary means by which to determine a person's race. Many state legislatures codified this acceptance into law during the first three decades of the twentieth century. With the 1930 census, the Census Bureau abandoned its efforts to divide blacks along racial lines and followed suit. As a result of the widespread acceptance of the one-drop rule, the recognition of racial distinctions among blacks disappeared. Therefore, at the commencement of the civil rights era and the creation of affirmative action programs, the one-drop rule was at its zenith. Part III of this chapter will discuss the rise of the one-drop rule.

Until recently, race was also a socially ascribed identity that American society imposed upon the individual, not a matter of self-identification. Since Hispanics/Latinos were still classified by their race in 1960, according to the census figures, whites and blacks constituted 99.4 percent of all Americans.[8] Although not always accurate, the one-drop rule allowed Americans to determine a person's race based on his or her appearance. Thus, racial identity was socially ascribed. However, a decade after the Supreme Court's decision in *Brown v. Board of Education*, the Court began to strike down antimiscegenation statutes, culminating with its 1967 decision in *Loving v. Virginia*.[9] As time passed, the number of interracial relationships involving blacks, and subsequently the numbers of Black Multiracials, increased. These increases were occurring at the same time that the United States was experiencing its first massive wave of immigration of people of color from the rest of the world. As a result, the one-drop rule was losing its ability to accurately determine the race of someone based on physical appearance. Also, the federal government's collection of official racial and ethnic statistics was drifting towards embracing the concept of race as a product of self-identification rather than a socially ascribed characteristic. Responding to these developments, by the late 1980s, individuals in mixed-race sexual relationships and their progeny created a movement that sought to add a separate "multiracial" category on all federal and state forms for mixed-race individuals to select. As discussed in Chapter One, the concerns of the Multiracial Movement impacted the 1997 Revisions, which changed the way the federal government collects and reports racial and ethnic data. These changes first went into effect for the 2000 census. The 1997 Revisions required that all federal programs adopt regulations that reflected the changes it made. The DOE adopted the Final Guidance with an implementation date of 2010–11 academic year. Those new regulations mandated that educational institutions use forms to collect racial and ethnic data, which provide individuals with the ability to designate all of their racial and ethnic groups. Individuals who indicate that they are Hispanic/Latino are reported as such by educational institutions to the DOE, regardless of the racial categories they also choose.

However, non-Hispanics/Latinos that designate two or more racial groups are reported in counts of a new "Two or More Races" category. The result is that those with some African ancestry who, for themselves or on behalf of their children or guardians, identify with more than one race or ethnicity, are no longer considered black. Thus, not only has the federal government abandoned the one-drop rule, but it has also compelled educational institutions to abandon it as well. The demise of the one-drop rule means that self-identified Black Multiracials are no longer classified by educational institutions as simply black. Part IV of this chapter will chronicle the demise of the one-drop rule and the rise of Black Multiracials.

As noted in Part I, evidence suggests that Black Multiracials are overrepresented among blacks at selective higher education programs. Yet the sociocultural differences between Black Multiracials and Ascendant Blacks reveal the fact that Black Multiracials, in general, have far fewer experiences related to the history of racial discrimination of blacks in United States than Ascendant Blacks. As Justice O'Connor noted in her opinion in *Grutter*,[10] these experiences are of particular importance to the Law School's mission and explain why such individuals are less likely to be admitted in meaningful numbers on criteria that ignore those experiences. Part V will explain the sociocultural differences between Black Multiracials and Ascendant Blacks, which suggests that Ascendant Blacks, in general, have far more experience of the black history of discrimination than Black Multiracials. This, along with the fact that Ascendant Blacks are more likely underrepresented, provides the justification for why Ascendant Blacks should receive more positive consideration in the admissions process than Black Multiracials.

# I. Increasing Interracial Sexual Relationships and Black Multiracials since the Institution of Affirmative Action

Black Multiracials are the products of interracial sexual relationships involving blacks. Before the institution of affirmative action programs, American public opinion had a very negative view of such relationships. However, over the past fifty years, American society has increasing come to accept interracial marriages and interracial cohabitation arrangements. The first section of this part will discuss both the growing acceptance and numbers of interracial sexual relations. The growing numbers of these relationships, predictably, led to an increase in the percentage of Black Multiracials among blacks, especially with regard to the young. The second section will briefly discuss the percentages of Black Multiracials reported by the Census Bureau on the 2000 and 2010 censuses. Even though the DOE did not require colleges and universities to separate Black Multiracials from other blacks until the fall of 2010, during the previous decade scholars and commentators pointed to evidence of the growing percentage of Black Multiracials among black students enrolled in selective higher education programs. The third section of this part discusses that evidence. Given what we know about family characteristics that aid in educational success, there are several reasons why Black Multiracials are likely to do better in American educational institutions than Ascendant Blacks. The fourth section discusses the differences in family characteristics between the families of Black Multiracial and single-race black children. My primary purpose in pointing to the differences in income, parental education, and two-parent households, however, is to demonstrate that these differences are not temporary and passing. Given that the number of Black Multiracials who are approaching the age at which most people attend colleges and universities is on a steep upward trajectory, no matter how overrepresented Black Multiracials are among black students now, the magnitude of the overrepresentation at selective higher education institutions could increase significantly over the next fifteen years.

## A. Increasing Acceptance and Number of Interracial Sexual Relationships

Since the origination of affirmative action policies, the acceptance of interracial marriages involving blacks has skyrocketed. For example, in 1958, only 4 percent of whites approved of interracial marriage between blacks and whites.[11] As for blacks, as one commentator on interracial marriage and the law put it, "desegregation on the marriage front seemed far less pressing a matter than did progress in educational opportunity or voting rights."[12] Surveys in the 1960s showed that about 92 percent of whites stated they would not consider marrying an African American. As late as 1965, 48 percent of whites in a national poll expressed approval of antimiscegenation laws.[13] In the South, the feeling was even stronger with 72 percent of whites and 30 percent of blacks favorably embracing such laws. However, in a 1997 Gallup poll, 77 percent of blacks and 61 percent of whites indicated their approval of interracial marriages.[14] The percentage of those who accepted interracial marriages continued to increase during the twenty-first century.[15] This is especially true among younger adults, those in their prime reproductive years. According to a 2010

Pew Research Center Report, almost all Millennials (18- to 29-year-olds) accept interracial dating and marriage. The Report noted that 92 percent of white and 88 percent of black Millennials said that they would be fine with a family member marrying someone outside of their racial group.[16]

As societal objections to interracial marriages decreased, the number of such marriages increased. Of the almost twelve million blacks over the age of fifteen in the country in 1960,[17] only 51,000 were married to whites.[18] Black women were slightly more likely to have a white spouse than black men.[19] The percentage of blacks with a spouse of another race, however, increased during the latter decades of the twentieth century, from 1.1 percent in 1970, to 2.4 percent in 1980, to 4.1 percent in 1990. Since the 2000 census allowed respondents to designate all of their racial categories, looking at the percentage of blacks married outside of the race is a little more complicated now. Nevertheless, the percentage of black out-marriages continued to increase, with 7.0 percent of single-race blacks marrying outside of their race.[20]

Viewing the increasing percentage of blacks who marry outside of their race obscures the differences in interracial marriage rates broken down by gender. Among racial minorities, blacks are the only group where the men are more likely to marry outside of their race than the women.[21] In fact, while single-race black men were more likely to marry outside of their race than Asian men, Asian woman were five times more likely to marry outside of their race than black women.[22] Whereas the percentage of married black males who were married outside of their race increased from 1.5 percent in 1970 to 5.8 percent in 1990, for married black women the percentages only increased from 0.8 percent in 1970 to 2.3 percent in 1990.[23] Data from the 2000 census also revealed that while 9.7 percent of married single-race black men reported having a spouse of another race, only 4.1 percent of married single-race black women reported the same.[24]

Younger blacks are even more likely to marry or cohabitate outside of their race. A study comparing census data from 1990 and 2000 of married couples between the ages of 20 and 34 pointed out that native-born, single-race African American men in the studied age range who married outside of the race increased from 8.3 to 14.2 percent.[25] For native-born, single-race black women, the increase was from 3.3 to 5 percent.[26] While many individuals will get married, many will cohabitate. It has contributed to a reduction in marriage rates in early adulthood and an increase in the average age of first marriage. The study also saw similar increases in the percentage of blacks involved in interracial cohabitation arrangements. The percentage of black males in interracial cohabitation arrangements grew between 1990 and 2000 from 14.7 to 21.9 percent, and for black women from 5.6 to 6.2 percent.[27]

Interracial marriages of blacks have continued to rise since the turn of the century. According to a Pew Research Center Report, in 2010 about 9 percent of married blacks married outside of their race.[28] This percentage continued to be significantly higher for black males than for black females, 12.5 compared to 5.5. Interracial marriages also made up a much larger percentage of new marriages by blacks than existing marriages. Thus, among 2010 newlyweds, 23.6 percent of black males and 9.3 percent of black females married outside of their race.[29]

## B. Increasing Numbers of Black Multiracials

Increases in interracial marriage and cohabitation have led to an increase in the percentage of blacks who have a nonblack parent. As discussed more fully in Chapter One, it was not until 2000 that the census forms allowed individuals to designate all of the racial and ethnic categories that applied to them. According to the 2010 census, 7.4 percent of blacks[30] (up from 4.8 percent in 2000[31]) indicated another racial category, over two and a half times the 2.9 percent (up from 2.4 percent in 2000) of the American population as a whole.[32] As one might expect, the younger blacks are, the more likely they are to be multiracial. The latest census figures for 2012 showed that the percentage of mixed-race blacks between the ages of 20 and 24 was only 7.9 percent.[33] However, the percentage of mixed-race blacks among blacks between the ages of 15 and 19 was 8.9 percent, 10 and 14 it increased to 10.9 percent, between the ages of 5 and 9 to 15.0 percent, and for those under the age of 5, it was 19.1 percent.[34]

Of the blacks who indicated at least one other racial category, 93 percent checked only two such boxes.[35] The largest combination of Black Multiracials reported on the 2000 census was black-white. There were 784,764 black-white individuals. Another 706,525 individuals checked the black box and one other racial box (black and some other race 417,249,[36] black and American Indian 182,494, black and Asian 106,782[37]). According to the 2010 census, the black-white combination was once again the largest combination of Black Multiracials. The 1,834,212 black-white individuals constituted 59.3 percent of Black Multiracials.[38]

## C. Evidence of Overrepresentation of Black Multiracials Attending Selective Higher Education Institutions

Even though selective higher education undergraduate institutions were not required to provide individuals with the ability to designate all of their racial and ethnic categories until the 2010–11 academic year, there is some evidence of the overrepresentation of Black Multiracials at selective colleges and universities before then. For example, a group of researchers led by Princeton sociologist Douglas S. Massey published a study of the incoming 1999 freshmen class at twenty-eight selective colleges and universities that were chosen to try to mirror the ones studied by William G. Bowen and Derek Bok in their influential book, *Shape of the River*.[39] The Massey study pointed out that Black Multiracials made up 17 percent of those black freshmen,[40] even though according to 2000 census figures, only 5.3 percent of blacks between the ages of 15 and 19 were multiracial.[41] At a gathering of black alumni in 2003, Harvard professors Lani Guiner and Henry Louis Gates noted that Black Multiracials and Black Immigrants together comprised two-thirds of Harvard's black undergraduate population. Thus, only 180 of the 530 black undergraduates at Harvard during the 2003–04 academic year were Ascendant Blacks.[42] In addition, a 2007 survey of college freshmen that entered the thirty-one elite colleges and universities comprising the Consortium on Financing Higher Education (COFHE)[43] revealed that 23 percent of black students were Black Multiracials.[44] In contrast, according to the 2000 census count, in 2007, multiracials only accounted for 6.3 percent of the black population between the ages of 17 and 21.[45]

As discussed in Chapter One, the Final Guidance went into effect for the fall of 2010. However, in the data that institutions report to the DOE, Black Multiracials are placed in either the Hispanic/Latino or the Two or More Races category. Thus, although the number of Black Multiracials in a given student body is not separately reported to the DOE, each individual institution should be able to generate statistics that provide separate counts for those students enrolled who designated black as one of their racial/ethnic categories. For example, 42 percent of the black students enrolled as freshmen starting at Yale in the falls of 2011–14 were Multiracial (54 percent in 2014), at the University of Virginia for the same years it was 21.5 percent (with 22.4 percent in 2014) and at Indiana University Bloomington, Black Multiracials made up 18.4 percent of all black undergraduate students on campus in the fall of 2013.[46] However, many Black Multiracials may strategically check only the black racial box on their admissions forms, even though they also identify with other racial categories.[47] Thus, these percentages could understate the number and percentages of Black Multiracials among blacks enrolled.

Other data suggest that Black Multiracials are overrepresented among blacks in graduate school as well. Census data from 2000 showed that 14.3 percent of the black only population over the age of twenty-five had attained at least a bachelor's degree, compared to 23.8 percent of Black-White Biracials.[48] Since Black Multiracials are more likely to graduate from college than Ascendant

Blacks, they almost certainly make up a larger percentage of the pool of blacks qualified for graduate study.

There is also evidence that Black Multiracials outperform single-race blacks on standardized tests used to determine graduate admissions. With respect to those taking the LSAT, figures from the Law School Admissions Council (LSAC) for the years 2010 to 2013 showed that of the about 42,450 individuals who indicated some black ancestry and took the LSAT, 9.5 percent were multiracials.[49] The percentage of Black Multiracials actually increased every year going from 6.7 percent in 2010 to 10.7 percent in 2013.[50] The number and percentage of each black racial group that scored over 150, 155, and 160 are listed in the table.

**BLACK LSAT SCORES BY RACE, 2010 to 2013**[51]

| Racial Group | # over 150 | % over 150 | # over 155 | % over 155 | # over 160 | % over 160 |
|---|---|---|---|---|---|---|
| **Single-Race Blacks** | 9,941 | 25.9 | 4,602 | 12.0 | 1,925 | 5.0 |
| **Total Black Multiracial** | 1,750 | 43.3 | 997 | 24.6 | 480 | 11.9 |
| Black Hispanic | 357 | 34.9 | 189 | 18.5 | 74 | 7.2 |
| Black/American Indian | 155 | 27.6 | 65 | 11.9 | * | * |
| Black/Asian | 194 | 46.7 | 100 | 24.1 | 57 | 13.7 |
| Black/White | 675 | 57.1 | 437 | 37.0 | 247 | 20.9 |
| Black/Two or More Groups | 369 | 43.1 | 206 | 24.1 | 95 | 11.1 |

From these statistics, it is clear that Black Multiracials outperform single-race blacks on the LSAT. What is most interesting is that the median LSAT score of black-white multiracials appears to exceed the LSAT median scores for all test takers. For comparison, the mean LSAT score for over 105,000 test takers for 2011–12 was 150.66.[52] However, 57.1 percent of black-white test takers exceeded 150.[53]

The above evidence suggests that Black Multiracials are significantly overrepresented among black students admitted to selective higher education institutions today. In addition, based on the 2012 census figures, the percentage of Black Multiracials among blacks who will be of law school age will increase by almost 90 percent between 2012 and 2027.[54]

## D. Parental Educational Levels and Higher Family Incomes Explain Part of the Overrepresentation of Black Multiracials

A number of studies on the educational attainment of multiracials concluded that their academic outcomes fall between those of their ancestral groups.[55] Other researchers have found that black-white multiracials have educational achievement levels that approximate those of whites and, thus, are significantly higher than those of blacks.[56] Melissa Herman found that black-white multiracials who identify as black had lower educational achievements than those who identified as white. She also found that black-Asian multiracials do better in school than single-race blacks, but not as well as Asians, and that black-Asian multiracials are also less likely to self-identify as black than black-white multiracials. The reported LSAT data above tends to confirm many of these findings about academic performance. Black Multiracials, as a group, scored higher than single-race blacks. Black-white multiracials' scores were similar to those of whites, and black-Asian multiracials did better than single-race blacks, but not as well as Asians.[57]

The fact that Black Multiracials are overrepresented among black students at selective higher education programs and may perform better on traditional measures of academic success should come as no surprise. Given what we know about family characteristics that aid in educational success, there are several reasons why Black Multiracials are likely to outperform single-race blacks. Black Multiracials tend to come from homes with higher levels of parental academic achievement and more family income than single-race blacks. Black Multiracials may also benefit from less of a cultural conflict than single-race blacks between their home experiences and the culture embedded in educational institutions. However, those cultural differences will be explored in Part V, which discusses why Ascendant Blacks should receive more positive consideration in the admissions process than Black Multiracials.

## 1. Black Multiracials Tend to Have Parents with Higher Levels of Academic Achievement

Studies have pointed out that "black/white intermarriages tend to occur when the white spouse trades the privilege of racial status for the higher status of a better-educated black partner."[58] According to 1990 Census Bureau statistics, 13 percent of married black males with some graduate school education and 10 percent with some undergraduate education were involved in interracial marriages. This contrasts with only 7 percent of high school graduates and 6 percent of high school dropouts. For married black women, 6 percent of those with some graduate education, 5 percent of those who were college graduates, and 4 percent of those with some undergraduate education were in interracial marriages. This contrasts with only 3 percent of those who were either high school dropouts or only high school graduates.[59] Statistics from 2008 show this tendency has continued. Whereas only 17.9 percent of single-race blacks have a parent with at least a bachelor's degree, for Black Multiracial children the figure is 23.6 percent.[60] Similarly, single-race blacks are 50 percent more likely than Black Multiracials to be born to parents, neither of which finished high school, 20.3 percent compared to 13.5 percent.[61]

Research on the standardized tests used to determine admission to selective higher education programs demonstrates that test takers growing up in families with higher levels of parental education outperform others. For example, the College Board reported that students whose highest level of parental education was an associate's degree scored 30 points higher on the SAT in 2000 and 50 points higher in 2010 than those whose highest level of parental education was a high school diploma.[62] Between 2000 and 2010, the SAT added a writing component to the critical reading and math component. This increased the total possible points from 1600 to 2400. The difference in SAT scores related to parental education mushroomed to 79 and 127 points, respectively, when the comparison was between students whose highest level of parental education was a bachelor's degree and those whose parents only had an associate's degree.[63]

Parents who are familiar with the process of obtaining a college degree are also more likely to ensure that their children take the appropriate classes in high school and provide them with the educational experiences necessary to prepare them to perform well on standardized tests. Based on 2013 SAT scores, those who took more English and language arts classes, more math courses, and more sciences courses scored higher on the SAT than those who did not.[64] Those students who took the PSAT their junior year (or earlier) scored 213 points higher than those who never took the PSAT.[65]

## 2. Black Multiracials Tend to Come from Families with More Income

According to the 2008 census data, Black Multiracials were much more likely to live in families with incomes over $50,000 and $100,000 than single-race black children, 41.7 percent and 17 percent, respectively.[66] In contrast, only 32.5 percent of single-race black children lived in families with incomes over $50,000 and only 10.3 percent in families with incomes over $100,000.[67] In addition, whereas only 26.2 percent of Black Multiracial children lived in families whose income was below the poverty level, 35.2 percent of single-race black children did. Black Multiracial children are also 20 percent more likely to live in families that own their own home (as opposed to renting) than single-race black children,[68] and almost 40 percent more likely to be covered by health insurance.[69]

Higher levels of family income correlate positively with performance on standardized tests used for college admission. For example, comparing SAT scores of individuals from families with incomes of $40,000 to $50,000 with those from families with incomes of $30,000 to $40,000, the College Board reported that test takers from the higher-income families scored 25 points higher in 2000 and 69 points higher in 2010 than test takers from the lower-income families.

Finally, Black Multiracial children were almost a third more likely to live with both parents than single-race black children.[70] Many single parents do an outstanding job raising their children; however, there are many educational advantages to two-parent families. Two parents allow for the sharing of child-rearing responsibilities such as day care, helping with homework, transporting children to and from school, and involving children in after school activities. An additional parent also increases the opportunities for the child to receive more parental attention at home. Two household incomes provide for greater economic stability for the child because the entire family income does not depend on the employment of just one adult. Research has shown that black children from two-parent homes have slightly higher grade point averages than those brought up in single-parent homes. For example, according to the National Household Education Surveys' Parent and Family Involvement Survey, black students from two-parent homes reported an average grade-point of 3.1, in comparison with those from mother-only homes of 3.0, father-only homes of 2.9, and no-parent homes of 2.7.[71]

## II. History of Antimiscegenation Measures and the Treatment of Mixed-Race Blacks during the Colonial and Antebellum Eras

Africans were not well known in England until the seventeenth century.[72] Therefore, seeking the origins of mixed-race black people in the United States takes us back to the first Africans to arrive in English North America. Those blacks were treated as indentured servants, and there was much mixing between blacks and whites. However, as a race-based system of slavery developed in colonial British North America, interracial unions created a problem because they blurred the boundary lines between the races.

From the beginning, the English colonies in North America, with perhaps the exception of the Lower South colony of South Carolina, were conceived as permanent white settlements. Attitudes about mixed-race blacks before the Civil War were primarily formulated in the Upper South and the North during the colonial period. The first permanent English colony was established in Jamestown in 1607. Maryland was the next Southern colony, founded in 1634, and North Carolina in 1653. In the 1660s, colonies in the Upper South started to enact measures to reduce interracial sexual relations between blacks and whites. Since the Northern economies were not based on slave labor, the number of slaves there was always small, never amounting to more than 5 percent of the overall population.[73] The New England colonies of Massachusetts (founded in 1620), New Hampshire (1623), Connecticut (1635), and Rhode Island (1636), for example, were settled primarily by farmers and artisans who arrived in the New World with families and strong religious convictions. They flocked to New England to create godly communities built on the centrality of the family.[74] With such small numbers of blacks, Northern colonies were not as concerned about the problems created by large numbers of slaves, including potential slave rebellions or the need to consider whether mulattoes should constitute a buffer class between blacks and whites. Yet Northern colonies also banned miscegenation. The first section of this part will address efforts by colonial authorities to constrain interracial unions and the treatment of mixed-race blacks by the Upper South and North.

In contrast to the Upper South and the North, in the Lower South, mulattoes were often valued and appreciated on their own. This was especially the case in and around the major urban areas of Charleston, New Orleans, and Mobile.[75] There, many mulattoes were fathered by wealthy white males. Often these prosperous fathers recognized and supported their mixed-race offspring. As a result, whites tended to draw more of a distinction between blacks and mulattoes, especially the more affluent ones, in the urban areas of the Lower South.[76] The second section of this part will discuss the treatment of mixed-race blacks in the major urban areas of the Lower South during the colonial and antebellum periods.

## A. Antimiscegenation Measures and the Treatment of Mixed-Race Blacks in the Upper South and North

A dozen years after the founding of Jamestown, the first record of blacks in English North America appears. The legal and social distinctions between blacks and whites were minimal in the beginning. Since whites considerably outnumbered black slaves in the Upper South, whites did not feel overly threatened by them. Thus, whites did not feel the need for assistance from mulattoes as allies in case of slave rebellions. White indentured servants also often worked alongside black slaves, which could lead to interracial sexual relations. The white parents of mulattoes in the Upper South, however, were likely individuals with little means who primarily did menial labor. Because of this genealogy, elite whites were inclined to look down on the practice of miscegenation, disdain mulattoes, and generally recognize few distinctions between mulattoes and blacks.[77]

As time elapsed, the English colonies in the Upper South imported more and more Africans. As the English colonies moved toward the formation of a race-based system of slavery, interracial unions created an increasing problem because they blurred the boundary lines between the races. Until the second half of the seventeenth century, English authorities dealt with issues generated by interracial unions on an *ad hoc* basis. For example, the first reference to an African in the Virginia legislature was the recorded punishment in 1634 of Hugh Davis, a white man, who defiled *his* body because he lay with "a negro."[78] However, according to Edmund Morgan, "Up to and perhaps through the 1660s it is difficult to document any indisputably racist feeling about miscegenation."[79]

As the population of Africans grew, colonial governments enacted legal prohibitions against miscegenation. The Virginia General Assembly adopted the first antimiscegenation statute in 1662.[80] Although the law did not ban interracial marriage, Virginia sought to discourage miscegenation by doubling the fine imposed for fornication if the act was committed between a black person and a white person. Nevertheless, interracial marriages continued in Virginia after the enactment of the statute.[81] The distinction between fornication and marriage was not surprising. For much of American history, fornication—that is, sexual acts outside of the province of marriage—was punished as a criminal offense because of its sinful nature. Marriage, however, was a very important institution sanctioned by God and viewed as necessary for the stability and maintenance of a successful society.

The 1662 law also addressed the status of mixed-race children. For the first forty years, the status of such children in Virginia was uncertain. The preamble to the statute mentioned this uncertainty by noting that "doubts had arisen as to the status of children by an Englishman and a negro woman." This ambiguity resulted from two conflicting provisions of the English common law. The common law rule for children was that they took the status of their father.[82] However, livestock ownership passed through the mother.[83] The statute cleared up this doubt by stating, "be it enacted and declared ... that all children borne in this country shall be held bond or free according to the condition of the mother."[84] Thus, following the common law rule for livestock, biracial children of a black slave mother were also slaves. Over the next few decades the other British colonies would follow suit.[85]

Two years after Virginia adopted its first antimiscegenation law, Maryland—the other Chesapeake Bay colony—passed a statute to discourage miscegenation.[86] The Maryland statute's primary concern was about interracial sexual relationships that involved white women and black men. This concern would lie at the heart of much of the objection to miscegenation in the United States until the civil rights era. James Baldwin summed up this reality when talking to a white segregationist 300 years after the first miscegenation statutes were adopted: "You're not worried about me marrying your daughter. You're worried about me marrying your wife's daughter. I've been marrying your daughter ever since the days of slavery."[87]

The Maryland statute stated that "[d]iverse freeborne Englishwomen [who were] forgetful of their free Condition and to the disgrace of our Nation doe intermarry with Negro slaves...."[88] Previously, biracial children in Maryland took their legal status from their mothers. Thus, if the mother was free, so was the child. The Maryland statute, however, provided that children inherit the legal status from their father.[89] To further discourage black male–white female miscegenation, the statute also changed the status of the white females who married slaves to that of a slave for as long as the father of the child was a slave. As an ex post facto punishment, the statute went on to declare that the children of free-born women who were already married to slaves would serve the master of their parents until age thirty.[90]

There were a couple of significant issues with Maryland's new law that demanded attention. Since the Maryland law for determining the status of the child differed from that in Virginia, it created an incentive for interracial couples to move: white husbands and African wives in Virginia started to move to Maryland, and African husbands and white wives began to flee from Maryland to

Virginia.[91] Another problem with Maryland's initial provisions to discourage miscegenation was that it encouraged economically motivated slave owners to marry their black male slaves to white female indentured servants.[92] In so doing, the slave owner would come to own the white female, as well as the children of these unions. The reality of this provision became apparent to the founder of the colony, Lord Baltimore. He had a white female servant known as Irish Nell who was determined to marry a black slave. When Lord Baltimore confronted Nell with the effect of the statute, she responded that she would rather "marry the Negro under them circumstances than to marry his Lordship with his Country."[93] Disturbed by this experience, Lord Baltimore used his influence to have the law changed. In 1681, Maryland adopted a statute that said if the marriage of any free-born English or white woman to a slave had the permission of the master, such woman and her issue would be free. Thus, Maryland took away the economic incentive that slave owners had to mate white women with black slaves.[94] Maryland also adopted Virginia's rule that slave status depended on the status of the mother.

Regardless of how deep the antiracist sentiment against miscegenation ran in Virginia in the 1660s, by the 1690s it was palpable. In 1691, Virginia adopted a statute that banished from the colony any free English or other white man or woman who married a Negro, mulatto, or Indian man or woman, bound or free.[95] The preamble to the law made the rationale for the statute clear: "for the prevention of that abominable mixture and spurious issue which hereafter may increase in this dominion."[96] Thus, the statute left no doubt that Virginians were motivated by a desire to suppress the numbers of mixed-race children in their colony. Following Virginia, Maryland outlawed interracial marriages by adopting a similar statute the next year.[97]

In 1705, Virginia passed another law that provided less drastic, but more effective deterrents to interracial marriage.[98] The law substituted a six-month prison term and a fine for those who entered into interracial marriages. Since banishment from the colony reduced its much needed population, with the change in punishment Virginia did not lose a valuable laborer or two. The statute also provided that the minister who presided over the service be fined 10,000 pounds of tobacco. A free white woman who had an illegitimate child by a black or a mulatto was fined, and if she could not pay the fine, she was sold for a five-year term. However, if she was an indentured servant at the time, an additional two years was also added to her contract with her current sponsor. As for the child, though free, the statute made the child a servant for the benefit of the parish until age 30.

Virginia also passed the first blood fraction statute to define a person's race. The statute involved the first use by Virginia of the word "mulatto," which it took from the Spanish.[99] This law defined a "mulatto" as the child of a white person and an Indian, or the child, grandchild, or great-grandchild of a white person and a Negro.[100] In other words, blacks were full blooded, mixed-race blacks with more than one-eighth black ancestry were considered mulattoes, and with regard to black ancestry, anyone with less than one-eighth black blood was considered white. From the time that Virginia started to distinguish mulattoes from blacks, however, its laws dealing with Negro slaves also included "and mulattoes." In addition, free mulattoes possessed the same legal rights as free blacks. For example, at the same time that Virginia passed the law defining who was a mulatto, it passed a law that prohibited blacks, Indians, and mulattoes from holding office in the colony. By 1723, Virginia denied free mulattoes the right to vote and limited their access to firearms.[101] From a legal point of view in Virginia, individuals with one-eighth or more black blood were treated as black, even if they were legally classified as mulatto.

While the legal status of mulattoes was still in flux, in the minds of whites in Maryland, mulattoes were generally treated as blacks.[102] In 1715, Maryland expanded its antimiscegenation provisions to forbid ministers and magistrates from marrying a white person to any black or mulatto slave.[103] In 1755, Maryland conducted the only population count that included mulattoes done before 1850, which tallied 108,000 whites, 45,000 blacks, and 3,600 mulattoes (or 2.4 percent of the population, of which 1,500 were free).[104]

North Carolina, which Virginia colonists began to settle into in the 1650s, banned interracial marriage in 1715.[105] For North Carolina, the punishments for miscegenation fell mostly on white women who married outside of their race; they were subjected to harsher punishments for having mixed-blood illegitimate children.[106] In 1741, North Carolina amended its antimiscegenation marriage statute to proscribe marriages by any white person to any person with one-eighth or more black blood.[107]

Even though there were fewer blacks in the North, Northerners also expressed their disapproval of miscegenation. In 1704, New Jersey provided that any "Negro, Indian or mulatto slave [who] shall attempt by force or persuasion to ravish or have carnal knowledge of any white woman, maid or child" would, upon conviction, be castrated at the care and charge of his master.[108] In 1705, Massachusetts adopted an antimiscegenation law.[109] The following year, New York did so as well. In 1725–26, Pennsylvania banned all interracial marriages, punished whites who engaged in the practice, and decreed that the mulatto children of white women became servants until the age of thirty-one.[110]

By the signing of the Declaration of Independence, twelve of the thirteen colonies had banned interracial marriage, with South Carolina being the only exception.[111] Also with the exception of South Carolina, the British mainland colonies generally recognized little distinction between mulattoes and blacks. As in Virginia, even when colonies or states provided different legal definitions for mulattoes than for blacks, generally, the law assigned the same, usually limited, legal rights to free citizens of both groups.[112] Thus, in the Upper South and North during the colonial and antebellum periods, racial distinctions tended to be bimodal, drawn between either white-black or white-colored (which included blacks and mulattoes).

## B. Status of Mulattoes in the Lower South during the Antebellum Era

There were fewer mulattoes in the Lower South than in the Upper South. However, many of them were fathered by wealthy, white males who often recognized and supported their mixed-race offspring, so there were many affluent free mulattoes in the Lower South. Elite whites tended to treat the more affluent ones as a sort of intermediate class between black and white, and slave and free.[113] The mulattoes often dominated the free black communities, both in numbers and influence, until emancipation. As a result, mixed-race blacks were often valued and appreciated in the Lower South, especially around urban areas such as Charleston, New Orleans, and Mobile.[114]

### 1. Charleston, South Carolina

Attitudes about race mixing in South Carolina developed differently from the way they developed in the other English mainland colonies. To begin with, as in most of the island colonies, blacks outnumbered whites two to one in South Carolina.[115] In addition, Charleston was founded by colonists from Barbados who were seeking additional land for their profitable plantation businesses. As one early historian of Carolina stated, it was "the colony of a colony."[116] The Barbadians were the richest and most influential whites in early South Carolina and dominated its economic, political, and social life. Between 1670 and 1730, for example, six of the governors of the Carolina colony were from Barbados.[117] South Carolina's earliest slave code was also copied from that used in Barbados.[118]

In contrast to the whites who came to the English mainland colonies with families, white male colonists immigrated to the West Indies alone. The far greater gender imbalances between white men and white women in the island colonies led to widespread miscegenation involving white men and black women.[119] Barbados was also a constant military staging ground for British troops fighting against its European enemies in the Caribbean and North America. As a result, it was the one slave-based economy that did not need a yeoman class to deal with servile insurrections.[120] Like many of the British colonies in the West Indies, Barbados developed a society with a small population of wealthy planters, who had a large number of black slaves doing the bulk of the manual labor, and a small biracial group of free mulattoes in between. Thus, free mulattoes emerged as a separate class in Barbados, with whites holding them in higher regard than black slaves.

Crossing the color line in South Carolina was probably more common than in any other place in the English-speaking part of the United States.[121] The children of black parents were often accepted into white society, especially if their parents were wealthy and their complexion was light enough. In addition, the perception of who was white shifted toward more of an African admixture in South Carolina. People whose color and other physical features placed them in the black category in, say, Massachusetts, might look physically white in South Carolina.[122]

Even though the color line was permeable, mulattoes did not occupy a separate legal category in South Carolina. Like other free blacks, they lost the right to vote in 1721. But South Carolina was the one colony that did not adopt an antimiscegenation statute before the Revolutionary War.[123]

Most of the free blacks were considered to be industrious, sober, and hardworking with large families and considerable property. Thus, they were seen by the elite white community as a loyal and safe class of residents. While Charleston's white working class viewed the free black community as competition, its elite whites knew that the free black community served as a buffer zone between white masters and slaves.[124]

Whites in South Carolina continued to treat mulattoes well after the Revolutionary War. The results of a legislative commission that investigated the failed insurrection plot of Denmark Vesey in 1822 confirmed the high regard that whites had for mulattoes. Vesey, a free black man, recruited some nine thousand slaves to participate in what would have been the largest and most elaborate servile insurrection in U.S. history.[125] However, his potential uprising was exposed before it could be executed. The legislative commission that investigated the plot specifically noted the benefit and importance of mulattoes, who acted as a buffer between the whites and the masses of black slaves.[126]

## 2. New Orleans, Louisiana

The origins and history of Louisiana created the conditions for a greater mixture of people there than anywhere else in the United States.[127] France began colonizing Louisiana in 1699 and founded New Orleans in 1718.[128] At the time, Louisiana's territory included modern-day Alabama. Fourteen years before France started to colonize Louisiana, King Louis XIV issued the *Code Noir* to deal with a number of issues involving slavery in the French colonies.[129] Through Article IX of the Code, the French sought to encourage the creation of a mixed-race group that could serve as a buffer class between whites and blacks to reduce the possibility of servile insurrections.[130] Among the provisions of Article IX was the requirement that if an unmarried slave master had children by a slave woman, he must marry the slave, who, together with the children, would become free. By the middle of the eighteenth century, a tripartite racial division of blacks, whites, and mulattoes was firmly in place in New Orleans, and most people married within their respective racial group.[131]

Before the Seven Years' War, with the North American component known as the French and Indian War, France held vast colonial territories in North America on both sides of the Mississippi River. However, on the verge of losing the war in 1762, French King Louis XV signed the Treaty of Fontainebleau with his cousin, King Charles III of Spain, transferring the French territories west of the Mississippi River and New Orleans to Spain. The French viewed this transfer as a temporary strategic measure to prevent the British from acquiring the land and to safeguard those territories for later reacquisition.[132] Under the Treaty, the French held onto their territories east of the Mississippi River, which they ended up giving to Britain at the end of the War.

Six years after the Treaty of Fontainebleau, the Spanish took control of the French territories west of the Mississippi River and New Orleans. At that time, free blacks made up only 7 percent of the city of New Orleans' black population. By 1805, they were more than 37 percent of the black population.[133] A number of free blacks and mulattoes immigrated to New Orleans from Haiti during Haiti's liberation struggles with France from 1791 to 1806.[134] But the main reason for the dramatic increase in free blacks was that Spanish law made it easier than French law for slaves to obtain their freedom.[135]

Napoleon Bonaparte reacquired the lands the French had transferred to Spain in 1800,[136] but sold France's holdings to the United States three years later. When Louisiana was purchased by the United States, New Orleans still had a three-tiered racial division of blacks, whites, and Colored Creoles. The Colored Creole Community in New Orleans was different in terms of education, wealth, history, and social standing than any other community of free people of color in the United States.[137] For example, the 1830 census revealed that nearly one thousand members of the Colored Creole Community owned almost 4,400 slaves, which was 4 percent of the slaves in Louisiana.[138] Colored Creoles viewed themselves primarily as Afro-European (also in some cases with Native American genes). They generally claimed the French language as their mother tongue, practiced Catholicism, and usually married others within their community.[139] These Colored Creoles were normally free persons, many of whom did not have slave parents.[140] In fact, New Orleans not only had "quadroon balls," which were popular dances limited to white men and free mulatto women, but also the institution of *plaçage*, where wealthy white men carried on long-term extramarital relationships with women of color.[141] Thus, in antebellum Louisiana, mulattoes enjoyed a presumption of free status, whereas blacks were presumed to be slaves.[142]

### 3. Mobile, Alabama

The British took control of Alabama after the French and Indian War. However, because they set apart much of it for use by Native Americans, most of Anglo Alabama was not open to white migration until after the passage of the Indian Removal Act of 1830.[143] Half of the free blacks in Alabama resided in the southwestern counties of Mobile and Baldwin, which bordered the Florida panhandle to the east and were the Alabama counties closest to New Orleans to the west. The cultural heritages of these counties primarily stemmed from French and Spanish influences, rather than English.[144]

Calculations made from 1860 census data showed that 78 percent of the free Negroes were mulatto, making Alabama's free black community second only to Louisiana in terms of the percentage who were products of miscegenation.[145] The free black population was a much larger percentage of blacks living in Latin-influenced Alabama as opposed to the Anglo Alabama. For example, according to Gary Mills, who exhaustively studied the 5,614 free blacks in antebellum Alabama, the portion of the black population that was free in Latin Alabama ranged from 15.3 percent in 1830 to 8.1 percent in 1860. In contrast, the portion of blacks who were free in Anglo Alabama remained below one percent during that time.[146]

Although Alabama did not pass a statute to ban interracial marriages until 1852, evidence from the 1860 census records showed that each of the three racial groups generally married within their respective group. Mills noted that about half of the marriages involving those with black ancestry were between men and women of similar racial composition, about 13 percent were unions between mulattoes and blacks, and about a third were between blacks and whites.[147] Alabama's laws also distinguished between colored and black in such matters as intermarriage, association, civil rights, and public education.[148]

## III. The Rise of the One-Drop Rule

Since most states tied some legal rights to race, from the late eighteenth century until the start of the twentieth century legal proceedings to address racial identity were common in local American courts.[149] By the start of the nineteenth century, the states had embraced three different legal methods to determine a person's race: blood fractions, appearance, and personal associations, with appearance as the most important.[150] States enacted a variety of blood fraction statutes to specify the quantum of blood that separated whites from blacks and mulattoes. The most common blood fraction for determining if a person was nonwhite was one-eighth or more Negro blood.[151] This remained the case through the early part of the twentieth century; by then, almost all states had adopted a statutory definition of race based on blood fractions. However, it was often impossible to determine a person's black blood fraction. Another problem with blood fraction laws was that they could contradict physical appearance. Thus, blood fraction laws tended to be used in conjunction with physical appearance. The third method used to determine race was a person's associations. Courts would sometimes give weight to the fact that a person only associated with whites as proof that the person was white, though this was normally combined with physical appearance as well.

The one-drop rule developed first in the North during the antebellum period. Before 1830, there was no mention of it.[152] Nor was there any mention of "white-looking black people," a concept that only makes sense when using something like the one-drop rule to determine a person's race. According to Frank Sweet, events such as the publication in 1829 of David Walker's *Appeal in Four Articles*, which called for blacks to resist slavery, and Nat Turner's 1831 revolt in Southampton County, Virginia, generated concern among white mainstream society that black sympathizers might be secretly among them.[153] However, it would take some time before the one-drop rule achieved national acceptance.

This part will discuss the rise of the one-drop rule. The first section will address the rise of a new scientific theory in the 1840s, which argued that blacks and whites were separate species. According to this theory, mixed-race blacks were the products of interspecies mating. Thus, they would be physically, and possibly mentally and morally, inferior to their black or white parents. Such a theory added a new scientific urgency for the need to prevent miscegenation and the number of mixed-race individuals.

Before the question of whether blacks were a separate species could be completely resolved, the Civil War led to the abolition of slavery, the addition of the Reconstruction Amendments to the Constitution, and passage by Congress of five major civil rights measures, including the Civil Rights Act of 1866. These new measures granted blacks unprecedented legal rights. The Fourteenth Amendment and the Civil Rights Act of 1866 also created concerns about the continued validity of antimiscegenation legislation. However, the Supreme Court's opinion in *Pace v. Alabama*[154] resolved any lingering doubts about such measures. The second section will discuss the reassertion of the validity of antimiscegenation measures despite the new legal rights blacks obtained during Reconstruction.

The Civil War also created the conditions that allowed for the first mass studies of physical differences of the races that included mulattoes. Scientific opinion interpreted the results of these studies as finding that although mixed-race blacks with enough white blood might be more intelligent than the full-blooded blacks, because of their physical infirmities and lack of morals, all things considered, mulattoes were worse than full-blooded blacks. The results of these studies helped to crystallize and substantiate earlier concerns about miscegenation and facilitated the acceptance of the one-drop rule by the entire nation as the principal means of determining a person's race. The third section of this part will discuss the scientific concerns about miscegenation after abolition that helped to lead to the rise of the one-drop rule.

Robert Park and Everett Stonequist conducted the first psychological studies of the development of the psyche of mixed-race individuals in the 1920s and 1930s. These studies suggested that for multiracial individuals to achieve a healthy psychological identity, they needed to embrace one racial heritage almost to the exclusion of the other. Given the physical appearance of most mixed-race people and the dominance of the one-drop rule, that meant their black ancestry. The last section of this part will discuss these early studies.

## A. The Rise of Scientific Concerns about the Nature of Mulattoes

Since the beginning of slavery, many religious believers argued that God was against miscegenation. They pointed to the story of the destruction of the Tower of Babel to explain that God objected to the amalgamation of humanity.[155] Thus, God placed whites on one continent, blacks on another, and erected land, sea, and language barriers to keep them apart. These racial groups only came together on a continent populated by Native Americans because of mankind's desires. Puritans also believed in a view of history in which they analogized themselves to God's first chosen people, the Israelites. They were the people of a New Exodus, who, like the Israelites, were on a journey through the Wilderness that would lead to the establishment of a New Israel.[156] Since God repeatedly warned his Chosen People not to mix with the original inhabitants of the Promise Land, the Puritans also attempted to abide by this injunction.[157] Thus, they also viewed miscegenation to be against the Will of God.

Beyond the longstanding religious objections to miscegenation, a scientific debate emerged in the 1840s that generated additional concerns. Until then, the dominant scientific belief about the unity of the human races was derived from the Book of Genesis, which indicated that all humans descended from Adam and Eve. Also, St. Paul proclaimed in Acts that God "hath made of one blood all nations of men for to dwell on all the face of the earth."[158] As these monogenesists argued, though blacks may differ physically and mentally from whites, they were of the same species. South Carolinian Lutheran minister John Bachman, who was also a trustee and the first professor of natural history of the College of Charleston, summarized the position of these theological naturalists.[159] He noted that when different species of animals produced a hybrid, by art or accident, these hybrids became extinct in a very short period of time. As a result, no group of animals has ever developed from the commingling of two or more species. Consequently, the creation of the various species of animals is an act of Divine Power alone. The fact that all the races of humankind produce fertile progeny is one of the most powerful and undeniable arguments in favor of the unity of the human races.[160]

In contrast to the monogenesists, polygenesists argued that humankind originated as the result of different acts of creation in several different places in the world. Thus, the differences among the human races were divisions of species, not varieties. Louis Agassiz, a Harvard professor who founded and directed the Museum of Comparative Zoology, and Samuel Morton, a Philadelphia physician, were the best known of the early polygenesists.[161] When asked if his theory of polygenesis contradicted the account of creation of Adam in the Book of Genesis, Agassiz responded that the Genesis account spoke only of the creation of the Caucasian race.[162] Morton measured a large collection of human skulls of blacks and whites, some of which dated back to Ancient Egypt, and concluded that racial distinctions were permanent and that blacks and whites were different species.

Josiah C. Nott, a Southern surgeon from Mobile, Alabama, figured prominently in the monogenesists-polygenesists debate. He followed up on the work of Morton and published a short piece in 1843 in the prestigious *Boston Medical and Surgical Journal*. Nott made the provocative claim that the mulatto was a hybrid. By "hybrid," Nott meant the offspring of two distinct species, like a mule from a horse and a donkey.[163] Nott contended that mulattoes were shorter lived than either blacks or whites; mulatto women were more delicate and subject to many chronic female diseases; mulatto women were bad breeders because many of them would not conceive at all, and a large portion of the children from those that did conceive would die at an early age; and if the two sexes interbred, they would be less prolific.[164] Nott went on to assert that each successive generation of mixed-race people would become more degenerate. Thus, his conclusions about blacks with 50 percent white blood applied with even more force to quadroons (blacks with 75 percent white blood).[165]

Nott's assertions challenged three of the dominant notions of the day. Nott argued that blacks and whites were different species, not simply different varieties of the same species. He also argued that hybrids could simply be less fertile and feebler than their parents, as opposed to sterile. And mulattoes might actually be inferior to full-bloodied blacks, not better.[166]

The controversy sparked by Nott's work coincided with debates about the results of the 1840 census, which showed significantly higher rates of mental illness among the black population than among the white.[167] Because of the disputes surrounding the 1840 census, Congress sought the advice of several social scientists when preparing the 1850 census.[168] The census form of 1850 was the first one to add a "mulatto" category for mixed-race blacks.[169] Congressional testimony about the 1850 census revealed that this category and other questions about race were added, in part, because of the efforts by scientists like Nott and supportive legislators to gather information on mulattoes.[170]

According to the 1850 census, 11.2 percent of the black population and 1.8 percent of the total population was mixed,[171] and almost 86 percent of them lived in the South.[172] However, because many mixed-race blacks were the offspring of white slave master fathers, they were far more likely to be free than other blacks. Of the approximately 406,000 mulattoes, about 159,000 or nearly 40 percent were free.[173] Mulattoes constituted 1 in 3 of the free blacks nationally, but only 7.6 percent of the total slave population. Over half of the mulattoes lived in the Upper South, with Virginia being the home of almost a fifth of them.[174] Also, mixed-race blacks made up about 35 percent of the free blacks in the Upper South, while just over one third of the mulattoes were reported as living in the Lower South,[175] and less than 10 percent of them were free. Nevertheless, they tended to dominate the free black communities in the Lower South, where they made up 75 percent of that population,[176] including Louisiana where 15,000 of the 18,000 free blacks were mulattoes.[177]

Nott continued his efforts to establish the belief that blacks and whites were separate species during the 1850s. In 1854, he published his coedited book, the *Types of Mankind*, with G.R. Gliddon.[178] This 800-page defense of Morton's theory of polygenesis and white supremacy was a contemporary best seller in the field of anthropology. Before the Civil War, Nott helped to get French aristocrat Count Arthur de Gobineau's book published in English,[179] and it was highly regarded in the United States.[180] Gobineau asserted that all of the high civilizations of humanity were products of the white race. The white race had a peculiar racial characteristic that produced a people with reflective energy, energetic intelligence, a feeling for utility, unusual perseverance, great physical power, an extraordinary instinct for order, a love of liberty and life, and a hatred of despotism. Among the other issues that Gobineau dealt with in his book were the laws that explain the rise and fall of civilizations.[181] Gobineau claimed that a society's abundance was based upon its ability to preserve the blood of the noble group that created it. When their blood is mixed with that of degenerate groups, it inevitably led to the destruction of that society.

## B. The Validity of Antimiscegenation Measures in Light of Major Legal Changes during Reconstruction

With the end of the Civil War and the abolition of slavery, the need to maintain racial categories to support a race-based system of slavery no longer existed. Over the next ten years, the United States enacted the Reconstruction Amendments, and Congress passed five major civil rights measures, including the Civil Rights Act of 1866.[182] The passage of the Civil Rights Act of 1866 and the Fourteenth Amendment created questions about the continued validity of antimiscegenation marriage statutes. The argument from the Civil Rights Act noted that the Act provided that blacks were to have the same rights to contract that whites had. Since marriage was a contract, the right to enter it could not be denied due to the race of the parties.[183] The Fourteenth Amendment argument was derived from the privileges and immunities clause and the equal protection clause, which many believed abrogated antimiscegenation statutes.

Five states repealed their antimiscegenation marriage laws during this time: New Mexico in 1866, Louisiana in 1868, South Carolina in 1868, Washington in 1868, and Mississippi in 1870.[184] Arkansas, Illinois, and Florida left their antimiscegenation marriage statutes out of their state code compilations.[185] Courts in Texas and Alabama struck down their antimiscegenation marriage statutes. Of the states that removed their legal bans on interracial marriage after the Civil War, seven were states of the former Confederacy.[186] One scholar writing in 1870 went so far as to say, "With the recent extinction of slavery, many of these [antimiscegenation] laws have passed into oblivion...."[187]

A number of state courts that addressed antimiscegenation provisions, however, upheld their state's statutes.[188] A decision of particular note was the 1871 Indiana Supreme Court opinion in *State v. Gibson*, in which the court rejected the notion that the Civil Rights Act of 1866 or any clause in the Fourteenth Amendment abrogated the state's antimiscegenation marriage statute. With respect to the Civil Rights Act argument, the court stated that although marriage was treated as a civil contract in the state, it was much more. Marriage was a public institution established by God and recognized by all Christian nations as essential to the peace, happiness, and well-being of society. Thus, the right of the states to regulate and control such an important God-given, civilizing, and Christianizing institution could not be surrendered to regulation by the federal government.[189] In an opinion that foreshadowed the Supreme Court's opinion in the *Slaughterhouse cases* two years later, the court agreed that the privileges and immunities clause gave black people the right to make and enforce contracts, but it applied only to the limited areas where the federal government had exclusive jurisdiction, like the District of Columbia and federal territories. The Alabama Supreme Court cited the *Gibson* opinion in an 1876 decision, when it overturned its 1872 decision that had struck down the state's antimiscegenation marriage statute.[190] Noting that Northern states did not look at the recent constitutional amendments as depriving them of the power to regulate against interracial marriages, the Alabama Supreme Court upheld its statute prohibiting interracial marriage.[191]

The United States Supreme Court removed all remaining doubt about the legitimacy of antimiscegenation measures when it rejected the equal protection argument against such restrictions in its 1883 decision in *Pace v. Alabama*.[192] The Court upheld an Alabama law that made interracial adultery or fornication a much more serious crime than intra-racial adultery or fornication. This issue did not involve the Civil Rights Act of 1866 because interracial adultery or fornication was a criminal act, unlike interracial marriage, which was a contract. According to the Court, since the black person engaged in the interracial sex act received the same punishment as the white person, whatever discrimination existed in the statute was directed at the offense, not at the person of any particular color. Thus, the statute did not violate the equal protection clause.

At least thirty-eight states eventually enacted antimiscegenation statutes.[193] In both the North and South, the statutes normally banned only marriages between blacks and whites. However, in the West where antimiscegenation statutes were enacted in the late nineteenth century, some of the prohibitions extended the ban to cover whites who intermarried with Native Americans, Chinese, Filipinos, Hawaiians, Hindus, Japanese, and Koreans.[194]

## C. The Rise of the One-Drop Rule: Scientific Concerns about Miscegenation after Abolition and the Civil War

As Peggy Pascoe noted, miscegenation laws were "the foundation of the larger racial projects of white supremacy and white purity" after Reconstruction.[195] The strongest justification for racial segregation was the fear of the consequences of miscegenation.[196] Wide-scale studies of racial differences among Civil War soldiers conducted by agencies of the U.S. government during the War validated this fear. The autopsies and anthropological studies carried out were the first mass studies of physical differences of the races that also included mulattoes. The results of these studies were important because they helped to crystallize and substantiate earlier concerns about miscegenation.[197] Expert scientific opinion interpreted this evidence about racial differences as affirming the notion that interracial breeding corrupted the races. From these scientific observations, surgeons and physicians generally concluded that mulattoes with enough white blood might be more intelligent than the full-blooded blacks; however, because of their physical infirmities and lack of morals, all things considered, mulattoes were worse than full-blooded blacks.

One of the federal agencies involved in the work of physical anthropology was the U.S. Sanitary Commission. President Abraham Lincoln created the Commission to study the physical and moral conditions of federal troops and to offer suggestions for how to improve army life. Dr. Sanford Hunt, a surgeon in the U.S. military during the war, prepared a report for the Sanitary Commission that discussed the results of 405 autopsies he conducted on deceased soldiers. In 1869, Hunt published the report as an influential article, "The Negro as Soldier," in the prestigious London *Anthropological Review*. Nearly all subsequent late-nineteenth-century studies on racial inferiority of blacks pointed to this report to justify their conclusions.[198]

At the time of Hunt's publication, scientists recognized three methods to determine the mental capacities of the races.[199] One was by external measurements of the cranium. The downside of this method was that it could not account for the thickness of the skull. The second method, the one employed by Samuel Morton, was to measure the internal space of the skull. However, as those engaged in scientific investigations became more professional, the researchers who had studied the shapes and sizes of the skulls began to focus more attention on the weight of the brain. Previous work in this area had always assumed that intelligence correlated with the size of the brain. Now the weight of the brain was deemed a direct, better, and more accurate measure of innate intellectual ability than the size of the cranium or the interior volume of the skull.

Hunt's article confirmed the implications from Morton's earlier findings: whites had larger brains than blacks. Hunt, however, went further and classified the brains that he weighed based on the fraction of white blood of the soldiers that he autopsied. Thus, Hunt reported the average brain weights for full-blooded whites and those with three-fourths, one-half, one-quarter, one-eighth, and one-sixteenth white blood, as well as those who were full-blooded blacks. Hunt found that the average weight of the brain of the white solider was more than five ounces heavier than that of the average black. He also found that the average weight of the brains of quadroons (those with three-fourths white blood) was closest to that of the average brain for whites, only three ounces lighter. The person who was 50 percent black and 50 percent white had a slightly heavier brain than the full-blooded black. However, Hunt found that those with only one-quarter, one-eighth, or one-sixteenth white blood had lighter brains than the full-blooded black person.[200] Hunt also found that "the percentage of exceptionally small brains is largest among negroes having but a small proportion of white blood."[201] Thus, Hunt concluded, "Slight intermixtures of white blood diminish the negro brain from its normal standard; but, when the infusion of white blood amounts to one-half, it determines a positive increase in the negro brain, which in the quadroon is only three ounces below the white standard."[202] Researchers understood Hunt's work to "establish" that blacks with at least 50 percent white blood were more intelligent than full-blooded blacks, but those blacks with less than this amount were not as intelligent as full-blooded blacks. Since mulattoes were not expected to breed with whites, but with other mulattoes or blacks, miscegenation by whites with any blacks would prove to have negative consequences for generations to come.

Benjamin Gould performed several anthropometric studies of Civil War soldiers for the Sanitary Commission as well.[203] He also published his findings in 1869.[204] Gould discovered that the lung capacity of the black soldier was less than that of the white, but greater than that of the mulatto. Comparisons of the head size, weight, and height led Gould to conclude that mulattoes were physically inferior to both blacks and whites. In discussing mulattoes in his report, Gould stated:

> The curious and important fact that the mulattoes, or men of mixed-race, occupy so frequently in the scale of progression a place outside of, rather than intermediate between, those races from the combination of which they have sprung cannot fail to attract attention. The well-known phenomenon of their inferior vitality may stand, possibly, in some connection with the fact thus brought to light.[205]

Another federal agency that published data on physical measurements conducted on troops during the Civil War was the Provost Marshal General's Bureau. In 1875, the Bureau released its report on the examinations of more than a million recruits, drafted men, substitutes, and enrolled men in military service during the Civil War.[206] Though its conclusions varied at times from those of the Sanitary Commission, the Bureau's findings generally corroborated those of the Commission, but on a much larger scale.[207] Part of the results of this report included a study of questionnaires sent to military medical doctors regarding their observations of black and mulatto recruits, including their physical builds, intellects, and abilities to perform military service. The answers of the doctors confirmed the belief that mulattoes were physically inferior and, thus, less capable of enduring the hardships of military service than either black or white recruits.[208]

Joseph LeConte, a former student of Agassiz, member of the faculty of several universities, including the University of California,[209] and president of the American Association for the Advancement of Science,[210] published two notable articles in 1879 and 1880.[211] LeConte argued that although the mulatto was intellectually superior to the pure black, he did not retain the physical capacity of either the white or the black race. Building on work of earlier race scholars such as Josiah C. Nott, George R. Gliddon, and Sanford Hunt, LeConte concluded that the mulatto was an inferior breed that would eventually perish in the natural course of the race struggle.[212]

Writing in the 1890s, Frederick Hoffman, a noted scholar on the racial characteristics of blacks, argued that the product of black-white interbreeding possessed the least vital force of all the races. Hoffman stated that miscegenation was a positive hindrance to the social, mental, and moral development of the black race. He went so far as to assert that the consequences of black-white interbreeding "demand race purity and a stern reprobation of any infusion of white blood."[213] Although Hoffman conceded that the mulatto was undoubtedly intellectually superior to the pure black, he noted this did not compensate for the deterioration in the physical and moral capacity. "Morally, the mulatto cannot be said to be superior to the pure black ... most of the illicit intercourse between whites and coloreds is with mulatto women and seldom with those of the pure type."[214] Hoffman was noting the popular belief shared by both blacks and whites that most interracial contact occurred mainly between the irresponsible underclass. Since white urban owners of theaters and nightclubs preferred light-skinned blacks as prostitutes, chorus girls, and singers, mulatto women were viewed by both black and white communities as less respectable.[215]

Nathanial Shaler, one of the most prominent Harvard professors and dean of the university's Lawrence Scientific School, wrote extensively on race in the late nineteenth and early twentieth centuries. Shaler argued that the anthropometric studies confirmed that not only was the black race a separate species from whites, but it had reached a point in its evolutionary development beyond which its further development could only result from imitating the master race, not from their own innate motives.[216] Shaler also noted that common opinion agreed that the products of unions between a pure black and white, on average, had shorter life spans and were less fertile than those of the races of either parent.[217] Shaler went on to assert that mulattoes grew up with disharmonic features. Their body frames were too large for their small hearts and kidneys, and their large teeth were tightly crowded into an undersized mouth. And Edward Youman, one of Herbert Spencer's devotees, concluded that mixing the northern European with the inferior races, including the black, would be extremely damaging to any society that did so.[218]

Herbert Hovenkamp accurately summarized the view that existed among the biological scientists in the early part of the twentieth century. For them, the "mulatto was an outcast in both worlds—too civilized to be comfortable with the black, but too primitive to live with the white without giving offense."[219] Even though the mulatto might be considered more physically attractive than the pure-blood black and often more intelligent, he was considered to be constitutionally weak, prone to disease, and less fertile.[220]

In one of the most significant segregation decisions by a lower court to reach the United States Supreme Court,[221] the Kentucky Supreme Court addressed the conviction of Berea College for violating a statute in that state that banned educating black and white students together.[222] In upholding the conviction of Berea College, the Kentucky Supreme Court compared interracial marriage to incestuous marriages and marriages by "idiots."

> Marriage by members of one race with those of the other is prohibited by statutes. It is admitted freely in argument that the subject of marriage is one of the very first importance to society; that it may be regulated by law even as among members of the same race. Inbreeding is known to lower the mental and physical vigor of the offspring. So incestuous marriages are prohibited. Others not incestuous, but involving the probable effect upon the vitality of the offspring, are prohibited also, and marriages by idiots. Still other inhibitions, such as age, and so forth, are imposed, all of which look to the well-being of the future generations. No one questions the validity of such statutes, enacted as they confessedly are, under the police power of the state. Upon the same considerations this same power has been exercised to prohibit the intermarriage of the two races.[223]

The Court went on to point out that racial prejudice serves an important function because it was "nature's guard to prevent amalgamation of the races."[224]

Although the scientific evidence did not distinguish between mulattoes with a white mother from those with a black mother, the hallmark of the concern about antimiscegenation was the protection of white womanhood. Thus, the double standard from slavery continued, where white men were far more likely than white women to be involved in interracial relationships.

The popular horror regarding miscegenation reached its apogee in the five decades spanning the turn of the last century. At the beginning of the nineteenth century, Jean Baptiste Lamarck noted the unconscious striving of organisms to improve their species, thus the male of the species possessed an instinctive drive to mate with the best female possible.[225] In the Darwinian era of the late nineteenth century, Neo-Lamarckian biologists applied this notion to miscegenation. They argued that these innate drives meant that black males would find themselves sexually attracted to white woman. Combating this natural urge was, therefore, a legitimate matter of social policy. Lynching was one possible means to do so. From 1882 until 1927, over 3,500 black men and 76 black women were lynched.[226] Although there is little doubt that many blacks were lynched because they were disrespectful or represented an economic threat to whites, the main reason given to justify these acts was that black males raped or attempted to rape white women.

Fueled by concerns about the horror of miscegenation, the one-drop rule became the unwritten law for determining race by the end of the nineteenth century.[227] In discussing the embrace of the one-drop rule, Booker T. Washington stated at this time:

> It is a fact that, if a person is known to have one per cent of African blood in his veins, he ceases to be a white man. The ninety-nine percent of Caucasian blood does not weigh by the side of the one per cent of African blood. The white blood counts for nothing. The person is a Negro every time.[228]

In 1910, Tennessee became the first state to codify the accepted practice of defining who was black based on the one-drop rule into its statutory definition of race. It was followed by Louisiana later that year, Texas and Arkansas in 1911, then Mississippi in 1917, North Carolina in 1923, Virginia in 1924, Alabama and Georgia in 1927, and Oklahoma in 1931. In addition, at least seven other states—Indiana, Kentucky, Maryland, Missouri, Nebraska, North Dakota, and Utah—amended their blood fraction statutes to classify a person as black who had as little as one-sixteenth or one-thirty-second black blood.[229] With the 1930 census, the Census Bureau also abandoned its inclusion of any categories for mixed-race individuals and adopted the one-drop rule.

## D. The Marginal Man Hypothesis: Mixed-Race Blacks Encouraged to Identify with Only Their African Ancestry

The earliest psychological studies of the development of mixed-race individuals were conducted in the 1920s and 1930s by Robert Park and his student, Everett Stonequist. Before World War I, racial scientists generally assumed that race and culture were fused together. Park and Stonequist, however, attributed the differences between mulattoes and blacks to social and cultural conditions, as opposed to biology. Park developed what he called the "marginal man hypothesis."[230] He concluded that mulattoes were destined to experience social and psychological stress because they existed between social worlds. The deepseated anxiety that results from their racial marginality "initiates a process of disorganization which finds expression in statistics of delinquency, crime, suicide and mental instability."[231] Yet, this did not necessarily mean that they were not intelligent. These scholars asserted that mulattoes were likely more intelligent than blacks because the crises of marginality made them more self-conscious and reflective. The dual biological and cultural situation they inhabited generated a situation in which they continually encountered conflicting feelings of pride and shame, love and hate. This conflict was the central feature of the organization of their life. The heightened sensitivity caused by this conflict, however, led to increased self-consciousness and race consciousness. Mixed-race blacks were, therefore, more driven to resolve this problem and, thus, more likely to become leaders of the Black Community. As Park argued, "Twenty per cent of mixed bloods among the American Negroes have produced 85 per cent of the race's superior men."[232] Park and Stonequist also felt that mulattoes would benefit from greater contact with the dominant culture and lower likelihood of experiencing color prejudice.

Stonequist asserted that multiracial identity would always be problematic because of the societal issues regarding race. These problems would include inferiority complexes, exaggerated self-consciousness, restlessness, and discontent.[233] For multiracial individuals to achieve a healthy psychological identity that embraced both races was impossible.[234] Stonequist noted that one of these social worlds was always dominant, so the mixed-race person identified with one social world or racial heritage to the near total exclusion of the other. Given the physical appearance of most mixed-race people and the dominance of the one-drop rule, this meant that mixed race people should identify with their black ancestry.

## IV. The Demise of the One-Drop Rule and the Rise of Black Multiracials

As affirmative action policies commenced, opposition to miscegenation remained strong. Until the middle of the twentieth century, about thirty states continued to ban interracial marriages of blacks with whites.[235] As an example of the depth of the anti-miscegenation sentiment, in the summer of 1963, former President Harry S. Truman, who was renowned for his decision to integrate the armed forces, expressed his displeasure about interracial marriage to a New York reporter. When asked if he thought interracial marriage would one day become widespread, Truman responded, "I hope not, I don't believe in it."[236]

Having been in use throughout the nation for six decades, the one-drop rule was now at its zenith. According to 1960 census figures, 88.8 percent of all Americans were classified as white and 10.6 percent as black.[237] With 99.4 percent of Americans viewed as either black or white, this was essentially a two-race society. Because a person's physical appearance may not reveal the fact that they had a very small quantum of black blood, it was possible for some blacks to pass as white.[238] Nevertheless, the use of the one-drop rule and the biracial nature of American society meant that Americans, in the overwhelming majority of cases, could determine a person's race based on their physical appearance. Thus, as affirmative action commenced, race was not only a socially ascribed identity, but simply put, there was no concept of a Black Multiracial person. As Angela Onwuachi-Willig has recently pointed out, the one-drop rule remains a strong force in both social and legal arenas.[239] Nevertheless, it is clearly in the process of rapidly disintegrating. This part is going to chronicle the attenuation of the one-drop rule and the concomitant rise of Black Multiracials.

In the 1960s, the Supreme Court struck down antimiscegenation statutes, culminating with its 1967 decision in *Loving v. Virginia*.[240] The first section of this part discusses the Court's decisions to abrogate these measures. As time passed from these decisions, the number of interracial relationships involving blacks increased, as did the number of Black Multiracials. The increasing numbers of interracial couples and Black Multiracials led to the rise of the Multiracial Movement, which wanted to add a separate multiracial category to all local, state, and federal government forms that sought to collect racial and ethnic data, but especially the forms for the 2000 census. The second section will discuss the rise of the Multiracial Movement. The Multiracial Movement coalesced with two other significant developments that helped to generate the conditions for the recognition that Black Multiracials could be separated from single-race blacks: the federal government's move toward adopting self-identification as the way to determine race/ethnicity and the massive immigration of people of color. In an effort to improve the accuracy of racial and ethnic data, the Census Bureau switched from sending enumerators to people's homes to fill out census forms, to sending out forms designed to be completed by heads of households and sent back to the Bureau. This change started the federal government and the rest of society on the road to providing individuals with the right to choose their racial identity. For official federal governmental purposes, race is now a self-identified trait, not one that is socially ascribed. The third section will discuss the federal government's move to self-identification of race. Although the change by the federal government might not alone have provided Black Multiracials with the ability to select a racial identity separate from single-race blacks, the federal government's movement occurred during the same time that new immigrants from Asia, Latin America, the Middle East, and North Africa were changing the face and complexion of American society. For the past fifty years, large numbers of people of color have entered the United States. Increasingly, a person's race is no longer obvious from their physical appearance. Thus, Americans are losing the ability to socially ascribe race, even if they want to continue to employ the one-drop rule. "Racially ambiguous blacks" have increasingly gained control over their racial identity because they more and more encounter the question "What are you?" with regard to their racial identity. The fourth section discusses how immigration undermined the ability to socially ascribe a person's race and, therefore, increased the ability of Black Multiracials to self-identify their race.

## A. *The Supreme Court Strikes Down Antimiscegenation Statutes*

Although willing to strike down school segregation of young children in its 1954 decision in *Brown v. Board of Education*,[241] the Supreme Court showed considerable reluctance in taking up the question of antimiscegenation statutes. A few months after the Court's decision in *Brown*, it declined to hear the case of a black woman convicted of violating the Alabama antimiscegenation statute.[242] Two years later, the Court again declined to take up a similar case from Virginia.[243]

In 1964, however, the Supreme Court changed its posture. A jury convicted a black man, Dewey McLaughlin, and a white woman, Connie Hoffman, of violating a Florida statute that made it a crime for an interracial couple to habitually live in and occupy the same room at night.[244] This statute authorized a greater punishment for this crime when committed by a black-white interracial couple than other couples. The judge sentenced McLaughlin and Hoffman to thirty days in jail and fined them $150. The statute treated a black-white interracial couple differently than other couples, but it punished both the white and black parties involved the same.

The Florida Supreme Court upheld the antimiscegenation statute and the convictions based on the 1883 U.S. Supreme Court decision in *Pace v. Alabama*.[245] On appeal to the U.S. Supreme Court, Florida also argued that the statute was ancillary to and served the interests of its antimiscegenation marriage law. The Supreme Court rejected its former rationale expressed in *Pace* to support the statute. It also went on to reject the argument that the statute could be upheld as ancillary to the statute that banned interracial marriage, without addressing whether an antimiscegenation marriage statute itself was valid.[246]

The Supreme Court finally struck the death knell for antimiscegenation marriage statutes with its 1967 decision in *Loving v. Virginia*.[247] Richard (a white man) and Mildred (a black woman) crossed into the District of Columbia and were married under its laws, which allowed interracial marriage.[248] The Lovings then returned to Virginia and established their marital abode in Caroline County.[249] In the fall of 1958, a grand jury issued an indictment charging the Lovings with violating the Racial Integrity Act that prohibited interracial marriages in Virginia.[250] On January 6, 1959, the Lovings pled guilty to the charge and were sentenced to one year in jail.[251] The trial judge, however, suspended the sentence for a period of twenty-five years on the condition that the Lovings leave the state and not return to Virginia during that time.[252] To justify his decision, the trial court judge stated in his opinion:

> Almighty God created the races white, black, yellow, malay and red, and he placed them on separate continents. And but for the interference with his arrangement there would be no cause for such marriages. The fact that he separated the races shows that he did not intend for the races to mix.[253]

The Lovings moved back to the District of Columbia.[254] However, five years later, desiring to return to their home in Virginia, they sought to have their convictions vacated on the ground that the Act they were convicted under was repugnant to the Fourteenth Amendment.[255] The Virginia Supreme Court of Appeals once again upheld the constitutionality of the Racial Integrity Act.[256]

In a unanimous opinion written by Chief Justice Earl Warren, the U.S. Supreme Court stated that the clear and central purpose of the Fourteenth Amendment was to eliminate all official state sources of invidious discrimination.[257] According to Warren, the Racial Integrity Act was not justified by any purpose independent of invidious racial discrimination.[258] Warren went on to note that Virginia only prohibits interracial marriages involving white persons,[259] which further demonstrated that the racial classifications standing on their own justifications were measures designed to maintain white supremacy.[260]

## B. The Rise of the Multiracial Movement

With the striking down of antimiscegenation statutes, the number of blacks involved in interracial marriages began to increase. By the late 1980s, individuals in black-white marriages[261] and multiracial groups like A Place for Us (APFU), the Association of MultiEthnic Americans (AMEA), and Project RACE (Reclassify All Children Equally) spearheaded efforts to add a "multiracial" option to all local, state, and federal forms, but especially for the 2000 census.[262] According to Kim Williams, at the height of the Multiracial Movement these groups had about 3,500 adult members, excluding students, throughout the country.[263] But only about twenty Movement leaders were responsible for the effort to add a multiracial category to the 2000 census.[264]

Steve and Ruth Bryant White founded APFU in 1984. They created the organization after Steve, who is white, asked his minister to marry them. The minister refused because Ruth was black.[265] One of Steve's friends also provided him with a list of reasons for why he should not marry. At the top of the list was the fact that Ruth was black. The Whites started APFU to support and encourage interactions involving interracial relationships. In 1990, APFU revised its mission statement to include, as a goal, working with other multiracial groups to add a multiracial category on all official forms until *all* racial categories from such forms were eliminated.[266]

In 1988, more than thirty multiracial organizations came together to create the first nationwide multiracial advocacy group, the AMEA.[267] The AMEA sought respect and recognition for multiracial/multiethnic individuals and advocated for the addition of a multiracial category on all government forms. In its first year, the AMEA actually sought to convince the federal government to add a new category, "Other," to the Directive 15 categories, principally for multiracial individuals. Civil rights forces, including the EEOC and the Civil Rights Division of the Department of Justice, opposed this effort. OMB decided not to take any action and concluded that it needed to conduct or authorize more testing before it could institute such a change.[268]

Susan Graham, a white woman from Marietta, Georgia, founded Project RACE in 1991. The objective of Project RACE was to get a "multiracial" classification on all forms used by local, state, and federal governmental units to collect racial data for school, employment, medical, and other purposes. Susan's husband, Gordon Graham, a black news anchor and reporter for CNN, helped to publicize the efforts of Project RACE.[269] Susan started Project RACE after her experience with the Census Bureau when she tried to find out from the Bureau how to report her mixed-race son on the 1990 census form. Eventually, a Census Bureau official told Susan to use her race "because in cases like these, we always know who the mother is, not the father."[270]

In 1992, a Conference was held in recognition of the twenty-fifth anniversary of the Supreme Court's decision in *Loving v. Virginia*. The conference drew nearly 400 multiracial individuals to Bethesda, Maryland, to attend the first national gathering of the multiracial community.[271] The meeting centered on organizing a lobbying effort aimed at convincing the federal government to modify its existing racial classifications. Specifically, the group wanted the Census Bureau to add a multiracial category on the 2000 census questionnaire.

Multiracial advocates generally argued that mixed-race individuals viewed themselves as multiracial rather than belonging to a single racial or ethnic group. A "multiracial" designation was, therefore, a better reflection of the true understanding of the multiracial person's racial identity. In a complete reversal of the earlier marginal man hypothesis, these groups pointed to the psychological problems created for biracial children who were forced to identify with one parent more than the other. They also noted that the one-drop rule does not apply to any other racial or ethnic group and appears only to exist in the United States.[272] In addition, the rule, used so long to classify any person with any black blood as black, was inherently racist.[273]

Black civil rights leaders, including Jesse Jackson, Kwesi Mfume for the Congressional Black Caucus, and the NAACP, opposed the addition of a multiracial category.[274] Among the concerns black leaders expressed were that many blacks would designate themselves as multiracial to escape the social stigma of identifying themselves as Black/African American. They were also concerned about the impact on efforts to dismantle racial discrimination that would result if a multiracial category were included, because the number of blacks among the population would appear to decrease. One study estimated that about 70 percent of the U.S. black population had multiracial ancestry, and other studies placed the percentage even higher.[275] Opponents of the multiracial category also argued that although the one-drop rule was a product of racism, it had become a means of mobilizing communities of color to organize against white race privilege.[276] A number of civil rights groups, including the NAACP, the National Urban League, the Lawyer's Committee on Civil Rights under the Law, and the Joint Center for Political and Economic Studies, signed onto the 1994 Coalition Statement.[277] The Statement noted that a multiracial category may have unanticipated adverse consequences for blacks. The Coalition Statement went on to oppose any action by OMB that would disaggregate the current black population.

Multiracial organizations were undaunted by these concerns and by opposition from civil rights groups. In 1995, multiracial activists were able to get legislation introduced in eleven different states to require the addition of a multiracial category to these various state's administrative or educational forms.[278] By the end of 1996, five states—Ohio, Illinois, Georgia, Indiana, and Michigan—had enacted such laws.[279]

Charles Michael Byrd, of black, white, and Cherokee heritage, launched an Internet website called *Interracial Voice*. Though not a member of any established multiracial association, he organized the first multiracial solidarity march held on the Mall in Washington, D.C., in July of 1996. The stated objective of the march was to petition the federal government for a multiracial category on the 2000 census.

In the early part of 1997, Susan Graham was able to talk with Newt Gingrich, Speaker of the House of Representatives. Graham resided in Gingrich's congressional district, and Gingrich knew of Graham because she had been instrumental in the successful effort to get a multiracial category added to the Georgia state forms. During the meeting, Gingrich embraced the effort to get a multiracial category on the census. Gingrich felt that the multiracial option was a step toward the eventual elimination of racial and ethnic categories.[280]

Even though OMB ultimately rejected the multiracial category for the census, in the 1997 Revisions it did allow individuals the ability to check more than one race category on forms used to collect the data reported to the federal government. Not all multiracial group advocates agreed that this was a step forward. The AMEA accepted the decision to allow individuals to choose more than one racial category, but Susan Graham of Project RACE felt that this was not enough. Ruth and Steve White and Charles Byrd returned to their original positions of trying to get beyond racial categories altogether.[281]

As subsequent federal agencies began to adopt their regulations to comply with 1997 Revisions, multiracial advocates achieved a partial victory that may not have been apparent when OMB rejected the multiracial category. As noted in Chapter One, when the EEOC and the DOE adopted their regulations, they concluded that it would be too onerous a burden to ask all employers and educational institutions to report the separate races of those in the Hispanic/Latino or Two or More Races categories. Thus, multiracials who also indicate that they are Hispanic/Latino, are lumped in with other Hispanics/Latinos and cannot be separated out from these aggregate counts. Non-Hispanic/Latinos who check multiple races are all lumped into a Two or More Races category. Although there is no multiracial category for individuals to check on forms, with regard to employers, educational institutions, and others reporting racial and ethnic data to various federal agencies, the Two or More Races category effectively functions as a multiracial category for non-Hispanic/Latino multiracials.

## C. The Federal Government's Move to Self-Identification of Race

Another development that paralleled the increases in interracial sexual relationships and Black Multiracials was the federal government's move to allow individuals to self-identify their race. For much of American history, race was not a matter of self-identification, but a socially ascribed characteristic. With the one-drop rule firmly in place, mixed-race blacks were treated as black regardless of how they might otherwise have identified themselves. However, to remedy the undercounting of blacks in the 1950 census, the Census Bureau decided to adopt the practice of requiring the head of the household to fill out the form. Thus, over 80 percent of American households received an advanced copy of the 1960 census form that was to be filled out and then given to census enumerators when they arrived.[282] The 1970 census form was the first designed to be completed by respondents without any oversight from census enumerators.[283]

The Census Bureau viewed the change to self-reporting as an improvement in the accuracy of racial statistics, but this change also began the process of changing the meaning of racial identification. Asking heads of households to fill out census forms generated the question for them of how they identify their own race and those of their family members. "This procedural change caused a shift in the meaning of racial categorization, from race as a feature of how others (such as census enumerators) perceive an individual to race as a product of how the individual sees himself or herself."[284]

Although Directive 15 indicated that an individual's racial/ethnic category should be the one that most closely reflects their recognition in their community, the race identification question on the 1980 census form said, "Fill the circle for the category with which the person most closely identifies."[285] And the 1990 census form said, "Fill ONE circle for the race that the person considers himself/herself to be."[286] Though the 1980 and 1990 census suggested self-identification, those forms limited a person's choice to only one racial category. The 1997 Revisions specifically embraced self-identification as the preferred means of determine a person's race and allowed individuals to choose all of the racial categories that apply to them.

## D. Immigration Has Changed the Face and Complexion of American Society

Whether the change in how the federal government requires racial and ethnic data to be collected in the 1997 Revisions would have been enough to cause Americans to abandon the one-drop rule in their day-to-day interactions with each other remains an open question. However, the increase in Black Multiracials and the movement by the federal government to self-identification of race and ethnicity occurred as American society was experiencing massive waves of immigration of people of color from the rest of the world.

Immigration during the past fifty years has fundamentally altered the predominantly dual race nature of American society and literally changed the face and complexion of America. America is now home to individuals with an array of facial features, hair textures, and colors. In 2010, non-Hispanic/Latino whites (which include those from the Middle East and North Africa) made up only 63.7 percent of the population, and single-race blacks made up another 12.6 percent.[287] Thus, those who were not simply black or white have increased from less than 1 percent of the population in 1960 to more than 23 percent, which is a percentage that is almost double that of single-race blacks in the country.

There are plenty of people who, by the application of the one-drop rule, look black but are from such places as the Caribbean, Latin America, the Middle East, North Africa, or Asia. One of the major consequences of immigration for racial identification in the United States is that even for those who want to socially ascribe race, appearance is no longer a reliable way to do so. Blacks with lighter complexions or less obvious African facial features are increasingly interacting with people who can no longer assume that they are black based on their physical appearance. This new uncertainty about a person's racial identity has meant that to determine a person's race, people have to ask. A person with some African ancestry is increasingly able to respond to such a question by saying, "I am black" or "I am multiracial" or "It depends" or "I am _____ (fill in the blank)" or "I am just me." In other words, many Black Multiracials, as well as other racially ambiguous blacks, can exercise a certain amount of choice in deciding their racial identity, because it is increasingly a function of choice, as opposed to social ascription.

## V. Why Ascendant Blacks Should Receive More Positive Consideration in the Admissions Process

For good or bad, in the aftermath of the Supreme Court's decisions in *Fisher* and *Schuette*, it is clear that Black Multiracials have a choice to make about their racial identity when they apply to selective higher education programs. Clearly some (many, most) Black Multiracials do truly self-identify as only black. However, there are some (many, most) who consider themselves multiracials and will self-identify as such and, thus, on their applications will be viewed as Hispanics/Latinos or Two or More Races. Others may consider themselves multiracial, but by being strategic about their admissions prospects, choose to self-identify as only black. Some evidence of this is present in the breakdown of blacks by race who took the 2012 LSAT. According to the 2010 census, almost 60 percent of Black Multiracials are black-white individuals. Yet on the 2012 LSAT, this combination only constituted 31.2 percent (338 of the 1081) of Black Multiracial test takers.[288] This may reflect strategic box checking by many Black Multiracials, especially black-white ones, who thought it best not to reveal their white ancestry. I do not mean to address whether this choice is right or wrong; what I am pointing out is that it exists. Because it exists, the concept of their race has changed for purposes of admission from what it was for mixed-race blacks when affirmative action began. This new racial landscape for Black Multiracials has rendered obsolete the old ways of employing race in the admissions process with regard to them and single-race blacks. In addition, the growing percentages of Black Multiracials who are approaching the age at which most people attend higher education institutions makes it urgent that selective higher education institutions address this new phenomena.

Black Multiracials, especially if their nonblack parent is white or Asian, may have less cultural discontinuities with educational institutions and school officials than other black students. This might also aid their academic performance.[289] However, the sociocultural differences between Black Multiracials and Ascendant Blacks reveal the fact that Black Multiracials, in general, have far fewer experiences derived from the history of discrimination of blacks in United States than Ascendant Blacks. This along with the fact that Ascendant Blacks are far more likely to be underrepresented, offers valid explanations for why Ascendant Blacks should receive more positive consideration in the admissions process than Black Multiracials. The following sections shall discuss several overlapping sociocultural differences between Black Multiracials and Ascendant Blacks to demonstrate how much more "our Nation's struggle with racial inequality"[290] affected the experiences of Ascendant Blacks when contrasted with Black Multiracials.

## A. The Ancestry of Black Multiracials Means That They Have Fewer Experiences Than Ascendant Blacks

Many of the parents and almost all of the grandparents of Ascendant Blacks experienced what America was like before the Supreme Court's opinion in *Brown v. Board of Education*, the passage of the Civil Rights Act of 1964, the Voting Rights Act of 1965, the Civil Rights Movement, and the Black Consciousness Movement. Thus, their ancestors lived through the period of time when segregation and conscious racial discrimination were the explicit law of the land in many areas of the country and, if it was not the law, where segregation still formed part of customary American business, educational, political, and social practices. For Ascendant Blacks, discussions about the victimization of blacks throughout American history are about their mothers, fathers, aunts, uncles, grandparents, great grandparents, great aunts, great uncles, and their earlier ancestors. For Ascendant Blacks, the history of discrimination in the United States is the history of their family tree. Black Multiracials clearly experience the impact of the history of racial discrimination, but the fact that one of their parents is not black means that half of their ancestral tree was not subjected to the victimization visited on blacks as a result of America's history of racial discrimination. Therefore, the historical experiences of blacks may simply be less important to Black Multiracials than it is to Ascendant Blacks. It also means that, in general, they will have had less experience with that history than Ascendant Blacks.

## B. Research on the Racial Identity Formation of Black Multiracials Suggests They Are Less Likely to Identify Only as Black

Black Multiracials are increasingly able to choose a racial identity that is separate from that of other blacks. As Professor Nancy Leong put it, "ultimately, while many multiracial people seem to identify with their minority background to some extent, or at least to a greater extent than with their white background, it seems inaccurate to argue that they are indistinguishable from monoracial members of the minority group with respect to the contribution to diversity they might make."[291]

Research exploring the identity formation of multiracial individuals suggests that they may understand their racial identity in a variety of ways. In addition to a singular identity (either exclusively black or exclusively white), which some research subjects chose, other options include a border identity (exclusively biracial), a protean identity (sometimes black, sometimes white, sometimes biracial), and a transcendent identity (no racial identity).[292] Research also suggests that individuals choose one (or several) identity(ies) based on social networks or appearance.[293] Another probable explanation for this phenomenon is that multiracial people may identify themselves differently in different contexts.[294] In short, Black Multiracials need not especially choose a single racial/ethnic identity because they have several.[295]

Some Black Multiracials may altogether reject the notion that they should be perceived as black. For example, Tiger Woods is a prominent example of a mixed-race individual with some black ancestry who openly considers himself "multiracial" as opposed to "black."[296] Under the one-drop rule, Woods is considered black. But his mother is of Thai, Chinese, and Dutch ancestry, and his father is a mixture of African American, Chinese, and Native American ancestry.[297] Thus, Woods embraces multiple racial identities. As another multiracial person put it, "We multiracial people have the right to make an individual choice about our racial identity. Just because it, at the same time, may threaten many blacks because of ongoing historical issues doesn't mean we should deny our white or other ancestries."[298]

Melissa Herman's study of a large sample of multiracials from 14 to 19 years old found that, when forced to choose one race, 68 percent of black-white students chose black.[299] A study that drew on data from the National Longitudinal Study of Adolescent Health found that only 59.5 percent of students who identified themselves as black-white multiracials at home described themselves the same way at school; over one-fifth identified themselves as black when at school, with 7.4 percent describing themselves as belonging to three or more racial groups, and about 5 percent as "other."[300] Another study found that multiracial students at a predominately white university who were black and another race did not identify as strongly with being black as single-race blacks.[301] The study found that biracial black students were less likely to feel close to other black students and more likely to report extreme or considerable alienation from black students on campus. While 54 percent of single-race black students reported that all or most of their close friends on campus were other black students, none of the biracial students did so. Some 40 percent of the biracial black students described negative experiences with other blacks, compared to only 12 percent of the single-race black students. A different study of 177 college students from Detroit who had one black and one white parent found that over 60 percent of these students saw themselves as neither black nor white, but something of a hybrid.[302]

Studies have also found that those from higher socioeconomic backgrounds are more likely to identify themselves as multiracial.[303] A more recent study that included a significant number of individuals with black and white parents found that 42.1 percent viewed themselves as biracial, as did others. An additional 34.2 percent viewed themselves as biracial even though others did not see them that way.[304] No doubt as American society becomes increasingly willing to accept multiracial identities, it is likely that the numbers of Black Multiracials who consider their racial identity to be multiracial will increase.[305]

Black Multiracials appear to be more likely than blacks to embrace concepts of individuality and colorblindness, so they are less likely to see their race and ethnicity as essential parts of their identity.[306] In addition, there may be negative psychological consequences for multiracials who adopt a monoracial identity. Some research suggests that if multiracials embrace a single-race identity, this can lead to feelings of guilt, disloyalty, oppression, and lower self-esteem.[307] If embracing a multiracial identity decreases psychological problems, this will provide additional motivation for Black Multiracials to embrace all of their racial identities.

The social science studies on multiracial identity clearly demonstrate that Black Multiracials increasingly do not view racial identity in the same way that Ascendant Blacks do. They are also less likely to have deeply rooted connections to other blacks. What's more, this sense may increase among those Black Multiracials coming from higher socioeconomic families, the ones most likely to be admitted to selective higher education institutions. As having experiences related to the history of discrimination inflicted on blacks requires an identification of oneself as black, to the extent that Black Multiracials do not identify as black, they are clearly having less experiences of race that are steeped in the history of racial discrimination than Ascendant Blacks.

## C. Many Black Multiracials Grow Up in Households without any Blacks

For some time, a large proportion of black children have grown up in single-parent homes in the United States. For example, in 2005, only 35 percent of black children lived with both parents.[308] According to the American Community Survey, only 31 percent of black children now live in homes with both parents; some 53 percent of black children live in homes with only a mother, and 7 percent live in homes with only a father.[309] Even though Black Multiracial children are 30 percent more likely to live with both parents,[310] like other black children, a significant percentage will grow up in single-parent households headed by women. Since black males are two to three times more likely to engage in interracial marriages or cohabitation arrangements than black females, if Black Multiracials are raised by a single parent, it is far more likely that the single parent is a nonblack female.

Many of these Black Multiracials growing up in households without a black parent may receive a cultural orientation that deemphasizes their connection to the historical struggle against racial oppression in the United States. Clearly, without a black parent in the home, they will have far fewer experiences that are shaped by America's history of racial discrimination than Ascendant Blacks.

## D. Black Multiracials May Also Have Divided Loyalties

Black Multiracials, understandably, may be concerned with the conditions and circumstances of their nonblack relatives. They may, quite correctly, spend much of their time engaged in activities with that side of their families, including outings, celebrations, and vacations. In addition, Black Multiracials will also be interested in the welfare of their nonblack relatives and assisting them when they can. Providing such assistance is certainly understandable, but unlike when Ascendant Blacks are helping their black relatives, this is not related to the history of discrimination experienced by blacks. As a result, Black Multiracials are spending less time engaged with the historical experience of discrimination suffered by blacks than Ascendant Blacks when participating in family activities or addressing family concerns.

## E. Conclusion

All of the reasons above strongly suggest that, in general (but with recognition that there will certainly be important individual differences), Ascendant Blacks are likely to have more significant experiences derived from the history of racial discrimination in the United States than Black Multiracials. In addition, Ascendant Blacks are more likely to advance the objectives of diversity in higher education than many Black Multiracials. I do not ignore the fact that many blacks with a nonblack parent have been critical in the historic struggle against racial oppression in the United States and are very important leaders in the Black Community today. But the concern of this book is not with the inclusion of Black Multiracials on affirmative action programs. Rather it is with the virtual elimination of Ascendant Blacks from the campuses of selective higher education programs. Room in affirmative action should, of course, continue to exist for Black Multiracials, but selective higher education programs must address the growing underrepresentation of Ascendant Blacks.

## Conclusion

At the commencement of affirmative action, the one-drop rule was at its pinnacle. As a result, race was a visible characteristic that, for the overwhelming majority of Americans, could easily be determined based on physical appearance. Thus, a person's racial identity was socially ascribed. Black Multiracials were not distinguished from other blacks; they were simply lighter skinned blacks.

Since the institution of affirmative action policies, several developments regarding racial identification have occurred that have allowed Black Multiracials to choose a separate racial identity from that of other blacks. The elimination of antimiscegenation statutes helped to foster the growing societal acceptance of interracial relationships involving blacks. That greater acceptance increased not only the number of such relationships, but also the number of Black Multiracials. At the same time that the number of Black Multiracials was increasing, the federal government increasingly turned to self-identification as the principal means by which to determine a person's racial identity. America was also experiencing its first significant wave of immigrants of color. This increased immigration of people of color from the rest of the world reduced the ability of those who continued to employ the one-drop rule to determine a person's race based on appearance. As a result, racially ambiguous blacks, including many Black Multiracials, are having more and more experiences where their racial identification is a matter over which they exercise increasing control. Thus, unlike when affirmative action programs commenced, Black Multiracials are increasingly given the choice about how they will identify their race. It is the fact that they can now make this choice, regardless of what that choice might be, that has dramatically altered the admissions landscape for them. Because Black Multiracials can choose their racial identity, policies and procedures based on their inability to do so are increasingly obsolete.

In addition to the fact that Ascendant Blacks are more likely underrepresented in selective higher education institutions than Black Multiracials, an outgrowth of the new reality is that Black Multiracials, in general, have considerably fewer experiences shaped by the history of discrimination suffered by blacks in the U.S. than Ascendant Blacks. These two reasons provide valid justifications for why Ascendant Blacks should receive more positive consideration in the admissions process than Black Multiracials.

Chapter Four

# Black Immigrants: Why They Should Not Be Preferred over Ascendant Blacks

This chapter will explore the differences between Black Immigrants and Ascendant Blacks based upon the Supreme Court's acceptance of the use of racial classifications to obtain a critical mass of underrepresented minorities with a history of discrimination. Since the adoption of affirmative action policies, the number of foreign-born blacks in the United States has exploded. In 1960, the 125,000 foreign-born blacks in the country made up less than 1 percent of the black population. As of 2012, however, the 3,900,000 foreign-born blacks made up almost 10 percent of the black population. Simply put, because of the minimal numbers of foreign-born blacks in the United States when affirmative action policies began, there was little reason to think about whether they differed in significant ways from other blacks for purposes of affirmative action. With an over thirty-fold increase, however, in the numbers of foreign-born blacks, their impact for purposes of affirmative action should no longer be ignored.

This chapter will discuss the differences between Black Immigrants and Ascendant Blacks. In so doing, it will not argue that Black Immigrants should receive no positive consideration in the admissions process. Rather it will argue that Ascendant Blacks should be preferred over Black Immigrants to such an extent as to assure the inclusion of a substantial presence of Ascendant Blacks in the student bodies of selective higher education institutions. Following Justice O'Connor's rationale, there are two reasons that Ascendant Blacks should receive preference over Black Immigrants. First, Ascendant Blacks are far more likely to be underrepresented in many, if not most, of the nation's selective higher education institutions than Black Immigrants. Second, the history of discrimination suffered by blacks in the United States affected the ancestors of Ascendant Blacks, as well as Ascendant Blacks themselves, far more than it did Black Immigrants. As a result, in general, Ascendant Blacks will have far more experiences with both aspects of the history of discrimination suffered by blacks in the United States than Black Immigrants.

Part I of this chapter will focus on the increasing numbers of foreign-born blacks in the country since affirmative action. It will also discuss the evidence of the overrepresentation of Black Immigrants among black students attending selective higher education programs. Given what educational research has long told us about family characteristics that aid in educational attainment, there are several reasons why Black Immigrants are likely to do better in American educational institutions than Ascendant Blacks. Children of foreign-born blacks tend to come from families with more income and better-educated parents than the children of native blacks. Some scholars have also argued that the educational performances of children of foreign-born blacks may benefit from certain sociocultural advantages as well.[1] For example, foreign-born blacks who come to the United States bring with them intact cultures developed in their countries of origin. However, to live with subordination, U.S.-born blacks developed coping mechanisms, which are often perceived as oppositional to those of the dominant group.[2] For over two decades, this oppositional theory has been one of the most popular cultural explanations for the low academic achievement of black youth in American schools.[3] Other scholars downplay the sociocultural factors as explanations for the lower educational performance and focus their attention on the other family characteristics noted above.[4] Even though the academic impact of the sociocultural differences between Black Immigrants and Ascendant Blacks is disputed among educational researchers, these differences are very relevant for the discussion that comes in Part IV, which deals with why Ascendant Blacks should be preferred to Black Immigrants in the admissions process. Part I will conclude by discussing the reasons why Black Immigrants are likely to enjoy more academic success than Ascendant Blacks, but the sociocultural differences will be addressed in the fourth part.

Although blacks have always constituted a significant portion of the American population, before the institution of affirmative action policies, not many blacks voluntarily immigrated to the United States. Part II of this chapter will discuss the history of black migration (forced and voluntary) into the United States from the colonial period until the advent in the 1960s of affirmative action policies for admission to the United States.

The adoption of affirmative action policies by selective higher education programs occurred about the same time that many countries with black majorities in the Caribbean and Africa were gaining their independence and Congress enacted the Family Reunification and Refugee Law, also known as the Hart-Cellar Act.[5] These developments, along with subsequent immigration reforms, reshaped American immigration policies and led to significant increases in the numbers of blacks immigrating into the country. Part III of this chapter will discuss these changes that led to an outburst of immigration by blacks into the United States over the past fifty years.

Foreign-born blacks have their negative experiences with racism in the United States, yet they may not have the same psychological, sociological, and philosophical reactions as Ascendant Blacks. So, while Black Immigrants share the commonality of being descendants of Africa with Ascendant Blacks, there are a number of very important social and cultural differences between the two groups. These differences make it clear that Ascendant Blacks have far more experiences than Black Immigrants with both aspects of the history of discrimination suffered by blacks in the United States. Part IV, thus, discusses the differences between Ascendant Blacks and Black Immigrants that justify Ascendant Blacks receiving preference in the admissions process of selective higher education institutions over Black Immigrants.

# I. Increasing Numbers of Black Immigrants since the Institution of Affirmative Action

Since the origination of affirmative action policies, the number of foreign-born blacks in the United States has exploded. The percentage of foreign-born among the black population is at its highest level since the days of the influence on the black population of the Transatlantic Slave Trade. The first section will discuss the current numbers of foreign-born blacks and how they are distributed throughout the country.

The reason that university admissions committees have historically lumped all blacks into a unified Black/African/African American category derives from the legacy of racial discrimination in the United States that viewed all blacks alike, regardless of racial or ethnic differences. Also, the black civil rights movement of the 1960s coincided with the founding of independent black nations in the Caribbean and Africa. This resulted in the emergence of a TransAfrica movement on both sides of the Atlantic, which asserted that all blacks had a common history and destiny. Thus, like 1960s mainstream culture, blacks generally did not distinguish recent arrivals from native-born blacks. Even though colleges and universities have not typically separated their Black Immigrants from other blacks, evidence has emerged over the past fifteen years that points to the overrepresentation of Black Immigrants among black students in selective higher education programs. This is discussed in the second section.

Given what we know about family characteristics that aid in educational success, there are several reasons why Black Immigrants are likely to do better in American educational institutions than Ascendant Blacks. The third section discusses the differences in family characteristics of the families of children with foreign- or native-born blacks. My primary purpose in pointing to the differences in income, parental education, and two-parent households, however, is to demonstrate that the overrepresentation of Black Immigrants among black students at selective higher education institutions is likely to persist. In other words, these differences are not temporary and passing. With the dramatic increase over the past fifty years in the number of foreign-born blacks in the country, the portion of Black Immigrants among blacks approaching the age at which most people attend colleges and universities is on a steep upward trajectory. Thus, no matter how overrepresented Black Immigrants are now, given their increasing proportion among blacks approaching college age, the magnitude of the overrepresentation at selective higher education institutions will increase significantly over the next fifteen years.

## A. *Increasing Numbers of Foreign-Born Blacks*

Since the origination of affirmative action admissions policies, the number of foreign-born blacks in the United States has substantially increased. The 1960 census recorded only 125,000 blacks not born in this country, constituting about 0.7 percent of the black population.[6] The portion of blacks that were foreign-born increased to 1.1 percent in 1970, to 3.1 percent in 1980, to 4.9 percent in 1990, to 6.1 percent in 2000, and to 8.0 percent in 2005.[7] The 2010 census recorded almost 3,600,000 foreign-born blacks, constituting 8.8 percent of the black population, but the latest census figures from 2012 put their numbers at 3,900,000 and nearly 10 percent of the black population.[8] In addition, foreign-born blacks also have at least one million U.S.-born children.[9] These new black faces are likely to have an even larger impact on the ethnic ancestry of the black population in the future, because foreign-born black women tend to have more children than native black women. For example, in 2004, a decade ago, approximately one out of every six black children was born to a foreign-born mother.[10] In Massachusetts where one out of every three blacks is currently foreign-born, since 2008, a majority of black babies born there have been to the immigrant mothers.[11]

Foreign-born blacks come primarily from two regions of the world, Africa and the Caribbean. Substantial black immigration from Africa, however, is of more recent origin than Caribbean immigration. In 1980, Africans made up less than 10 percent of the foreign-born blacks, and over three quarters of them have come to the United States since 1990.[12] Between 2000 and 2009, the African born black population in this country increased by 92 percent, in contrast the Caribbean born black population only increased by 19 percent.[13] As of 2009, approximately 33 percent of the foreign-born blacks were born in Africa and 52 percent were from the Caribbean.[14] The countries that sent the largest percentage of African born immigrants were Nigeria (19), Ethiopia (13), Ghana (10), and Kenya, Somalia and Liberia (all at 6); for Caribbean countries it is Jamaica (36), Haiti (31), and Trinidad and Tobago (11).[15]

Foreign-born blacks are unevenly distributed in the country. For example, in 2008, they made up 1 percent or less of the black population in the Southern states of Arkansas, Alabama, Louisiana, Mississippi, and South Carolina and between 1 to 3 percent in Illinois, Indiana, Kentucky, Michigan, Missouri, West Virginia, and Wisconsin.[16] By contrast, in 2007, almost half of the foreign-born blacks, including 62 percent of Caribbean-born blacks, lived either in the New York City area or in the Miami area.[17] In 2008, with a percentage of 31.8, Massachusetts had the highest percentage of blacks that were foreign-born within their state followed by North Dakota (27), New York (26.9), Rhode Island (26.2), Maine (25), Minnesota (23.7), Vermont (23.7), Utah (21.3), and Florida (19.3).[18] In 2007, West Indians were far more concentrated in certain states than African immigrants. Over 70 percent of West Indians resided in only three states: New York at 37 percent, Florida at 27 percent, and New Jersey at 7 percent; in contrast, foreign-born Africans have spread throughout the country. New York at 11 percent was home to the largest portion, followed by Maryland at 10 percent and Texas at 8 percent.[19]

## B. Evidence of Overrepresentation of Black Immigrants Attending Selective Higher Education Institutions

The substantial increase in immigration by blacks from other parts of the world has also had a significant impact on the ethnic ancestry of blacks on college campuses throughout the country. In accordance with Department of Education regulations, higher education institutions typically place foreign-born individuals on student visas in a separate category from their other students.[20] But these institutions have not separated Black Immigrants, who are American citizens or have permanent residency status, from other blacks. In the past dozen years, evidence has emerged that Black Immigrants are overrepresented among black students in higher education. In general, studies also suggest that the more selective a college or university, the higher the proportion of Black Immigrants among the black students attending that institution.

According to Census Bureau statistics, only 2 percent of black children under the age of 18 are foreign-born, but approximately 12.7 percent have at least one parent born in a foreign country.[21] Even though non-Hispanic, foreign-born whites make up about the same percentage of the white population as foreign-born blacks make up of the black population,[22] both of the above percentages for blacks are approximately double the rates for whites.[23] Further, according to 2004 census statistics, more than 12 percent of all black undergraduate students enrolled in U.S. colleges and universities were born outside of the United States—this is nearly four times the rate for whites.[24] Also, 20.9 percent of black undergraduates had at least one parent born outside of the United States.[25] For enrolled black graduate students, 18.7 percent, more than one in six, were born outside the United States.[26] This contrasts with only 6.3 percent for white students.[27] And more than one in four, or 27.4 percent, of black graduate students had at least one foreign-born parent.[28]

Beyond the overrepresentation of Black Immigrants on college campuses in general, there is evidence to suggest that they constitute an even disproportionately larger percentage of black students at selective higher education institutions. A 2006 article discussing baseline data from a study of freshmen who enrolled in twenty-eight selective colleges and universities in 1999 focused heavily on the differences between Black Immigrants and other blacks at these institutions.[29] This article noted that although only 13 percent of black eighteen- or nineteen-year-olds at the time were first- or second-generation immigrants, they made up 27 percent of the black freshmen at these selective colleges and universities.[30] The portion of Black Immigrants was actually higher at the ten most selective schools in the study, constituting 35.6 percent of the black students.[31] And it was even higher at the four Ivy League schools (Columbia, Princeton, University of Pennsylvania, and Yale), where they comprised 40.6 percent of the black students enrolled.[32] According to Dr. Michael T. Nettles, Vice President for Policy Evaluation and Research at the Educational Testing Service, a decade ago, "If Blacks are typically 5 and 6 percent of the population at elite colleges, then the representation of native U.S. born African Americans might be closer to 3 percent."[33]

Another study by Pamela R. Bennett of Johns Hopkins University and Amy Lutz of Syracuse University looked at high school graduates who were Black Immigrants, native blacks, and whites to determine where they attended college. Looking at data from the National Education Longitudinal Study,[34] Bennett and Lutz found that a larger percentage of Black Immigrants attended college than either native blacks or whites, 75.1 percent compared to 60.2 and 72.5 percent, respectively.[35] In addition, the Black Immigrants were almost four times more likely to enroll in selective colleges and universities than other blacks. The study found that 9.2 percent of the Black Immigrants enrolled in selective colleges, compared to only 2.4 percent of other black high school graduates (and 7.3 percent of the white high school graduates).[36]

As noted earlier, no matter how large the overrepresentation of Black Immigrants among black students at selective higher education institutions is today, it is likely to get larger in the future. For example, the number of black children under the age of ten who live with a foreign-born black parent has more than doubled from 363,000 in 1990 to an average of 813,000 between the years 2005 to 2009. As a result, during this time period the percentage of these children has increased from 7 to 12 percent, respectively, among blacks under the age of ten.[37]

## C. Why Black Immigrants Perform Better Academically than Ascendant Blacks

Foreign-born blacks share with Ascendant Blacks the commonality of being descendants of Africa. Nevertheless, there are a number of very important economic, social, and cultural differences between the two groups.[38] Children of foreign-born blacks tend to come from families with more income and better-educated parents than the children of native blacks. In addition, the children of foreign-born blacks are also more likely to grow up with both parents than Ascendant Blacks.

As early as the 1920s, James Weldon Johnson—author of *Lift Every Voice and Sing* and Executive Secretary of the NAACP—pointed to the success of West Indians in New York City. He noted that they were sober-minded, had a genius for business, and were almost completely different in these respects from the average rural black of the South.[39] Other scholars also noted the economic success of West Indians in the 1960s and 1970s.[40] For example, Nathan Glazer and Patrick Moynihan in their 1963 book, *Beyond the Melting Pot*, noted that "the ethos of West Indians, in contrast to that of the Southern Negro, emphasized savings, hard work, investment, and education."[41] They also pointed out that since West Indian blacks come from countries where they are in the ethnic majority, they see blacks integrated at all levels of the political, economic, and social strata. As a result, West Indians are more confident about their abilities than native blacks. Thomas Sowell noted that in 1968, the median family income of the general black population was only 62 percent of the national average, but for West Indians it was 94 percent.[42] He also pointed out that West Indian blacks have long had higher incomes, higher levels of educational attainment, better occupational status, and were far more likely to own a business than American blacks.

Like Black Multiracials, Black Immigrants tend to grow up in homes with higher levels of parental education and family income than the children of native blacks. In addition, Black Immigrants are also more likely to live in two-parent families than the children of native blacks. These advantages explain part of the reason why Black Immigrants are overrepresented among blacks at selective higher education institutions.

## 1. Black Immigrants Tend to Have Parents with Higher Levels of Academic Attainment

One advantage that the children of foreign-born blacks have over native blacks is having parents with higher levels of education. In 2000, foreign-born African immigrants' average educational attainment level of fourteen years not only exceeded that of both West Indian blacks at 12.6 years and native blacks at 12.4 years, but also of whites and Asians at 13.5 years and 13.9 years, respectively.[43] The children of foreign-born blacks are also more likely to grow up in homes with parents with college degrees than are Ascendant Blacks. As one commentator who studied African immigrants to the United States put it, "education is the cultural capital that most African immigrants bring with them to the United States."[44] The 2000 census revealed that foreign-born blacks from Africa averaged the highest percentage of college graduates of any group in the United States. At that time, the college graduation rate for African immigrants over the age of twenty-five was 43.8 percent, compared to 42.5 percent for Asian Americans, 28.9 percent for immigrants from Europe, Russia, and Canada, 23.1 percent for the United States population as a whole,[45] and 14.3 percent for blacks as a whole.[46] However, from 2000 to 2005, there was a dramatic increase in the number of African-born foreign blacks in the country; over 40 percent of African-born foreign blacks in the United States in 2005 arrived in those previous five years.[47] One of the consequences was that the portion of Africans in the country over the age of twenty-five with college degrees slipped to 38 percent.[48] In contrast at that time, only 20 percent of West Indians and 16 percent of native blacks over the age of twenty-five had a college degree.[49]

The parental education advantage that the children of foreign-born blacks have over those of native blacks for the group who will soon be of college age continues. According to a study by the Migration Policy Institute, for the period of 2005–09, 33 percent of the children of foreign-born blacks under the age of ten had a father with a college degree, compared to only 18 percent of native blacks. For mothers, the respective figures were 26 percent compared to 15 percent.[50]

For a variety of reasons, many of the foreign-born blacks will not find jobs in the United States that are commensurate with their educational achievement and abilities. For example, an immigrant who practiced medicine or law in his or her native country cannot simply start a new practice in the United States without complying with additional educational and/or licensing requirements. In addition, the employment opportunities of foreign-born blacks will also suffer as a result of racism. So even as they earn more than native blacks, they do not earn nearly as much as Asians or whites or as much as their educational credentials would dictate. Nevertheless, these highly educated foreign-born black individuals are still likely to have a better understanding of what it takes to guide and motivate their children to pursue a college education than native blacks with less education. The college educated foreign-born blacks are aware of the importance of a degree and have gone through the process of obtaining one for themselves.

## 2. Black Immigrants Tend to Come from Families with More Income

Another advantage in the pursuit of highly valued educational credentials that the children of foreign-born blacks have over the children of native blacks is greater family income. In 2000, the median household income of foreign-born blacks from the Caribbean was $43,650, and for their African counterparts was $42,900.[51] Both of these figures substantially outpaced that of native blacks at only $33,790.[52] Foreign-born blacks from the Caribbean and Africa were also less likely to be unemployed (7.3 and 8.7 percent, respectively, compared to 11.2 percent) and live below the poverty level (22.1 and 18.8 percent, respectively, compared to 30.4 percent) than native blacks.[53]

## 3. Children of Foreign-Born Blacks Are More Likely to Grow up with Two Parents

The children of foreign-born blacks are also more likely to grow up with both parents than the children of native blacks. In 2004, 68.8 percent of black babies were born to single mothers.[54] One report of foreign-born blacks noted that according to the 2000 census data, only 44 percent of African American children were living with both parents.[55] In contrast, data from the 2000 census showed that 76 percent of African immigrant children (whether born in the United States or abroad) and 65 percent of Caribbean immigrant children were living with both parents.[56] And figures from 2005–09 showed that 71 percent of black children under the age of ten in immigrant families were growing up in households with both parents, in comparison to only 39 percent of native black children.[57]

## II. History of Black Migration Before the Adoption of Affirmative Action Policies

The first act of Congress that allowed the United States to generate immigration records did not become effective until January 1, 1820.[58] This Congressional act required the captain or master of any vessel from a foreign country arriving at a port in the United States, or in any of its territories, to submit a list of passengers to the collector of customs.[59] Between 1820 and 1970, official records show that over forty-five million people voluntarily immigrated to the United States.[60] A number of black West Indians came in two separate waves before the 1960s. However, during this 150-year period, only about 76,000 Africans immigrated to the United States.[61] Prior to the 1970s, the largest numbers of African immigrants came from Egypt and Morocco (ethnically Arab and racially classified as white).[62] Thus, many, if not most, of the Africans who immigrated before 1970 were classified as white.

This part will discuss black migration into the United States from the colonial period until the origin of affirmative action, which roughly coincides with the passage by Congress in 1965 of the Hart-Cellar Act. The first section of this part will discuss that migration before the abolition of slavery. The second section will discuss the immigration of blacks from the end of the Civil War until the implementation of restrictive immigration reforms that culminated with the passage of the Immigration Act of 1924. The third section discusses the period from the impact of those reforms through the 1960s on U.S. immigration, in general, and on black immigration, in particular.

### A. Black Migration Before the Abolition of Slavery

The first blacks to come to the North American mainland with Europeans came with Spanish explorers in the sixteenth century.[63] However, the first blacks did not arrive in English North America until 1619.[64] Even today, the overwhelming majority of blacks to arrive in what is now the United States came because of the Transatlantic Slave Trade, which Congress outlawed as of January 1, 1808.[65]

Historians estimate that Europeans and Americans transported between eleven and twelve million Africans to the New World. So great was the Transatlantic Slave Trade that by 1850, a third of the people of African descent lived outside of the continent.[66] Yet only about half a million disembarked onto the soil of what is now the United States.[67] In contrast, slave transport ships brought an estimated 4.6 million blacks to the West Indies.[68]

During the United States' era of chattel slavery, very few black Africans voluntarily immigrated to this country. Only a small number of black Africans had the capacity to come voluntarily. Those who could would have found America an uninviting destination.[69] For example, Congress's first restrictive immigration measure, the Naturalization Act of 1790, limited citizenship to free white persons.[70] Moreover, at the time of the Constitutional Convention, slave owners held over 92 percent of blacks in the country in bondage.[71] This situation changed little by the eve of the Civil War, with 89 percent of blacks held as slaves and 92 percent of them living in states that legalized slavery.[72] Free blacks also presented special problems in slaveholding states, so Southern legislatures adopted laws to restrict both their numbers and their legal rights. Although slavery did not exist in many of the Northern states during much of the antebellum period, blacks in the North encountered plenty of racist sentiments from whites there. In these states, blacks found themselves locked into the bottom of the racial caste system by custom, if not by explicit law.

Even with minimal voluntary immigration, blacks constituted a significant portion of the population of the United States during the antebellum period. In the first census, conducted in 1790, blacks comprised nearly 20 percent of the 3.9 million Americans.[73] On the eve of the Civil War, the 4.4 million blacks in the country made up 14.1 percent of the United States population.[74]

## B. Black Immigration from the Abolition of Slavery to the Immigration Reforms of the 1920s

After the Civil War, Congress expanded the coverage of the Naturalization Act of 1790 to include those of African nativity or African descent.[75] In addition, Section 1 of the Fourteenth Amendment made anyone born in the United States a citizen of the country and the state in which they resided.[76] This part of the constitutional amendment reversed the holding of the 1857 Supreme Court decision in *Dred Scott*, which concluded that blacks, slave or free, could not be citizens of the United States.[77] However, Congress continued to limit naturalization to only those of either the black or white races.[78]

Coinciding with the end of slavery was increased immigration from the only group of Africans that voluntarily immigrated to the United States in large numbers before the institution of affirmative action programs: the Cape Verdeans.[79] Cape Verde is an archipelago of ten islands off the northwest coast of Africa, near Mauritania and Senegal. The islands were prone to drought and contained little fertile agricultural soil.[80] As a result, when Portuguese sailors arrived in the mid-fifteenth century, the islands were uninhabited. Portugal made Cape Verde an important transportation hub for its Transatlantic Slave Trade. Most of the Portuguese who populated the islands, however, were criminals or political exiles.[81] They soon started to reproduce with slave women and created a unique mixed-race population and culture.

By the late eighteenth or early nineteenth century, the whaling industry began looking for ways to reduce costs. Ship captains started to replace American sailors with more affordable Cape Verdean laborers. Despite poor wages and difficult working conditions, Cape Verdean men jumped at the opportunity to escape the famine, drought, and colonial mismanagement common to the islands. Stops in New Bedford, Massachusetts and Providence, Rhode Island, became settling points for Cape Verdean immigration. Before the beginning of the Civil War, between five hundred and one thousand Cape Verdeans immigrated to the United States.[82] The collapse of the whaling industry, however, made whaling sailors obsolete. The Cape Verdeans in America pooled their resources and converted whaling boats into passenger and cargo ships. These converted ships started to make voyages between New Bedford, Providence, and Cape Verde. Mary Halter found that over 23,000 Cape Verdeans arrived in New Bedford alone between 1860 and 1934.[83] However, after World War I, the Portuguese government issued decrees restricting the movement of men eligible for military service, which included those on Cape Verde. When coupled with the restrictive immigration laws the United States adopted in the early 1920s, immigration from Cape Verde came to a virtual end by the mid 1930s.[84]

Up to the enactment of the Immigration Act of 1924, the United States had allowed unlimited immigration from the Western Hemisphere.[85] The first wave of Caribbean blacks that voluntarily immigrated to the United States, about 85,000, came in the first three decades of the twentieth century.[86] The number of legal entrants increased every year and peaked at over 12,000 in 1924. Although many West Indians emigrated directly from the islands, a number also came to America after working on the Panama Canal.[87]

Black Caribbean immigrants settled mainly in New York and a few other cities, including Miami and Boston. In 1910, New York was primarily a city of foreign-born European immigrants; most native blacks were still living in the South. Thus, the 80,000 native blacks in New York made up only about 2 percent of the population.[88] The 12,000 foreign-born blacks in New York in 1910, increased to 37,000 by 1920 and at the time represented almost a quarter of the blacks in the city at the time.[89] In general, these West Indians came from a highly selective segment of the population, with a large portion of them being professionals. Despite the fact that blacks were less than 3 percent of the New York's population, they confronted a virulent racism.[90] Thus, the Caribbean blacks played a significant role in the intellectual, political, and economic leadership of the Black Community in New York City, including being disproportionately involved in the black radical and black nationalist struggles of the time. The Great Depression, however, virtually stopped this wave of Caribbean immigration.

## C. Restrictive Immigration Reforms and Black Immigration after the 1920s

From 1820 to 1870, about 7,500,000 people arrived in port in the United States, and almost all of them were from northern and western Europe. Twenty percent of them departed from Great Britain.[91] Another third were from Ireland, where many people sought to escape the effects of the potato famine that struck there in the mid-1840s.[92] Another third were Germans, many of whom came to the United States to escape economic hardship; others fled political unrest caused by riots, rebellions, and revolution.[93]

Between 1850 and 1880, approximately 225,000 Chinese immigrated to the United States.[94] This was the first significant wave of Asian immigration.[95] In the spring of 1882, however, Congress passed the Chinese Exclusion Act, placing a ten-year moratorium on Chinese labor and, thereby, restricted Chinese immigration. Congress extended the Act for another ten years in 1892, and made the moratorium permanent in 1902. Congress also added additional registration requirements on the Chinese already in the country.[96] As Chinese immigration fell in the 1890s, Japanese immigration began to increase. Between 1881 and 1890, only about 2,300 people from Japan immigrated into the United States. That number increased to nearly 26,000 between 1891 and 1900, and to nearly 130,000 from 1900 to 1910.[97] The United States reached a sort of gentlemen's agreement with Japan in 1908 that slowed Japanese immigration.[98] In 1917, the United States established an Asiatic barred zone that excluded immigrants from Afghanistan to the Pacific, with the exception of Japan and the Philippines, which was an American territory.[99] However, none of the restrictions on Asian immigrants applied to blacks. This in part derived from the short-lived positive post-Civil War sentiment toward blacks and the relative invisibility of blacks as immigrants.[100]

The massive immigration from southern and eastern Europe after 1880 triggered more discriminatory immigration reforms. Driven by the economic need for labor created by the rapid industrialization of America's urban areas and advances in transportation technology, including developments for oceangoing steam ships, immigration into the United States exploded after 1880. Between 1881 and 1920, almost 23.5 million people poured into the country, over three times the number that came in the fifty years between 1820 and 1870.[101] The majority of these European immigrants came from southern and eastern Europe, as opposed to northern and western Europe, including 4.1 million Italians, 4.1 million Austria-Hungarians, and 3.2 million former Soviets (including the now-independent republics).[102] This flood of immigrants also brought different religious faiths. Between 1900 and 1930, the U.S. Catholic population doubled to 24 million.[103] The Jewish population also skyrocketed from 229,000 in 1887 to over 4.2 million forty years later, increasing the Jewish portion of the American population from 0.5 to 3 percent.[104]

Congress responded to the wave of immigration from southern and eastern Europe by enacting further immigration measures. The Anglo-Teutonic American ruling class feared that immigration from those parts of Europe diluted their "superior" culture.[105] Ellwood P. Cubberley, one of the most influential educators of the early twentieth century, captured the general sentiment of many Americans about these newcomers. He described the southern and eastern European immigrants as "[i]lliterate, docile, lacking in self-reliance and initiative, and not possessing the Anglo-Teutonic conceptions of law, order, and government."[106] Cubberley went on to note that the coming of these immigrants tremendously diluted the national stock and corrupted civic life.[107] Thus, proponents of restrictive immigration measures stressed the racial superiority of Anglo-Saxon and Teutonic people, the inability to assimilate the new foreigners from southern and eastern Europe, and the threats to national unity these new immigrants posed.[108]

In this climate of rising concerns about the quantity and quality of immigrants coming into the nation, in 1921, Congress passed a temporary measure that imposed a limit on annual immigration of 350,000 and quota limits for various countries.[109] The Immigration Act of 1924 superseded the 1921 law and went into effect in 1929. That Act contained a quota system for most countries that limited the number of foreign-born individuals from any given European country to 2 percent of people from that country of origin in the American population, based on the 1890 census counts.[110] The 1890 census counts were used because that census occurred before most of the southern and eastern Europeans had arrived in the country. As a result, 126,000 of the 153,700 immigrants per year who could enter the United States from countries subject to the quota limits[111] were to come from northern and western European countries.[112]

The 1924 Immigration Act also continued the limitations on immigration from Asia that were already in place and virtually eliminated the possibility of immigration of blacks from Africa. At the time, the only independent countries in Africa were Liberia and Ethiopia, with almost no immigrants from these countries in the United States.[113] All the rest of Africa was under European colonial control, and the colonial powers did not grant many Africans European citizenship. However, Congress did provide that one hundred immigrants from each Liberia and Ethiopia could enter the United States per year.[114]

The Immigration Act of 1924 established a nonquota category that applied to immigrants born in independent countries in the western hemisphere, including Canada, the Canal Zone, Cuba, the Dominican Republic, Haiti, Mexico, and Newfoundland.[115] British West Indians were able to enter the United States under the quotas for Great Britain. However, in 1952, the McCarran-Walter Act prohibited colonial subjects from using the quota of the home country. This eliminated the ability of British West Indians to immigrate because they were not coming from independent countries and could no longer come as British subjects. With the passage of this law, the majority of British West Indian migration shifted to Great Britain for a time.[116] Only a small wave of Caribbeans arrived in the United States between 1930 and the early 1960s.[117]

## III. Modern Wave of Black Migration

With the Great Depression, immigration into the United States would probably have fallen anyway in the 1930s; Congressional reforms of the 1920s assured that it would. For forty years after the passage of the Immigration Act of 1924, Congress seldom turned its attention to overseas immigration reform.[118] During this time, the percentage of foreign-born Americans fell to its lowest level on record. In 1970, just over 9.6 million foreign-born people resided in the United States, constituting only 4.7 percent of the population.[119] In contrast, the portion of foreign-born Americans stood at 13.2 percent in 1920[120] and 12.9 percent in 2010.[121]

When it comes to immigration, some factors pull individuals to certain receiving countries, and different factors push them away from sending countries. Countries that receive a lot of immigrants normally have high wages and standards of living, good employment prospects, and favorable immigration legislation. Conversely, unfavorable conditions that push individuals to seek to leave their home countries include government instability, poverty, disease, and war.[122] The first section of this part will discuss international conditions that made immigration to the United States desirable to blacks. The second section will focus on the major changes in American immigration law, starting with the Hart-Cellar Act. The third section will discuss the specific changes in American immigration law that provided for the increase in the number of foreign-born blacks. Some of these changes benefitted West Indians more, while others helped to increase the number of African immigrants.

## A. International Conditions that Contributed to the Modern Wave of Black Immigration into the United States

Globalization is a significant pull factor drawing blacks to the United States from other parts of the world. Globalization has created a complex network of trade, finance, and technology relations that has allowed greater movement of goods and services and of people. The global economy also includes a division of labor among countries, with the Western industrial nations looking to the developing world to supply needed workers and professionals.

In addition to globalization, a number of international developments combined with changes in U.S. immigration laws to create massive waves of voluntary black immigrants. First, although many black migrants might have found European countries, especially the United Kingdom, attractive destinations, restrictions on immigration enacted there in the 1960s and 1970s helped to redirect many of them to the United States. Second, as Caribbean countries gained independence from colonial rule in the 1960s, they also gained control over the ability to determine their countries' emigration policies. This control, coupled with favorable U.S. immigration laws for the Western Hemisphere, sparked the modern wave of black migration from the Caribbean to the United States. Finally, the failure of economic progress to materialize in many of the newly independent nations of Africa, combined with endemic civil wars, poverty, and disease on the African continent, led many there to seek new places to live, including locations in the United States.

### 1. Restrictive Immigration Measures Enacted in Europe, Especially in the United Kingdom

As American immigration policies were starting to liberalize in the 1960s, the United Kingdom and other countries in Western Europe were adopting laws limiting immigration into their countries from much of the world outside of Western Europe, including the Caribbean and Africa. Post-World War II Europe suffered a labor shortage and sought willing immigrants to rebuild war-torn countries. For example, France actively recruited Africans from its former colonies of Senegal, Mali, and Mauritania.[123] Other countries in Western Europe also engaged in large-scale labor recruitment through the 1960s. In addition, as African nations gained their independence from their former European colonial masters, many Africans looked to Europe as an immigration choice, in part because of the cultural and economic ties that remained between the colonizers and their former subjects.[124] However, these pro-immigration policies started to end in the United Kingdom in the 1960s and in other parts of Europe after 1973. For example, France was the largest importer of African immigrants until 1974, when the government banned legal immigration.[125]

Many foreign-born blacks in the United States are English-speaking people from Commonwealth countries. In 2005, the seven leading countries of origin of foreign-born blacks were Jamaica (568,000), Haiti (478,000), Trinidad and Tobago (167,000), Nigeria (160,000), Guyana (128,000), Ethiopia (105,000), and Ghana (75,000).[126] Five of these countries are also members of the British Commonwealth.[127] Many immigrants from these countries saw the United Kingdom as an attractive destination. However, hostility toward immigrants of color in the United Kingdom starting in the late 1950s led to restrictive immigration measures there. These measures helped to redirect many English-speaking would-be black immigrants from the United Kingdom to the United States.

Before the start of World War II, only about 2,000 blacks were living in Great Britain and virtually all of them were in England.[128] The large majority of Britain's cities remained almost entirely white, and half of the United Kingdom's population had never met a black person.[129] Despite all the years when the sun never set on the British Empire, Britain simply had no experience of substantial colonial immigration prior to World War II. People moved from Britain to other places in the Empire, not the other way around. In the late 1940s, only about 20,000 to 30,000 colonials had come to Britain, and most of them were of European descent from Australia, Canada, New Zealand, and South Africa.[130] Britain enacted the British Nationality Act of 1948, which made it clear that all subjects in the British Empire had the right to live and work in Britain without visas. With this Act, Britain opened its borders to 600 million people in the developing world[131] and sparked a wave of immigration.[132] However, nonwhite ethnic groups from the British colonies in the West Indies, Africa, and the Indian subcontinent were not as welcome as their counterparts of European descent from Australia, Canada, and New Zealand. Many whites in Britain saw these colored immigrants as inferior.[133] Although employers reluctantly employed nonwhite immigrant workers, these workers encountered constant prejudice and discrimination.[134]

At this time, the United States may have been the preferred destination for many West Indian immigrants, but the adoption by Congress of the McCarran-Walter Act in 1952 substantially reduced their ability to immigrate here for a time.[135] As a result, more of them went to Britain. The percentage of black and

Asian immigrants in Britain remained small throughout the 1950s, reaching only one-fourth of one percent of the British population in 1960.[136] Even though the British government was concerned about nonwhite immigration during this time, the government did not enact restrictive legislation. This was partly because of the continued labor shortage, partly because Britain wanted to maintain a public image of an open society,[137] and partly because of a romantic attachment to the old Empire that saw all British subjects as having equal rights.[138] Nevertheless, concern about nonwhite immigration continued to increase. Social elites, conservatives, and their followers preached that blacks (the term "black" in Britain would come to include those from the South Asian subcontinent as well)[139] were lazy, quarrelsome, criminal, unskilled, and unenterprising, thus provoking racial prejudice.[140] Large-scale violence directed at immigrants broke out in August of 1958 in Nottingham. The altercation ignited growing tension between the poor indigenous populations of Nottingham and recent immigrants from the Caribbean.[141] It began after a fight outside of a pub when white youth went on what they described as a "nigger-hunt." The crowd was estimated at 1,500 to 4,000 people. A week later, on September 1st, the Caribbean neighborhood of Notting Hill experienced the worst civil unrest of the 1950s.[142] There were also smaller riots in Paddington, Birmingham, and London. The riots were the result of social discontent that many whites blamed on nonwhite immigrants.[143] Since the victims, on the whole, were Afro-Caribbeans, commentators interpreted the riots as evidence that the British had reached their threshold of tolerance and would not accept more nonwhite immigrants. Thus, the riots brought immigration reform to the forefront of political attention.

Politicians publicly began to express concern about nonwhite immigration. Winston Churchill thought that black immigration could produce a "magpie society and that would never do."[144] Other conservative politicians were more explicit in their condemnation of nonwhite immigration. For example, Parliament member Sir Cyril Osborne used explicitly racist rhetoric in the House of Commons on October 29, 1958: "It is time someone spoke out for the white man in this country, and I propose to do so.... I refer to the urgent need for restriction upon immigration into this country, particularly of coloured immigrants."[145]

Until 1962, colonial subjects and UK residents were treated the same for purposes of entering Britain, and colonial subjects were considered by the law to be full British subjects.[146] In 1962, Britain began enacting measures to limit and reduce the number of nonwhite immigrants. Four immigrant control acts gradually reduced the ability of nonwhite colonial subjects to immigrate to Britain. Pass laws and voucher systems were also introduced to restrict immigration of people of color and induce them to repatriate back to their native countries.[147] The first such act was the Importance of the Commonwealth Act in 1962 that ended the unlimited right of any colonial subject to migrate to Britain. The Act also set up a system to limit immigration to those who already secured employment in Britain, possessed special skills that were in short supply, or included in part of a large undifferentiated group whose numbers were determined in accordance with the labor needs of the Britain's economy.[148] The Commonwealth Act, however, failed to stem the tide and led to a boom in applications, with over 319,000 of them in the first sixteen months.[149] The more liberal Labour Party, which had strongly opposed the 1962 Act, afterward endorsed immigration reform.[150] Thus, in response to so many applicants, Britain abolished nonpriority vouchers and limited the job offer and special skill vouchers to 8,500 per year.[151]

Throughout the 1960s, Britain continued to restrict immigration of nonwhites. For example, to limit immigration in response to the Kenyan crisis where that government expelled British subjects from South Asia, Britain adopted the Commonwealth Immigrants Act in 1968. That Act limited those South Asians from Kenya who could immigrate to Britain. To do so such British subjects needed to have substantial connections with Britain by birth or ancestry to a British national for admission, unless they obtained the permission of immigration authorities.[152] It was during this time that Conservative Member of Parliament Enoch Powell delivered his infamous "Rivers of Blood" speech expressing opposition to colored immigration into Britain. In the speech Powell castigated journalists who supported strengthening antidiscrimination legislation before Parliament, which according to Powell blinds the country to the rising peril of nonwhite immigration it confronted. "To enact legislation of this kind is to risk throwing a match onto gunpowder." It would be used to discriminate against the indigenous white British population. Powell advocated voluntary reemigration of the immigrants and compared allowing the inflow of these immigrants to continue to "a nation busily engaged in heaping up its own funeral pyre."[153]

The Immigration Act of 1971 brought permanent migration from the Asian subcontinent, Africa, and the Caribbean to a halt.[154] It ended the right of nonwhite citizens of the Commonwealth to settle in Britain, while strengthening the rights of white settlers in the Commonwealth to do so. Thus, the Act actually increased the number of those who could enter Britain without restriction, but only for those of European descent.[155] An additional factor was the Act's effective date—January 1, 1973, was the same day that Britain entered the European Economic Community (EEC). As a member of the EEC, Britain removed restrictions on entering the country from citizens of the countries in the European Community, including former adversaries like

France, Germany, Italy, and Spain. Also in the 1980s, Britain passed legislation that even prevented the entry of husbands and male fiancés of British citizens, unless they could demonstrate that the primary purpose of their marriage was not for settlement.[156]

## 2. Causes of Caribbean Immigration to the United States

Prior to the passage of the Hart-Cellar Act in 1965, the United States still allowed unlimited immigration for people from independent countries in the Western Hemisphere. However, European countries controlled most of the islands of the West Indies. Since the McCarran-Walter Act prevented colonial subjects from using the quotas of their home countries, legal immigration of blacks from the Caribbean was severely restricted. Nevertheless, the growth of American economic and political power in the twentieth century made it a natural destination for people of the Caribbean.

In the 1960s, many Caribbean countries gained their independence from European powers, starting with Jamaica and Trinidad and Tobago in 1962, and Guyana in 1966. Thus, they were the first Anglophone countries in the Caribbean to gain control of their emigration policies. They could take advantage of American immigration laws that allowed unlimited immigration from independent countries of the Western Hemisphere until it changed because of the Hart-Cellar Act, which went into effect on July 1, 1968. The Hart-Cellar Act also included an annual quota of 120,000 visas for the Western Hemisphere. With independence, these newly created Caribbean nations also could take full advantage of this quota. U.S. immigrants from the above three countries constitute the largest number of foreign-born blacks from Anglophone Caribbean nations living in the United States today.[157]

As noted, Great Britain sought to restrict immigration in the 1960s. Thus, independence, liberal American immigration laws for the Western Hemisphere, and restrictions on immigration in Europe, especially in Great Britain, combined to facilitate an explosion of immigration from the Caribbean to the United States. In the first ten years following the Hart-Cellar reforms, more West Indians immigrated to the United States than in the previous seventy years.[158] And by the early 1980s, about 50,000 legal immigrants arrived each year from Anglophone Caribbean nations and an additional 6,000 to 10,000 from Haiti.[159] In the 1980s, over 200,000 Jamaicans migrated to the United States, which was 9 percent of that country's total population. Guyana also sent a large percentage of its population; by the end of the 1980s, the New York City Department of Urban Planning estimated that about 8 percent of Guyana's population resided in that city alone.[160]

## 3. Causes of African Immigration to the United States

The period following the end of colonial rule in sub-Saharan Africa was a time of great hope and expectation on the continent of Africa.[161] In 1957, Ghana became only the third independent sub-Saharan African nation, but within a dozen years, thirty-five other sub-Saharan African countries gained their independence from European colonial rule.[162]

People in these newly independent nations were not only excited about self-rule, but also hoped and expected improvements in their daily lives, including better access to healthcare, education, and robust economic development. The political rhetoric of nationalist leaders also raised hopes for rapid progress. In many new African nations, political leaders justified single-party rule as a means to provide stable government and implement programs for socioeconomic growth. However, instead of producing stable pro-growth governments, many one-party states fostered corruption by political leaders, nepotism, and the establishment of repressive dictatorial regimes. Thus, significant economic improvement did not materialize after independence in most sub-Saharan African countries.

As the European economies were seeking to limit immigration, the failures of the new African economies were becoming more and more apparent. In addition, the African populations were growing at the rate of about 3 percent a year between 1969 and 1979, but most of their economies were growing at less than 1 percent a year.[163] Economic crises in sub-Saharan Africa increased in the 1980s, along with mounting national debt and falling foreign investments. By the end of the 1980s, many African countries were forced into structural adjustment programs by the International Monetary Fund to try and stabilize their economies. Poverty in these countries remained rampant. Some estimates put as much as two-thirds of Africa's population below the poverty line.[164]

The pressures of rapid population growth, lack of economic development, poverty, disease, and illiteracy also created very dangerous conditions in many African countries, which often produced riots, civil strife, other forms of political violence, and warfare. Armed conflicts have plagued the African continent since World War II. From the end of that war to the late 1990s, there were 130 armed conflicts on the continent, with only three between distinct countries.[165] During the 1980s, for example, two thirds of all war victims were in Africa. One third of all African countries were involved in a military conflict in 1991.[166] By 1994, Africa had surpassed Asia as the region of the world with the most refugees, and eight of the ten countries with the most living refugees were in sub-Saharan Africa in 1995.[167] Although most of these refugees ended up in other African countries, like Côte d'Ivoire, Nigeria, and

South Africa,[168] some of them came into the United States. Thus, many Africans who came to the United States sought to leave their native land to escape government corruption, poverty, disease, unemployment, and armed violence.

## B. Changes in U.S. Immigration Law Starting with the Passage of the Hart-Cellar Act

President John F. Kennedy introduced legislation to change American immigration law.[169] Congress eventually enacted the Hart-Cellar Act in 1965. By terminating the quota system contained in the 1924 Immigration Act, the Hart-Cellar Act reconfigured U.S. immigration policy.[170] The Act shifted immigration policies away from the quota system to emphasizing family reunification and professional qualifications. Visas based on family preferences continue to constitute the majority granted in any given year. The second most popular U.S. visas are employment-based visas,[171] which favor immigrants with desired skills, regardless of their country of origin. Although the Hart-Cellar Act also included a preference for refugees, originally this provision primarily benefitted Southeast Asians, Cubans, and others fleeing Communism.[172]

Other revisions to immigration law adopted by Congress after the Hart-Cellar Act also liberalized immigration policies. For example, the Immigration and Nationality Act Amendments of October 20, 1976, made it easier for foreigners to obtain visas to study, reunite with family, or market their skills in the United States.[173] The Refugee Act of March 17, 1980, changed America's refugee policy to conform to United Nations protocols for refugees. Instead of admitting refugees only from communist countries, America began admitting increasing numbers of refugees created by conflicts other than those related to the Cold War. Congress passed the Immigration Reform and Control Act in 1986,[174] the main purposes of which were to curtail illegal immigration, legalize immigrants already in the country, and impose sanctions on employers who hired undocumented workers.[175] This Act authorized the conferring of initially temporary, then permanent resident alien status on foreigners who had resided in the United States unlawfully before January 1, 1982. The 1990 Immigration Act increased the number of immigrants admitted into the United States for their valued job skills. As part of this Act, Congress also set up the Diversity Visa Program, which went into effect on October 1, 1994,[176] with the goal of providing an avenue for immigration from countries not well represented in the United States. Under the program, 50,000 people from such areas could receive visas each year.[177] To qualify for a diversity visa, a person had to be a citizen from one of the underrepresented countries and in possession of at least a high school diploma.[178]

The above changes in American immigration law combined with various international developments to create the conditions for a dramatic increase in immigration to the United States. Approximately 5 million immigrants flooded into the United States in the 1970s, followed by another 8 million in the 1980s.[179] Estimates put the number of immigrants arriving in the 1990s between 12 and 15 million.[180] According to the 2000 census, there were 31 million foreign-born individuals living in the United States, constituting over 11 percent of the American population.[181] The number of foreign-born people has continued to grow. By 2010, almost 40 million foreign-born individuals were living in the United States and made up 12.9 percent of the total population.[182]

## C. Specific Changes to U.S. Immigration Law that Benefitted Black Immigration

Two waves of West Indians had already come to the United States by 1960. The three Anglophone West Indian nations with the largest number of U.S. immigrants—Jamaica, Trinidad and Tobago, and Guyana—were also the first to gain their independence in the 1960s. These countries were able to take advantage of the nonquota provisions for independent nations of the Western Hemisphere that existed at the time. They were also able to take advantage of the 120,000-visa quota reserved for the Western Hemisphere in the Hart-Cellar Act. Thus, the change in American immigration policies to emphasizing family reunification benefitted the black immigrants from the Caribbean more than it did immigrants from Africa. Those West Indians already here used these changes to bring their relatives. For example, over 80 percent of the foreign-born black immigrants from Haiti and the English-speaking Caribbean countries from 2001 to 2006 came because of family relations, in contrast to just 40 percent of African immigrants.[183]

Congress primarily sought to curtail illegal immigration from Latin America when it included provisions in the Immigration Reform and Control Act passed in 1986 to confer legal status on foreigners unlawfully in the country before January 1, 1982. Nevertheless, the Act also benefitted a number of foreign-born blacks. About 100,000 English-speaking Caribbean residents obtained legal status under the 1986 Act.[184] Even though Africans constituted less than 1 percent of those granted amnesty pursuant to this provision, that still amounted to almost 40,000 individuals.[185]

In contrast to the West Indians (other than the Haitians), a large percentage of African immigrants to the United States came because of expanded refugee policies. In 2007, about a quarter of African immigrants were refugees, in contrast to only 7 percent of all immigrants.[186] According to a 2005 Census Report, the following eleven countries in Africa accounted for 70 percent of the African-born blacks in the United States: Eritrea, Ethiopia, Liberia, Nigeria, Sierra Leone, Somalia, Sudan, Cameroon, Ghana, Kenya, and Guinea.[187] War was an important push factor driving people to leave in the first seven of these countries. Although less than 6 percent of the over 1.7 million refugees admitted to the United States between 1983 and 2000 came from Africa, Africans accounted for over 25 percent of the 321,000 refugees admitted during the years 2001–05.[188] Whereas 29 percent of African immigrants between 2001 and 2006 consisted of refugees or asylum seekers, only about 3 percent of Caribbean immigrants (mostly from Haiti) were refugees or asylum seekers.[189]

African immigrants are also more likely to take advantage of the Diversity Visa Program. As part of the Immigration Act of 1990, Congress also set up the Diversity Visa Program,[190] which emerged from a series of similar, temporary programs that Congress created in the 1980s.[191] Between 1998 and 2006, sub-Saharan Africans received 27 percent of the diversity visas awarded,[192] even though Africans accounted for only 10 percent of all legal immigrants.[193]

## IV. Why Ascendant Blacks Should Receive More Positive Consideration in the Admissions Process of Selective Higher Education Institutions

Since the institution of affirmative action, the number of Black Immigrants enrolled in selective higher education institutions has exploded. This increase also obscures the magnitude of the underrepresentation of Ascendant Blacks at these institutions. In addition, the growing proportions of blacks who are Black Immigrants and who are approaching the age at which most people attend higher education institutions has changed the dynamics of the continued notion of lumping Black Immigrants with Ascendant Blacks. Thus, it is urgent that selective higher education institutions address this new phenomenon. In effect, the new ethnic landscape for blacks has rendered obsolete the current ways of employing race in the admissions process with regard to Black Immigrants and Ascendant Blacks. Now, Black Immigrants are no longer the minor exception to the rule on affirmative action, but the exception that has altered the rule.

Following Justice O'Connor's rationale, there are two reasons that Ascendant Blacks should receive preference over Black Immigrants. First, Ascendant Blacks are far more likely to be underrepresented in many, if not most, of the nation's selective higher education institutions than Black Immigrants. Second, the history of discrimination suffered by blacks in the United States affected the ancestors of Ascendant Blacks, as well as Ascendant Blacks themselves, far more than it did Black Immigrants. As a result, in general, Ascendant Blacks will have far more experiences with both aspects of the history of discrimination suffered by blacks in the United States than Black Immigrants. Therefore, Ascendant Blacks should be preferred over Black Immigrants in the admissions process.

As discussed in detail in Chapter Two, one aspect of the experience of historical discrimination for African Americans is the experience of what it means to be "raced" or branded as inferior.[194] The other aspect is the active engagement in a collective struggle against their racial oppression. The term "Black Immigrants" includes foreign-born blacks who come to the United States as adults (Adult Black Immigrants), foreign-born blacks who immigrated with relatives or guardians as children, and U.S.-born children with at least one foreign-born black parent (the latter two groups will be referred to as Next-Generation Black Immigrants). There are important differences between Adult Black Immigrants and Next-Generation Black Immigrants. Nevertheless, Ascendant Blacks, in general, have far more of the relevant experiences for taking account of race in the admissions process than Black Immigrants. The first section of this part shall discuss the sociocultural differences between Adult Black Immigrants and Ascendant Blacks. For the Next-Generation Black Immigrants who came of age in the United States, their experiences with the history of racial discrimination is likely to be more acute than that of Adult Black Immigrants. However, like Black Multiracials, at least half of their ancestry does not come from the line of blacks who experienced the history of discrimination endured by blacks in the United States. The second section shall focus on the differences between the experiences of Next-Generation Black Immigrants and Ascendant Blacks.

## A. *Sociocultural Differences Between Adult Black Immigrants and Ascendant Blacks*

Foreign-born blacks have their negative experiences with racism in the United States. If any doubt exists, just recall the incidents of Haitian immigrant Abner Louima, who was brutalized and sodomized with a broken broomstick by New York City Police, and Amadou Diallo from Guinea, who the police shot nineteen times because they thought he was reaching for a gun instead of his wallet. However, many foreign-born blacks may assert an ethnic identity in the United States as opposed to a black identity in order to make a case that they are distinct from Ascendant Blacks.[195] In addition, having grown up and matured in their countries of origin, Adult Black Immigrants do not have the same extensive years of experiences with the historical discrimination encountered by Ascendent Blacks in the United States. Even when Adult Black Immigrants encounter or address racism, many of them do not experience the same psychological, sociological, and philosophical reactions to it. This is because they do not come from a line of ancestors that grew up in the United States.[196]

This section shall discuss the sociocultural differences between Adult Black Immigrants and Ascendant Blacks to demonstrate how much more "our Nation's struggle with racial inequality"[197] affects the experiences of Ascendant Blacks when contrasted with Adult Black Immigrants. Adult Black Immigrants encounter conflicting sociological forces in the United States. They come to a land with a long history of voluntary immigration, yet they also come to a place where their race places them at the bottom of a racial hierarchy. As a result, Adult Black Immigrants do not fit within the historic traditions of voluntary immigrants from Europe or within the historic traditions of blacks in the United States. This section will start by discussing the unique sociocultural status of foreign-born blacks in the United States and continue with discussions of several overlapping sociocultural differences between Adult Black Immigrants and Ascendant Blacks. As voluntary immigrants, Adult Black Immigrants tend to have a more optimistic and positive outlook on their conditions in American society than Ascendant Blacks. In addition, because Adult Black Immigrants mature in their home country, they do not bring with them to the United States the oppositional aspect to mainstream American culture that developed in Ascendant Black culture with the history of resistance to racial oppression. Also, most foreign-born blacks come from countries with substantial black majorities, so race does not play nearly as important of a role in their psychological and emotional development as it does for Ascendant Blacks. Coming from countries with substantial black majorities, Adult Black Immigrants are familiar with seeing blacks wield significant economic, political, and educational authority. This may provide them with the empowering expectation that success in society is not tied to race, an idea that Ascendant Blacks with their experience growing up in the United States find much more difficult to embrace. Finally, the reasons that Adult Black Immigrants immigrate to the United States militates against them having experiences rooted in the history of racial discrimination suffered by blacks.

## 1. Adult Black Immigrants Occupy a Unique Sociocultural Status

For most nations of the world, national identity is the product of a long historical process.[198] This process binds a people together through shared experiences, beliefs, and values. The United States, however, is unlike other countries, because almost all Americans are from other parts of the world or are descendants of people from other parts of the world. In the United States, people from different racial, ethnic, and religious groups with traditions of long-standing grievances and animosities towards each other live in relative peace and harmony. The United States has done a better job than any other country at integrating into one society so many disparate racial, ethnic, and religious groups who elsewhere in the world have been enemies. Many commentators have pointed out this American exceptionalism. For example, Margaret Thatcher, the former Prime Minister of the United Kingdom, noted when discussing the United States, "No other nation has so successfully combined people of different races and nations into a single culture."[199]

What makes the United States different from other countries is that it came into existence at a particular moment in time and was the product of a deliberate and conscious act based on explicit political principles. Those principles were first enunciated in the Declaration of Independence:

> We hold these truths to be self-evident, that all men are created equal, that they are endowed by their Creator with certain unalienable rights, that among these are life, liberty and the pursuit of happiness. That to secure these rights, governments are instituted among men, deriving their just powers from the consent of the governed.[200]

These principles are also used to articulate why we adopted our Constitution. As the preamble of the U.S. Constitution states:

> We the People of the United States, in Order to form a more perfect Union, establish Justice, insure domestic Tranquility, provide for the common defence, promote the general Welfare, and secure the Blessings of Liberty to ourselves and our Posterity, do ordain and establish this Constitution for the United States of America.

In expressing these core American values four score and seven years after the founding of the Republic, Abraham Lincoln stated in his Gettysburg Address—perhaps the most famous speech by an American president—that "our fathers brought forth on this continent, a new nation, conceived in Liberty, and dedicated to the proposition that all men are created equal."[201] Thus, from the very beginning, the American identity has centered on adherence to a set of shared political ideals that embrace liberty, equality, democracy, and respect for individual rights.[202] While America has not yet achieved the "perfect union," these ideals are ones that any immigrant can adhere to, regardless of their race, ethnicity, creed, or color.

Recall the massive immigration discussed earlier that occurred between 1880 and 1920. The classic assimilation model used to explain what happens to the descendants of immigrants into the United States over succeeding generations derives from the experiences of those southern and eastern Europeans.[203] Under this theory, first-generation immigrants seldom obtain socioeconomic parity with native-born Americans. They are disadvantaged by a number of factors, including their lack of English proficiency, knowledge about the United States and how its institutions function, and prejudice and hostility from native-born American citizens. Their children, however, are educated and socialized into mainstream American culture. As a result, the second-generation immigrants are more successful than their parents. Succeeding generations of immigrants become more and more acculturated. This continued exposure to American culture leads them to adopt an American identity and lose much of their immigrant cultural heritage. Thus, as Professors Alexander Alienkoff and Rubén Rumbaut point out, the traditional immigrant narrative regarding social incorporation in the United States is also a transition from out-group to in-group through integration and assimilation over time.[204]

In contrast to the voluntary immigrant narrative, blacks in the United States formed their cultural identity within the context of a long historical process that responded to conditions of oppression and exploitation. The greater part of the experience of the Black Community is that of a group whose liberty, equality, freedom, and individual rights were sacrificed on the altar of the American ideals for the benefit of other Americans. As Malcolm X once remarked, "We didn't land on Plymouth Rock..., Plymouth Rock landed on us."[205] This historic experience produced a counterculture among African Americans (discussed at length in Chapter Two) in which the primary goal was not adherence to American ideals, but the liberation of black people in the United States from racial oppression.

For foreign-born blacks, there is another migration narrative. Foreign-born blacks confront two countervailing social forces when they immigrate to the United States.[206] On the one hand, this is a country of voluntary immigrants in whose footsteps they follow and many of whose experiences they share. Yet, because of the negative meanings attached to blackness throughout much of American history, there is a racial hierarchy in the United States with blacks at the bottom. Thus, foreign-born blacks also confront negative social forces that are tied to the perception of their race. Segmented immigration theory, developed by Alejandro Portes and his colleagues,[207] as opposed to the classical immigration theory, asserts that foreign-born blacks and their children benefit more from maintaining their ethnic orientation rather than assimilating to the cultural norms of their native black neighbors.[208] Thus, for white ethnics who failed to progress economically, their ethnic identity was sort of a consolation prize. But, maintaining ethnic identity of both first- and second-generation black immigrants becomes a source of economic and social advancement. Therefore, foreign-born blacks do not fit within the tradition of immigration from European countries. More importantly, however, they do not fit within the tradition of deprivation in the United States that blacks here have historically experienced.

## 2. Foreign-Born Blacks Tend to Have a More Optimistic Outlook

Although West Indians and Africans were also victimized by European colonialism and slavery, their settlement in the United States is in large part the result of voluntary immigration. Nigerian-born and America-educated Professor John Ogbu was the leading proponent of the theory that voluntary immigrants, like foreign-born blacks, develop a very different cultural orientation to their host society than involuntary minorities, like Ascendant Blacks.[209] In his groundbreaking work in educational anthropology, Ogbu studied the cultures and educational performances of minority groups in several countries. He separated minority groups into voluntary immigrants, those who choose to migrate to their new countries, and involuntary minorities, those incorporated into their societies through slavery, conquest, or colonization. Ogbu found that caste-like involuntary minority groups exist all over the world. According to Ogbu, two historical forces help shape the cultures of ethnic minority groups in their dominant host society: their initial terms of incorporation into society and their pattern of adaptive responses to the discriminatory treatment by members of the dominant group after their incorporation.[210]

Voluntary immigrants generally move to their host country hoping for greater economic or educational opportunities or more political or religious freedoms than were available at home. They tend to compare their economic, educational, political, and social conditions in their host country to what they left behind. Generally, this assessment allows them to develop a positive comparative framework for interpreting their experiences and conditions in their host country. Many voluntary immigrants who do not believe they are better off, simply exercise the option of returning to their native land. Thus, the more successful ones are more likely to remain.

In contrast to voluntary immigrants, involuntary minority groups are incorporated into their present society through conquest, slavery, or exploitation.

Without the voluntary aspect of their original incorporation, involuntary minorities differ from voluntary immigrants in their perceptions, interpretations, and responses to their situation in their host society. Unlike voluntary immigrants, involuntary minorities cannot refer to a native homeland to generate a positive comparative framework for their condition. Instead, they compare themselves to the dominant group. Since the dominant group is generally better off, this comparative approach often produces a negative interpretation of their experiences and conditions. Involuntary minorities perceive themselves as victims of institutionalized discrimination perpetuated against them by dominant group members. As a result, involuntary minorities distrust members of the dominant group and the institutions they control.

Both voluntary immigrants and involuntary minorities frequently face prejudice and discrimination in their host society. When confronted with this discrimination, voluntary immigrants tend to interpret the educational, economic, political, and social barriers they face as temporary. They also tend to interpret prejudice and discrimination in their host country as the result of their being foreigners. Voluntary immigrants tend to believe they can overcome these obstacles in time, with hard work and more education. Voluntary immigrants may also view prejudice and discrimination as the price they must pay for the benefits they enjoy. In their cost-benefit analysis, voluntary immigrants weigh the negative consequences of prejudice and discrimination against the positive educational, economic, religious, or social benefits they receive and often conclude that, on balance, they are better off.

Involuntary minorities respond to prejudice and discrimination differently than voluntary immigrants. Involuntary minorities do not have the luxury of being able to understand prejudice or discrimination as a consequence of their temporary status as foreigners. The prejudice and discrimination they experience in society and educational institutions relates to their history as members of a victimized group. Consequently, the experience of prejudice and discrimination is not part of a cost-benefit analysis. Rather, involuntary minorities are more likely to perceive discrimination as adding insult to injury. Thus, as Ogbu notes, voluntary immigrants, like foreign-born blacks in the United States, tend to be more optimistic and positive about their experiences in their host countries than involuntary minority groups, like Ascendant Blacks. A number of other researchers have confirmed Ogbu's assessment about the optimism of foreign-born blacks.[211]

Ogbu found involuntary minority groups throughout the world who continued to suffer from the effects of their initial incorporation into their host societies decades, if not centuries, later. For example, there is an approximately 15-point IQ difference between blacks and whites in the United States.[212] The same 15-point difference shows up in comparisons between a number of involuntary minorities and the dominant group in their host societies, including the Maori of New Zealand, the Burakumin of Japan (a group that is racially indistinguishable from other Japanese but isolated as a disparaged group), the Dalits in India,[213] and Oriental Jews in Israel.[214] This 15-point gap also showed up in comparisons between Protestants and Catholics in Northern Ireland.[215]

Consider the following account by Claude Fischer and his colleagues in the sociology department at the University of California–Berkeley of a particular minority group they studied:

> Members of a minority, many of whom were brought to the country as slave labor, are at the bottom of the social ladder. They do the dirty work, when they have work. The rest of the society considers them violent and stupid and discriminates against them. Over the years, tension between minority and majority has occasionally broken out in deadly riots. In the past, minority children were compelled to go to segregated schools and did poorly academically. Even now, minority children drop out of school relatively early and often get into trouble with the law. Schools with many minority children are seen as problem ridden, so majority parents sometimes move out of the school district or send their children to private schools. And as might be expected, the minority children do worse on standardized tests than majority children.[216]

This may sound like it is describing African Americans in the United States, but the authors are actually discussing the Korean minority in Japan. Japan overran Korea in 1904, annexed it in 1910, and held it until the end of World War II. The Japanese sent a number of Koreans to Japan to provide a supply of cheap labor and relegated those Koreans to the bottom of Japanese society.[217] During the peak of this colonial period, the Korean Community in Japan reached two million people.[218] Although most Koreans returned to their native land after World War II, many stayed in Japan where they continue to occupy a nebulous place in society. Even though Korean descendants continue to struggle in Japanese society, in the United States, where both groups are voluntary immigrants, both groups achieve substantial economic and educational success.

Being voluntary immigrants, foreign-born blacks tend to have a more positive outlook on their experiences in the United States than native blacks. A a result, foreign-born blacks would not experience nearly as much of the historical discrimination that is the result of being branded as inferior as native blacks would experience. In addition, without the experience of being subjugated because of race, Adult Black Immigrants are also less likely than Ascendant Blacks to comprehend the need to engage in activities to eradicate the continuing effects of racism on blacks in the United States.

## 3. Foreign-Born Blacks Have a Less Oppositional Culture than Native-Born Blacks

The differences between the culture created by Ascendant Blacks and mainstream U.S. culture arose after the forcible incorporation of Ascendant Blacks into American society.[219] To live with racial subordination, blacks developed a different outlook that attenuated the negative effects of mainstream culture. Thus, as demonstrated in Chapter Two, there is a certain amount of oppositional character between the culture of Ascendant Blacks and mainstream American culture. As Molefi Asante put it,

> The central fact of black history in United States is slavery and antislavery, which stands astride every meaningful rhetorical pathway like a giant elephant.... However, it is not only physical slavery that dominates the history of the United States but the exploitation of the African through ideological impositions. Europe is insulated into every aspect of black existence, even the sacred process of naming. Black discourse, therefore, to be healthy discourse, is resistance.[220]

As with other voluntary immigrants, the goal of finding a better life is, generally, what brought Adult Black Immigrants to the United States in the first place. When they arrive in the United States, they arrive with their own sense of culture developed in their countries of origin. Thus, they come with reference points, a sense of connectedness, and a feeling of belonging that derives from their homeland. The cultures of Adult Black Immigrants in their native countries did not evolve in response to the racial discrimination experienced in America. In addition, Adult Black Immigrants were not exposed to the demeaning racialized experiences that native blacks have experienced throughout U.S. history, so they enter this country devoid of the animus toward the majority culture and the oppositional aspect of the black experience in the United States. As a result, cultural and language differences between Adult Black Immigrants and the dominant American culture are not oppositional. Not being oppositional, the indigenous cultures that Adult Black Immigrants bring with them do not reflect the aspect of the historical experience of being black that is a product of the subjugation of black people in the United States, nor the active engagement in a collective struggle against white supremacy.

In addition, as Professor Kenneth Karst noted, the oppositional nature in the United States worked both ways.[221] Many in American society may see some foreign-born blacks, particularly Adult Black Immigrants, as belonging to a separate group than Ascendant Blacks.[222] To these individuals in American society, foreign-born blacks may seem more polite, less hostile, more solicitous, and easier to get along with than Ascendant Blacks. A growing number of studies have shown that employers prefer hiring immigrants, including black ones, over native blacks.[223] Thus, foreign-born blacks may often experience what it is to be a "model minority." The result is that these foreign-born blacks are experiencing less of the effect of the history of racial oppression of blacks in the United States than Ascendant Blacks.

## 4. Race Is Not as Salient a Feature of the Experience of Foreign-Born Blacks as It Is for Native-Born Blacks

The historic bipolar racial distinctions of white and black that developed in the United States do not neatly apply in Caribbean countries. English-speaking blacks from the Caribbean are coming from countries with long histories where the overwhelming majority of people are of African descent. If we apply the historic bipolar racial distinction developed in the United States to determine race, the overwhelming majority of Adult Black Immigrants come from countries where they are by far the largest racial group. For example, the British had several colonies in the Caribbean during the time of the Transatlantic Slave Trade. Trinidad was the only one of the British Caribbean colonies where fewer than 80 percent of its population was enslaved.[224] In Jamaica, by 1739, blacks outnumbered whites ten to one. Haiti gained its independence from France in 1804 and has been a predominantly black independent nation for over two centuries. Even today, people of African ancestry are the overwhelming majorities in Caribbean countries, with the exception of Trinidad and Guyana, where the East Indians make up 40 and 50 percent of the population, respectively. As for Africa, Nigeria has the smallest percentage of black people among the sub-Saharan countries: blacks constitute 64 percent of the population, with another 35 percent classified as colored.[225]

Race is more of a continuum in Caribbean countries, where factors other than color and physical characteristics, such as class, are considered.[226] Different islands, and even different parts of various islands, developed their own unique ways of determining racial differences. Thus, many people who would be labeled black in the United States would not be so labeled in their Caribbean societies.

Because the overwhelming majority of Adult Black Immigrants come from countries with populations that are predominately of people of color, race does not operate as an important characteristic that divides people in their native societies. Foreign-born blacks from Africa, for example, define themselves primarily in relation to their ethnic or kinship group, not their race.[227] Race, therefore, is not as important a factor in the lives of Adult Black Immigrants before immigrating to the United States as it is for blacks born in the United States. This means that Adult Black Immigrants are much less likely than Ascendant Blacks to identify themselves in terms of their race.[228] One person aptly stated the experience of many foreign-born blacks coming to America: "It was not a matter of color in the Caribbean; it was a matter of the have and have-nots. You came here; it was definitely a matter of black and white. We really haven't been discriminated against in Jamaica."[229]

In addition, as Ogbu asserted, many Adult Black Immigrants may attribute the discrimination that they experience once they arrive in the United States as stemming from their status as an immigrant, rather than their race. In her noteworthy study on Caribbean immigrant culture, Mary C. Waters found that "the movement to the United States makes [West Indian immigrant] reactions to discrimination and prejudice more likely to resemble those of other voluntary immigrants than to those of black Americans."[230]

To experience what it means to be branded as inferior because of one's race requires that you identify yourself in racial terms. In addition, to experience what it is to be involved in the active engagement in a collective struggle against white supremacy and racial subjugation also requires identifying oneself with being black. Thus, to the extent that Adult Black Immigrants do not identify themselves primarily in racial terms, they do not experience either aspect of the historical experience of blacks in the United States.

## 5. Foreign-Born Blacks are Used to Seeing Blacks Occupy All Positions in the Socioeconomic Order

Haiti won its independence from France over 200 years ago, but many of the English-speaking Caribbean countries from which the largest numbers of foreign-born blacks emigrated gained their independence during the 1960s.[231] Over the past forty to fifty years, blacks have also controlled most of the governments of sub-Saharan African countries. To the extent that people in these countries still suffer from exploitation, for some time it has been as the hands of other blacks or at the hands of black-run Western institutions like multinational corporations. Thus, the visible oppressors of black people in majority-black foreign countries are almost all black themselves.[232] Since black people have mediated and exercised power in these countries for two generations, in modern Caribbean and African societies, socioeconomic hierarchy is divorced from race. There are plenty of black role models of social achievement, which can provide foreign-born blacks with a greater sense of motivation to aspire to positions of prestige in society,[233] or at least, less of a sense that when one aspires to such a position, one will stand out because of their race. Associating powerlessness with black skin, therefore, is not part of the cultural experience of Adult Black Immigrants. Thus, while blacks who are successful in the United States may encounter alienation from other blacks, in the countries where the overwhelming majority of black immigrants came from success does not challenge racial identity.[234]

The historical experience of blacks in America is very different from that of foreign-born blacks in their native countries. Both aspects of the historical black experience in the United States are based upon the recognition that black people are not the primary ones that mediate and exercise power. To the extent that Adult Black Immigrants do not associate powerlessness or struggle against oppression with black skin, they do not share in the experience of the history of racial oppression of blacks in the United States.

## 6. The Reasons Foreign-Born Blacks Come to the United States Militates against Experiences Related to the History of Discrimination

Adult Black Immigrants come to America for the same reasons that other immigrants come to America. These reasons reflect a desire to improve their social, economic, political, or educational standing. "They wanted to make a better life for themselves, and they realized they could make more money in the United States or receive a more valuable education than they could back home."[235] Ronald Takaki has argued that the immigrants who arrive in a new country are self-sorting populations who have more resources geared toward success than the ones who stayed behind.[236] For example, those coming to the United States must be able to make the expensive trip, so they are already in a better economic position to take advantage of opportunities that exist here than the ones who remained at home. This selective migration theory asserts that immigrants are different from those who do not make the sacrifice necessary to leave their familiar environment in search of a better life in a new country.

For the immigrant, the decision to move to the United States comes at a high personal cost. What justifies this sacrifice by Adult Black Immigrants is success in obtaining social, economic, political, or educational advancements. This provides them with a powerful motive to make the decision pay off. One researcher who studied African immigrants, for example, found that African immigrants tend to participate only selectively in American society and do not intend to assimilate into it.

The African immigrant is a sojourner and stranger in America and often does not aspire to naturalize or assimilate. Becoming culturally and economically integrated is not a major goal. Most African immigrants have one goal in mind, and this they pursue with relentless vigor—the goal of achieving economic independence and self-sufficiency and funneling their assets to Africa to start a business or retire.[237]

Adult Black Immigrants, understandably, may also be motivated to immigrate in order to assist their relatives and other people they care about in their countries of origin. There is ample proof of this concern on the part of foreign-born blacks. Remittances received by relatives and friends from natives living abroad are a major source of income for many developing nations in Africa and the Caribbean.[238]

The motives of Adult Black Immigrants for coming to the United States suggest that they are often less likely to concern themselves with engaging in a collective struggle to overcome the racial oppression of American blacks. Even if they experience discrimination because of their race, they are likely to view that as part of the cost of pursuing the goals that brought them to America as opposed to seeing it as a reason to engage in a collective struggle against it. Thus, Adult Black Immigrants are far less likely to spend as much of their time engaged in the collective struggle against racial oppression in the United States than Ascendant Blacks who do not share these motives.

## B. Differences between Next-Generation Black Immigrants and Ascendant Blacks

The term "Black Immigrants" includes Adult Black Immigrants and Next-Generation Black Immigrants, and there are many differences between the two.[239] Because Next-Generation Black Immigrants come of age in the United States, they are less likely to return to their family's country of origin if they do not achieve socioeconomic success. In addition, Next-Generation Black Immigrants may have a harder time developing an optimistic outlook on their socioeconomic condition in the United States because they may not necessarily compare their success here to the conditions that exist in their parent's country of origin. While growing up in the United States, Next-Generation Black Immigrants are exposed to more of the oppositional culture of Ascendant Blacks than their parents. Next-Generation Black Immigrants have less of the experience of growing up in a more favorable racial climate than their foreign-born parents, so they are less likely than their parents to see blacks occupying all positions in the socioeconomic order and more likely to come to understand and appreciate that in the United States, black skin is associated with a lack of power and access. Next-Generation Black Immigrants are not self-selected immigrants who chose to come to the United States, so they may not possess the same motivation to succeed that the Adult Black Immigrant generation possessed. It may also be harder for Next-Generation Black Immigrants to distinguish themselves from Ascendant Blacks, especially if they are from the Caribbean and have English surnames, because they are less likely to have a foreign-sounding accent.

Ethnic identities for the Next-Generation Black Immigrants are often situational, fluid, and contextual, but Mary Waters has described three ideal ethnic identities taken by the children of foreign-born West Indian blacks.[240] Some will assert a strong ethnic identity that involves distancing themselves from native black Americans. Others will stress their national origins and their parents' experience in their home country, without the need to distance themselves. Still others will adopt an ethnic identity that identifies with that of native black Americans. Thus, like Black Multiracials, Next-Generation Black Immigrants show some flexibility in choosing their ethnic identities to fit the occasion.

For Next-Generation Black Immigrants, their foreign-born parent(s) and their foreign heritage are likely to have a very important impact on their experiences of race in the United States. As Professor Leonard Baynes (now Dean of the University of Houston Law Center), the son of two West Indian parents who was born and raised in the United States, noted,

> Since I grew up in this culture, I do not speak with an accent, and most people do not know that I am of Caribbean ancestry unless I tell them. However, at times, culturally I do not feel American. This should be no surprise since I am a child of immigrants. Like many other people whose parents may have emigrated here from other countries, I feel that I sometimes straddle the cultures of my parents and that of their adopted home.[241]

Scholars still debate the final stage of assimilation of white ethnics into American society, but the classic assimilation model has long supported the notion that higher social and economic status is attached to becoming more American.[242] Yet the assimilation of foreign-born blacks would imply becoming more like native blacks, a group stigmatized and victimized by oppression in the United States for centuries. Segmented assimilation literature discusses how immigrants attempt to shield their children from the negative Americanizing influences of disadvantaged minority youth.[243] The parents believe that growing up in the midst of poor native blacks puts their children at risk of being negatively influenced by the oppositional outlook that exists among native blacks. Thus, foreign-born black parents may attempt to foster a separate ethnic identity in their children from that of Ascendant Blacks. One study of blacks at selective colleges and universities confirms this possibility. It revealed that Black Immigrants were considerably less likely to self-identify as black or African American than native blacks.[244] In Mary Waters' study of West Indian immigrants, she found that middle-class families and the institutions that supported them worked to maintain a distinct West Indian identity, with sharp cultural boundaries around their group.[245] Middle-class, second-generation West Indians assert their separate cultural identities from African Americans in order to claim the benefits of being a "model minority."[246] However, young Caribbean blacks who identify with native blacks tended to do so by adopting "oppositional" cultural norms.[247] They also tended to see fewer rewards for their efforts and, like native blacks, focused more on the impact of racial discrimination that limited their opportunities.[248] So it stands to reason that the Next-Generation Black Immigrants who identify the most with Ascendant Blacks may be less likely to be admitted into selective higher education programs than the ones who do not.

A major aspect of the psychology of second-generation children of immigrants is the perception that one of the main reasons their parent(s) immigrated was to improve their children's future. So although Next-Generation Black Immigrants may lack the motive to succeed that their parents possessed, understanding the sacrifices of their parents on their behalf may provide them with a different powerful reason to succeed.[249]

Even though Next-Generation Black Immigrants have had very different experiences with race in the United States than their foreign-born parents, some evidence suggests that second-generation Black Immigrants are even more successful than their parents. Thomas Sowell pointed out as early as 1970 that second-generation West Indians in New York City exceeded the socioeconomic status not only of other West Indians, but also of the U.S. population as a whole in terms of family income, education, and proportion in the professions.[250] Researchers Xue Lan Rong and Frank Brown have found that second-generation black immigrants obtain higher levels of education than their foreign-born parents.[251] Using data from the 1990 census, Matthis Kalmijn found that English-speaking Caribbean immigrant men fared better economically and in terms of social occupation than African American men; furthermore, the second-generation, English-speaking Caribbean men did even better than the immigrating generation of Caribbean men.[252] Census Bureau data from 2009 also showed that, of foreign-born blacks between the ages of twenty-five and thirty-four, 30 percent have a bachelor's degree or higher; in comparison, it was 42 percent for second-generation blacks, but only 18 percent for the third or later generations.[253]

Historically, as succeeding generations of foreign-born blacks were born and raised in the United States, the head start that the immigrating and second generations possessed appeared to be lost by the third generation.[254] However, we must place the evidence about this loss in its proper historical context. As noted earlier, only 125,000 foreign-born blacks were recorded in the 1960 census,[255] so the prior third-generation descendants of foreign-born blacks were unable to benefit from the increasing numbers of foreign-born blacks coming to the United States since the 1960s. For example, Jamaicans came to the United States in three distinct waves. As of 2004, over 571,000 have come in this current third wave, far more than in the first two waves combined.[256] The greater numbers of foreign-born blacks in the United States today may influence these historic trends. So many more Black Immigrants should make Americans more sensitive to ethnic distinctions within the Black Community. It also means that third-generation Black immigrants are more and more likely to grow up alongside others from their countries of origin, which will thereby help them to maintain their ethnic identity. In addition, the astonishing advancements in communications technology over the past fifty years will enable the Black Immigrants in America to remain connected to events and in contact with families and friends in their countries of origin. The Internet provides a constant source of news that can keep Black Immigrants up to date about developing conditions in their countries of origin. With access to broadband computer services, email, Internet telephone services, and even video communication services, Black Immigrants can remain routinely in touch with families and friends that are thousands of miles away at very little cost. These technological changes provide Black Immigrants and their third-generation descendants with far greater ability to remain connected to their families and cultural heritage than prior generations.[257]

Although Next-Generation Black Immigrants' experience of the history of racial discrimination is likely to be more acute than that of Adult Black Immigrants, it is not as acute as that of Ascendant Blacks. The distinction between Ascendant Blacks and Next-Generation Black Immigrants is the distinction between those with two native-born black parents and those with at least one foreign-born black parent. By definition, the ancestries of both parents of Ascendant Blacks suffered through the American history of segregation and, probably, slavery as well. Ascendant Blacks have a far greater ancestral connection to the history of discrimination in the United States than Next-Generation Black Immigrants. Thus, many Black Immigrants are less likely than Ascendant Blacks to offer the unique contributions to the character of education sought by selective higher education institutions when they seek to enroll a critical mass of students from groups historically oppressed in the United States.

## Conclusion

This chapter explored the differences between Black Immigrants and Ascendant Blacks that justify a preference for Ascendant Blacks in the admissions process of selective higher education programs. There are two reasons why selective higher education programs should prefer Ascendant Blacks to Black Immigrants in their admissions process. Available evidence about the ethnic characteristics of blacks enrolled in selective higher education programs suggests that Ascendant Blacks are far more likely to be underrepresented in the student bodies of these institutions than Black Immigrants. In addition, simply put, Black Immigrants do not have as great a connection as Ascendant Blacks to the history of discrimination against blacks in the United States. Therefore, Ascendant Blacks have far more experiences and are more likely to identify with that history. It is not that the experiences of Black Immigrants should not be valued in their own regard. Rather, admissions committees should not value their experiences as members of "underrepresented minorities with a history of discrimination" to the same extent that such experiences are valued for Ascendant Blacks.

# Chapter Five

# Proposal for Changes in the Admissions Process

The primary concern of this Proposal is not that Black Multiracials and Black Immigrants receive positive consideration for their racial/ethnic ancestry in the admissions process. Nor is the primary worry that Black Multiracials or Black Immigrants are somewhat overrepresented among black students who attend selective higher education programs. This Proposal is motivated by the substantial reduction of Ascendant Blacks attending the nation's selective higher education programs. Thus, the goals of this Proposal are twofold. This Proposal is intended to provide selective higher education programs with a greater probability of including a "substantial presence" of Ascendant Blacks in their student bodies. In addition, this Proposal will also increase the chances that the student bodies of these educational institutions include a critical mass of individuals with some black ancestry who have sufficient experiences of the history of racial oppression of blacks in the United States to allow them to influence the education of all students. Without achieving the second goal, selective higher education programs may not achieve the benefits of diversity on their college campuses articulated by the U.S. Supreme Court in *Grutter v. Bollinger*.

Under the Final Guidance, educational institutions must include in their counts of Hispanics/Latinos that they report to the DOE, those who answer "yes" to the Hispanic/Latino question, even if they indicate Black/African American as one of their racial categories (Black Hispanics). They must also include in their counts of those in the Two or More Races categories, the non-Hispanics/Latinos who indicate that they are Black/African American and at least one other racial category (Blacks with Two or More Races). Throughout this book, the term "Black Multiracial" has referred to blacks who have a nonblack parent, so the term includes both Black Hispanic and Blacks with Two or More Races. This Proposal takes into account both the unfolding impact of the Final Guidance and the changing racial and ethnic ancestry of blacks benefitting from affirmative action. Thus, for the purpose of discussing the Proposal, it is necessary to maintain the separation of Black Multiracials into Black Hispanic and Blacks with Two or More Races.

The Final Guidance has rejected the view of treating all blacks alike. It, effectively, divides those with some black ancestry into three categories: Black/African American, Black Hispanics, and Blacks with Two or More Races. Thus, the Final Guidance allows admissions officials to separate out Black Multiracial applicants from Black/African Americans. However, it does not allow educational institutions to separate those in the Black/African American category into Black Immigrants and Ascendant Blacks. Part I of this chapter will discuss two changes to the admissions forms of selective higher education institutions. First, selective higher education programs need to change their forms in order to disaggregate those who are lumped in their Black/African American category into Ascendant Blacks and Black Immigrants. They also need to provide individuals who indicate that they have some black ancestry with the opportunity to submit a supplemental statement discussing their experiences with both aspects of the historical experiences of blacks in the United States.

Another important distinction to note is that the DOE requires educational institutions to determine race and ethnicity based on self-identification. Yet, in this book the terms "Ascendant Black," "Black Immigrant," and "Black Multiracial" are based upon parentage, not self-identification. Thus, in determining whether applicants with some black ancestry are Black Hispanics, Blacks with Two or More Races, Black Immigrants, or Ascendant Blacks, admissions officials should take account of more than just the boxes an applicant checks. They should consider all of the application materials provided for a given applicant.

Part II of this chapter will lay out an approach to determine which applicants who check the Black/African American category should receive positive consideration due to their racial/ethnic heritage and how much they should receive. The approach rejects the current biological method based on applicant box checking; rather, it is a hybrid approach that takes into account both the racial/ethnic ancestry of applicants with some African ancestry and their experiences with both aspects of the historical experience of blacks in the United States. Selective higher education programs should seek to include a substantial presence of Ascendant Blacks in their student bodies and a critical mass of individuals with some black ancestry who have sufficient experiences of both aspects of the history of discrimination suffered by blacks in the United States. I recognize that the terms "substantial presence" and "sufficient experience" are vague. The Supreme Court, however, has emphatically rejected quotas, so it is inadvisable to assign a percentage to the concept of substantial presence. The important thrust of this book is to sensitize readers about the need to abandon the concept of treating all blacks alike for admissions purposes, because doing so obscures the declining proportions of Ascendant Blacks who are actually in their student bodies. Thus, the term substantial presence should be understood in light of the need to ensure that there are enough Ascendant Blacks so that the student body can appreciate their experiences. With regard to determining which applicants with some black ancestry have had sufficient experiences of the history of racial oppression of blacks in the US, admissions officials should seek to ensure that these are individuals who have had enough experiences that they are knowledgeable about and have a substantial appreciation of the history of racial oppression that blacks have encountered in the US.

This proposal will have different impacts on the admissions prospects of Black Hispanics, Blacks with Two or More Races, Black Immigrants, and Ascendant Blacks. Part III addresses the impact of the Proposal on these various groups of blacks.

# I. Changes to Admissions Forms

The Proposal calls for changes to the admissions process that involves modifying the admissions forms of selective higher education institutions. Two changes are recommended. By following the requirements for gathering racial/ethnic data laid out in the Final Guidance, selective higher education institutions will lump Black Immigrants with Ascendant Blacks in the Black/African American category. Thus, the first recommendation is that these institutions should alter their application forms so that they can distinguish Black Immigrants from Ascendant Blacks. The second recommendation is that they alter the application forms to provide those who indicate Black/African American as one of their racial categories with the option of submitting a supplemental statement that discusses their experiences with both aspects of the black historical experience with discrimination.

The Final Guidance requires all educational institutions to allow students to address whether they are Hispanic/Latino and to check any of the five different racial boxes that apply. Looking at the way the Hispanic/Latino ethnic question and the racial question are written on the Common Application and the Universal College Application forms provide good examples of how selective colleges and universities have changed their admissions forms to comply with this requirement of the Final Guidance. The Common Application form is being used by 500 American colleges and universities in forty-seven states and the District of Columbia.[1] For 2012/13, over 720,000 applicants filled out this form.[2] The Universal College Application form is accepted by forty-three institutions.[3]

The Common Application form for 2013/14 made significant changes to how racial and ethnic information has handled from the prior year. Under this revised form, respondents are asked the following ethnicity question: "Are you Hispanic/Latino? __ Yes, __ No."[4] If the applicant checks yes, then they are asked: "Which best describes your background?

|                 |     |
|-----------------|-----|
| Central America | ___ |
| Cuba            | ___ |
| Mexico          | ___ |
| Puerto Rico     | ___ |
| South America   | ___ |
| Spain           | ___ |
| Other           | ___ |

The racial identification question is as follows:

"Regardless of your answer to the prior question, please indicate how you identify yourself. (Select one or more.)

_____ American Indian or Alaska Native (Which best describes your American Indian or Alaskan Native background?

|                                                 |     |
|-------------------------------------------------|-----|
| Alaska Native                                   | ___ |
| Chippewa                                        | ___ |
| Choctaw                                         | ___ |
| Cherokee                                        | ___ |
| Navajo                                          | ___ |
| Sioux                                           | ___ |
| Other (Specify other American Indian or Alaskan Native background)) | _____ |

Are you Enrolled? __ Yes __ No
Tribal Enrollment Number_____

_____ Asian (Which best describes your Asian background?

|             |     |
|-------------|-----|
| China       | ___ |
| India       | ___ |
| Japan       | ___ |
| Korea       | ___ |
| Pakistan    | ___ |
| Philippines | ___ |

|  |  |
|---|---|
| Vietnam | \_\_\_ |
| Other East Asia | \_\_\_ |
| Other South Asia | \_\_\_ |
| Other Southeast Asia) | \_\_\_ |

\_\_\_\_\_ Black or African American (Which best describes your Black or African American background?

|  |  |
|---|---|
| U.S./African American | \_\_\_ |
| Africa | \_\_\_ |
| Caribbean | \_\_\_ |
| Other (Specify other Black or African American background) _____) | |

\_\_\_\_\_ Native Hawaiian or Other Pacific Islander (Which best describes your Native Hawaiian or Other Pacific Islander background?

|  |  |
|---|---|
| Guam | \_\_\_ |
| Hawaii | \_\_\_ |
| Samoa | \_\_\_ |
| Other Pacific Islands (excluding Philippines) \_\_\_\_\_ | |
| Other (Specify other Native Hawaiian or Other Pacific Islander background) _____) | |

\_\_\_\_\_ White (Which best describes your White background?

|  |  |
|---|---|
| Europe | \_\_\_ |
| Middle East | \_\_\_ |
| Other (Specify other White background) _____)"[5] | |

Thus, given the way the Common Application form was modified for the 2013/14 academic year, selective higher education institutions that use this form can already separate those in the Black or African American category into Black Immigrants and Ascendant Blacks. Therefore, they do not need to modify their applications to be able to make these distinctions among their black applicants.

On the Universal College Application form for the 2013/14 academic year, respondents are asked the following ethnicity question: "Are you Hispanic or Latino? \_\_ Yes \_\_ No (country of family's origin _____)."[6] The racial identification question follows:

How would you describe your racial background? (select one or more of the following categories):

\_\_\_\_\_ Asian (country of family's origin _____)
\_\_\_\_\_ Native Hawaiian or Other Pacific Islander
\_\_\_\_\_ Black or African American
\_\_\_\_\_ White
\_\_\_\_\_ American Indian or Alaska Native (enrolled _____)
(Tribal affiliation _____)[7]

While the Universal College Application form was modified to comply with the Final Guidance, the modifications do not allow selective higher education institutions that use it to distinguish Black Immigrants from Black/African American. However, the Final Guidance allows educational institutions to collect additional information regarding ethnic subcategories for each of the racial categories, including Black/African American, for their own purposes as long as they can aggregate that information back into the required reporting racial category.[8] Thus, those selective higher education programs that use the Universal Common Application form should seek to have it modified so that they can separate Ascendant Blacks from Black Immigrants. The Universal Application form should be modified for the Black or African American category to look something like following:

"Black or African American (country or countries of family's origin _____)"

For those selective higher education institutions that use their own application forms or other standardized application forms, they should make certain that their forms allow them to distinguish Black Immigrants from Ascendant Blacks. They could follow the comprehensive approach to questions about race and ethnicity used by the Common Application form. Alternatively, they could use the less detailed approach I suggested for the Universal College Application form, with appropriate modifications for ethnic subcategories of those checking Black/African Americans discussed above.

The second change for the admissions form relates to allowing applicants who check the Black/African American racial box with the opportunity to add a supplemental statement that addresses their experiences with both aspects of the history of discrimination in the United States. The directions for the supplemental statement should stress the need for applicants to discuss both how they have experienced such discrimination and how they have fought against racial oppression in the United States. The question on the application form could read something like this:

**For those who have indicated Black/African American:** We believe that it is important to include in our student body meaningful numbers of blacks who have had substantial experiences derived from the historic experience of the Black Community in the United States with race discrimination and the struggle by blacks seeking to attenuate the effects of that history of discrimination. Thus, we invite you, at your option, to submit a supplemental statement that discusses both your experiences of being negatively impacted by the legacy of discrimination in the United States suffered by blacks and your efforts to assist our society in overcoming that legacy. Among the experiences that are relevant would be your participation in activities or organizations dedicated to attenuation of the continuing effects of history of discrimination in the United States, experiences in your life where race made a huge difference, and experiences that you have had with individuals you met because of race.

## II. The Proposal's Hybrid Approach to Positive Consideration in the Admissions Process

After changing their admissions forms, selective higher education institutions should alter how they determine positive consideration during their admissions process for those who check the Black/African American category. Before the Final Guidance, selective higher education programs generally did not distinguish among black applicants; they normally employed a purely biological approach to awarding positive consideration in the admissions process based on the applicant's self-selection of the black racial box. This Proposal rejects the purely biological approach for several reasons. First, the Final Guidance effectively creates three categories for those with some black ancestry: Black/African American, Black Hispanic, and Blacks with Two or More Races. As a result, the Final Guidance required admissions officials to reevaluate the concept of treating all blacks alike for admissions purposes. Second, relying purely on box-checking self-identification to determine race/ethnic identification and the experiences an applicant has with both aspects of the history of racial discrimination suffered by blacks is simply inadequate. Normally, the appropriate way to determine a person's race/ethnicity is by self-identification. The problem with self-identification in the context of applying to selective higher education institutions, however, is the possibility that individuals will choose the box for their racial identification primarily for the strategic purpose of improving their admissions prospects. Thus, those with black ancestry who truly identify themselves as multiracial, Hispanic/Latino, or as an immigrant may decide to select only the Black/African American racial box because it is likely to improve their chances for admissions. Third, a simple box-checking, biological approach tells admissions officials little about the experiences an applicant with some black ancestry has had with racial discrimination in the United States.

Since the concern that this Proposal seeks to address is the virtual ethnic cleansing of Ascendant Blacks from the campuses of selective higher education institutions, it is not necessary to assert that positive consideration in the admissions process should be limited to Ascendant Blacks. To do so would also ignore the tremendous contributions of those blacks with mixed heritage or of foreign-born blacks and their children over the centuries to the collective struggle against racial oppression of blacks in the United States.

This Proposal suggests a hybrid approach to the determination of how much positive consideration an applicant with African ancestry should receive in the admissions process. In determining that amount, selective higher education admissions officials should take account both of the racial/ethnic ancestry of blacks and of their experiences of both aspects of the historical experience of discrimination of blacks in the United States. Admissions officials should give positive consideration to Ascendant Blacks as part of the holistic evaluation of their applications because of the ancestral connection that Ascendant Blacks have to the historical struggle against racial oppression in the United States. They are the racial/ethnic group of blacks most affected by that history. In addition, it is the ascendancy of this group of blacks out of slavery and segregation that made possible not only affirmative action, but also the dramatic increases in interracial cohabitation, mixed-race blacks, the immigration of foreign-born blacks into the United States, and Black Immigrants over the past fifty years. Thus, Ascendant Blacks have the strongest connection to the history of discrimination suffered by blacks.

Any applicant with some black ancestry should also receive positive consideration in the admissions process based on his or her supplemental statement. The more significant and impactful the applicant's experiences with both aspects of the history of discrimination in the United States, as revealed on his or her supplemental statement and other aspects of the application, including their extracurricular activities, the more positive consideration the applicant should receive. Ascendant Blacks who submit a supplemental statement demonstrating sufficient experience should receive what amounts to double-positive consideration, some based on their ancestry and some based on their experiences.

For a Black Hispanic applicant who does not submit a supplemental statement, or submits one that does not indicate sufficient experience, admissions committees should treat their applications in a manner consistent with how they treated the applications of other Hispanics/Latinos. A Black with Two or More Races or a Black Immigrant applicant who does not submit a supplemental statement, or submits a supplemental statement that does not indicate sufficient experience, should not receive any positive consideration in the admissions process based on their racial ancestry. This does not mean that admissions committees should reject such an applicant. Rather, in evaluating such an applicant, admissions committees simply should not provide any positive consideration in making the admissions decision based on their being a member of an underrepresented minority group with a history of discrimination.

As with any holistic evaluation of a particular candidate, no admissions process can quantify the amount of positive consideration that a particular applicant should receive because of his or her racial/ethnic ancestry.[9] Each admissions committee must determine this as they grapple with each individual applicant who has some African ancestry. However, the general goals of this revised admissions process are twofold. The first is to assure a substantial presence of Ascendant Blacks in the student body. The second aims to make certain that a critical mass of individuals sufficiently experienced with the history of racial oppression of blacks in the United States is included in the student body. The latter group includes all those who received positive consideration, both Ascendant Blacks—regardless of whether they submit a supplemental statement—and all the others who check the Black or African American racial box and submit an adequate supplemental statement.

## III. How the Proposal Applies to Various Black Racial/Ethnic Groups

This part discusses how the Proposal will apply to the four different groups with some black ancestry: Black Hispanics, Blacks with Two or More Races, Black Immigrants, and Ascendant Blacks. Because of the Final Guidance, individuals with some black ancestry who also indicate that they are Hispanic/Latino are reported by educational institutions in their counts of Hispanics/Latinos, but not of blacks. The first section of this part discusses how the Proposal applies to Black Hispanics. The second section of this part addresses how the Proposal applies to Blacks with Two or More Races. Since the Proposal calls for the addition of ethnic subcategories on the application forms, it will be possible for selective higher education programs to separate those blacks in the Black/African American category into Black Immigrants and Ascendant Blacks. The third section addresses how the Proposal will affect the admissions prospects of Black Immigrants. The fourth section discusses the implications of the Proposal for Ascendant Blacks.

## A. Implications for the Admissions Prospects of Black Hispanic Applicants

The Final Guidance requires the use of the two-question format for collecting data on race and ethnicity. This format separates the Hispanic/Latino ethnicity question from the question about a person's racial categories. For the purpose of reporting race and ethnicity to the DOE, the Final Guidance requires educational institutions to report Black Hispanics as Hispanic/Latino. The DOE noted that this approach would result in more accurate reporting of data on individuals who are Hispanic/Latino.[10]

As pointed out by researchers C. Anthony Broh and Stephen D. Minicucci, "prior to the Final Guidance, institutions of higher education almost universally exercised their discretion ... and used one question to record race and ethnicity with 'Hispanic' listed as an item among the other race categories."[11] This format required Black Hispanics to choose between designating their racial/ethnic category as Black or Hispanic/Latino. Using the one-question format, therefore, did not create the problem of classifying someone as Hispanic/Latino who identified more with their race than their ethnicity. In addition, the common practice of many educational institutions that allowed individuals to check more than one racial/ethnic box was to classify students who indicated that they were both black and Hispanic/Latino as black.[12]

If admissions officials chose to treat Black Hispanics as if they were Black/African American, they will be applying the one-drop rule and ignoring the expressed racial/ethnic identity of the applicant. Admissions officials will also confront the question of whether it is fair to treat a Black Hispanic like they were Black/African American. Since this person would count in the total of Hispanic/Latino students reported to the DOE, and not Black/African American students, it could come at the expense of another Hispanic/Latino who may even have higher standardized test scores.

Under the Proposal, selective higher education institutions should treat as an Ascendant Black any Black Hispanic applicant who includes a supplemental statement indicating sufficient experience of both aspects of the history of discrimination of blacks. Black Hispanics who submit a supplemental statement are choosing to identify with the historic struggle to eradicate racial oppression of blacks. By doing so, they are indicating that their race is important to them. Therefore, admissions committees should view these individuals as expressing a preference for their race over their Hispanic/Latino ethnicity and treat them as such in the admissions process. By treating Black Hispanics in this way, the Proposal also restores some of the ability to those who could self-identify as Hispanic/Latino or black before the implementation of the Final Guidance to choose whether their race is more important to them than their ethnicity. In addition, it may very well be that some Black Hispanics would be considered Ascendant Blacks as that term is defined in this book, because even though at least one of their parents is Hispanic/Latino, that parent may also have some black ancestry. Although the number of Black Hispanics who would classify as Ascendant Blacks might be small,[13] it does seem reasonable to presume that the ones who submit an adequate supplemental statement should be so classified.

When selective higher education programs use race and ethnic classifications for determining admissions, they must employ an individualized admissions process.[14] However, there is little doubt that admissions officials—at least in their minds—compare the standardized test scores and grade point averages of a particular applicant from a given racial/ethnic group to the scores and grade point averages of other applicants of the same racial/ethnic group.[15] Thus, treating a Black Hispanic as an Ascendant Black could make a difference in their admissions prospects because Hispanic/Latinos often score higher than blacks on standardized tests. For example, the average combined SAT math, critical reading, and writing score of blacks in 2013 was 1278. In contrast, the combined SAT scores for the various Hispanic/Latino groups were 1355 for Mexican Americans, 1354 for Puerto Ricans, and 1355 for other Latinos.[16] Thus, being treated as an Ascendant Black should improve their admissions prospects. They should also count in the effort to obtain a substantial presence of Ascendant Blacks.

Selective higher education institutions should treat Black Hispanics who do not submit a supplemental statement with sufficient experience as Hispanic/Latino for the purpose of admissions. These individuals have not indicated that their racial identify is more important than their Hispanic/Latino identity. But, treating a Black Hispanic in this way could reduce their admissions prospects from what they would be if this applicant were treated as Black/African American.

## B. Implications for the Admissions Prospects of Blacks with Two or More Races

As discussed in Chapter Two, the Final Guidance mandates that all educational institutions collecting racial and ethnic data use forms that allow individuals the ability to indicate all the racial categories that apply to them. This requirement traces back to efforts by multiracial groups to add a multiracial category on the 2000 census. The multiracial movement sought to assert a racial identity for Black Multiracials that was different from that of single-race blacks. Thus, the issue about how to treat Blacks with Two or More Races for purposes of affirmative action is a necessary outgrowth of this effort.

For some Blacks with Two or More Races, choosing to identify with all of their racial groups may reflect a positive desire to embrace their entire heritage. This Proposal provides Blacks with Two or More Races with a choice about whether they want to write about their identification with the historic struggle by blacks in the United States. Some Blacks with Two or More Races do see themselves as black and very much embrace their African ancestry. As Professor Christine Hickman pointed out, mixed-race blacks often fought against the system of racial domination, and the Black Community used the one-drop rule to solidify its own unity by embracing mixed-race blacks as part of the Community.[17] Walter White, the Executive Secretary of the NAACP from 1931 to 1955, provides an excellent example of a person with black heritage who was light enough to pass as white, but not only consciously choose to identify as black, he became one of black America's greatest champions for racial justice.[18] White stated in his autobiography:

> I am a Negro. My skin is white, my eyes are blue, my hair is blond. The traits of my race are nowhere visible upon me.... I am not white. There is nothing within my mind and heart which tempts me to think that I am. Yet I realize acutely that the only characteristic which matters to either the white or the colored race—the appearance of whiteness—is mine.[19]

There is little doubt that Blacks with Two or More Races who identify with the historic struggle of blacks in the U.S., like Walter White, would gladly submit a supplemental statement discussing their experiences with both aspects of the history of racial discrimination of blacks in the United States. Blacks with Two or More Races who submit a supplemental statement that reveals sufficient experience should receive positive consideration based on their statement and other aspects in their applications. The more meaningful the experiences, the greater the positive consideration admissions officials should award. In addition, they should count in the efforts of the selective higher education program to obtain a critical mass of underrepresented minorities with a history of discrimination.

Because of the persistent gaps on standardized test scores, providing positive consideration in the admissions process for Blacks with Two or More Races and counting them in the total number of those with black ancestry in the effort to obtain a critical mass of blacks could significantly increase their admissions prospects. As noted earlier, the average combined SAT math, critical reading, and writing score of blacks in 2013 was 1278. In contrast, the average combined SAT scores for American Indians and Alaskan Natives was 1427; whites scored 1576; and Asian Americans scored 1645.[20] Thus, changing the comparative group of a Black with Two or More Races applicant from the Two or More Races category to the Black/African American category should significantly aid their admissions prospects. White/Asian Two or More Races individuals will likely constitute a significant proportion of those in the Two or More Races category,[21] so the Two or More Races applicants' average standardized test scores will be much higher than those of the Black/African American category.

For some Blacks with Two or More Races, checking all of their racial categories could reflect the negative desire to partially reject being considered black. If they choose not to submit a supplemental statement that reveals sufficient experience, then their choice should be respected. Thus, they should not receive any positive consideration because they are a member of an underrepresented minority with a history of racial discrimination. Evidence suggests that Black Multiracials are not under-represented in selective higher education programs. In addition, admissions officials cannot be certain that they have adequate experiences of both aspects of the history of racial discrimination of blacks in the United States. Nor should those applicants be included in counts of blacks used to determine whether a selective higher education program has obtained a critical mass of underrepresented minorities with a history of discrimination. However, this does not mean that these individuals will not be admitted. Even without any positive consideration of race, many Blacks with Two or More Races, especially black/white ones based on the LSAT data revealed by LSAC discussed in Chapter Three, will have the test scores and GPAs to be admitted without consideration of race.

No doubt many admissions officials will be tempted to treat Blacks with Two or More Races as Black/African American, despite the fact that their applications indicate multiple racial categories. Treating Blacks with Two or More Races as if they are Black/African American applicants for admissions purposes contradicts much research regarding the racial identity of Black Multiracials. Research exploring the identity formation of multiracial individuals suggests that many of them may understand their racial identity in a variety of ways that are different from Ascendant Blacks. Also, treating Blacks with Two or More Races as black would, effectively, ignore the racial information that such applicants provided on their application forms. Ignoring this information would deny them their right of self-identification. It also involves a blatant application of the racist aspect of the one-drop rule. Furthermore, by doing so, admissions officials are providing positive consideration in the admissions process to someone who may not be seeking it, which may very well come at the expense of another who has had significantly more experiences with both aspects of the history of black oppression in the United States. Finally, ignoring the self-proclaimed racial categories of Blacks with Two or More Races would nullify much of the rationale of the OMB and DOE when they decided it was best to use self-identification to determine a person's race and provide them the ability to indicate all of their racial categories.

The impact of this Proposal on the admissions prospects of Blacks with Two or More Races will vary. Regardless of this proposal, because of the implementation of the Final Guidance, admissions officials have to decide if they should treat them as Black/African Americans. I suspect that in the first few years of the implementation of the Final Guidance, many admissions officials may compare Blacks with Two or More Races to Black/African Americans. During this initial period, when admissions officials are questioned about how many black students are enrolled in their particular educational program, they may also report the number of Black Multiracial students along with the number of Black/African American students. In other words, they may respond by saying, for example, "We have enrolled sixteen black students, of whom five are also multiracial." Regardless of how officials make admissions decisions for Blacks with Two or More Races over the next few years, as time passes from the effective date of the Final Guidance, the tendency of admissions officials to compare Blacks with Two or More Races to others in the Two or More Races category will likely increase. As the years pass, educational institutions will become increasingly familiar with addressing the racial/ethnic reporting categories of the Final Guidance. As admissions officials come to understand that Blacks with Two or More Races no longer increase their numbers of Black/African American students, the educational institutions may come to look at them in a different light. Thus, for many Blacks with Two or More Races who embrace their African ancestry, this Proposal may, in the long run, greatly assist their admissions prospects.

## C. Implications for the Admissions Prospects of Black Immigrant Applicants

Currently, many selective higher education programs do not have a way to easily distinguish Black Immigrants from Ascendant Blacks among those who check only the Black/African American racial box. As a result, Black Immigrants are treated as if they have experiences with both aspects of the history of blacks in the United States, regardless of whether they actually do. The Proposal allows Black Immigrants the ability to let admissions officials know what their ethnic identity is and whether they identify with the historic struggle of blacks in the United States.

Under this Proposal, admissions officials should treat Black Immigrant applicants like Blacks with Two or More Races applicants. Historically, many black individuals with foreign-born black parent(s) have been leaders in the struggle against racial oppression of blacks in the United States. These individuals not only identified with this struggle, they added their voices, commitments, motivations, and talents. Thus, any attempt to discuss the changing ethnic ancestries of blacks on affirmative action must be sensitive to the reality that the success to date in that struggle is also because of the large contributions of blacks with black foreign-born parents.

Black Immigrants who submit a supplemental statement revealing sufficient experiences with both aspects of the history of discrimination of blacks in the United States, should receive positive consideration based on their statement and other aspects in their applications. The more meaningful the experiences, the greater the positive consideration they should receive. In addition, they should count in the efforts of the selective higher education program to obtain a critical mass of underrepresented minorities with a history of discrimination. However, as with Blacks with Two or More Races, if Black Immigrants chose not to submit an adequate supplemental statement, it does not mean that they would not be admitted. Some Black Immigrants will have academic records that will justify their admission even though they are not treated as members of an underrepresented minority group with a history of discrimination. Others may express other individual factors that would make them valued members of the student body. However, Black Immigrants who do not submit a supplemental statement should not be viewed as contributing to the effort of a selective higher education institution to obtain a critical mass of underrepresented minorities with a history of discrimination.

## *D. Implications for the Admissions Prospects of Ascendant Black Applicants*

Under the Proposal, Ascendant Blacks would receive positive consideration based on their ancestry. Those who submit a supplemental statement that reveals sufficient experiences can also receive positive consideration for their experiences of both aspects of the history of discrimination that blacks have suffered in the United States. Thus, Ascendant Blacks who submit an adequate supplemental statement can receive what amounts to double-positive consideration, some based on their ancestry and some based on their experiences.

One of the primary goals of the Proposal is to provide selective higher education programs with a greater probability of including a substantial presence of Ascendant Blacks in their student bodies. This is brought about because admissions officials are placing more weight on the experiences that they can bring to the student body. Thus, implementation of the Proposal should significantly increase the admissions prospects of Ascendant Blacks.

## Conclusion: Limitations of the Proposal

The Proposal takes into account the unfolding impact of the Final Guidance and the changing racial and ethnic ancestry of blacks benefitting from affirmative action. Because the Final Guidance divides Black Multiracials into Black Hispanics and Blacks with Two or More Races, the Proposal had to address how each of these groups would be treated in the admissions process. In addition, it is important to note that the way the Census Bureau and the DOE determine racial and ethnic classifications is based on self-identification. However, in this book the terms "Ascendant Black," "Black Multiracial," and "Black Immigrant" are based upon parentage, not self-identification.

The Proposal suggests that selective higher education programs change their admissions forms so that they can distinguish Black Immigrants from Ascendant Blacks in the Black/African American category. It also suggests that these programs provide applicants with some black ancestry the opportunity to submit a supplemental statement discussing their experiences with both aspects of the historical experience of blacks in the United States.

The Proposal rejects the purely biological box-checking approach of awarding positive consideration in the admissions process to those with black ancestry. Instead, it proposes a hybrid approach. Admissions officials should provide Ascendant Blacks with positive consideration because of their ancestral connection to the historical experiences of blacks in the United States. In addition, admissions officials should also take into account the experiences that a particular applicant with black ancestry has that derive from both aspects of the history of discrimination experienced by blacks in the United States. If the applicant reveals sufficient experiences of both aspects in the supplemental statement and the other information that is part of his or her admissions file, then the applicant should receive positive consideration for being a member of an underrepresented minority group with a history of discrimination. The more significant and impactful that experience has been to the applicant, the greater the positive consideration. Ascendant Blacks who submit an adequate supplemental statement would receive what amounts to double-positive consideration, some based on ancestry and some based on experiences.

Admittedly, the above proposal is still open to the possibility that individuals with some black ancestry will attempt to game the system by revealing only the portion of their racial/ethnic identity that maximizes their admissions prospects. Given the fact that the definition of Ascendant Blacks is based on having two black parents, as defined by the one-drop rule, if other information in a person's application discloses that they do not fit this definition of Ascendant Black, admissions officials should take account of that information and treat the applicant in accordance with the actual parental background revealed by such information. Also, applicants might falsify or manufacture evidence indicating that they have had substantial experience with both aspects of the history of discrimination that blacks have encountered. Beyond the minimal requirements contained in the Proposal, to further reduce the ability of individuals to falsify their racial and ethnic ancestry, or to eliminate the ability of applicants to manufacture stories regarding their experiences would require that selective higher education institutions establish intrusive and cumbersome measures to acquire some kind of independent verification or documentation regarding an applicant's racial/ethnic ancestry and experiences. Both admissions officials and applicants are likely to consider more intrusive measures abhorrent. So although the Proposal is not perfect, adding the burden of composing a supplemental statement should function as a disincentive for those who otherwise merely have to check a box to receive positive consideration based on African ancestry. Also, selective higher educational programs would have the right to sanction applicants for misrepresentation under the general prohibition against falsifying their application.

# Conclusion

This book has discussed the changing racial and ethnic ancestry of blacks benefiting from affirmative action. It has pointed to the evidence of the current overrepresentation of Black Multiracials and Black Immigrants among blacks attending selective higher education institutions. No matter how overrepresented these groups are now, given the increases in the numbers and percentages of Black Multiracials and Black Immigrants among blacks approaching college age, if current trends continue, Ascendant Blacks will be virtually eliminated from the campuses of many, if not most, of these programs.

While this book suggests changes in the admissions process in order to respond to the changing racial and ethnic ancestry of blacks at selective higher education programs, its primary goal is to spark discussions about these changes and their implications. I recognize that such discussions run counter to the Post-Racial/Colorblind thinking that is coming to dominate issues about race in the United States. In this time where Barack Obama serves as the popularly elected President of the United States, there are many who would desire to say that our battle against racism has been fought and won. I also understand that within the Black Community discussions about the changing racial and ethnic ancestry of blacks on affirmative action are particularly difficult because of their implications for the unity of that community. The history of the dominant experience of blacks in America is of a group of people united by the common trait of their race. For almost all of the 20th Century, race was a socially ascribed characteristic and those with any black blood were considered black. Also, throughout its history, American society has treated black people who were recent voluntary immigrants from Jamaica or Nigeria as if they were descendants of those blacks brought to the United States as a result of the Trans-Atlantic Slave Trade. Thus, the need to talk about the changing racial and ethnic ancestry of blacks on affirmative action reveals the fact that the Black Community in the United States may have reached a critical juncture in its existence. It stands at a point in the collective struggle against racial subordination that may threaten its racial and ethnic solidarity forever. After all, to discuss the changing racial and ethnic ancestry of Blacks on affirmative action requires blacks (and others) consciously to think about the racial and ethnic ancestry of black people. Blacks are compelled to think about whether to view their brothers and sisters of mixed parentage with different eyes than those with two parents who suffered as victims of the historic racial oppression in the United States their entire lives. They are also required to consider whether they should do the same with their black brothers and sisters from the Mother Country, West Indies, or other parts of the world. As a result, a forthright and honest discussion of the changing racial and ethnic nature of blacks on affirmative action cannot help but literally pit father against son, mother against daughter, half-brother against half-brother, half-sister against half-sister, and husband against wife. Yet, despite these concerns, what is at stake in these discussions (or lack thereof) are issues of paramount importance to all of America. We are not only discussing which blacks will come to occupy the most prestigious social positions in American society in the next generation, but also who will influence the education of all others that come to occupy those prestigious positions with them.

I want to conclude, however, by reiterating one point succinctly captured in the title of the book. American society does not arrive at the point where there is a need to discuss the changing racial and ethnic ancestry of blacks on affirmative action without a lessening of the grip of racism in the United States. When affirmative action began in the 1960s, people of African descent were still called Negroes or colored out of respect; and coon, darkie and even black as an insult. America and her descendants from Africa were just entering the Civil Rights Movement, but we had not yet gotten to the Black Consciousness Movement, the Afrocentric Movement, the Multicultural Movement, the Diversity Movement, or the Post-Racial Movement. The institution of affirmative action was contemporaneous with the passage of the Civil Rights Act of 1964, the most sweeping piece of civil rights legislation in the country's history, and the Voting Rights Act of 1965. At the time of the commencement of affirmative action, most Negroes in the South had been disenfranchised for the entire twentieth century. There were only five or six Negroes serving in Congress and none had been elected from any of the eleven states that made up the former Confederacy during the 20th century. Segregation and conscious racial discrimination still formed part of customary American business, educational, political, and social practices. Discrimination based on race in employment, merchandising stores, eating establishments, places of entertainment, and hotels and motels was generally accepted as a fact of life. Negroes seldom occupied positions above the most menial levels in American businesses and corporations. What later became known as the glass ceiling was a firmly implanted, outright concrete barrier in the 1960s. As affirmative action commenced, only a handful of blacks attended the prestigious colleges and universities of this country and almost none of them taught there. In mid-1960s, we were just beginning to dismantle separate water fountains, waiting rooms, transportation facilities, rest rooms, hospitals, and cemeteries for whites and coloreds. I briefly recount the conditions that existed as affirmative action programs were being instituted by selective higher education programs to point out that we should enthusiastically engage in the discussions about the changing racial and ethnic ancestry of blacks on affirmative action and what to do about it. Such discussions are necessary *because of our success*, not our failure, in combatting the continuing effects of our society's history of racial discrimination.

# Endnotes

## Foreword by Dennis J. Shields

1. The process at the University of Iowa College of Law had a higher level of faculty committee involvement in admissions decision-making.
2. The Brazilian Supreme Court upheld the setting of quotas for access to higher education for the African-Brazilian descendants of slaves.
3. No doubt I benefitted in some ways from the impact of the *Bakke* decision.

## Introduction

1. WILLIAM BOWEN & DEREK BOK, THE SHAPE OF THE RIVER 4 (1998).
2. Ernest Gellhorn, *The Law Schools & the Negro*, 1968 DUKE L.J. 1069, 1077–85 (1968).
3. BOWEN, *supra* note 1, at 5–6.
4. Barbara A Noah, *A Prescription for Racial Equality in Medicine*, 40 CONN. L. REV. 675, 698–99 (2008).
5. *Id.*
6. *See* Campbell Gibson & Kay Jung, *Historical Census Statistics on Population Totals by Race, 1790 to 1990, and by Hispanic Origin, 1970 to 1990, for the United States, Regions, Divisions, and States*, at tbl.1 (United States Census Bureau, Working Paper Series No. 56, 2002).
7. *See id.* The author further wants to note that both the words "Hispanic" and "Latino" are used in this book as English language words. "Latino" has its translation in the Spanish language and is masculine in gender and the feminine gender translation is "Latina." English language nouns, however, do not have gender. Thus, for the English language, Latino refers to both males and females while Spanish language data collection should use the masculine ("Latino") and feminine ("Latina") nomenclature, such as "Latino/a."
8. *See id.*
9. "Twenty-two states, including many Northern states, still had anti-miscegenation laws in the early 1960s." F. JAMES DAVIS, WHO IS BLACK?: ONE NATION'S DEFINITION 68 (1991).
10. BUREAU OF THE CENSUS, THE SOCIAL AND ECONOMIC STATUS OF THE BLACK POPULATION IN THE UNITED STATES: AN HISTORICAL VIEW, 1790–1978: CURRENT POPULATION REPORTS, SPECIAL STUDIES, SERIES P-23, No. 80, 16 tbl.10 (showing of the 18,849,000 blacks in 1960, 37 percent were under the age of fifteen, thus there were approximately 11,875,000 blacks over the age of 15 (63 percent x 18,849,000)) (1979).

11. G. Reginald Daniel, More Than Black?: Multiracial Identity and the New Racial Order 98 (2001).

12. C. Matthew Snipp, *Racial Measurement in the American Census: Past Practices and Implications for the Future*, 29 Ann. Rev. Soc. 563, 568 (2003).

13. The Census Bureau sent advanced copies of the 1960 census form to over 80 percent of American households who filled them out and then gave them to census enumerators when they showed up. *See id.* The 1970 census form was the first designed to be completed by respondents alone without any assistance from census enumerators. *See* Sharon M. Lee & Barry Edmonston, *New Marriages, New Families: U.S. Racial and Hispanic Intermarriage*, Population Bull., June 2005, at 9.

14. Light-skinned blacks had long been passing as white in the United States. For example, a conservative estimate put the number of blacks who were able to successfully pass as white between 1880 and 1925 at approximately 90,000 people. F. James Davis, *supra* note 9, at 56.

15. The term foreign-born refers to any United States resident who was born outside the United States or its territories, except for people who were born abroad to parents who were United States citizens. Mary Mederios Kent, *Immigration and America's Black Population*, 62 Population Bull. 5 Box 1 (December 2007).

16. *See* Campbell J. Gibson & Emily Lennon, *Historical Census Statistics on the Foreign-Born Population of the United States: 1850–1990*, at tbl.8 (U.S. Census Bureau, Working Paper Series No. 29, 1999).

17. *See* F. James Davis, *supra* note 9, at 78 (1991).

18. Ghana (1957); Guinea (1958); Chad, Benin, Nigeria, Ivory Coast, Madagascar, Central African Republic, Mali, Niger, Senegal, Burkina Faso, Mauritania, Togo, Zaire, Somalia, Congo, Gabon, Cameroon (1960); Sierra Leone (1961), South Africa (under minority rule until 1995); Burundi, Rwanda, Uganda (1962); Kenya, Tanzania (1963); Malawi, Zambia (1964); Gambia (1965); Botswana, Lesotho (1966); Equatorial Guinea, Mauritius, Swaziland (1968); Guinea-Bissau (1969). *See* Indigenous People of Africa and America, *available at* http://ipoaa.com/african_independence.htm (last visited April 29, 2014).

19. Jennifer V. Jackson & Mary E. Cothran, *Black versus Black: The Relationships among African, African American, and African Caribbean Persons*, 33 J. of Black Stud. 576, 578 (2003).

20. There are different ways to define "Black Multiracials." One can follow self-identification or can determine who is multiracial based on the race of their parents. The problem with self-identification in the context of applying to selective higher education institutions is the possibility that individuals will choose their racial identification for strategic purposes of getting admitted as opposed to how they truly self-identify. Since the primary concern here is about the reduction in the number and percentage of Ascendant Blacks, Black Multiracials in this book refers to those with one black and one non-black parent.

21. I wish to also specifically acknowledge the insightful article written by Angela Onwuachi-Willig. *See* Angela Onwuachi-Willig, *The Admission of Legacy Blacks*, 60 Vand. L. Rev. 1141, 1149 n.27 (2007). She and the late Professor Derrick Bell of New York University School of Law and others use the terms "descendants" and "legacy Blacks" to denote these blacks to make the connection between their ancestral lineage as descended from blacks who were enslaved and segregated. *Id.* at 1149 n.27.

22. The term "Ascendants" is also used by African Americans who left America to repatriate in the Republic of Ghana. This term was first mentioned to me in the summer of 2007 by Seestah Imaakus and Brother El Shabazz, the owners and operators of Hotel One Africa located in the city of Cape Coast, Ghana. One Africa is a facility located between

Cape Coast Castle (the main British administrative castle during the Tran-Atlantic Slave Trade) and Elmina Castle (the first permanent European structure built in Africa) on the Ghanaian coast. Their lifelong mission is to assist Ascendant Blacks as they go through the experience of going through those castles.

23. *See* KIM WILLIAMS, MARK ONE OR MORE: CIVIL RIGHTS IN MULTIRACIAL AMERICA 89 (2008).

24. *Loving v. Virginia*, 388 U.S. 1 (1967).

25. *Id.*

26. In the General Social Survey conducted in 2002, only 10 percent of Americans and 4 percent of young adults objected to interracial marriage. *See* Michael J. Rosenfield, *CCF Briefing Paper: Interracial Marriage 40 years after Loving v. Virginia* (2007).

27. *See* PEW RESEARCH CTR. PUBLICATIONS, *Almost All Millennials Accept Interracial Dating and Marriage* (2010).

28. *See* Paul Taylor, Wendy Wang, Kim Parker, Jeffrey S. Passel, Eileen Patten & Seth Motel, Pew Research Ctr., *The Rise of Intermarriage: Rates, Characteristics Vary by Race and Gender* 11 (2012).

29. *Id.* For black men, these represent substantial increases from the 15.7 percent figure in 2000 and 7.9 percent in 1980. While it also increased for black women, the increase went from 7.1 percent in 2000 and 3.0 percent in 1980. *See* Jeffrey S. Passel et al., Pew Research Center, *Marrying Out: One-in-Seven New U.S. Marriages is Interracial or Interethnic* 11–12 (2010). With respect to blacks having a white spouse, more recent statistics show a similar trend. In 2010, 8.5 percent of married black men had white spouses, an increase from 6.6 percent in 2005. U.S. Census Bureau, *America's Families and Living Arrangements* (2010), *available at* http://www.census.gov/hhes/families/. While, only 3.9 percent of black women were married to white men, an increase from 2.8 percent in 2005. *Id.* According to a recent N.Y. Times article, intermarriages between blacks and whites "make up 1 in 60 new marriages today, compared with fewer than 1 in 1,000" a half century ago. Sam Roberts, *Black Women See Fewer Black Men at the Altar*, N.Y. TIMES, June 4, 2010, at A12.

30. *See* KAREN R. HUMES, NICHOLAS A. JONES & ROBERTO R. RAMIREZ, OVERVIEW OF RACE AND HISPANIC ORIGIN 2010, 6 tbl.2 (2011).

31. *See* CensusScope.org, *United States Multiracial Profile*, http://www.censusscope.org/us/print_chart_multi.html. (last visited Apr. 29, 2014).

32. *See* Overview of Race and Hispanic Origin: 2010, 8 (2011) available at www.census.gov/prod/cen2010/briefs/c2010bR-02.pdf.

33. According to the 2012 Census Bureau figures, of the 3,588,000 individuals between the ages of 20 and 24 who were classified as Black Alone or in Combination, 3,303,000 were Black in Combination. Thus, the percentage of Black in Combination to total blacks was 7.9 percent (285,000 (3,588,000—3,303,000))/3,588,000. For Black Alone or in Combination see U.S. Census Bureau, tbl.1. *Population by Sex and Age, for Black Alone and White Alone, Not Hispanic: 2012* (Numbers in thousands). For Black in Combination see U.S. Census Bureau, tbl.29. *Population by Sex and Age, for Black Alone or in Combination and White Alone, Not Hispanic: 2012* (Numbers in thousands Civilian non-institutionalized population). Then subtract the totals of Black Alone or in Combination from the total for Black Alone.

34. For ages 15 to 19, the corresponding figures were 8.9 percent (322,000 (3,624,000–3,302,000))/3,624,000; For ages 10 and 14 the corresponding figures were 10.9 percent (384,00 (3,511,000–3,127,000))/3,511,000; for ages 5 to 9 the corresponding figures were

15.0 percent (532,000 (3,545,000−3,013,000))/3,545,000); for under the age of five the corresponding figures were 19.1 percent (718,000 (3,769,000−3,051,000))/ 3,769,000). *Id.*

35. Campbell Gibson & Emily Lennon, *Race and Hispanic Origin of the Population of Nativity: 1850 to 1990* (1999).

36. *Id.*

37. U.S. Census Bureau, The Black Alone Population in the United States: 2012 tbl.7; *Nativity and Citizenship Status by Sex, for Black Alone and White Alone, Not Hispanic*: 2012 (2012).

38. *Id.*

39. Jeffrey S. Passel, *Demography of Immigrant Youth: Past, Present and Future, in* The Future of Children 19, 30 (2011).

40. *See* Mary Mederios Kent, *supra* note 15, at 4. (asserting that the figure drops to just 13 percent of black children if only non-Hispanic blacks are considered). For Massachusetts statistics see Maria Sacchetti, *The Changing Face Of Citizenship* in the Boston Globe March 25, 2014.

41. *Fisher v. University of Texas*, 133 S. Ct. 2411 (2013).

42. *Schuette v. Coalition to Defend Affirmative Action*, 134 S.Ct. 1623 (2014).

43. *Grutter v. Bollinger*, 539 U.S. 306 (2003).

44. *Id.* at 343.

45. *See, e.g., id.* at 375 (Thomas, J., concurring in part and dissenting in part) ("The Court also holds that racial discrimination in admissions should be given another twenty-five years before it is deemed no longer narrowly tailored to the Law School's fabricated compelling state interest.").

46. *See id.* at 346 (Ginsburg, J., concurring) ("From today's vantage point, one may hope, but not firmly forecast, that over the next generation's span, progress toward nondiscrimination and genuinely equal opportunity will make it safe to sunset affirmative action.").

47. During oral arguments in *Fisher v. University of Texas*, both Chief Justice Roberts and Justice Scalia raised questions about mixed-race Hispanic/Latinos and how they were counted. Tr. of oral argument, *Fisher v. Univ. of Texas at Austin*, at 32–35.

48. *See* C. Anthony Broh & Stephen D. Minicucci, Racial Identity and Government Classification: A Better Solution 5 (2008). They also had to be either a United States citizen or a permanent United States resident. The average number of Africans who were enrolled in higher education institutions who are also on student visas in the United States from 2001 to 2006 was approximately 33,100 per year. West Indians accounted for less than half of this number with an annual amount of 14,100. However, these statistics do not include the race of the students. Most, but not all, are black. Census 2000 statistics suggest, for example, that many students studying in the United States from Kenya may be of South Asian origin. Thus, foreign-born blacks on student visas make up less than fifty thousand individuals on college campuses. Even if these foreign-born blacks on student visas are included in the counts of Black Immigrants at colleges and universities, they make up a small percentage of black students. In contrast to their numbers, there were nearly 2.5 million blacks enrolled in college in 2007. *See* U.S. Census Bureau, College Enrollment—Summary by Sex, Race, and Hispanic Origin: 2007.

49. Daryl Fears, *In Diversity Push, Top Universities Enrolling More Black Immigrants*, The Washington Post, Mar, 6, 2007, at 2.

50. I use the terms "Negroes," "Coloreds," "Black", or "African American" in the historic and inclusive sense of referring to people in the United States who are of African descent.

I will also be citing to various statistical reports and documents throughout this book. They will employ different terminology for Blacks. When I do so, I will use the terms that were used in those reports and documents.

51. *See* Angela Onwuachi-Willig, *supra* note 21; Kevin Brown & Jeannie Bell, *Demise of the Talented Tenth: Affirmative Action and the Increasing Underrepresentation of Ascendant Blacks at Selective Higher Educational Institutions*, 69 Ohio St. L.J. 1227 (2008); and Luis Fuentes-Rohwer, *Merit and Race*, New York Times Opinion Pages, (Nov. 29, 2010). *See also* Curtis Valentine, *Rethinking the Achievement Gap: Lessons From the African Diaspora*, Washington Post, September 2, 2012.

52. *Grutter*, *supra* note 43.

53. The following academic year, 350 of the 530 black undergraduate students who attended Harvard were either Black Multiracials or Black Immigrants. Ronald Roach, *Drawing Upon the Diaspora*, Diverse Issues in Higher Educ. (Aug. 25, 2005).

54. *Id.* (discussing Douglas S. Massey et al., The Source of the River: The Social Origins of Freshman at America's Selective Colleges and Universities (2003)).

55. *Id.*

56. Broh, *supra* note 48, at 5.

57. The thirty-one institutions that are part of COFHE are among the most prestigious in the country. They are Amherst College, Barnard College, Brown University, Bryn Mawr College, Carleton College, Columbia University, Cornell University, Dartmouth College, Duke University, Georgetown University, Harvard University, Johns Hopkins University, MIT, Mount Holyoke College, Northwestern University, Oberlin College, Pomona College, Princeton University, Rice University, Smith College, Stanford University, Swarthmore College, Trinity College, University of Chicago, University of Pennsylvania, University of Rochester, Washington University in St. Louis, Wellesley College, Wesleyan University, Williams College, and Yale University. *See* Consortium on Financing Higher Educ., http://web.mit.edu/cofhe/ (last visited March 29, 2014).

58. Broh, *supra* note 48, at 5. Broh and Minicucci provided an alternative way for colleges and universities to maintain internal statistics on the racial and ethnic makeup of their students, even though these statistics differed from what these educational institutions are required to report to the Department of Education. Under their alternative approach, Broh and Minicucci classified any multiracial student who had indicated that they were black as "Black" and not as Hispanic/Latino or "Two or More Races" as required by the Final Guidance. *Id.* at 23–24. From this, they calculated that 5.3 percent of the students were black (self-reported as monoracial or multiracial) as opposed to 4.1 percent that would be reported as black under the Final Guidance. *Id.* at 25 fig.17. Thus, some twenty-three percent of the black students will therefore be classified as either Hispanic/Latino or Two or More Races under the Final Guidance. While black-only students constituted 77 percent (4.1 percent/5.3 percent) of the black students, black/white students comprised 14.7 percent (0.78 percent/5.3 percent) of the black students. Another 4 percent were black/Latino, 2 percent were black/Asian, and 1.9 percent as black and Native American. *Id.* at 17 fig.2.

59. There were 1,298 black students on campus and an additional 318 Two or More Races students who also indicated black. *See Indiana University Institutional Research and Reporting Fall 2013 Student Degree Seeking Enrollment by Race and Ethnicity*, available at https://www.iu.edu/~uirr/doc/diversity/student/1-IU_BL_base_05_13.pdf (last visited Jan. 21, 2014).

60. A 2006 article also discussed baseline data from the National Longitudinal Survey of Freshmen students who entered twenty-eight selective colleges and universities in 1999. *See generally* Douglas S. Massey et al., *Black Immigrants and Black Natives Attending Selective Colleges and Universities in the United States*, 113 AM. J. EDUC. 243, 245–48 (2006) (analyzing data from the National Longitudinal Survey of Freshman to study black immigrants and native-born blacks attending selective colleges and universities in the United States).

61. *A Solid Percentage of Black Students at U.S. Colleges and Universities Are Foreign Born*, 54 J. BLACKS HIGHER EDUC. 22 (Jan. 2006).

62. Pamela R. Bennett & Amy Lutz, *How African American Is the Net Black Advantage? Differences in College Attendance Among Immigrant Blacks, Native Blacks, and Whites*, 80 SOCIOL. EDUC. 70, 90 (2009). This study looked at a nationally representative sample of eighth graders drawn from the National Educational Longitudinal Study who were first surveyed in 1988. There were four follow-up surveys conducted in 1990, 1992, 1994, and 2000. Bennett and Lutz stopped their research at the 1994 data set. This set of data was two years after the students should have entered college. They found that while 9.2 percent of Black Immigrants attended selective colleges and universities, only 2.4 percent of other blacks did. *Id.* at 70, 79.

63. Ronald Roach, *supra* note 53.

64. SIMON CHENG & SEENA MOSTAFAVIPOUR, THE DIFFERENCES AND SIMILARITIES BETWEEN BIRACIAL AND MONORACIAL COUPLES: A SOCIODEMOGRAPHIC SKETCH BASED ON THE CENSUS 2000 6 (2005).

65. Kevin Brown, *Change in Racial and Ethnic Classifications is Here: Proposal to Address Race and Ethnic Ancestry of Blacks for Affirmative Action Admissions Purposes*, 31 HAMLINE J. PUB. L. & POL'Y 143, 149–51 (2009).

66. *Id.*

67. Scholars have interpreted the way that African Americans' culture affects their educational performance in different ways. For example, the Afrocentrist argued that the Eurocentric bias of the traditional educational curriculum was responsible for the poor performance of black schoolchildren. Scholars like John H. Whorter argue that the problem of African American culture is the "stranglehold of Victimology, Separatism, and Anti-Intellectualism." *See* JOHN H. MCWHORTER, LOSING THE RACE (2000). Nigerian-born educational anthropologist, John Ogbu, draws distinctions between the cultures of involuntary minorities like African Americans and voluntary immigrants. He notes that involuntary minorities throughout the world have difficulty succeeding in education. Their situation is unfavorably contrasted to that of voluntary immigrants who generally come to the host country in search of better economic, political, or religious motivations. *See* John U. Ogbu, *Immigrant and Involuntary Minorities in Comparative Perspectives*, *in* MINORITY STATUS AND SCHOOLING: A COMPARATIVE STUDY OF IMMIGRANT AND INVOLUNTARY MINORITIES 37, 37–61 (Margaret A. Gibson & John U. Ogbu eds., 1991).

68. I am using the term "ethnic cleansing" of Ascendant Blacks in the sense of the elimination of this racial/ethnic group of blacks from the campuses and classrooms of our nation's selective higher education institutions. *See* Andrew Bell-Fialkoff, *A Brief History of Ethnic Cleansing*, 72 FOREIGN AFFAIRS 110 (1993) ("[E]thnic cleansing [ … ] defies easy definition.… At the most general level, however, ethnic cleansing can be understood as the expulsion of a population from a given territory.")

69. For recent books on affirmative action see SHERYLL CASHIN, PLACE, NOT RACE! A NEW VISION OF OPPORTUNITY IN AMERICA (2014), RANDALL KENNEDY, FOR DISCRIMINA-

TION: RACE, AFFIRMATIVE ACTION, AND THE LAW (2013), and RICHARD SANDER AND STUART TAYLOR, JR., MISMATCH: HOW AFFIRMATIVE ACTION HURTS STUDENTS IT'S INTENDED TO HELP, AND WHY UNIVERSITIES WON'T ADMIT IT (2012).

70. *Grutter*, supra note 43.
71. *Id.*
72. *Id.*
73. *Id.* at 319.
74. *Id.*
75. *Id.*
76. *Id.* at 330.
77. *Id.*
78. *Id.* at 333, 338 (emphasis added).
79. *See* Lewis Gordon, *Thinking through Identities: Black Peoples, Race Labels, and Ethnic Consciousness*, in THE OTHER AFRICAN AMERICANS: CONTEMPORARY AFRICAN AND CARIBBEAN IMMIGRANTS IN THE UNITED STATES 83 (Yoku Shaw-Taylor & Steven A. Tuch, eds., 2007) (arguing that concern about the underrepresentation of Ascendant Blacks benefitting from affirmative action is xenophobic and underappreciates the impact of the legacy of slavery on other blacks and how American foreign policy has harmed the development of Caribbean countries). *See also* Leonard M. Baynes, *Who Is Black Enough for You: The Story of One Black Man and His Family's Pursuit of the American Dream*, 11 GEO. IMMIGR. L.J. 97, 128 (1996) ("The only difference is that our [black West Indians'] slavery did not occur in the United States."); Camille A. Nelson, *Carriers of Globalization: Loss of Home and Self Within the African Diaspora*, 55 FLA. L. REV. 539, 573–74 (2003) (noting the slavery in colonial Jamaica); *cf.* Hope Lewis, *Lionheart Gals Facing the Dragon: The Human Rights of Inter/National Black Women in the United States*, 76 OR. L. REV. 567, 619 (1997) ("The impact of that history, along with the related histories of global imperialism and neo-colonialism, continues to plague modern-day Blacks whether they are descended from slaves in the United States, Latin America, or the Caribbean....").
80. *See, e.g.*, Kendall Thomas, *Comments at Frontiers of Legal Thought Conference* (Jan. 26, 1990), *quoted in* Charles R. Lawrence III, *If He Hollers Let Him Go: Regulating Racist Speech on Campus*, 1990 DUKE L. J. 431, *in* MARI J. MATSUDA, CHARLES R. LAWRENCE III, RICHARD DELGADO & KIMBERLÉ W. CRENSHAW, WORDS THAT WOUND 53, 61 (1993); *see also* D. Marvin Jones, *Darkness Made Visible: Law, Metaphor, and the Racial Self*, 82 GEO. L. J. 437 (1993) (arguing that racial categories are neither objective nor natural, but ideological and constructed. In these terms race is not so much a category but a practice: people are raced).
81. "Final Guidance, on Maintaining, Collecting, and Reporting Racial and Ethnic Data to the United States Department of Education," 72 FED. REG. 59266 (Oct.19, 2007).
82. The purpose of the Final Guidance is to "obtain more accurate information about the increasing number of students who identify with more than one race." *Id.* at 59267.
83. KERRY ANN ROCKQUEMORE & DAVID BRUNSMA, BEYOND BLACK: BIRACIAL IDENTITY IN AMERICA 1–17 (2002).
84. In the summer of 1997, I spent seven weeks traveling through South Africa. In the summer of 1998, I spent three weeks with the Law Faculty of the University of Witwatersrand and four weeks with the Law Faculty of the University of Capetown. In the summer of 1999 and 2000, I spent ten days on each visit, mostly in Johannesburg and Soweto.
85. John C. Duncan, Jr., *Two "Wrongs" Do/Can Make A Right: Remembering Mathematics, Physics, & Various Legal Analogies (Two Negatives Make A Positive; Are Remedies Wrong?)*

*The Law Has Made Him Equal, But Man Has Not*, 43 BRANDEIS L.J. 511, 517 n.18 (2005).

86. *See generally* Devesh Kapur & John McHale, *Globalization at Work: Migration's New Payoff*, 139 FOREIGN POL'Y 48 (2003). In Jamaica, for example, migrants, who primarily live in the U.S., send an average of $640 per year back to families in Jamaica. This represents a substantial percentage of household income. *See* Alex Glennie and Laura Chappell, *Jamaica: From Diverse Beginning to Diaspora in the Developed World* (2010) (published by Migration Policy Institute).

87. *Regents of the University of California v. Bakke*, 438 U.S. 265, 312 fn 48 (1978) (quoting Bowen, *Admissions and the Relevance of Race*, PRINCETON ALUMNI WEEKLY, Sept. 26, 1977, at 7, 9).

88. *See* RAINER SPENCER, REPRODUCING RACE: THE PARADOX OF GENERATION MIX 144 (2010).

89. EUGENE ROBINSON, DISINTEGRATION: THE SPLINTERING OF BLACK AMERICA (2010).

90. *Id*.

91. According to Forbes Magazine, Oprah Winfrey was #184 on its list of 400 Richest Americans with a net worth of $2.9 billion. *See* FORBES, THE FORBES 400: THE RICHEST PEOPLE IN AMERICA (Luisa Kroll and Kerry A. Dolan eds., Sept. 16, 2013).

92. According to Forbes inaugural list of the Wealthiest Black Americans, after Oprah Winfrey comes Tiger Woods with a net worth of approximately $600 million, Robert Johnson worth $550 million, Michael Jordan worth $525 million followed by Magic Johnson worth $500 million and Bill Cosby worth $450 million. *See* MATTHEW MILLER, FORBES, THE WEALTHIEST BLACK AMERICANS (May 6, 2009).

93. For additional heads of corporations run by blacks, see *Ebony Power 150*, EBONY MAG., May 2009, at 74.

94. *See* 100 Highest Paid Celebrities in the World: Power List 2011, (Oprah Winfrey #1, Tiger Woods #14, Kobe Bryant #24 and LeBron James #29), *available at* http://www.ranker.com/list/100-highest-paid-celebrities-in-the-world-power-list-2011/worlds-richest-people-lists.

95. *See* Karin Chenoweth, *African American College Presidents in Decline*, DIVERSE ISSUES IN HIGHER EDUC. (July 13, 2007).

96. There have been at least eight black Miss Americas with the last one, Caressa Cameron, crowned in January 2010. *See* Joanne Fowler, *Caressa Cameron of Virginia Crowned Miss America*, PEOPLE (Jan. 31, 2010), http://www.people.com/people/article/0,,20340574,00.htm. The other seven were Vanessa Williams (1984); Suzanne Charles (1984); Debbye Turner (1990); Marjorie Judith Vincent (1991); Kimberly Aiken (1994); Erika Harold (2003) (Erika was born in 1980 to a white father and a mother who was part African American and part Native American. Carol Brennan, *Erika Harold Biography*, *available at* http://biography.jrank.org/pages/2852/Harold-Erika.html#ixzz0JFeloz8x&D (last visited Oct. 18, 2010)); and Erica Dunlap (2004). *See* ELWOOD WATSON, THERE SHE IS MISS AMERICA: THE POLITICS OF SEX, BEAUTY, AND RACE IN AMERICA'S MOST FAMOUS PAGEANT (2004); *see also* Elwood Watson, *Miss America's Racial Milestones*, DIVERSE ISSUES IN HIGHER EDUC. (Jan. 14, 2009). In 2012, Nina Meriwether became the sixth black woman to win the Miss USA pageant. The other five are 2008 Crystle Stewart; 2007 Rachel Smith—half black and half white; 2002 Shauntay Hinton; 1995 Chelsi Smith—black father and white mother; and 1993 Kenya Moore. *Crystle Stewart crowned Miss USA*, THE DAILY VOICE: BLACK AMERICA'S DAILY NEWS SOURCE, April 12, 2008.

97. *See* Jennifer E. Manning, *Membership of the 113th Congress: A Profile* 7 (from Congressional Research Service), *available at* https://www.fas.org/sgp/crs/misc/R42964.pdf (last

visited Dec. 15, 2013).

98. Tim Scott was appointed on January 2, 2013, by South Carolina Governor Nikki Halley to serve out the term of Jim DeMint who resigned to run the Heritage Foundation. William Maurice Cowans served in the Senate from January 30, 2013 until July 16, 2013. He was appointed by Governor Deval Patrick to fill the vacancy left by John Kerry who resigned to become Secretary of State. Cory Booker, the former Mayor of Newark, was sworn in on October 31, 2013. He won the special election in October 16, 2013 to succeed Frank Lautenberg who died in office.

99. There have been four black governors in America's history. In addition to Deval Patrick and David Patterson, the other two were P.B.S. Pinchback who served as governor of Louisiana for thirty-six days in 1872–1873 and L. Douglas Wilder who was elected governor of Virginia in 1990. *See Spitzer Successor will be Nation's 4th Black Governor*, CNN POLITICS, Mar. 10, 2008, http://articles.cnn.com/2008-03-10/politics/paterson.bio_1_lieutenant-governor-black-governor-hofstra-law-school?_s=PM:POLITICS.

100. *See* EBONY MAG., Mar. 2008, at Cover.

101. *See, e.g.*, Peter Wallsten, *Election 2008: The Presidential Vote/News Analysis*, L.A. TIMES, Nov. 5, 2008, at 11; Craig Gordon, *Analysis: How Obama Won It*, NEWSDAY, Nov. 5, 2008, at W04; Kevin Sack, *After Decades, A Time to Reap*, N. Y. TIMES, Nov. 5, 2008, at A1; John B. Judis, *It's A Wrap: The 2008 Campaign*, L. A. TIMES, Nov. 9, 2008, at 34.

102. *Parents Involved in Community Schools v. Seattle School Dist. No. 1*, 551 U.S. 701, 787 (2007) (Kennedy, J. concurring in part and concurring in the judgment).

103. John Rolfe's casual reference to the arrival of black slaves in Jamestown, Virginia twelve years later is generally regarded as the first time Africans were imported into British North America. The Norfolk-born first recorder of the Virginia Colony, wrote "[a]bout the last of August, came in a dutch man of warre that sold us twenty Negars.". CAPTAIN JOHN SMITH, THE GENERALL HISTORIE OF VIRGINIA, NEW ENGLAND, AND THE SUMMER ISLES, VOL. 1 246–47(Glasgow: James MacLehose & Sons, 1907). This account can also be found printed in CIVIL RIGHTS AND AFRICAN AMERICANS 4 (Albert P. Blaustein & Robert L. Zangrando eds., 1991).

104. *See* Charles Lawrence, *The Id, the Ego and Equal Protection: Reckoning with Unconscious Racism*, 39 STAN. L. REV. 317 (1987).

105. Patricia J. Williams, *Spirit-Murdering the Messenger: The Discourse of Fingerpointing as the Law's Response to Racism*, 42 U. MIAMI L. REV. 127, 151 (1987) (observing that racism is "spirit-murder"); *see also* Adrien Katherine Wing & Sylke Merchan, *Rape, Ethnicity, and Culture: Spirit Injury from Bosnia to Black America*, 25 COLUM. HUM. RTS. L. REV. 1, 2 (1993).

106. *See, e.g.*, Barbara Flagg, *Was Blind, But Now I See: White Race Consciousness and the Requirement of Discriminatory Intent*, 91 MICH. L. REV. 953 (1993); *see also* Stephanie M. Wildman & Adrienne D. Davis, *Language and Silence: Making Systems of Privilege Visible*, 35 SANTA CLARA L. REV. 881 (1995).

107. *See* DeLoggio Admissions Achievement Program, *Race and Ethnicity, available at* http://www.deloggio.com/diversty/race.html (last visited Feb. 24, 2014). In addition, some researchers have observed that multiracial individuals are more likely to identify with the minority component of their background when forced to choose in constrained, high-stakes settings and when they have specific knowledge of how such race-conscious data will be used— i.e., in the context of LSAT pre-law school testing, as opposed to being asked to "check all that apply" once in law school. A.T. Panter et al., *It Matters How and When You Ask: Self-Reported*

*Race/Ethnicity of Incoming Law Students*, 15 CULT. DIV. & ETHNIC MIN. PSYCH. 51, 63 (2009).

108. Selective higher education institutions may also want to add additional ethnic subcategories for its Hispanic/Latino, Asian, and Native Hawaiian or Other Pacific Islander applicants. Admission forms typically ask for applicants who want to check the American Indian or Alaska Native box to include their tribe. The definitions under the Final Guidance for this box says "[a] person having origins in any of the original peoples of North and South America (including Central America), and who maintains tribal affiliation or community attachment." *See Final Guidance, supra* note 81, at 59274. Thus, educational institutions must gather tribal information about those in the American Indian or Alaska Native box.

109. According to American Community Survey results from 2008–09, a third of the almost 3.3 million foreign-born black were from Africa and 52 percent were from the Caribbean. *See* Randy Capps, Kristen McCabe, and Michael Fix, *Diverse Streams: Black African Migration to the United States* 3 tbl. 1 (2012), published by the Migration Policy Institute, *available at* http://www.migrationpolicy.org/research/CBI-african-migration-united-states?pdf=africanmigrationus.pdf (last visited Feb. 22, 2014).

110. *See* DeLoggio Admissions Achievement Program, *supra* note 107.

111. *See Gratz v. Bollinger*, 539 U.S. 244 (2003) (striking down a system that provided numerical points in the admissions process based on race and ethnicity because it failed to preclude admissions counselors from conducting the type of individualized consideration described in the Court's opinion in *Grutter*).

112. *See* SPENCER, *supra* note 88, at 144.

113. For a recent book that proposes substituting low-opportunity neighborhoods for race as a plus factor in admissions decisions, *see* SHERYLL CASHIN, PLACE, NOT RACE: A NEW VISION OF OPPORTUNITY IN AMERICA (2014).

114. *See* Office for Civil Rights, U.S. Dep't of Educ., Race-Neutral Alternatives in Postsecondary Education: Innovative Approaches to Diversity (Feb. 2004) (noting that economically disadvantaged students are twenty-five times less likely to be found on selective college campuses as economically advantaged students); *see also* ANTHONY CARNEVALE AND STEPHEN J. ROSE, SOCIOECONOMIC STATUS, RACE/ETHNICITY, AND SELECTIVE COLLEGE ADMISSIONS 106 (2003) from the Century Foundation, *available at* http://tcf.org/assets/downloads/tcf-carnrose.pdf.

115. For a discussion of these issues and Hispanic/Latinos see Kevin Brown and Tom I. Romero, II, *The Social Reconstruction of Race & Ethnicity of the Nation's Law Students: A Request to the ABA, AALS and LSAC For Changes In New Reporting Requirement* 2011 MICH. ST. L. REV. 1133 (2011). For an excellent recent book discussing racism in Latin America, see TANYA KATERI HERNANDEZ, RACIAL SUBORDINATION IN LATIN AMERICA: THE ROLE OF THE STATE, CUSTOMARY LAW, AND THE NEW CIVIL RIGHTS RESPONSE (2013).

116. *See* CollegeBoard, *2013 College-Bound Seniors: Total Group Profile Report* 3 tbl.8 (2013). The average combined SAT math, critical reading, and writing score of the various Hispanic/Latino groups were 1355 for Mexican Americans, 1354 for Puerto Ricans, and 1355 for other Latinos.

117. The 2010 MCAT scores for applicants to medical schools broken down by race (with standard deviations) are as follows: Mexican American 26.3 (5.5); Puerto Rican 21.4 (6.3); Cuban 26.6 (5.6); Other Hispanic or Latino 25.8 (5.4); Multiple Hispanic or Latino 25.6 (5.4); Black or African American 22.2 (5.8); Asian 29.3 (5.3); American Indian or Alaska Native 25.4 (4.5); Native Hawaiian or Other Pacific Islander 25.6 (6.3); White 29.0 (4.8); Other Race 28.6 (6.1); More Than One Race 28.6 (5.8) and all 28.3 (5.5). See Association of American Medical Colleges website under *Applicants and Matriculants Data Table 19: MCAT Scores*

*and GPAs for Applicants and Matriculants to U.S. Medical Schools by Race and Ethnicity, 2010.*
118. Kevin Brown and Tom I. Romero II, *supra* note 115.
119. *Id.*

# Chapter One

1. *See, e.g.,* Ariela J. Gross, What Blood Won't Tell: A History of Race on Trial in America 3 (2008) and Frank W. Sweet, Legal History of the Color Line: The Rise and Triumph of the One-Drop Rule (2005).

2. Department of Education, *Final Guidance, on Maintain, Collecting and Reporting Racial and Ethnic Data to the Department of Education,* Fed. Reg., 59266, Oct. 19, 2007 (hereinafter, the Final Guidance.)

3. For example, almost 350 public and private colleges accepted the Common Application form for the incoming 2009–10 freshmen class and almost 80 institutions accepted the Universal College Application form. Both of these forms lump all black students into a single "African-American/African/Black." *See* Kevin Brown, *Should Black Immigrants Be Favored Over Black Hispanics and Black Multiracials in the Admissions Processes of Selective Higher Education Programs?,* 54 How. L.J. 255, 256 n.3 (2011).

4. *See* C. Anthony Broh and Stephen D. Minicucci, *Racial Identity and Government Classification: A Better Solution 1* (2008).

5. *Id.*

6. *See Final Guidance, supra* note 2, at 59267.

7. The definition of Hispanic or Latino is "a person of Cuban, Mexican, Puerto Rican, South or Central American, or other Spanish culture or origin, regardless of race." *Final Guidance, supra* note 2, at 59266–79.

8. *See* Broh, *supra* note 4, at 2.

9. *See* Katherine K. Wallman, Suzann Evinger & Susan Schechter, *Measuring Our Nation's Diversity: Developing a Common Language for Data on Race/Ethnicity,* 90 Am. J. Pub. Health 1704 (2000).

10. C. Matthew Snipp, *Racial Measurement in the American Census: Past Practices and Implications for the Future,* 29 Ann. Rev. Soc. 563, 566 (2003).

11. *See* U.S. Const. art. I, §2, cl. 3.

12. U.S. Const. art. II, §1, cl. 2 states: "Each State shall appoint, in such Manner as the Legislature thereof may direct, a Number of Electors, equal to the whole Number of Senators and Representatives to which the State may be entitled in the Congress: but no Senator or Representative, or Person holding an Office of Trust or Profit under the United States, shall be appointed an Elector."

13. *See* Campbell Gibson and Kay Jung, *Historical Census Statistics On Population Totals By Race, 1790 to 1990, and By Hispanic Origin, 1970 to 1990, For Large Cities And Other Urban Places In The United States,* Table 1-A. (United States Census Bureau, Working Paper Series No. 76, 2005).

14. For a copies of the census forms from 1790 to 1840, see Census Forms, available at http://www.ancestry.com/download/forms. (last visited Mar. 30, 2014).

15. Jennifer Lee & Frank D. Bean, The Diversity Paradox: Immigration and the

COLOR LINE IN TWENTY-FIRST CENTURY AMERICA 38 (2010).

16. MELISSA NOBLES, SHADES OF CITIZENSHIP: RACE AND THE CENSUS IN MODERN POLITICS 32 (2000).

17. *Id.* at 33.

18. Snipp, *supra* note 10, at 563, 565.

19. *See* U.S. State Department website of former Secretaries of State, Abel Parker Upshur, http://history.state.gov/departmenthistory/people/upshur-abel-parker. (last visited Mar. 30, 2014).

20. Nancy Krieger, *Shades of Difference: Theoretical Underpinnings of the Medical Controversy on Black/White Differences in the United States, 1830–1870* 17 INT. J. HEALTH SERV. 259, 265 (1987).

21. NOBLES, *supra* note 16, at 34.

22. Snipp, *supra* note 10, at 563, 566.

23. NOBLES, *supra* note 16, at 35–6.

24. *See* Christine Hickman, *The Devil and the One Drop Rule: Racial Categories, African Americans and the U.S. Census,* 95 MICH. L. REV. 1162, 1184–5 (1996–97).

25. To see census forms throughout the years and accompanying questions, see http://usa.ipums.org/usa/voliii/tEnumForm.shtml. (last visited Mar. 30, 2014).

26. *See* Gibson and Jung, *supra* note 13.

27. To see the list of questions raised on the census, including those about race or color, see U.S. Census Bureau history http://www.census.gov/history/www/through_the_decades/index_of_questions/1900_1.html (last visited Mar. 30, 2014).

28. B. EDMONSTON & C. SCHULTZE, MODERNIZING THE U.S. CENSUS 144 (1994).

29. Snipp, *supra* note 10, at 563, 567.

30. Snipp, *supra* note 10, at 563.

31. M.J. ANDERSON & S.E. FEINBERG, WHO COUNTS: THE POLITICS OF CENSUS-TAKING 29–30 (1999).

32. *Id.* at 30.

33. Snipp, *supra* note 10, at 563, 569.

34. *See* Sharon M. Lee & Barry Edmonston, *New Marriages, New Families: U.S. Racial and Hispanic Intermarriage,* Population Bull., at 9, June 2005.

35. Snipp, *supra* note 10, at 563, 570.

36. Nancy Leong, *Multiracial Identity and Affirmative Action,* 12 ASIAN PAC. AM. L. J. 1, 3 (2007).

37. Instructions for 1930 census with definition for "Mexican" available at https://usa.ipums.org/usa/voliii/inst1930.shtml (date last visited March 30, 2014).

38. *Id.*

39. NOBLES, *supra* note 16, at 73. According to the 1930 census, the total American population was 122,775,046. *See* Gibson and Jung, *supra* note 13.

40. Instructions for 1940 census, *supra* note 25.

41. NOBLES, *supra* note 16, at 74.

42. *See* Betsy Guzmán, U.S. Census Bureau, The Hispanic Population, Census 2000 Brief 1 (2001).

43. *See* Jorge Chapa, *Hispanic\Latino Ethnicity and Identifiers,* Encyclopedia of the U.S. Census. (Margo Andersen, editor-in-chief, Jorge Chapa, Connie Citro & Joe Salvo, editorial board (Congressional Quarterly Press: Washington, DC, 2000).

44. *Id.*

45. Alex M. Saragoza, Concepcion R. Juarez, Abel Valenzuela Jr., & Oscar Gonzalez, *History And Public Policy: Title VII and the Use of the Hispanic Classification*, 5 LA RAZA L. J. 1, 11–12 (1992).

46. 113 CONG. REC. S16101 (1967) (statement of Rep. González).

47. *See* Chapa, *supra* note 43.

48. *Id.*

49. *See* U.S. Census Bureau, *Hispanic Population of the United States, Hispanic Population in the United States 1970 to 2050*.

50. Snipp, *supra* note 10, at 563, 572.

51. G. REGINALD DANIEL, MORE THAN BLACK?: MULTIRACIAL IDENTITY AND THE NEW RACIAL ORDER 98 (2001).

52. REYNOLDS FARLEY, IDENTIFYING WITH MULTIPLE RACES: A SOCIAL MOVEMENT THAT SUCCEEDED BUT FAILED? in THE CHANGING TERRAIN OF RACE AND ETHNICITY 126 (Maria Krysan & Amanda E. Lewis, eds., 2004).

53. *See* Alice Robbin, *The Politics Of Representation In The US National Statistical System: Origins Of Minority Population Interest Group Participation* 27 J. GOV. INFORM. 431, 433–34 (2000).

54. *See* Wallman, *supra* note 9, at 1704.

55. *See Final Guidance*, *supra* note 2, at 59270.

56. *See* Wallman, *supra* note 9, at 1704.

57. President, Executive Order, "To Facilitate Coordination of Federal Education Programs, Executive Order 11185," CODE OF FEDERAL REGISTER, TITLE 3: THE PRESIDENT, 1964 AND 1965 COMPILATION (1967): 260 (revoked by: EO 12553, Feb. 25, 1986).

58. *See* REPORT OF THE AD HOC COMMITTEE ON RACIAL AND ETHNIC DEFINITIONS OF THE FEDERAL INTERAGENCY COMMITTEE ON EDUCATION, 8 (April 1975).

59. *Id.*

60. In *U.S. v. Bhagat Singh Thind*, 261 U.S. 204 (1923), the Supreme Court rejected an argument that a "high caste Hindu" from the Punjab would be considered a "white person" for purposes of the Naturalization Act that at the time provided that only white persons and those of African descent could become naturalized citizens.

61. Report of Ad Hoc Comm. on Racial and Ethnic Def., *supra* note 58.

62. *Id.*

63. *Id.*

64. RAINER SPENCER, SPURIOUS ISSUES: RACE AND MULTIRACIAL IDENTITY POLITICS IN THE UNITED STATES 68 (1999).

65. *Id.* at 42–43.

66. DIRECTIVE No. 15 RACE AND ETHNIC STANDARDS FOR FEDERAL STATISTICS AND ADMINISTRATIVE REPORTING (as adopted on May 12, 1977).

67. For a more complete retelling of the change of the name of Directive No. 15 see SPENCER, *supra* note 64, at 70–71.

68. Directive No. 15, *supra* note 66.

69. *Id.*

70. SPENCER, *supra* note 64, at 78.

71. OFFICE OF MANAGEMENT AND BUDGET: Revisions to the Standards for the Classification of Federal Data on Race and Ethnicity *Federal Register* Notice, October 30, 1997. (hereinafter 1997 Revisions).

72. *See* SPENCER, *supra* note 64, at 70–73.

73. Committee on National Statistics, National Research Council, Spotlight on Heterogeneity: The Federal Standards for Racial and Ethnic Classification 37 (1996); DVORA YANOW, CONSTRUCTING "RACE" AND "ETHNICITY" IN AMERICA: CATEGORY-MAKING IN PUBLIC POLICY AND ADMINISTRATION 42–46 (2003).

74. *See* Wallman, *supra* note 9, at 1704. Katherine K. Wallman directed the review of the standards.

75. Wendy D. Roth, *The End of the One-Drop Rule? Labeling of Multiracial Children in Black Intermarriages*, 20 SOC. F. 35, 38 (2005).

76. For a listing of the steps taken see OMB Revisions, see *supra* note 71.

77. YANOW, *supra* note 73, at 38–39.

78. *See* Wallman, *supra* note 9, at 1704.

79. 1997 Revisions, *supra* note 71.

80. *Id.*

81. *See* Wallman, *supra* note 9, at 1704.

82. 1997 Revisions, *supra* note 71.

83. *See* FARLEY, *supra* note 52, at 134.

84. About 15.4 million respondents checked just the Some Other Race (SOR) category and 3.2 million checked SOR along with another racial category on the 2000 census. Approximately 97.0 percent of those who just checked SOR also responded that they were Hispanic or Latino. Over 90% of those who checked SOR and another racial category also indicated that they were Hispanic or Latino. "Thus it is clear that reporting of SOR is highly related to how Hispanics report in race." Jorge del Pinal, Elizabeth Martin, Claudette Bennett & Art Cresce, *Overview of Results of New Race and Hispanic Origin Questions in Census 2000,* (2007); *See also* Sharon M. Lee & Barry Edmonston, *supra* note 34, at 12 tbl.2.

85. PINAL, *supra* note 84, at 715.

86. Karen Humes, Nicholas A. Jones, and Roberto Ramirez, *Overview of Race and Hispanic Origin: 2010,* 6 tbl 2 (2011).

87. *See* Wallman, *supra* note 9, at 1704.

88. *See* KIM M. WILLIAMS, MARK ONE OR MORE: CIVIL RIGHTS IN MULTIRACIAL AMERICA 112 (2006).

89. KERRY ANN ROCKQUEMORE & DAVID BRUNSMA, BEYOND BLACK: BIRACIAL IDENTITY IN AMERICA 102 (2002). *See also* WILLIAMS, *supra* note 88, at 7–8.

90. *Id.* at 1–17.

91. Committee on National Statistics, *National Research Council, Spotlight on Heterogeneity: The Federal Standards for Racial and Ethnic Classification* 37–40 (1996).

92. *See* F. JAMES DAVIS, WHO IS BLACK: ONE NATION'S DEFINITION 21 (1991). *See also* JON MICHAEL SPENCER, THE NEW COLORED PEOPLE: THE MIXED-RACE MOVEMENT IN AMERICA 156 (1997) (pointing to a study that estimated that about 70% of the black population of the United States has multiracial ancestry).

93. Maria P. P. Root, *Within, Between, and Beyond Race, in* RACIALLY MIXED PEOPLE IN AMERICA 9, (Maria P. P. Root ed., 1991).

94. *See* Executive Office of the President, Office of Management and Budget, Tabulation Working Group of the Interagency Committee for the Review of Standards of Data on Race and Ethnicity, *Provisional Guidance on the Implementation of the 1997 Standards for Federal Data on Race and Ethnicity,* FED. REG., Appendix C page 88–90, Dec. 15, 2000.

95. *See* Sonya M. Tafoya, Hans Johnson, & Laura E. Hill, *Who Chooses to Choose Two?*

*in* THE AMERICAN PEOPLE: 2000 CENSUS 332 (Richard Farley & John Haaga, ed., 2005).

96. *See* Wallman, *supra* note 9, at 1705

97. 1997 Revisions, *supra* note 71.

98. *See* FARLEY, *supra* note 52, at 134.

99. Humes, *supra* note 86 at 4 tbl 1.

100. For a listing of the 57 categories and their populations, see *CENSUSSCOPE, UNITED STATES MULTIRACIAL PROFILE* (2001), http://www.censusscope.org/us/print_chart_multi.html. (last visited Mar. 30, 2014).

101. *Id.*

102. *Id.*

103. *See* United States Census Bureau, *The Two or More Races Population: 2000, Census 2000 Brief*, at p. 9 (Nov. 2001).

104. Humes, *supra* note 86

105. *Id.*

106. *Final Guidance*, *supra* note 2, at 59274.

107. *Proposed Guidance on Maintaining, Collecting and Reporting Data on Race and Ethnicity to the U.S. Department of Education*, 71 FED. REG. at 44866 (hereinafter, the *Proposed Guidance*).

108. *Id.* at 44868.

109. *Id.*

110. *Id.*

111. Agency Information Collection Activities, Notice of Submission for OMB Review; Final Comment Request to the Equal Employment Opportunity Commission, 70 FED. REG. 71295 (Nov. 28, 2005).

112. *See EEO-1 Who Must File*, U.S. EQUAL EMP. OPPORTUNITY COMM'N from Commission website, *available* at http://www.eeoc.gov/employers/eeo1survey/whomustfile.cfm (Mar. 30, 2014).

113. *Id.*

114. *Id.*

115. Agency Information Collection Activities, *supra* note 111.

116. *Id.* at 71296–97.

117. *Id.* at 71296–98.

118. *Id.* at 71297.

119. *Id.*

120. *Id.* at 71296

121. *Id.* at 71297.

122. *Id.*

123. *Id.* at 71294, 71296.

124. *Id.*

125. *Id..*

126. *Id.*

127. For a listing of the 57 categories and their populations, see *CENSUSSCOPE, supra* note 100.

128. *Id.*

129. Employers began to use the revised survey for the reporting period beginning September 30, 2007.

130. *Proposed Guidance*, *supra* note 108, at 44871.

131. *Final Guidance, supra* note 2.
132. *Final Guidance, supra* note 2, at 59270. *But see* BROH & MINICUCCI, *supra* note 4, at 4 (arguing that this assumption was not tested).
133. *Final Guidance supra* note 2, at 59266–67.
134. *Id.* at 59270–71.
135. *Id.* at 59271.
136. *Id.*
137. *Id.* at 59267.
138. *Id.* at 59277.
139. *Id.*
140. *Id.* at 59271.
141. *Id.* at 59270.
142. *Id.* at 59274.
143. According to the 2000 Census, of the 3,093,824 individuals between the ages of 15 and 19 who were classified as Black or African American or Black or African American in Combination, 164,271 were classified as Black or African American in combination (164,271 / 3,093,824=5.3%); for ages 10 and 14, the corresponding figures were 210,794 of 3,332,324 (210,794 / 3,332,324=6.3%); for ages 5 to 9, they were 285,205 of 3,490,717 (285,205 / 3,490,717=8.1%); for under the age of five, they were 362,073 of 3,166,859 (362,073 / 3,166 859=11.4%). *See* Census 2000 PHC-T-8. Race and Hispanic or Latino Origin by Age and Sex for the United States: 2000, Table 3. Black or African American Population, by Age and Sex for the United States: 2000.
144. *See* WILLIAMS, *supra* note 88, at 114.
145. SHERYLL CASHIN, PLACE, NOT RACE! A NEW VISION OF OPPORTUNITY IN AMERICA.
146. *Grutter v. Bollinger*, 539 U.S. 306, 334 (2003).
147. This was one of the points that Chief Justice Rehnquist stressed in his dissenting opinion in *Grutter*. *Id.* at 382–86 (Rehnquist, C.J., dissenting).
148. The mean SAT scores for blacks in 2013 were Critical Reading 431, Mathematics 429, and Writing 418; for Mexican Americans they were 449, 464, and 442, respectively; for Puerto Ricans they were 456, 453, and 445, respectively; for other Latinos they were 450, 462, and 443, respectively; for American Indians and Alaskan Natives they were 480, 486, and 461, respectively; for whites 527, 534, and 515, respectively; and for Asian Americans 521, 597, and 527, respectively. *See* CollegeBoard, 2013 College-Bound Seniors: Total Group Profile Report 2 tbl.8 (2013).
149. SUSAN P. DALESSANDO ET AL., LSAT PERFORMANCE WITH REGIONAL, GENDER, AND RACIAL/ETHNIC BREAKDOWNS: 2005–2006 THROUGH 2011–2012 TESTING YEAR 20, TBL 4B (2012). The standard deviations of the various racial/ethnic groups were 8.68, 9.25, 9.68, 10.52, and 9.27, respectively. *Id.*
150. *Final Guidance, supra* note 2, at 59268.
151. *Id.*
152. *See* 1997 Revisions, *supra* note 71. (there was no discussion in the comments about separating Africans from African Americans or West Indians from African Americans, although there the separation of Cape Verdeans from African Americans was specifically rejected).
153. *See Final Guidance, supra* note 2, at 59267.

# Chapter Two

1. For recent books on affirmative action see SHERYLL CASHIN, PLACE, NOT RACE: A NEW VISION OF OPPORTUNITY IN AMERICA (2014); RANDALL KENNEDY, FOR DISCRIMINATION: RACE, AFFIRMATIVE ACTION, AND THE LAW (2013); and RICHARD SANDER AND STUART TAYLOR, JR., MISMATCH: HOW AFFIRMATIVE ACTION HURTS STUDENTS IT'S INTENDED TO HELP, AND WHY UNIVERSITIES WON'T ADMIT IT (2012).
2. Grutter v. Bollinger, 539 U.S. 306 (2003).
3. Id. at 306, 333, 338 (2003).
4. ROBERT J. COTTROL, THE LINGERING SHADOW: SLAVERY, RACE, AND LAW IN THE AMERICAN HEMISPHERE 5–6 (2013). For a discussion of different estimates of how many blacks were transported to North America see David Eltis, The U.S. Transatlantic Slave Trade, 1644–1867: An Assessment 54 CIVIL WAR HISTORY 347 (2008).
5. See David Eltis, supra note 4, at 357–8.
6. Id. at 347, 356.
7. See Ramón A. Gutiérrez, Changing Ethnic and Class Boundaries in America's Hispanic Past, in SOCIAL AND GENDER BOUNDARIES IN THE UNITED STATES 37 (Sucheng Chan ed., 1989).
8. I distinguish this view of the struggle of African Americans against racial oppression from those who view the black perspective as one of victimology. See, e.g., JOHN H. MCWHORTER, LOSING THE RACE: SELF-SABOTAGE IN BLACK AMERICA (2000). When I discuss this liberation perspective, it is not as an embrace of victimhood. Rather, it is a desire to eradicate the victimization that is a result of historical racial oppression. As such, it is derived from a perspective that takes the struggle against racial oppression, not the effect of that oppression, as its primary feature.
9. W. E. B. DuBois, "Three Centuries of Discrimination," The Crisis 54 (December 1947), 362–63.
10. See, e.g., Kendall Thomas, Comments at Frontiers of Legal Thought Conference, Duke Law School (Jan. 26, 1990), quoted in Charles R. Lawrence III, If He Hollers Let Him Go: Regulating Racist Speech on Campus, 1990 DUKE L. J. 431, in MARI J. MATSUDA, CHARLES R. LAWRENCE III, RICHARD DELGADO & KIMBERLÉ W. CRENSHAW, WORDS THAT WOUND 53, 61 (1993); see also D. Marvin Jones, Darkness Made Visible: Law, Metaphor, and the Racial Self, 82 GEO. L. J. 437 (1993) (arguing that racial categories are neither objective nor natural, but ideological and constructed. In these terms race is not so much a category but a practice: people are raced).
11. Mari Matsuda, Looking to the Bottom: Critical Legal Studies and Reparations, 22 HARV. C.R.-C.L. L. REV. 323, 335 (1987).
12. Letter from John Rolfe to Sir Edwin Sandys (Jan. 1619/1620), in 3 THE RECORDS OF THE VIRGINIA COMPANY OF LONDON 241, 243 (Susan M. Kingsbury ed., 1933), reprinted in PAUL FINKELMAN, THE LAW OF FREEDOM AND BONDAGE 9 (1986).
13. CAPTAINE JOHN SMITH, THE GENERALL HISTORIE OF VIRGINIA, NEW ENGLAND, AND THE SUMMER ISLES, VOL 1, at 246–7 (Glasgow: James MacLehose & Sons, 1907). This account can also be found printed in CIVIL RIGHTS AND AFRICAN-AMERICANS 4 (Albert P. Blaustein & Robert L. Zangrando eds., Northwestern Univ. Press 1991)(1968).
14. CLAUDINE L. FERRELL, THE ABOLITIONIST MOVEMENT 3 (2006).

15. Edmund S. Morgan, American Slavery, American Freedom: The Ordeal of Colonial Virginia 297–98 (1975).
16. V. T. Harlow, A History of Barbados, 1625–1685, 295 (1926).
17. Vincent Harding, There Is a River 8 (1985).
18. Ferrell, *supra* note 14, at 4.
19. Richard Kluger, Simple Justice: The History of Brown v. Board of Education and Black America's Struggle for Equality 31–33 (1976).
20. *See* Joe R. Feagin, Racist America: Roots, Current Realities, and Future Reparations 12 (2000).
21. *Dred Scott v. Sandford*, 60 U.S. 393, 407 (1857).
22. Bureau of the Census, U.S. Dep't of Commerce, Ser. P-23, No. 80, The Social and Economic Status of the Black Population in the United States: An Historical View, 1790–1978, at 254 (1979) (hereinafter Historical View).
23. *See* Campbell Gibson & Kay Jung, *Historical Census Statistics on Population Totals by Race, 1790 to 1990, and by Hispanic Origin, 1970 to 1990, for the United States, Regions, Divisions, and States, Table 4. South Region—Race and Hispanic Origin: 1790 to 1990* (United States Census Bureau, Working Paper Series No. 56, 2002).
24. For example, in one 1671 Virginia declaration, slaves were put in the same categories as sheep, horses, and cattle. *See* Feagin, *supra* note 20, at 41.
25. James H. Dorman & Robert R. Jones, The Afro-American Experience: A Cultural History Through Emancipation 118 (1974).
26. Calhoun, Speech in the U.S. Senate, 1837, *in* Paul Finkleman, Defending Slavery: Proslavery Thought in the Old South: A Brief History with Documents 54, 58–59 (2003).
27. William Jay, The Life of John Jay I, 231 (2 vols, 1833).
28. Leon Litwack, North of Slavery: The Negro in the Free States 14 (1961).
29. Northwest Ordinance of 1787, Art. 6, reprinted in Blaustein & Zangrando eds., *supra* note 13, at 47.
30. Howard Zinn: A People's History of the United States 1492 to Present 77 (5th ed. 2003).
31. Litwack, *supra* note 28, at 14.
32. *See generally id.*
33. *See* C. Van Woodward, The Strange Career of Jim Crow 20 (3d rev. ed. 1974). *See also* Bernard Grofman et al., Minority Representation and the Quest for Voting Equality 4, n1 (1992).
34. *See* Alexis de Tocqueville, Democracy in America 344 (George Lawrence trans., 1966).
35. *See, e.g.*, Daniel Raymond, Race, Slavery, and Fertility *reprinted in* 1 Racial Thought in America: From the Puritans to Abraham Lincoln 274 (Louis Ruchames ed., 1969)
36. James D. Lockett, *Abraham Lincoln and Colonization: An Episode that Ends in Tragedy at L'Ile a Vache, Haiti, 1863–4*, 21 J. Black Stud. 428 (1991).
37. *Id.* at 428, 429–30.
38. John Hope Franklin & Alfred A. Moss, Jr., From Slavery to Freedom: A History of Negro Americans 154–57 (6th ed. 1988).
39. Lockett, *supra* note 36, at 433.
40. Franklin & Moss, *supra* note 38, at 189.

41. Lockett, *supra* note 36, at 442.
42. W. E. B. DuBois, Black Reconstruction In America 1860–1880 56 (Macmillan 1992)(1935).
43. *See* Eric Foner, Reconstruction: America's Unfinished Revolution 1863–1877, 250–51 (1988).
44. U.S. Const. amend. XIV, §2. The section states in full: "Representatives shall be apportioned among the several States according to their respective numbers, counting the whole number of persons in each State, excluding Indians not taxed. But when the right to vote at any election for the choice of electors for President and Vice President of the United States, Representatives in Congress, the Executive and Judicial officers of a State, or the members of the Legislature thereof, is denied to any of the male inhabitants of such State, being twenty-one years of age, and citizens of the United States, or in any way abridged, except for participation in rebellion, or other crime, the basis of representation therein shall be reduced in the proportion which the number of such male citizens shall bear to the whole number of male citizens twenty-one years of age in such State."
45. The Civil Rights Act of 1866 (most important provisions were those that declared blacks citizens and granted equal rights to enter into contracts; to buy, sell, lease or rent property; to sue and be sued in court; and to give testimony in court); the Enforcement Act of May 31, 1870 (outlawed state actions intended to deprive blacks of the right to vote); the Enforcement Act of February 28, 1871 (amended the Enforcement Act of 1870 and was designed to eliminate fraudulent registration practices and establish a complex system of federal machinery to supervise elections in the states if the circuit court was petitioned); the Enforcement Act of April 20, 1871 (also known as the Ku Klux Klan Act, it was designed primarily to prevent intimidation of blacks by illegal action where states were unwilling or unable to provide such protection and gave the President the right to employ the militia and to suspend the right of habeas corpus when public safety was endangered by unlawful combinations); and the Civil Rights Act of 1875 (guaranteed to all persons, regardless of race or color, the full and equal enjoyment of inns, public conveyances, and public places of amusement. It also gave the right to sue for personal damages, gave federal courts exclusive jurisdiction over cases arising under the act and made it a misdemeanor to bar any qualified person from serving as a grand or petit juror).
46. Foner, *supra* note 43, at 425.
47. Bureau of the Census, U.S. Department of Commerce, Historical Statistics of the United States: Colonial Times to 1970 Part 1, Series A-195–209 (1975).
48. *See* Wang Xi, The Trial of Democracy: Black Suffrage Northern Republicans, 1860–1910, xviii (1997).
49. Burke Marshall, Federalism and Civil Rights 13–14 (1964) (quoting Judge Chrisman speaking at the 1890 Mississippi constitutional convention).
50. Sean Dennis Cashman, African-Americans and the Quest for Civil Rights 8 (1991).
51. *Williams v. Mississippi,* 170 U.S. 213 (1898).
52. *Guinn v. United States,* 238 U.S. 347 (1915).
53. *See Smith v. Allwright,* 321 U.S. 649 (1944).
54. Charles L. Black, *The Lawfulness of the Segregation Decisions,* 69 Yale L.J. 421, 424–25 (1960).
55. James Loewen, Sundown Towns: A Hidden Dimension of American Racism 29 (2005).

56. *Civil Rights Cases*, 109 U.S. 3 (1883).
57. C. Van Woodward, *supra* note 33, at 97.
58. *Plessy v. Ferguson*, 163 U.S. 537 (1896).
59. *Id.* at 544.
60. *Id.* at 552.
61. *Cumming v. Richmond County Bd. of Educ.*, 175 U.S. 528 (1899).
62. Jeannine Bell, Hate Thy Neighbor: Move-In Violence and the Persistence of Racial Segregation in American Housing 13 (2013).
63. Barbara Bair, *Though Justice Sleeps: 1880–1900, in* To Make Our World Anew: A History of African Americans From 1880, Vol. II 3 (2000).
64. Stephan Thernstrom & Abigail Thernstrom, America in Black and White: One Nation, Indivisible 17 (1997).
65. *Brown v. Board of Education*, 347 U.S. 483 (1954).
66. *See*, Lev. 25:44–46
67. *See, e.g.*, 1 Cor. 12:13; Titus 2:9–10; Philem.; Col. 3:22; Ephesians 6:5–6.
68. David M. Goldenberg, The Curse of Ham: Race and Slavery in Early Judaism, Christianity, and Islam 1 (2003).
69. *See* Genesis 4:1–16.
70. *See, e.g.*, Goldenberg, *supra* note 68, at 178–181.
71. Cornel West, Prophesy Deliverance! 57–58 (1982).
72. Benjamin Rush, *Observations Intended to Favor a Supposition that the Black Color (as it is Called) of the Negroes is Derived from Leprosy*, reprinted in Ruchames ed., *supra* note 35, at 218–225.
73. West, *supra* note 71, at 56–57.
74. *See* Feagin, *supra* note 20, at 81.
75. Herbert Hovenkamp, *Social Science and Segregation Before* Brown, 34 Duke L. J. 624, 651 (1985).
76. Stephen Jay Gould, The Mismeasure of Man 85–101 (1982).
77. For example, Johannes Kepler calculated the date of creation of the world as 3992 B.C., Martin Luther put it at 4000 B.C., but the most famous date was 4004 B.C., which was calculated by Irish archbishop James Ussher. The exact date was October 23, 4004 B.C. *See* David Livingston, Adam's Ancestors: Race, Religion & the Politics of Human Origins 5 (2008).
78. William H. Tucker, The Science and Politics of Racial Research 23–24 (1994).
79. Sanford B. Hunt, *The Negro as a Soldier*, 7 Anthropological Review: 40, 48–54 (1869).
80. Hovenkamp, *supra* note 75 at 624, 653–54.
81. Gould, *supra* note 76, at 188.
82. *Id.* at 227.
83. Melissa Nobles, Shades of Citizenship: Race and the Census in Modern Politics 74 (2000).
84. In 1939 the NAACP established the NAACP Legal Defense and Educational Fund, Inc., known later as the Legal Defense Fund or the Inc. Fund (LDF). After that time the LDF became responsible for the legal work. For a book discussing the history of the legal efforts of the NAACP and LDF, see Mark Tushnet, Making Civil Rights Law: Thurgood Marshall and the Supreme Court, 1936–1961 (1994).

85. *See, e.g., Gaines v. Canada*, 305 U.S. 337 (1938); *Sipuel v. Oklahoma State Board of Regents*, 332 U.S. 631 (1948); *Shelley v. Kraemer*, 334 U. S. 1 (1948); *Sweatt v. Painter*, 339 U. S. 629 (1950); and *McLaurin v. Oklahoma State Regents*, 339 U.S. 629 (1950).

86. K. B. Clark, Effect of Prejudice and Discrimination on Personality Development (Mid-century White House Conference on Children and Youth, 1950); E. Frazier, The Negro in the United States 674–81 (1949); G. Myrdal, An American Dilemma (1944); H. Witmer & R. Kotinsky, Personality in the Making: The Fact-finding Report of the Mid-century White House Conference on Children and Youth (1952); Isador Chein, *What Are the Psychological Effects of Segregation Under Conditions of Equal Facilities?* 3 Int'l J. Opinion and Attitude Res. 229 (1949); Brameld, Educational Costs, in Discrimination and National Welfare 44 (R. MacIver ed. 1949); Max Deutscher & Isador Chein, *The Psychological Effects of Enforced Segregation: A Survey of Social Science Opinion*, 26 J. PSYCHOL. 259 (1948); see *Brown I*, 347 U.S. at 494 n.11. For a copy of the brief filed by leading social scientists see *The Effects of Segregation and the Consequence of Desegregation: A Social Science Statement* reprinted at 37 Minn. L. Rev. 427 (1953).

87. *Brown*, 347 U.S. at 494.

88. *Brown*, 347 U.S. at 494 (quoting *Brown v. Bd. of Educ.*, 98 F. Supp. 797 (D. Kan. 1951)).

89. *Mayor & City Council of Baltimore v. Dawson*, 350 U.S. 877 (1955) (per curiam) (concluding that enforcement of racial segregation in enjoyment of public beaches and bathhouses maintained by public authorities of state and city was not a proper exercise of police powers); *Holmes v. Atlanta*, 350 U.S. 879 (1955) (per curiam) (declaring unconstitutional the City's refusal to permit blacks to play golf on city's public courses and prohibiting blacks from frequenting city parks maintained for white people's use); *Gayle v. Browder*, 352 U.S. 903 (1956) (per curiam) (striking statutes of the state of Alabama and local ordinances of the City of Montgomery, which required segregation on buses); and *New Orleans City Park Improvement Ass'n v. Detiege*, 358 U.S. 54 (1958) (per curiam) (enjoining the New Orleans City Park Improvement Association, a municipal corporation, from denying plaintiffs and other Negroes, solely on account of their race or color, the use of the facilities of the New Orleans City Park).

90. *See Green v. County School Board*, 391 U. S. 430, 435 (1968). In *Green*, the Supreme Court ordered school districts that had operated dual school systems to desegregate every aspect of their system and do it now. In ordering the taking account of race of students, faculty, staff, and administrators the Court justified this decision by stating that it was what the Court's opinion in *Brown* and the implementation decision rendered a year later, *Brown v. Board of Education*, 349 US 294 (1955), required. *Id* at 437–38.

91. 503 U.S. 467 (1992).

92. *Id.* at 485–86.

93. *See* U.S. Commission on Civil Rights, Twenty Years After Brown: Equality of Educational Opportunity 46 (1975).

94. *Green, supra* note 90, at 435.

95. For figures on school desegregation *see* Kevin Brown, Race, Law and Education in the Post-Desegregation Era: Four Perspectives on Desegregation and Resegregation 177, 206 (2005).

96. *See, e.g.,* James A. Banks. Multiethnic Education 99 (2d ed. 1988); Myra Sadker et al., *Gender and Educational Equality, in* Multicultural Education 106–23 (James A. Banks & Cherry A.M. Banks eds., 1989); Geneva Gay, *Achieving Educational Equality Through Curriculum Desegregation*, 72 Phi Delta Kappan 56, 57 (1990).

97. Banks, *supra* note 96, at 99.

98. President Lyndon B. Johnson, *To Fulfill These Rights*, Commencement Address at Howard University (June 4, 1965).

99. Richard Sander, Mismatch: How Affirmative Action Hurts Students It's Intended to Help, and Why Universities Won't Admit It (2012); *Fisher v. Texas*, 133 S. Ct. 2411, 2431 (2013) (Thomas, J. Concurring).

100. *Fisher, supra* note 99, at 2432 (2013) (Thomas, J. concurring).

101. *Regents of the Univ. of Calif. v. Bakke*, 438 U.S. 265, 407 (1978).

102. *See, e.g., Keyes v. Sch. Dist. No. 1*, 413 U.S. 189 (1973); (rejecting de facto segregation and embracing de jure (intentional) discrimination); *Milliken v. Bradley*, 418 U.S. 717 (1974) (generally rejecting interdistrict school desegregation remedies).

103. *See, e.g., Griggs v. Duke Power Co.*, 401 U.S. 424 (holding that Title VII of the Civil Rights Act of 1964 prohibits the use of tests that operate to exclude members of minority groups unless the employer demonstrates that the procedures are substantially related to job performance); *Palmer v. Thompson*, 403 U.S. 217 (1971) (rejecting an argument that equal protection clause violations should be based on motivation: "no case in this Court has held that a legislative act may violate equal protection solely because of the motivations for the men who voted for it."); *Lau v. Nichols*, 414 U.S. 563 (1974) (upholding regulations under Title VI from the Department of Health, Education and Welfare that barred discriminatory actions by educational institutions which have a discriminatory effect even though no purposeful design is present).

104. *See, e.g., Green supra* note 96, at 430 (1968) (requiring school districts that had operated dual school systems to take account of race of teachers, administrators, students in order to produce racially desegregated schools); *Swann v. Charlotte-Mecklenburg Board of Education*, 402 U.S. 1 (1971) (School authorities are traditionally charged with broad power to formulate and implement educational policy and might well conclude, for example, that in order to prepare students to live in a pluralistic society each school should have a prescribed ratio of Negro to white students reflecting the proportion for the district as a whole.); and *United Steelworkers of America v. Weber*, 443 U.S. 193 (1979) (upholding agreement between employer and labor union requiring an employer to reserve 50 percent of the openings in an in-plant craft training program for black craft workers as an acceptable measure to eliminate a manifest racial imbalance in the company's labor force).

105. *See e.g. Keyes, supra* note 102, at 189 (defining an unconstitutionally segregated school system as one based on discriminatory intent not *de facto* segregation); *Washington v. Davis*, 426 U.S. 229 (1976) (concluding that violations of equal protection principles by the federal government under the Fifth Amendment are based on discriminatory intent); *Village of Arlington Heights v. Metro. Hous. Dev. Corp.*, 429 U.S. 252 (1977) (holding that violations of the equal protection clause are based on discriminatory intent); *City of Richmond v. J.A. Croson Co.*, 488 U.S. 469, 493 (1989) (striking down minority set asides in government contracting under the equal protection clause); *Adarand Constructors, Inc. v. Pena*, 515 U.S. 200, 237 (1995) (stating that strict scrutiny applies whenever governmental entities at any level employ racial classifications); *Guardians Association v. Civil Service Commission of New York City*, 463 U.S. 582 (1983) (holding Section 601 of the 1964 Civil Rights Act only applies to intentional discrimination); and *Alexander v. Sandoval*, 532 U.S. 275, 281 (2001) (stating that Title VI itself directly reaches only instances of intentional discrimination and rejecting private rights of actions under the discriminatory effects regulations adopted pursuant to Section 602 of the 1964 Civil Rights Act).

106. *Bakke, supra* note 101.

107. *Id.* at 298.
108. *Id.*
109. *Adarand,* 515 U.S. 200 (1995).
110. *Id.* at 242 (Thomas, J., concurring).
111. *Croson,* 488 U.S. 469 (1989), at 493.
112. *See, e.g.,* Justice O'Connor's opinion in *City of Richmond v. Croson. Id.* ("may in fact ... lead to a politics of racial hostility"); in *Shaw v. Reno,* 509 U.S. 630, 643 (a majority of the Court stated that racial and ethnic classifications have a tendency to stigmatize individuals, polarize society, and incite racial hostilit[ies].)
113. *Miller v. Johnson,* 515 U.S. 900 (1995).
114. *Id.* at 914 (citation omitted) (quoting *Metro Broadcasting, Inc. v. FCC,* 497 U.S. 547, 636 (1990) (Kennedy, J., dissenting)).
115. *Croson, supra* note 111, at 493.
116. *See Parents Involved in Cmty. Sch. v. Seattle Sch. Dist. No. 1,* 551 U.S. 701, 782–98 (2007) (Kennedy, J., concurring in part and concurring in judgment).
117. For a discussion of the change in judicial philosophy that evidences a special concern for the educational rights of black children to one that is based more on racially neutral decision making and colorblindness, see KEVIN BROWN, *supra* note 95, at 199–270.
118. *See Washington,* and *Village of Arlington Heights.* The Court has also concluded that Section 601 of the 1964 Civil Rights Act only outlaws intentional discriminatory conduct. *See Guardians Association, supra* note 105. The Supreme Court reiterated this position in *Alexander, supra* note 105, at 281 (quoting *Alexander v. Choate,* 469 U.S. 287, 293 (1985)).
119. *Croson, supra* note 111.
120. *Id.* and *Adarand,* 515 U.S. 200 (1995).
121. *Wygant v. Jackson Board of Education,* 467 U. S. 267 (1986).
122. *Miller v. Johnson,* 515 U. S. 900 (1995).
123. *Parents Involved, supra* note 116.
124. *See* David Kairys, *Unconscious Racism,* 83 TEMP. L. REV. 857, 862 (2011).
125. Black family income was also less than that of Hispanic/Latino household income of $39,005. In contrast, white non-Hispanic household income was $57,009 and Asian household income was $68,636. *See* Carmen DeNavas-Walt, Bernadette D. Proctor and Jessica C. Smith, *Income, Poverty, and Health Insurance Coverage in the United States: 2012 Current Population Reports,* 6 tbl 1 (Sept. 2013).
126. *See* U.S. Census Bureau, Historical Income Tables: People, Black CPS Population and Per Capita Income Table P-1B, *available at* http://www.census.gov/hhes/www/income/data/historical/people/index.html. Per capita income for blacks is actually 19.4 percent higher than the per capita income of Hispanics of $16,125. *See id.* U.S. Census Bureau, Historical Income Tables: People, Hispanic of Any Race CPS Population and Per Capita Income Table P-1B, *available at* http://www.census.gov/hhes/www/income/data/historical/people/index.html. The per capita income for whites is $33,434; *see id.* U.S. Census Bureau, Historical Income Tables: People, White non-Hispanic CPS Population and Per Capita Income, Table P-1; and for Asians it is $31,905; *see id.* Census Bureau, Historical Income Tables: People, Asian CPS Population and Per Capita Income, Table P-1A.
127. U.S. Bureau of Labor Statistics, *BLS Reports Report 1044 Labor Force Characteristics by Race and Ethnicity, 2012,* 6 chart 4 (Oct. 2013).

128. U.S. Census Bureau, Table 3. Poverty Status of People, by Age, Race, and Hispanic Origin: 1959 to 2012, *available at* http://www.census.gov/hhes/www/poverty/data/historical/people.html.

129. U.S. Census Bureau, Table 2. Poverty Status of People by Family Relationship, Race, and Hispanic Origin: 1959 to 2012, *available at* http://www.census.gov/hhes/www/poverty/data/historical/people.html.

130. Signe-Mary McKernan, Caroline Ratcliffe, Eugene Steuerle, and Sisi Zhang, *Less than Equal, Racial Disparities in Wealth Accumulation* Urban Institute 1 (2013), *available at* http://www.urban.org/UploadedPDF/412802-Less-Than-Equal-Racial-Disparities-in-Wealth-Accumulation.pdf (date last visited January 30, 2013). The average wealth of a Hispanic/Latino family was $110,000. *Id.*

131. Robert Stillwell and Jennifer Stable, *Public School Graduates and Dropouts from the Common Core of Data: School Year 2009–10: First Look (Provisional Data)*, 4, U.S. Department of Education (2013). These high school graduation rates are based on receipt of a diploma. Therefore, they exclude from high school graduates those that only receive a certificate of completion or its equivalent.

132. For Hispanic/Latinos, the percentage is only 13.9 percent. *See* U.S. Census Bureau, Educational Attainment by Race and Hispanic Origin: 1970 to 2010, 9 tbl 2.

133. Michelle Alexander, The New Jim Crow: Mass Incarceration In An Age Of Colorblindness 6 (2010).

134. Heather C. West, *Prison Inmates at Midyear 2009-Statistical Tables*, U.S. Dept. of Justice Bureau of Justice Statistics, (June 2010), at 19 tbl.16.

135. For Hispanic/Latinos men, the corresponding figure is 1,822. *Id.* at 2.

136. For Latino men, their lifetime imprisonment rate is 1 in 6 and for Latino women it is 1 in 45. *See* The Sentencing Project, Racial Disparity: Lifetime Likelihood of Imprisonment, *available at* http://www.sentencingproject.org/template/page.cfm?id=122. (last visited Mar. 30, 2014).

137. The Henry J. Kaiser Family Foundation, Life Expectancy at Birth (in years) by Race/Ethnicity, available at http://kff.org/other/state-indicator/life-expectancy-by-re/. (date last visited March 30, 2014).

138. *See, e.g.*, Thernstrom & Thernstrom, *supra* note 64 (urging colorblind public policies).

139. *See, e.g.*, James McWhorter, *supra* note 8, at 10 (disputing the argument that black people get paid less than whites for the same job).

140. Richard Henstein and Charles Murray, The Bell Curve: Intelligence and Class Structure in American Life (1994).

141. *See* Roland G. Fryer Jr. and Steven D. Fevitt, *Understanding the Black-White Test Score Gap in the First Two Years of School*, 86 Rev. Econ. and Stats. 447, 448 (2004).

142. *See* Natasha Warikoo & Prudence Carter, *Cultural Explanations for Racial and Ethnic Stratification in Academic Achievement: A Call for a New and Improved Theory*, 79 Rev. of Educ. Res. 366, 370 (2009). There is a growing amount of literature that argues this is overemphasized. *See, e.g.*, James W. Ainsworth-Darnell & Douglas B. Downey, *Assessing the Oppositional Culture Explanation for Racial/Ethnic Differences in School Performance*, 63 Am. Sociological Rev. 536, 536–53 (1998); Karolyn Tyson, William Darity & Domini R. Castellino, *It's Not a 'Black Thing': Understanding the Burden of Acting White and Other Dilemmas of High Achievement.* 70 Am. Sociological Rev. 582, 582–605 (2005). *See also* Pamela R. Bennett & Amy Lutz, *How African American Is the Net Black Advantage? Differ-*

*ences in College Attendance Among Immigrant Blacks, Native Blacks, and Whites* 80 SOCIOLOGY OF EDUC. 70, 90 (2009).

143. The oppositional nature in the United States worked both ways. Professor Karst noted that in the South, which is the American ancestral home for the overwhelming majority of African Americans, to identify oneself as white meant, above all, to identify oneself as not black. *See* KENNETH L. KARST, BELONGING TO AMERICA 17 (1989). *See also* Amuzie Chimezie, *Black Bi-Culturality*, 9 W. J. BLACK STUD. 224 (1985) (defining and discussing black bi-culturality).

144. *See, e.g.,* Pamela R. Bennett & Amy Lutz, *supra* note 142, at 79.

145. Roland G. Fryer, Jr. and Steven D. Levitt, *supra* note 142, at 447.

146. MCWHORTER, *supra* note 8, at 2.

147. *Id.* at 83.

148. MARTIN DELANY, THE CONDITION, ELEVATION, EMIGRATION AND DESTINY OF THE COLORED PEOPLE OF THE UNITED STATES (1852).

149. *See* STEPHEN TUCK, WE AIN'T WHAT WE OUGHT TO BE: THE BLACK FREEDOM STRUGGLE FROM EMANCIPATION TO OBAMA 2 (2010).

150. HARDING, *supra* note 17, at 3.

151. Normal losses attendant to the crossing was 18–20% of the cargo. *See, e.g.,* DORMAN & JONES, *supra* note 25, at 81.

152. SAMUEL YEBOAH, THE IDEOLOGY OF RACISM: THE ORIGIN OF RACISM 41 (1988).

153. *See* EUGENE D. GENOVESE, ROLL, JORDAN, ROLL: THE WORLD THE SLAVES MADE 588 (1972).

154. HERBERT APTHEKER, AMERICAN NEGRO SLAVE REVOLTS 18 (6th ed. 1993).

155. *Id.* at 162.

156. *See* GENOVESE, *supra* note 153.

157. RONALD SEGAL, THE BLACK DIASPORA: FIVE CENTURIES OF THE BLACK EXPERIENCE OUTSIDE OF AFRICA 142 (1995).

158. MORGAN, *supra* note 15, at 308.

159. William M. Wiecek, *The Origins of the Law of Slavery in British North America* 17 CARDOZO L. REV. 1711, 1758 (1995).

160. 2 William W. Hening, *The Statutes at Large: Being a Collection of All the Laws of Virginia, from the First Session of the Legislature in the Year 1619*, at 481 (Act of 1680, ch. 10).

161. W. C. Rucker, *Westmoreland Slave Plot* (1687) (2012, April 3) *in* ENCYCLOPEDIA VIRGINIA. Retrieved from http://www.EncyclopediaVirginia.org/Westmoreland_Slave_Plot_1687. (last visited Mar. 30, 2014).

162. Wiecek, *supra* note 159, at 1711, 1768.

163. 1 The Colonial Laws of New York from the Year 1664 to the Revolution, 761–67 (1894).

164. SEGAL, *supra* note 157, at 142.

165. JANE LANDERS, BLACK SOCIETY IN SPANISH FLORIDA 1–2 (1999).

166. Patrick Riordan, *Finding Freedom in Florida: Native Peoples, African Americans, and Colonists, 1670–1816*, 75 THE FLORIDA HIST. QUART. 24, 31(1996).

167. *See, e.g.*, HARDING, *supra* note 17, at 34–35 (1981).

168. DANIEL RASMUSSEN, AMERICAN UPRISING: THE UNTOLD STORY OF AMERICA'S LARGEST SLAVE REVOLT 179 (2011).

169. HARDING, *supra* note 17, at 56. For a recent account of Gabriel Prosser's rebellion discussing the academic literature regarding the size of the rebellion, *see* MICHAEL L. NICHOLLS, WHISPERS OF REBELLION: NARRATING GABRIEL'S CONSPIRACY (2012).

170. Segal, *supra* note 157, at 142.
171. *See* Rasmussen, *supra* note 168, at 1.
172. Segal, *supra* note 157, at 145.
173. *See* David M. Robertson, The Buried Story of America's Largest Slave Rebellion and the Man Who Led It 4–8 (2000).
174. *See id.*
175. Kenneth S. Greenberg, *Introduction* in Nat Turner: A Slave Rebellion in History and Memory xi (Kenneth S. Greenberg ed., 2003).
176. *Id.*
177. Kenneth M. Stampp, The Peculiar Institution: Slavery In The Ante-Bellum South 219 (1956).
178. Harding, *supra* note 17 at 49.
179. John Ernest, A Nation Within A Nation: Organizing African American Communities Before the Civil War 19 (2011).
180. *See* John Hope Franklin & Loren Schweninger, Runaway Slaves: Rebels on the Plantation (1999).
181. *See* David Brion Davis, The Problem of Slavery in the Age of Revolution 1770–1823, 10 (2nd ed. 1999).
182. *See, e.g.*, Richard B. Morris, The American Revolution Reconsidered 76 (New York, 1967) and Ellen Gibson Wilson, The Loyal Blacks 21 (1976).
183. *See, e.g.*, Cassandra Pybus, *Jefferson's Faulty Math: The Question of Slave Defections in the American Revolution* 62 Wm. & Mary Quart. 243, 261 (2005) (pointing out that Jefferson made this estimate while he was in Paris and he over estimated his own losses).
184. *Id.* 245–47.
185. Franklin & Moss, *supra* note 38, at 70. *See also* Aptheker, *supra* note 154, at 218.
186. *See, e.g.*, R. J. M. Blackett, Building an Antislavery Wall: Black Americans in the Atlantic Abolitionist Movement 1830–1860, 7 (1983).
187. Tim McNeese, The Abolitionist Movement: Ending Slavery 82 (2008).
188. Catherine Clinton, Harriet Tubman: The Road to Freedom (2004).
189. Copy of Benjamin Banneker's letter to Thomas Jefferson, *available at* http://etext.virginia.edu/etcbin/toccer-new2?id=BanLett.sgm&images=images/modeng&data=/texts/english/modeng/parsed&tag=public&part=1&division=div1 (last visited Mar. 30, 2014).
190. For a copy of the petition, see http://www.pbs.org/wgbh/aia/part3/3h327t.html.
191. *See* Richard Newman, *Good Communications Corrects Bad Manners: The Banneker-Jefferson Dialogue and the Project of White Uplift* in Contesting Slavery: The Politics of Bondage and Freedom in the New American Nation 71 (John Craig Hammond and Matthew Mason eds., 2011).
192. Harding, *supra* note 17.
193. *See supra* notes 251 to 253 and accompanying text.
194. Kimberly Hayes Taylor, Profiles: Black Abolitionists and Freedom Fighters 27 (1996).
195. Wilson Jeremiah Moses, *Introduction* to Classical Black Nationalism: From the American Revolution to Marcus Garvey 13 (Wilson Jeremiah Moses ed., 1996).
196. *Id.* at 21–22.
197. Martin R. Delany, *The Condition, Elevation, Emigration, and Destiny of the Colored People of the United States* in Moses ed., *supra* note 195, at 101.

198. For Delany's views of American race relations, see M. DELANEY, *supra* note 148, at 159–73.

199. *See* DAVID WALKER'S APPEAL TO THE COLOURED CITIZENS OF THE WORLD, BUT IN PARTICULAR, AND VERY EXPRESSLY TO THOSE OF THE UNITED STATES OF AMERICA, INTRODUCTION BY JAMES TURNER 9 (1993).

200. ERNEST, *supra* note 179, at 24.

201. FERRELL, *supra* note 14, at 59.

202. *Id.* at 60.

203. Speech reprinted in Frederick Douglass, *The Life and Writings of Frederick Douglass*, vol. 2, Pre-Civil War Decade, 1850–1860 (New York: Philip S. Foner, International Publishers Co., Inc., 1950).

204. ADAM SMITH, AN INQUIRY INTO THE NATURE AND CAUSES OF THE WEALTH OF NATIONS 229 (Digirades.com; Reprint edition (Jan. 1, 2009)).

205. JOHN HOPE FRANKLIN AND LOREN SCHWENINGER, *supra* note 180, at 2.

206. *See* MORGAN, *supra* note 15, at 319.

207. DUBOIS, *supra* note 42, at 40. *See also* STAMPP, *supra* note 177, at 334–6, 126–7.

208. JOHN HOPE FRANKLIN AND LOREN SCHWENINGER, *supra* note 180, at 5.

209. ERNEST, *supra* note 179, at 15.

210. *See, e.g.,* BLACKETT, *supra* note 186, at 7.

211. FERRELL, *supra* note 14, at 61.

212. PHILLIP T. DROTNING, BLACK HEROES IN OUR NATION'S HISTORY: A TRIBUTE TO THOSE WHO HELPED SHAPE AMERICA 77 (1969).

213. *See* JAMES M. MCPHERSON, ORDEAL BY FIRE: THE CIVIL WAR AND RECONSTRUCTION 266 (1982).

214. NORALEE FRANKEL, BREAK THOSE CHAINS AT LAST: AFRICAN AMERICANS 1860–1880, 25 (1996).

215. Wang Xi, *supra* note 48, at 2169.

216. The Collected Works of Abraham Lincoln, Volume VI, p. 149–50 (ed. Roy P. Basler 1953) (emphasis in original).

217. JAMES M. MCPHERSON, THE NEGRO'S CIVIL WAR: HOW AMERICAN BLACKS FELT & ACTED DURING THE WAR FOR THE UNION 166–67 (1991).

218. *See* FONER, *supra* note 43, at 8.

219. MAULANA KARENGA, INTRODUCTION TO BLACK STUDIES 144 (2d ed. 1993).

220. MCPHERSON, *supra* note 217, at 241.

221. KARENGA, *supra* note 219, at 144.

222. MCPHERSON, *supra* note 217.

223. FRANKLIN & Moss, *supra* note 38, at 198.

224. *See* FONER, supra note 43, at 8.

225. CONG. GLOBE, 39th Cong., 1st Sess. 3453 (1866).

226. *See* Roy P. Basler ed., *supra* note 216, at Volume VII, p. 499–501 (Letter to Charles D. Robinson, August 17, 1864).

227. *See* FONER, supra note 43, at 75.

228. See *Slaughterhouse Cases*, 83 U.S. 36, 68 (1873).

229. *See* FONER, *supra* note 43, at 110–119.

230. *Black Republican* (Sept 1865) quoted by Leon Litwack *in* BEEN IN THE STORM SO LONG: THE AFTERMATH OF SLAVERY 536 (1980).

231. HARDING, *supra* note 17, at 302.

232. *Id.* at 104–05.

233. *See* FONER, *supra* note 43, at 282–83.

234. MICHAEL W. FITZGERALD, THE UNION LEAGUE MOVEMENT IN THE DEEP SOUTH: POLITICS AND AGRICULTURAL CHANGE DURING RECONSTRUCTION 4 (1989).

235. *See* FONER, *supra* note 43, at 282–83.

236. HARDING, *supra* note 17, at 292.

237. *See* MCPHERSON, *supra* note 213, at 535.

238. Xi, *supra* note 48, at 2153, 2213.

239. Approximately 500,000 blacks voted in the 1868 Presidential election. See *id.* at 2153, 2215. Of the 5,722,816 votes cast, Grant received 3,013,790. *See* 1868 Presidential General Election Data — National, *available at* http://uselectionatlas.org/RESULTS/data.php?year=1868&datatype=national&def=1&f=0&off=0&elect=0 (last visited Mar. 30, 2014).

240. U.S. CONST. amend. XV, § 1.

241. MICHAEL L. LEVINE, AFRICAN-AMERICANS AND CIVIL RIGHTS: FROM 1619 TO THE PRESENT 102 (1996).

242. FRANKEL, *supra* note 214, at 48.

243. *See* FONER, *supra* note 43, at 70.

244. *See id.* at 159.

245. *See id.* at 161.

246. ERNEST, *supra* note 179, at 56.

247. C. ERIC LINCOLN, RACE, RELIGION, AND THE CONTINUING AMERICAN DILEMMA 72 (1999).

248. *See* GENOVESE, *supra* note 153, at 189.

249. *See* Anthony E. Cook, *Beyond Critical Legal Studies: The Reconstructive Theology of Dr. Martin Luther King, Jr.*, 103 HARV. L. REV. 985, 1018 (1990).

250. Paul Lawrence Dunbar, *Hidden in Plain Sight: African American Secret Societies and Black Freemasonry*, 16 J. AFR. AM. STUD. 622, 623 (2011).

251. ERNEST, *supra* note 179.

252. TAYLOR, *supra* note 194, at 18.

253. ERNEST, *supra* note 179, at 62.

254. *Id.* at 16–17.

255. LINCOLN, *supra* note 247, at 69.

256. STANLEY K. SCHULTZ, THE CULTURE FACTORY: BOSTON PUBLIC SCHOOLS, 1789–1860, 172 (1973).

257. *Id.* at 161.

258. Arthur O. White, *The Black Leadership Class and Education in Antebellum Boston*, 42 J. NEGRO EDUC. 504, 505 (1973).

259. HOSEA EASTON, A TREATISE ON THE INTELLECTUAL CHARACTER AND CIVIL AND POLITICAL CONDITIONS OF THE COLORED PEOPLE OF THE UNITED STATES AND THE PREJUDICE EXERCISED TOWARD THEM 40–43 (Boston, Knapp 1837); see also SCHULTZ, *supra* note 256, at 160 (1973) (pointing to the fact that the lack of attendance at Boston schools by blacks was also a result of the deplorable economic condition of the black community in Boston).

260. Prince Hall et al., Petition to the Honorable Senate and House of Representatives of the Commonwealth of Massachusetts Bay in General Court Assembled (Oct. 17, 1787), *in* 1 A DOCUMENTARY HISTORY OF THE NEGRO PEOPLE IN THE UNITED STATES 19 (Herbert Aptheker ed., 1969).

261. Carter G. Woodson, The Education of the Negro Prior to 1861, 95 (1919). Woodson calls him "Primus Hall," but he is also known as "Prince Hall."

262. See website for Cheyney State, available at http://www.cheyney.edu/about-cheyney-university/ (date last visited March 30, 2014).

263. Lerone Bennett, Jr., Before the Mayflower: A History of Black America 641 (1987).

264. Henry Allen Bullock, A History of Negro Education in the South: From 1619 to the Present 29 (1967).

265. See Foner, supra note 43, at 366–67.

266. In 1917 the U.S. Bureau of Education published *Negro Education: A Study of Private and Higher Schools for Colored People in the United States*. The report was written by Thomas Jesse Jones and in two volumes it chronicled the conditions of the nation's black schools. His report was "the most comprehensive survey of segregated schools for its time." Robert A Margo, Race and Schooling in the South 1880–1950: An Economic History 21–23 (1990).

267. Diane Ravitch, The Troubled Crusade: American Education 1945–1980, 121 (1983).

268. Id.

269. Louis R. Harlan, Booker T. Washington: The Wizard of Tuskegee 1901–1915, 134 (1983).

270. Gil Kujovich, *Equal Opportunity in Higher Education and the Black Public College: The Era of Separate But Equal*, 72 Minn. L. Rev. 29, 42 (1987).

271. Benjamin Quarles, The Negro In The Making Of America 162–63 (1969).

272. Walter Recharde Allen and Joseph O. Jewell, *A Backward Glance Forward: Past, Present and Future Perspectives on Historically Black Colleges and Universities*, 25 Rev. High. Educ. 241, 244 (2002).

273. Bullock, supra note 264, at 33.

274. See National Center for Education, Historically Black Colleges and Universities, 1976 to 2001, 1 (2004).

275. Seventeen states and the District of Columbia were collectively referred to as the "segregationist states" because they maintained a rigid form of segregation. Kujovich, supra note 270, at 29, 30 n. 1. Eleven were part of the Confederacy: Alabama, Arkansas, Florida, Georgia, Louisiana, Mississippi, North Carolina, South Carolina, Tennessee, Texas, and Virginia. Id. Four of the segregationist states were the Border States during the Civil War: Delaware, Kentucky, Maryland, and Missouri. Id. At the time of the Civil War, slavery was legal in these states; however, they refused to secede from the Union. West Virginia, which was carved out of Virginia during the Civil War, was the 16th state and Oklahoma was the 17th state. Id.

276. Kujovich, supra note 270, at 113.

277. Id. at 113 n. 303.

278. Sabrina Hope King, *The Limited Presence of African-American Teachers*, 63 Rev. Educ. Res. 115, 124 (1993).

279. Moses, supra note 195, at 30.

280. E. David Cronon & John Hope Franklin, Black Moses: The Story of Marcus Garvey and the Universal Negro Improvement Association 48 (1960).

281. Levine, supra note 241, at 152–54.

282. Cronon & Franklin, supra note 280 at 4.

283. Adam Fairclough, Better Day Coming: Blacks and Equality 1890 to 2000, 112–13 (2001).

284. HISTORICAL VIEW, *supra* note 22, at 13.

285. For copies of the 103 issues of the Freedom Journal, see Wisconsin Historical Society website for African American Newspapers and Periodicals, available at http://www.wisconsinhistory.org/libraryarchives/aanp/freedom/volume1.asp (last visited Mar. 30, 2014).

286. ROBIN D.G. KELLEY AND EARL LEWIS, TO MAKE OUR OWN WORLD ANEW 387 (2000).

287. *Id.* at 384.

288. University of Virginia, *The History of African-American Newspapers*, available at http://cti.itc.virginia.edu/~aas405a/newspaper.html (last visited Mar. 30, 2014).

289. Bennett, *supra* note 263.

290. A'LELIA BUNDLES, ON HER OWN GROUND: THE LIFE AND TIMES OF MADAM C. J. WALKER (2002).

291. Bennett, *supra* note 263, at 329.

292. *Id.* at 292, 510.

293. *Id.* at 291.

294. *Id.* at 515.

295. KELLEY & LEWIS, *supra* note 286, at 394.

296. NANCY J. WEISS, THE NATIONAL URBAN LEAGUE 1910–1940, 64 (1974).

297. KARENGA, *supra* note 219.

298. MANNING MARABLE, W. E. B. DU BOIS: BLACK RADICAL DEMOCRAT 32 (1986).

299. *Id.*

300. National Medical Association, *History*, available at http://www.nmanet.org/index.php?option=com_content&view=article&id=3&Itemid=4 (last accessed Sept. 14, 2013) (last visited Mar. 30, 2014).

301. National Dental Association, *NDA History*, available at http://ndaonline.org/about-nda/ (last visited Mar. 30, 2014).

302. *Id.*

303. *Id.*

304. G. Estelle Massey, *The National Association of Colored Graduate Nurses*, 33 Am. J. of Nurs., 534 (1933).

305. MinorityNurse.com, *Eyes on the Prize*, available at http://www.minoritynurse.com/article/eyes-prize (last visited Mar. 30, 2014).

306. Walter J. Leonard, *The Development of the Black Bar*, 407 Annals of the Am. Aca. of Pol. and Soc. Sc., 140 (1973).

307. National Bar Association, *Our History*, available at http://www.nationalbar.org/our_history (last visited Mar. 30, 2014).

308. *Id.*

309. The Legal Advocate, *Wrap Up: National Bar Association 87th Annual Convention*, available at http://blog.nita.org/2012/08/01/wrap-up-national-bar-association-87th-annual-convention/ (last visited Mar. 30, 2014).

310. National Technical Association, Inc., *History*, available at http://www.ntaonline.org/aboutus/history.html (last visited Mar. 30, 2014).

311. National Banker's Association, *History*, available at http://www.nationalbankers.org/history.asp (last visited Mar. 30, 2014).

312. National Newspaper Publishers Association, *NNPA History*, available at http://nnpa.org/about-us/nnpa-history/ (last visited Mar. 30, 2014).

313. Sigma Pi Phi Fraternity, *History of the Boulé*, available at https://www.sigmapiphi.org/home/history_of_the_boule/ (last visited Mar. 30, 2014).

314. EARNESTINE GREEN MCNEALEY, THE PEARLS OF ALPHA KAPPA ALPHA: A HISTORY OF AMERICA'S FIRST BLACK SORORITY, ALPHA KAPPA ALPHA SORORITY, INCORPORATED. 2010

315. *Id.* at 28.

316. See website of Phi Eta Psi Fraternity, *available at* http://phietapsi1965.com/index.php/about-phi-eta-psi/founding-fathers/the-birth-of-phi-eta-psi-fraternity (last visited Mar. 30, 2014).

317. Lawrence C. Ross, *The Divine Nine: The History of African American Fraternities and Sororities,* cover flap (2001).

318. See PAULA J. GIDDINGS, IDA: A SWORD AMONG LIONS: IDA B. WELLS AND THE CAMPAIGN AGAINST LYNCHING 5 (2008).

319. Wells was a truly remarkable woman who worked tirelessly for the liberation of the Black Community. She was not only one of those who issued the call that led to the creation of the NAACP and started her own Ida B. Wells Clubs, but also worked with Marcus Garvey and rallied black Chicagoans to support A. Philip Randolph's Brotherhood of Sleeping Car Porters and Maids. *See id.*

320. TUCK, *supra* note 149, at 99.

321. MARABLE, *supra* note 298, at 55.

322. *See* KLUGER, *supra* note 19, at 95–6.

323. MARABLE, *supra* note 298, at 56–57.

324. *See* KLUGER, *supra* note 19, at 96.

325. *Id.* at 97.

326. WARREN D. ST. JAMES, NAACP: TRIUMPHS OF A PRESSURE GROUP 1909–1980, 113 (2d ed. 1980).

327. MARABLE, *supra* note 298, at 76.

328. *Id.* at 78, 97.

329. *See* KLUGER, *supra* note 19, at 143.

330. 238 U.S. 347 (1915).

331. 245 U.S. 60 (1917). The NAACP also filed an amicus brief in *Guinn v. United States*, 238 U.S. 347 (1915), where the Supreme Court struck down the grandfather clause. The case was actually argued in front of the Supreme Court by the Solicitor General, John W. Davis. See KLUGER, *supra* note 19, at 103.

332. MARK TUSHNET MAKING CIVIL RIGHTS LAW: THURGOOD MARSHALL AND THE SUPREME COURT, 1936–1961 (1994).

333. *Smith v. Allwright*, 321 U.S. 649 (1944).

334. *Shelley v. Kraemer*, 334 U.S. 1 (1948).

335. Bennett, *supra* note 263, at 431.

336. FAIRCLOUGH, *supra* note 283, at 112–154.

337. *Id.*

338. Executive Order 8802 (issued June 25, 1951).

339. *See* FEAGIN, *supra* note 20, at 60.

340. FAIRCLOUGH, *supra* note 283, at 112–208.

341. To Secure These Rights: The Report of the President's Committee on Civil Rights available at trumanlibrary.org/civilrights/srights1.htm.

342. MARABLE, *supra* note 298.

343. *Id.* at 176.

344. *Brown v. Board of Education*, 347 U.S. 483 (1954).

345. *See Missouri ex rel. Gaines v. Canada*, 305 U.S. 337 (1938); *Sipuel v. Board of Regents*, 332 U.S. 631 (1948); *Sweatt v. Painter*, 339 U.S. 629 (1950); *McLaurin v. Oklahoma State Regents*, 339 U.S. 637 (1950). The Supreme Court cases addressing segregation in graduate and professional schools were actually preceded by the decision of the highest court in Maryland striking down segregation at the University of Maryland. *Pearson v. Murray*, 169 Md. 78, 182 A. 590 (Md. 1936). Donald Murray, an African American graduate of Amherst College, applied to the University of Maryland Law School, which denied him admission because of his race. *Id.* at 590. While Maryland did not provide any legal training for African Americans, it quickly appropriated $10,000 to fund an out-of-state scholarship program. *Id.* at 593. The Maryland Court of Appeals ruled that the program was insufficient to provide Murray with equal educational opportunities.

346. *See* Social Science Statement, *supra* note 87, at 431.

347. *DeFunis v. Odegaard*, 416 U.S. 312, 336 (1974), (Douglass, J., dissenting).

348. Randall Kennedy, *Martin Luther King's Constitution: A Legal History of the Montgomery Bus Boycott*, 98 YALE L.J. 999, 1019–20 (1989).

349. *Id.* at 999, 1022.

350. *Gayle v. Browder*, 352 U.S. 903 (1956).

351. For an account of the Nashville sit-in movement, see DAVID HALBERSTAM, THE CHILDREN (1998).

352. EYES ON THE PRIZE CIVIL RIGHTS READER (Clayborne Carson, David J. Garrow, Gerald Gill, Vincent Harding, & Darlene Clark Hine, eds., 1997).

353. *See* Jack Greenberg, *Report On Roma Education Today: From Slavery To Segregation And Beyond* 110 COLUM. L. REV. 919, 986 (2010).

354. *See* RAYMOND ARSENAULT, FREEDOM RIDERS: 1961 AND THE STRUGGLE FOR RACIAL JUSTICE 7 (2006)

355. A complete list of the demands of the organizers of the March on Washington is available at http://www.crmvet.org/docs/moworg2.pdf (last visited Mar. 30, 2014).

356. The bill passed the Senate on May 26, 1965 and the House on July 9, 1965. After resolving differences between the House and Senate versions of the bill in conference committee, the House passed the Conference Report on August 3 and the Senate the following day.

357. *See* EDWARD G. CARMINES, ISSUE EVOLUTION: RACE AND THE TRANSFORMATION OF AMERICAN POLITICS 49 TABLE 2.2 (1990).

358. John Kendle, *Players boycott AFL All-Star Game,* on website for the Official History of Pro Football Hall of Fame, posted on February 18, 2010 and available at http://www.profootballhof.com/history/2010/2/18/players-boycott-afl-all-star-game/ (last visited Mar. 30, 2014).

359. *Clay v. U. S.,* 403 U.S. 698 (1971).

360. *See* TUCK, *supra* note 149 at 328. Carmichael was not the first to use the term "Black Power." Several others, including Adam Clayton Powell and Richard Wright, had also used the term. *Id* at 329.

361. *See Id.* at 329, 330.

362. DELANEY, *supra* note 148.

363. *See* TUCK, *supra* note 149, at 333.

364. H. CRUSE, REBELLION OR REVOLUTION? 211 (1968).

365. ELIJAH MUHAMMED, MESSAGE TO THE BLACK MAN xiv (1965).

366. *See* TUCK, *supra* note 149, at 338.

367. *Id.* at 356.

368. *See* David Kairys, *Unconscious Racism*, 83 TEMPLE L. REV. 857, 862 (2011).
369. *Washington*, 426 U.S. at 248.
370. *Id.* at 248 fn 14 (quoting from Frank I. Goodman, *De Facto School·Segregation: A Constitutional and Empirical Analysis*, 60 Calif. L. Rev. 275, 300 (1972),
371. EUGENE ROBINSON, DISINTEGRATION: THE SPLINTERING OF BLACK AMERICA (2010).
372. *See* Jennifer E. Manning, *Membership of the 113th Congress: A Profile* 7 (from Congressional Research Service).
373. Tim Scott was appointed on January 2, 2013, by South Carolina Governor Nikki Halley to serve out the term of Jim DeMint who resigned to run the Heritage Foundation. William Maurice Cowans served in the Senate from January 30, 2013, until July 16, 2013. He was appointed by Governor Deval Patrick to fill the vacancy left by John Kerry, who resigned to become Secretary of State. Cory Booker, the former Mayor of Newark, was sworn in on October 31, 2013. He won the special election in October 16, 2013, to succeed Frank Lautenberg who died in office.
374. *See* Mario L. Barnes, Erwin Chemerinsky & Trina Jones, *Post-Race Equal Protection?*, 98 GEO. L.J. 967, 968 (2010)(describing "postrace" as a term that has been widely used to characterize a belief in the "declining significance of race in the United States" and "postracialism" as "a set of beliefs that coalesce to posit that racial discrimination is rare and aberrant behavior as evidenced by America's and Americans' pronounced racial progress"); Sumi Cho, *Post Racialism*, 94 IOWA L. REV. 1589, 1594 (2009) (finding that "post-racialism in its current iteration is a twenty-first century ideology that reflects a belief that due to significant racial progress that has been made, the state need not engage in race-based decision making or adopt race-based remedies"); Gregory S. Parks & Jeffrey J. Rachlinski, *Implicit Bias, Election '08, and the Myth of a Post-Racial America*, 37 FLA. ST. U. L. REV. 659, 660 (2010).
375. *See supra* notes 125 to 137 and accompanying text.
376. *See, e.g.,* Girardeau A. Spann, *Disparate Impact,* 98 GEO. L.J. 1133, 1134 (2010) (asserting that "the post-racial claim ultimately serves to legitimate the practice of continued discrimination against racial minorities").
377. *See* Sherrilyn A. Ifill, *Summer of Our Discontent,* THE ROOT (Aug. 19, 2013).
378. *See, e.g.,* MCWHORTER, *supra* note 8, at 10 (disputing the argument that black people get paid less than whites for the same job).
379. *See, e.g.,* SONIA NIETO, AFFIRMING DIVERSITY: THE SOCIOPOLITICAL CONTEXT OF MULTICULTURAL EDUCATION (1992) and JODY ARMOUR, NEGROPHOBIA AND REASONABLE RACISM (2000).
380. Charles Lawrence III, *The Id, the Ego, and Equal Protection: Reckoning with Unconscious Racism,* 39 STAN. L. REV. 317 (1987). Other scholars have also pointed to unconscious racism including Timothy Davis, *Racism in Athletics: Subtle Yet Persistent,* 21 U. ARK. L. REV. 881 (1999); Angela J. Davis, *Prosecution and Race: The Power and Privilege of Discretion,* 67 FORDHAM L. REV. 13 (1998); and Richard Delgado, *Words that Wound: A Tort Action for Racial Insults, Epithets and Name-Calling,* 17 HARV. C.R.-C.L. L. REV. 133 (1982).
381. *See, e.g.,* Neil Gotanda, *A Critique of "Our Constitution is Color-Blind"* 44 STAN. L. REV. 1, 54 (1991).
382. *See* Russell J. Skiba, Suzanne E. Eckes, and Kevin Brown, *African American Disproportionality In School Discipline: The Divide Between Best Evidence And Legal Remedy,* 54 N.Y.L. SCH. L. REV. 1071 (2009).
383. *Grimes v. Sobol,* 832 F. Supp. 704 (S.D.N.Y. 1993), *aff'd Grimes* by and through *Grimes v. Sobol,* 37 F.3d 857 (2d Cir. 1994).

384. Randall Kennedy, *McCleskey v. Kemp: Race, Capital Punishment, and the Supreme Court* 101 HARV. L. REV. 1388 (1988).

385. *McCleskey v. Kemp*, 481 U.S. 279, 286–87 (1987).

386. *Id.*

387. *Id.* at 287.

388. *Id.* at 321 (Brennan, J., dissenting)

389. *McCleskey v. Kemp*, 481 U.S. at 297–98 (citing *Personnel Administrator of Mass. v. Feeney*, 442 U.S. 256, 279 (1979)).

390. *McCleskey*, 481 U.S. at 308.

391. Tanya Kateri Hernandez, *Multiracial Discourse: Racial Classifications in an Era of Color-Blind Jurisprudence*, 57 MD. L. REV. 97, 141–45 (1998).

392. Kennedy, *supra* note 384, at 1388.

393. SHERYLL CASHIN, PLACE, NOT RACE: A NEW VISION OF OPPORTUNITY IN AMERICA (2014).

394. *Id.* at 334.

395. *See, e.g.,* Brief filed in *Grutter v. Bollinger* of Amici Curiae on Behalf of a Committee of Concerned Black Graduates of ABA Accredited Law Schools: Vicky L. Beasley, Devon W. Carbado, Tasha L. Cooper, Kimberlé Crenshaw, Luke Harris, Shavar Jeffries, Sidney Majalya, Wanda R. Stansbury, Jory Steele, et al., in Support of Respondents 5 (2003).

396. *DeFunis, supra* note 346, at 336 (1974, Douglass, J., dissenting).

# Chapter Three

1. THOMAS DIXON, JR., THE LEOPARD'S SPOTS: A ROMANCE OF THE WHITE MAN'S BURDEN—1865–1900, 243 (1902). Niel Gotanda also ties the one-drop rule to the notion of racial purity of whites in his path breaking article, *A Critique of "Our Constitution is Color-Blind,"* 44 STAN. L. REV. 1, 25–27 (1991).

2. *See* Campbell Gibson & Kay Jung, *Historical Census Statistics on Population Totals by Race, 1790 to 1990, and by Hispanic Origin, 1970 to 1990, for the United States, Regions, Divisions, and States*, at tbl.1 (United States Census Bureau, Working Paper Series No. 56, 2002).

3. For example, one website that provides valuable advice to students applying for law school specifically states in its section for multiracial applicants "if a school lets you identify only one racial category, check the box that indicates the most disadvantaged group: Native American or Black...." *See* DeLoggio Admissions Achievement Program, *Race and Ethnicity*, available at http://www.deloggio.com/diversty/race.html (last visited Mar. 30, 2014). In addition, some researchers have observed that multiracial individuals are more likely to identify with the minority component of their background when forced to choose in constrained, high-stakes settings and when they have specific knowledge of how such race-conscious data will be used — i.e., in the context of LSAT pre-law school testing, as opposed to being asked to "check all that apply" once in law school. A.T. Panter et al., *It Matters How and When You Ask: Self-Reported Race/Ethnicity of Incoming Law Students*, 15 CULT. DIV. & ETHNIC MIN. PSYCH. 51, 63 (2009).

4. *See Loving v. Virginia*, 388 U.S. 1, 5 (1967) (pointing to the fact that 16 states currently banned interracial marriage and 14 states repealed their laws banning interracial marriage over the past 15 years).

5. *See, e.g.*, Grace Kao and Marta Tienda, *Optimism and Achievement: The Educational Performance of Immigrant Youth*, 76 Soc. Sci. Quart. 1–19 (1995) (arguing that the academic success of children of immigrants is associated with immigrants' optimism) and Mary Waters, *Ethnic and Racial Identities of Second-Generation Black Immigrants in New York City* in The New Second Generation, 171–196 (Alejandro Portes ed., 1996) (concluding that because the children of West Indians are more optimistic, they tend to identify in ethnic terms as opposed to racial).

6. Carter G. Woodson, *The Beginnings of Miscegenation of the Whites and Blacks*, 3 J. Negro. Hist. 335, 339 (1918) also reprinted in Interracialism: Black-White Intermarriage in American History, Literature, and Law 42, 44 (Werner Sollors ed. 2000).

7. *West Chester & P. R. Co. v. Miles*, 55 Pa. 209 (1867).

8. *See* Gibson, *supra* note 2.

9. *See Loving v. Virginia*, *supra* note 4.

10. *Grutter v. Bollinger*, 539 U.S. 306, 333, 338 (2003).

11. *See* Kim Williams, Mark One or More: Civil Rights in Multiracial America 89 (2008).

12. Peter Wallenstein, Tell the Court I Love My Wife: Race, Marriage and Law—An American History 184–85 (2002).

13. Robert J. Sickels, Race, Marriage and the Law 117, 121 (1972).

14. *See* Maria Root, *The Color Of Love*, Am. Prospect, Apr. 8, 2002, at 54. *See also* Stephen & Abigail Thernstrom, *We Have Overcome*, New Republic, Oct. 13, 1997, at 23 (noting that the proportion of whites who would like to see interracial marriage outlawed has dropped from 62% to 16%); Another survey of American attitudes showed that in 1997, 67% of whites and 83% of African Americans approved of interracial marriages. *See* Howard Schuman, Charlotte Steeh, Lawrence Bobo & Maria Krysan, Racial Attitudes in America: Trends and Interpretations 285 (1997).

15. In the General Social Survey conducted in 2002, only 10 percent of Americans and 4 percent of young adults objected to interracial marriage. *See* Michael J. Rosenfield, *CCF Briefing Paper: Interracial Marriage 40 years after Loving v. Virginia* (2007).

16. *See* Pew Research Center Publications, *Almost All Millennials Accept Interracial Dating and Marriage* (2010).

17. Of the 18,849,000 blacks in 1960, 37 percent were under the age of fifteen, thus there were approximately 11,875,000 blacks over the age of fifteen (63 percent × 18,849,000). Bureau of the Census, *The Social and Economic Status of the Black Population in the United States: An Historical View, 1790–1978: Current Population Reports*, Special Studies, Series P-23, No. 80, 16 tbl.10 (1979).

18. U.S. Census Bureau, *Race of Wife by Race of Husband: 1960, 1970, 1980, 1991, and 1992*, tbl.1 (1998).

19. *Id.*

20. Sharon M. Lee & Barry Edmonston, *New Marriages, New Families: U.S. Racial and Hispanic Intermarriages*, 60 Population Bull. (Number 2) 1, 12 tbl.2 (2005).

21. *Id.* at 12.

22. The percentage of Asian men who married outside their race was only 9.5 percent, but for Asian woman it was 21.6 percent. *Id.*

23. *Id.*

24. *Id.* While the Census refers to blacks as "black only," I will refer to them throughout this book as single-race blacks and where the Census refers to "blacks in combination," I

will refer to them as mixed-race or Black Multiracials. There may be some lack of precision between the use of these terms in the text and their use by the Census Bureau. Since the Census Bureau allows individuals to self-identify, it uses these terms to refer to how individuals or their parents or guardians designate them. In the text, the term single-race blacks refers to those born to two black parents as determined by the one-drop rule and "Black Multiracials" refers to those blacks with a black and a non-black parent. Thus, this book bases these terms on parents ancestry, not self-identification.

25. *See* Zhenchao Qian & Daniel T. Lichter, *Social Boundaries and Marital Assimilation: Interpreting Trends in Racial and Ethnic Intermarriage*, 72 AM. SOC. REV. 68, 79 (2007).

26. *Id.*

27. *Id.*

28. *See* Paul Taylor, Wendy Wang, Kim Parker, Jeffrey S. Passel, Eileen Patten & Seth Motel, Pew Research Ctr., *The Rise of Intermarriage: Rates, Characteristics Vary by Race and Gender* 11 (2012).

29. *Id.* For black men, these represent substantial increases from the 15.7 percent figure in 2000 and 7.9 percent in 1980. While it also increased for black women, the increase went from 7.1 percent in 2000 and 3.0 percent in 1980. *See* Jeffrey S. Passell et al., Pew Research Center, *Marrying Out: One-in-Seven New U.S. Marriages is Interracial or Interethnic* 11–12 (2010). With respect to blacks having a white spouse, more recent statistics show a similar trend. In 2010, 8.5 percent of married black men had white spouses, an increase from 6.6 percent in 2005. U.S. Census Bureau, *America's Families and Living Arrangements* (2010). While, only 3.9 percent of black women were married to white men, an increase from 2.8 percent in 2005. *Id.*

30. *See* Karen R. Humes, Nicholas A. Jones & Roberto R. Ramirez, *Overview of Race and Hispanic Origin 2010*, 6 tbl.2 (2011).

31. *See* CensusScope.org, *United States Multiracial Profile*, http://www.censusscope.org/us/print_chart_multi.html (last visited Mar. 30, 2014).

32. *See* Overview of Race and Hispanic Origin: 2010, 4 tbl 1 (2011) available at www.census.gov/prod/cen2010/briefs/c2010br-02.pdf.

33. According to the 2012 Census Bureau figures, of the 3,588,000 individuals between the ages of 20 and 24 who were classified as Black Alone or in Combination, 3,303,000 were Black in Combination. Thus, the percentage of Black in Combination to total blacks was 7.9% ((3,588,000–3,303,000)/3,588,000). For Black Alone or in Combination *see* U.S. Census Bureau, tbl.1. *Population by Sex and Age, for Black Alone and White Alone, Not Hispanic: 2012* (Numbers in thousands). For Black in Combination *see* U.S. Census Bureau, tbl.29. *Population by Sex and Age, for Black Alone or in Combination and White Alone, Not Hispanic: 2012* (Numbers in thousands Civilian non-institutionalized population). Then subtract the totals of Black Alone or in Combination from the total for Black Alone.

34. For ages 15 to 19, the corresponding figures were 8.9% ((3,624,000–3,302,000)/3,624,000); For ages 10 and 14 the corresponding figures were 10.9% ((3,511,000–3,127,000)/3,511,000); for ages 5 to 9 the corresponding figures were 15.0% ((3,545,000–3,013,000)/3,545,000); for under the age of five the corresponding figures were 19.1% ((3,769,000–3,051,000)/3,769,000). *Id.*

35. CensusScope, *supra* note 31.

36. Of those who checked the Some Other Race box on the 2000 Census, over 95% also identified themselves as Hispanic/Latino. Jorge del Pinal et al., *U.S. Census Bureau, Overview of Results of New Race and Hispanic Origin Questions in Census 2000*, at 4 (2007).

37. CensusScope.org, *supra* note 31.

38. U.S. Census Bureau, *2010 Census Shows America's Diversity* (Mar. 24, 2011).

39. Douglas S. Massey et al., The Source of the River: The Social Origins of Freshman at America's Selective Colleges and Universities (2003).

40. Ronald Roach, Drawing Upon the Diaspora, Diverse Issues In Higher Education, Aug. 25, 2005, at 39.

41. The number of Black or African American in Combination only who were between the ages of 15 and 19 was 164,271 and the total number of Black or African American was 3,093,824. So the percentage of Black Multiracials among total black students between ages 15 and 19 was 5.3% (164,271/3,093,824). *See* U.S. Census Bureau, *Black or African American Population, by Age and Sex for the United States: 2000*, tbl.3 (2002).

42. Roach, *supra* note 40.

43. The thirty-one institutions that are part of COFHE are among the most prestigious in the country. They are: Amherst College, Barnard College, Brown University, Bryn Mawr College, Carleton College, Columbia University, Cornell University, Dartmouth College, Duke University, Georgetown University, Harvard University, Johns Hopkins University, MIT, Mount Holyoke College, Northwestern University, Oberlin College, Pomona College, Princeton University, Rice University, Smith College, Stanford University, Swarthmore College, Trinity College, University of Chicago, University of Pennsylvania, University of Rochester, Washington University in St. Louis, Wellesley College, Wesleyan University, Williams College, and Yale University. Consortium on Financing Higher Education, *Home*, http://web.mit.edu/cofhe/ (last visited Mar. 30, 2014).

44. C. Anthony Broh & Stephen D. Minicucci, *Racial Identity and Government Classification: A Better Solution*, 17, figure 2 (2008). Broh and Minicucci provided an alternative way for colleges and universities to maintain internal statistics on the racial and ethnic make-up of their students, even though these statistics differed from what these educational institutions are required to report to the DOE under the Final Guidance.

45. Kevin Brown, *Should Black Immigrants Be Favored Over Black Hispanics and Black Multiracials in the Admissions Processes of Selective Higher Education Programs?*, 54 How. L.J. 255, 290 (2011).

46. The figures for Yale University came from Leilani Baxter, Research Associate, Office of Institutional Research. According to the figures, for the Fall of 2011, Black Multiracials were 40% of black students enrolled, 32% in 2012, 44% in 2013, and 54% in 2014 (email correspondence on file with author). And, for the University of Virginia, the figures came from George Stovall, Director, Institutional Assessment and Studies. According to the figures, for the Fall of 2011 there were 218 single-race blacks and 53 Black Multiracials. Thus, of the black students enrolled in the Fall of 2011, Black Multiracials made up 19.6% (53/(53+218)), for 2012 it was 21.7% (52/(52+188)), for 2013 it was 22.4% (59/(59+263)), and for 2014 it was also 22.4% (68/(68+304)) (email correspondence on file with author). There were 1,298 black students on the Bloomington campus of Indiana University and an additional 318 Two or More Races students who also indicated black. See Indiana University Institutional Research and Reporting Fall 2013 Student Degree Seeking Enrollment by Race and Ethnicity, available at https://www.iu.edu/~uirr/doc/diversity/student/1-IU_BL_base_05_13.pdf (last visited Mar. 30, 2014).

47. Deloggio Academic Achievement Program, *supra* note 3.

48. Kevin Brown & Jeannie Bell, *Demise of the Talented Tenth: Affirmative Action and the Increasing Underrepresentation of Ascendant Blacks at Selective Higher Educational Institutions*, 69 Ohio St. L.J. 1227 (2008). For Black/Asians the percentage is 24.1%. *Id* n 79.

49. *See* SONYA M. TAFOYA, HANS JOHNSON, & LAURA E. HILL, *Who Chooses to Choose Two?*, 340 fig 5, *in* THE AMERICAN PEOPLE: 2000 CENSUS (Richard Farley & John Haaga eds., 2005).

50. According to statistics obtained from Josiah Evans the Assistant Director of Social Science Research for LSAC (on file with author).

51. *Id.*

52. SUSAN P. DALESSANDO ET AL., LSAT PERFORMANCE WITH REGIONAL, GENDER, AND RACIAL/ETHNIC BREAKDOWNS: 2005–2006 THROUGH 2011–2012 TESTING YEAR 9, TBL 1 (2012).

53. The LSAT data on mean is actually from 2011–12, whereas the scores of black multiracials are from 2012. In addition, while the *mean* LSAT score for all test takers in 2011–-12 was 150.66, the *median* for black multiracials had to be higher than 150, since 56.8% scored 150 or above.

54. The percentage of mixed-race blacks among blacks between the ages of 15 and 19 in 2012 was 8.9 percent, but for those between the ages of 5 and 9 is 15 percent. *See supra* note 34 and accompanying text.

55. Mary E. Campbell, *Multiracial Groups and Educational Inequality: A Rainbow or a Divide?*, 56 SOC. PROBL. 425, 427 (2009).

56. *Id.* at 425, 428.

57. The scores of various racial and ethnic groups on for the 2011–12 LSAT takers were 141.84, for Latinos generally 146.32, for Puerto Ricans 138.05, for Asians 152.68, and for whites 152.8. DALESSANDO, *supra* note 52, at 20, tbl 4B.

58. Simon Cheng & Seena Mostafavipour, *The Differences and Similarities between Biracial and Monoracial Couples: A Sociodemographic Sketch Based on the Census 2000* 6 (Jan. 2005). According to 1990 statistics from the United States Census Bureau, 10 percent of black males with some college education and 13 percent of black males with some graduate school education who were married were in interracial marriages. *See The Effect of Higher Education on Interracial Marriage*, 16 J. BLACKS HIGH. EDUC. 55 (1997). This contrasts with only 6 percent of high school dropouts and 7 percent of high school graduates. For black women, 4 percent of those with some college education, 5 percent of those who were college graduates, and 6 percent of those with some graduate school education who were married were in interracial marriages. *Id.* This contrasts with only 3 percent of those who were either high school dropouts or just high school graduates. *Id.*

59. *Id.* at 55. *The Effect of Higher Education on Interracial Marriage*, 16 J. BLACKS HIGH. EDUC. 55 (1997).

60. Kevin Brown, *Change in Racial and Ethnic Classifications is Here: Proposal to Address Race and Ethnic Ancestry of Blacks for Affirmative Action Admissions Purposes*, 31 HAMLINE J. PUB. L. & POL'Y., 149–51 (2009).

61. *Id.* Between 2000 and 2010, the College Board also added a writing section to the SAT. As a result, the highest combined possible score increased from 1600 to 2400 points. This accounts for much of the substantial increase from 2000 to 2010.

62. For 2000 the difference was 30 points. *See* College Board, *2000 College-Bound Seniors: Total Group Profile Report* 7 tbl.4.2 (2000). The average SAT scores of those where the highest level of parental education is an associate degree is 979 (critical reading 488 and math 491). In contrast, those where the highest level of parental education is a high school diploma is 949 (critical reading 472 and math 477). For 2010 the difference was 50 points. *Id.* The average SAT scores of those where the highest level of parental education is an associate degree is 1442 (critical reading 482, math 491, and writing 469). In contrast, those

where the highest level of parental education is a high school diploma is 1392 (critical reading 464 math 475, and writing 453). *Id.* at 4, Table 11.

63. For 2000 the difference was 79 points. The average SAT scores of those where the highest level of parental education is an associate degree is 1058 (critical reading 525 and math 533). In contrast, those where the highest level of parental education is a high school diploma is 989 (critical reading 488 and math 491). *See id.* at 7, tbl. 4.2. For 2010, the difference was 127 points. The average SAT scores of those where the highest level of parental education a bachelor's degree is 1569 (critical reading 521, math 536, and writing 512). In contrast, those where the highest level of parental education is an associate degree is 1442 (critical reading 482, math 491, and writing 469). *Id.* at 4, tbl. 11.

64. *See* College Board, *2013 College-Bound Seniors: Total Group Profile Report.* For the benefit of more English and Language Arts classes and math courses, *see id.* at 6, tbl 15 and for more sciences courses *see id.* at 7, tbl 16.

65. *Id.* at 4 tbl.11.

66. Brown, *supra* note 60, at 149.

67. *Id.*

68. While almost 50% (49.9%) of multiracials live in families that own their home, only 41.4% of single-race blacks do. Figures calculated from U.S. Census Bureau, *America's Families and Living Arrangements: 2008, Tables C5*; *Nativity Status of Children Under 18 Years/1 and Presence of Parents by Race, and Hispanic Origin /2 for Selected Characteristics: 2008— Black alone* and *Tables C5. Nativity Status of Children Under 18 Years/1 and Presence of Parents by Race, and Hispanic Origin /2 for Selected Characteristics: 2008—Black alone or in combination with one or more other races.*

69. While 12.1% of single-race blacks were not covered by health insurance, only 7.4% of Black Multiracials did not have health insurance. *Id.*

70. Approximately 48.5% of multiracial children live with both parents compared to only 37.5% of single-race blacks children. *Id.*

71. Ivory Toldson, *Single Parents Aren't the Problem,* from THE ROOT (July 3, 2013).

72. ROBERT J. COTTOL, THE LONG LINGERING SHADOW: SLAVERY, RACE, AND THE LAW IN THE AMERICAN HEMISPHERE 83 (2013).

73. *Id.* at 91.

74. JOHN D'EMILIO & ESTELLE B. FREEDMAN, INTIMATE MATTERS: A HISTORY OF SEXUALITY IN AMERICA 3 (1997).

75. JOEL WILLIAMSON, NEW PEOPLE: MISCEGENATION AND MULATTOES IN THE UNITED STATES 14–15 (1995).

76. *Id.*

77. *But see* Howard Bodenhorn, *The Mulatto Advantage: The Biological Consequences of Complexion in Rural Antebellum Virginia,* 21 J. INTERDISCIPL. HIST. 33 (2002) (arguing that complexion differences were as important a determinant of socioeconomic status in the rural Upper South as in the urban Lower South).

78. Virginia Council, MINUTES OF THE COUNCIL AND GENERAL COURT OF COLONIAL VIRGINIA, 1622–1632, 1670–1676, WITH NOTES AND EXCERPTS FROM ORIGINAL COUNCIL AND GENERAL COURT RECORDS, INTO 1683, NOW LOST, 479 (H.R. McIlwaine, ed. 1924); *but see* FRANK W. SWEET, LEGAL HISTORY OF THE COLOR LINE: THE RISE AND TRIUMPH OF THE ONE-DROP RULE 120 (2005) (pointing out that "Davis was caught 'lying with a negro,' not 'lying with a *negress*'" and, thus, his offense could have involved homosexuality).

79. EDMUND S. MORGAN, AMERICAN SLAVERY, AMERICAN FREEDOM 333 (1975).

80. *See* F. JAMES DAVIS, WHO IS BLACK?: ONE'S NATION'S DEFINITION 33 (1991).

81. MORGAN, *supra* note 79, at 334.

82. Christine B. Hickman, *The Devil and the One Drop Rule: Racial Categories, African Americans, and the U.S. Census*, 95 MICH. L. REV. 1161, 1175 (1997).

83. SWEET, *supra* note 78, at 122.

84. A. Leon Higginbothan, Jr., & Barbara Kopytoff, *Racial Purity and Interracial Sex in the Law of Colonial and Antebellum Virginia*, 77 GEO. L.J. 1967 (1989).

85. SWEET, *supra* note 78.

86. *See* Laurence C. Nolan, *The Meaning of* Loving: *Marriage, Due Process and Equal Protection (1967–1990) as Equality and Marriage, from* Loving *to* Zablocki, 41 How. L.J. 247–48 (1998).

87. Frank H. Wu, *The Multiracial Classification Can Be Detrimental, in* INTERRACIAL AMERICA: OPPOSING VIEWPOINTS 38 (Eleanor Stanford, ed., 2006).

88. Jonathan L. Alpert, *The Origin of Slavery in the United States—The Maryland Precedent*, 14 AM. J. LEGAL HIST. 195 (1970).

89. William D. Zabel, *Interracial Marriage and the Law*, Atlantic Monthly 216 (Oct. 1965): 75–79.

90. *See* statute quoted in WOODSON, *supra* note 6, at 335–53.

91. SWEET, *supra* note 78, at 124.

92. ARTHUR WALLACE CALHOUN, A SOCIAL HISTORY OF THE AMERICAN FAMILY FROM COLONIAL TIMES TO THE PRESENT (1945).

93. Philip D. Morgan, *British Encounters with Africans and African-Americans, circa 1600–1780, in* STRANGERS WITHIN THE REALM: CULTURAL MARGINS OF THE FIRST BRITISH EMPIRE 172 (Bernard Bailyn & Philip D. Morgan, eds., 1991).

94. WOODSON, *supra* note 6, at 335–53.

95. WILLIAM WALLER HENING, THE STATUTES AT LARGE; BEING A COLLECTION OF ALL THE LAWS OF VIRGINIA, FROM THE FIRST SESSION OF THE LEGISLATURE IN THE YEAR 1619, VOL. 3, 86–87 (1823).

96. WOODSON, *supra* note 6, at 335–53.

97. SWEET, *supra* note 78, at 124–25.

98. MORGAN, *supra* note 79, at 335.

99. *See* Winthrop D. Jordan, *American Chiaroscuro: The Status and Definition of Mulattoes in the British Colonies*, 19 WILLIAM MARY QUART. 184 (1962).

100. HENING, *supra* note 95, at 252.

101. WILLIAMSON, *supra* note 75, at 9–10.

102. *Id.*, at 13.

103. *Id.* at 11.

104. *Id.* at 12–13.

105. SWEET, *supra* note 78, at 128.

106. Karen M. Woods, *"A Wicked and Mischievous Connection": The Origins of Indian-White Miscegenation Law*, 23 LEGAL STUD. F. 37, 52 (1999).

107. *Id.*

108. *An Act for Regulation Negro, Indian, and Mulatto Slaves Within This Province of New Jersey, Laws of New Jersey, C. ix*, 1704, *reprinted in* CIVIL RIGHTS AND AFRICAN AMERICANS 17–20 (Albert P. Blaustein & Robert L. Zangrando eds., 1991).

109. Zabel, *supra* note 89.

110. WILLIAMSON, *supra* note 75, at 9–10.

111. SWEET, *supra* note 78, at 128.
112. *See, e.g.,* CARL N. DEGLER, NEITHER BLACK NOR WHITE: SLAVERY AND RACE RELATIONS IN BRAZIL AND THE UNITED STATES 103 (1971).
113. WILLIAMSON, supra note 75, at 9–10.
114. *Id.*
115. COTTOL, *supra* note 72, at 90. Even as late as 1860, blacks constituted almost 60% of the population of South Carolina. *See* Gibson, *supra* note 2, at Table 55, *South Carolina-Race and Hispanic Origin: 1790 to 1990.*
116. PETER H. WOOD, BLACK MAJORITY: NEGROES IN COLONIAL SOUTH CAROLINA FROM 1670 THROUGH THE STONO REBELLION 34 (1974).
117. WILLIAMSON, *supra* note 75, at 9–10.
118. COTTOL, *supra* note 72, at 90.
119. Bodenhorn, *supra* note 77.
120. SWEET, *supra* note 78, at 189–90.
121. *Id.* at 187.
122. *Id.*
123. F. JAMES DAVIS, *supra* note 80, at 35.
124. LARRY KOGER, BLACK SLAVEOWNERS: FREE BLACK SLAVE MASTERS IN SOUTH CAROLINA, 1790–1860, 182 (1985).
125. *See* DAVID M. ROBERTSON, THE BURIED STORY OF AMERICA'S LARGEST SLAVE REBELLION AND THE MAN WHO LED IT 4 (2000).
126. F. JAMES DAVIS, *supra* note 80, at 35.
127. *See* Mark Golub, *Plessy as 'Passing': Judicial Responses to Ambiguously Raced Bodies in* Plessy v. Ferguson, 39 LAW & SOC'Y REV. 568 (2005).
128. Kimberly S. Hanger, *Origins of New Orleans Free Creoles of Color, in* CREOLES OF COLOR IN THE GULF SOUTH 4 (James H. Dormon ed., 1996).
129. An English translation of the "The Code Noir (The Black Code)," is available at http://chnm.gmu.edu/revolution/d/335/. (last visited Mar. 30, 2014) Carter G. Woodson called the *Code Noir* "the most human of all slave regulations." WOODSON, *supra* note 6, at 338.
130. SWEET, *supra* note 78, at 207.
131. Pierre Force, *The House on Bayou Road: Atlantic Creole Networks in the Eighteenth and Nineteenth Centuries,* 100 J. AM. HIST. 9 (2012).
132. JUNIUS P. RODRIGUES, THE LOUISIANA PURCHASE: A HISTORICAL AND GEOGRAPHICAL ENCYCLOPEDIA (2002).
133. IRA BERLIN, MANY THOUSANDS GONE: THE FIRST TWO CENTURIES OF SLAVERY IN NORTH AMERICA 333 (1998).
134. ERIC FONER, RECONSTRUCTION: AMERICA'S UNFINISHED REVOLUTION, 1863–1877, 47 (1988).
135. For a recent book discussing slavery in Latin America, *see* COTTOL, *supra* note 72.
136. DAVID OTTO, INSIDERS' GUIDE TO SHREVEPORT 159 (2010).
137. FONER, *supra* note 134, at 47.
138. WILLIAMSON, *supra* note 75, at 81–82.
139. Hanger, *supra* note 128, at 167.
140. *Id.*
141. ROGER A. FISCHER, THE SEGREGATION STRUGGLE IN LOUISIANA, 1862–77, 15 (1974).

142. David C. Rankin, *The Impact of the Civil War on the Free Colored Community of New Orleans*, 11 PERSPECT. AM. HIST. 381–82 (1977–78). *See also Adele v. Beauregard*, 1 Mart. (o.s.) 183 (1810).

143. Gary B. Mills, *Miscegenation and the Free Negro in Antebellum 'Anglo' Alabama: A Reexamination of Southern Race Relations*, 68 J. AM. HIST. 26 (JUNE 1981).

144. *Id.* at 19.

145. IRA BERLIN, SLAVES WITHOUT MASTERS: THE FREE NEGRO IN THE ANTEBELLUM SOUTH 105 (1974).

146. *See* MILLS, *supra* note 143, at 33.

147. *Id.* at 21.

148. For a brief survey of such laws in Alabama, *see* Virginia M. Gould, *The Free Creoles of Color of the Antebellum Gulf Ports of Mobile and Pensacola: A Struggle for the Middle Ground*, in CREOLES OF COLOR IN THE GULF SOUTH 28–50 (James H. Dormon ed., 1996).

149. ARIELA J. GROSS, WHAT BLOOD WON'T TELL: A HISTORY OF RACE ON TRIAL IN AMERICA 3 (2008).

150. SWEET, *supra* note 78, at 169.

151. PEGGY PASCO, WHAT COMES NATURALLY: MISCEGENATION LAW AND THE MAKING OF RACE IN AMERICA 116 (2009).

152. SWEET, *supra* note 78, at 325–46.

153. *Id.* at 328–36.

154. *Pace v. Alabama*, 106 U.S. 583 (1883).

155. Genesis 11:1–9.

156. Thomas M. Davis, *The Traditions of Puritan Typology*, in TYPOLOGY AND EARLY AMERICAN LITERATURE 44–45 (Sacvan Bercovitch ed., 1972).

157. WOODS, *supra* note 106, at 37, 45–47.

158. Acts 17: 26. *See also* William M. Wiecek, *The Origins of the Law of Slavery in British North America*, 17 CARDOZO L. REV. 1711, 1727 (1995).

159. *See* JOHN BACHMAN, SELECTED WRITINGS ON SCIENCE, RACE, AND RELIGION 1–20 (Gene Waddell ed., 2011).

160. *See* JOHN BACHMAN, THE DOCTRINE OF THE UNITY OF THE HUMAN RACE EXAMINED ON THE PRINCIPLES OF SCIENCE (Charleston: C. Canning, 1850); *portions reprinted* in RACIAL THOUGHT IN AMERICA, FROM THE PURITANS TO ABRAHAM LINCOLN 453 (Louis Ruchames ed., 1969).

161. STEPHEN JAY GOULD, THE MISMEASURE OF MAN 79 (1981).

162. KEVIN BROWN, RACE, LAW AND EDUCATION IN THE POST-DESEGREGATION ERA: FOUR PERSPECTIVES ON DESEGREGATION AND RESEGREGATION 67 (2005).

163. Josiah Clark Nott, *The Mulatto: A Hybrid: Probable Extermination of the Two Races If the Whites and Blacks are Allowed to Intermarry*, 29 BOSTON MED. SURG. J. 29 (1843).

164. Nott rested his conclusions in part on an 1842 article, also published in the *Boston Medical and Surgical Journal* by an author who only identified himself as "Philanthropist."

165. NOTT, *supra* note 163.

166. Nancy Krieger, *Shades of Difference: Theoretical Underpinnings of the Medical Controversy on Black/White Differences in the United States, 1830–1870*, 17 INT. J. HEALTH SERV. 265 (1987).

167. JENNIFER LEE & FRANK D. BEAN, THE DIVERSITY PARADOX: IMMIGRATION AND THE COLOR LINE IN TWENTY-FIRST CENTURY AMERICA 38 (2010).

168. MELISSA NOBLES, SHADES OF CITIZENSHIP: RACE AND THE CENSUS IN MODERN POLITICS 32–36 (2000).

169. C. Matthew Snipp, Racial Measurement in the American Census: Past Practices and Implications for the Future, 29 Ann. Rev. Soc. 563 (2003).
170. Nobles, *supra* note 168, at 36–42.
171. Williamson, *supra* note 75, at 25
172. *Id* at 25.
173. *Id.* at 24
174. *Id.* at 25.
175. *Id.*
176. *Id.*
177. Bart Landry, The New Black Middle Class 24 (1987).
178. Josiah Clark Nott et al., Types of Mankind: Or, Ethnological Researches, Based Upon the Ancient Monuments, Paintings, Sculptures and Crania of Races, and Upon Their Natural, Geographical, Philological and Biblical History 80 (1854).
179. Count Arthur de Gobineau, The Moral and Intellectual Diversity of Races, With Particular Reference to their Respective Influence in the Civil and Political History of Mankind (1856).
180. *See* Idus A. Newby, Jim Crow's Defense: Anti-Negro Thought in America, 1900–1930, 9 (1965).
181. *Id.*
182. The five acts were as follows: Civil Rights Act of 1866; the Enforcement Act of May 31, 1870; the Enforcement Act of February 28, 1871; the Enforcement Act of April 20, 1871; and the Civil Rights Act of 1875.
183. Pasco, *supra* note 151, at 40–44.
184. *Id.* at 40.
185. *Id.*
186. *Id.*
187. James Schoulder, Domestic Relations 29 (1870).
188. *See, e.g., State v. Gibson*, 36 Ind. 389 (1871) (upholding an Indiana miscegenation statute); *Kinney v. Commonwealth*, 71 Va. (30 Gratt.) 858 (1878) (upholding a lower court's decision that the marriage between a black person and a white person conducted in Washington D.C. was void in the state of Virginia).
189. *Gibson, supra* note 188.
190. The Alabama Supreme Court upheld an antimiscegenation statute in 1868. *See Ellis v. State*, 42 Ala. 525 (1868). This decision was handed down in June of 1868, before the 14th Amendment was certified on July 28, 1868. Four years later the Court reversed its decision in Ellis and declared that the state ban on interracial marriage was unlawful. *Burns v. State*, 48 Ala. 195, 197 (1877). However, in 1873, the Alabama Supreme Court reversed itself again and held that Congress did not intend the Civil Rights Act of 1866 to overturn anti-miscegenation laws. *Green v. State*, 58 Ala. 190 (1877).
191. *Id.*
192. *Pace v. Alabama, supra* note 154.
193. *See also* Rachel F. Moran, Interracial Intimacy: The Regulation of Race and Romance 17 (2001).
194. Pasco, *supra* note 151, at 6.
195. *Id.* at 2.
196. Zabel, *supra* note 89.

197. John G. Mencke, Mulattoes and Race Mixture: American Attitudes and Images, 1865–1918, 39 (1979).

198. John S. Haller, Jr., Outcasts From Evolution: Scientific Attitudes of Racial Inferiority, 1859–1900, 21 (1971). It may seem that autopsies of 405 soldiers seem like a small sample to establish the notion that the brains of blacks are smaller than those of whites and the brains of mixed-race blacks with less than 50% white blood are smaller than that of blacks. Keep in mind that the Kenneth Clark's doll studies used to establish the psychological damage that segregation caused in blacks drew on tests of only 253 children. The research by the psychologist purporting to show that African-Americans in public schools had lower self-esteem has been the subject of criticism. *See, e.g.,* William Cross, Shades of Black (1990) (arguing that the psychologist confused racial group preference with self-esteem, assuming that racial group preference would automatically correspond with self-esteem).

199. Sanford B. Hunt, *The Negro as a Soldier,* 7 Anthropol. Rev. 49–50 (January 1869).

200. *Id.* at 51.

201. *Id.* at 52.

202. *Id.*

203. Cedric J. Robinson, Forgeries of Memory and Meaning: Blacks and the Regimes of Race in American Theater and Film Before World War II 120 (2007).

204. Benjamin Apthorp Gould, Investigations in the Military and Anthropological Statistics of American Soldiers 471 (1869).

205. *Id.* at 319.

206. Jedediah H. Baxter, *Statistics, Medical and Anthropological, of the Provost-Marshal-General's Bureau: Derived From Records of the Examination for Military Service in the Armies of the United States During the Late War of the Rebellion of Over a Million Recruits, Drafted Men, Substitutes, and Enrolled Men* (Washington: Government Printing Office, 1875).

207. Haller, *supra* note 198, at 29.

208. *Id.* at 30.

209. *Id.*

210. Joseph LeConte, The Race Problem in the South (1892).

211. Joseph LeConte, "The Genesis of Sex," in *Popular Science Monthly* (Vol.16 December 1879): 167; "The Effect of Mixture of Races on Human Progress," in *Berkeley Quarterly* 1 (April 1880): 89–90.

212. Haller, *supra* note 198, at 161.

213. Frederick L. Hoffman, Race Traits and Tendencies of the American Negro 206–07 (1896).

214. *Id.* at 184.

215. F. James Davis, *supra* note 80, at 57 (1991).

216. Nathaniel Southgate Shaler, The Neighbor: The Natural History of Human Contacts 135 (1904).

217. *Id.* at 162.

218. Haller, *supra* note 198, at 131.

219. Herbert Hovenkamp, *Social Science and Segregation Before* Brown, 34 Duke L.J. 655 (1985).

220. Mencke, *supra* note 197, at 38.

221. *Berea College v. Kentucky,* 211 U.S. 45 (1908).

222. *Berea College v. Commonwealth*, 94 S.W. 623 (Ky. 1906), *aff'd*, *Berea College v. Kentucky*, 211 U.S. 45 (1908).

223. *Id.* at 625.

224. *Id.* at 626.

225. Hovenkamp, *supra* note 219, at 624, 655.

226. Joe R. Feagin, Racist America: Roots, Current Realities, and Future Reparations 60 (2000).

227. Mencke, *supra* note 197, at 37.

228. *Quoted in id.*

229. Sweet, *supra* note 78, at 318–19.

230. Robert Park, *Human Migration and the Marginal Man*, 33 Am. J. Sociol. 881 (1928).

231. Everett V. Stonequist, *The Problem of the Marginal Man*," 41 Am J. Sociol. 1, 12 (1935). E.V. Stonequist, The Marginal Man: A Study in Personality and Culture Conflict, 8 (1937).

232. Robert Park, *Mentality of Racial Hybrids*, 36 Am. J. Sociol. 534, 544 (1931).

233. Christine C. Iijima Hall, *Please Choose One: Ethnic Identity Choices for Biracial Individuals*, in Racially Mixed People in America 250–51 (Maria P. P. Root ed., 1992).

234. Stonequist, *supra* note 231, at 8.

235. *See Loving v. Virginia*, *supra* note 4 (pointing to the fact that 16 states currently banned interracial marriage and 14 states repealed their laws banning interracial marriage over the past 15 years).

236. Wallenstein, *supra* note 12, at 185.

237. *See* Gibson, *supra* note 2. The instructions for those enumerators stated, "A person of mixed white and Negro blood was to be returned as Negro, no matter how small the percentage of Negro blood." See Snipp, *supra* note 170.

238. Light skinned blacks had long been passing as white in the United States. For example, a conservative estimate put the number of blacks who were able to successfully pass as white between 1880 and 1925 at approximately 90,000 people. F. James Davis, *supra* note 80, at 56.

239. Angela Onwuachi-Willig, According to Our Hearts: Rhinelander v. Rhinelander and the Law of the Multiracial Family 13 (2013).

240. *Loving*, *supra* note 4.

241. *Brown v. Board of Education*, 347 U.S. 483 (1954).

242. *Jackson v. Alabama*, 348 U.S. 888 (1954) *cert. den.*

243. *Naim v. Naim*, 350 U.S. 985 (1956).

244. *McLaughlin v. State*, 153 So. 2d 1 (1963).

245. *Id.*

246. *Id.*

247. *Loving*, *supra* note 4. In 1924, Virginia adopted the Racial Integrity Act, which defined a person as white if they had "no trace whatsoever of any blood other than Caucasian; but persons who have only one-sixteenth or less of the blood of the American Indian ... shall be deemed to be white." Ch. 371, 1924 Va. Acts 535. A 1930 statute also defined as colored, anyone "in whom there is ascertainable any Negro blood." Ch. 85, 1930 Va. Acts 97.

248. *Id* at 2.

249. *Id.*

250. *Id.* at 2–3.

251. *Id.*

252. *Id.*

253. *Id.*
254. *Id.*
255. *Id.*
256. *Loving v. Commonwealth*, 147 S.E.2d 78, 83 (Va. 1966).
257. *Loving v. Virginia*, *supra* note 4.
258. *Id.* at 11.
259. *Id.* at 11, n. 11.
260. *Id.* at 11.
261. As Kim Williams, who extensively studied the movement to alter the federal forms to allow individuals to mark one or more boxes, stated, "Unexpectedly, I found that white, liberal, and suburban-based middle-class women (married to black men) held the leadership roles in most multiracial organizations. These white women helped to set an optimistic tone for multiracial activism; many believed that American racial polarization could be overcome by their example. Most of these women were looking for community—not for a census designation. Movement spokespeople reversed these priorities somewhat, although they parted ways after the OMB decision in 1997." *See* WILLIAMS, *supra* note 11, at 112.
262. KERRY ANN ROCKQUEMORE & DAVID BRUNSMA, BEYOND BLACK: BIRACIAL IDENTITY IN AMERICA 1–2 (2002). *See also* WILLIAMS, *supra* note 11, at 7–8.
263. *Id.*, at 15.
264. *Id.*
265. *See* Brown, *supra* note 45, at 277
266. *See* WILLIAMS, *supra* note 11, at 12.
267. *See* AMEA website, *at* http://www.ameasite.org/history.asp (last visited Mar. 30, 2014). The American MultiEthnic Association was the product of an effort to provide a multiracial option on official forms including Census forms. For a comprehensive history of the movement, *see* Naomi Mezey, *Erasure and Recognition: The Census, Race and the National Imagination*, 97 Nw. U. L. REV. 1701, 1749–52 (2003).
268. RAINER SPENCER, SPURIOUS ISSUES: RACE AND MULTIRACIAL IDENTITY POLITICS IN THE UNITED STATES 71, 126 (1999). *See also* Bijan Gilanshah, *Multiracial Minorities: Erasing the Color Line*, 12 LAW & INEQ. 183, 188 (1993).
269. *See* WILLIAMS, *supra* note 11, at 12.
270. *Id.*
271. Gilanshah, *supra* note 268, at 184.
272. *See* F. JAMES DAVIS, *supra* note 80, at 13.
273. ROCKQUEMORE & BRUNSMA, *supra* note 262, at 1–17.
274. *Id.* at 1–2.
275. *See* MICHAEL SPENCER, THE NEW COLORED PEOPLE: THE MIXED-RACE MOVEMENT IN AMERICA (1997). *See* F. JAMES DAVIS, *supra* note 80, at 21 (mentioning studies that place the percentage of blacks with white ancestry at between 75 and 90 percent).
276. *See* G. Reginald Daniel, *Black No More or More Than Black?: Multiracial Identity Politics and the Multiracial Movement* in RACIAL THINKING IN THE UNITED STATES 291 (Paul Spickard & G. Reginald Daniel eds., 2004). *See also*, HICKMAN, *supra* note 82 at 1162, 1184–85 (arguing that while the one-drop rule was a product of racism, it became a means of mobilizing communities of color to organize against white race privilege).
277. Coalition Statement on Proposed Modification of OMB Directive No. 15 (1994).
278. Alice Robbin, *Classifying Racial and Ethnic Group Data in the United States 1: The Politics of Negotiation and Accommodation*, 27 J. GOV. INFORM. 129–156 (2000).

279. *Id. See also* WILLIAMS, *supra* note 11, at 65–83. (discussing multiracial category legislation in states).

280. Jennifer Hochschild & Traci Burch, *Contingent Public Policies and Racial Hierarchy: Lessons from Immigration and Census Policies*, in POLITICAL CONTINGENCY: STUDYING THE UNEXPECTED, THE ACCIDENTAL, AND THE UNFORESEEN 156 (Ian Shapiro & Sonu Bedi eds., 2007).

281. *See* WILLIAMS, *supra* note 11, at 44. Charles Byrd would later write a book asserting that Krishna Consciousness was a way to get beyond the American fixation on race. CHARLES MICHAEL BYRD, THE BHAGAVAD-GITA IN BLACK AND WHITE: FROM MULATTO PRIDE TO KRISHNA CONSCIOUSNESS (2007).

282. SNIPP, *supra* note 169, at 569 (2003).

283. *See* Lee & Edmonston, *supra* note 20.

284. Nancy Leong, *Multiracial Identity and Affirmative Action*, 12 ASIAN PAC. AM. L. J. 1 (2006).

285. For a copy of the census forms throughout the years and accompanying questions, *see* http://usa.ipums.org/usa/voliii/tEnumForm.shtml (last visited Mar. 30, 2014).

286. *Id.*

287. *See* Humes, *supra* note 30.

288. According to statistics obtained from Josiah Evans the Assistant Director of Social Science Research for LSAC (on file with author).

289. Scholars have interpreted the way that African Americans' culture affects their educational performance in different ways. For example, the Afrocentrist argued that the Eurocentric bias of the traditional educational curriculum was responsible for the poor performance of black schoolchildren. Scholars like John H. Whorter argue that the problem of African American culture is the "stranglehold of Victimology, Separatism, and Anti-Intellectualism." *See* JOHN H. MCWHORTER, LOSING THE RACE (2000). Nigerian-born educational anthropologist, John Ogbu, draws distinctions between the cultures of involuntary minorities like African Americans and voluntary immigrants. He notes that involuntary minorities throughout the world have difficulty succeeding in education. Their situation is unfavorably contrasted to that of voluntary immigrants who generally come to the host country in search of better economic, political, or religious motivations. *See* John U. Ogbu, *Immigrant and Involuntary Minorities in Comparative Perspectives*, in MINORITY STATUS AND SCHOOLING: A COMPARATIVE STUDY OF IMMIGRANT AND INVOLUNTARY MINORITIES 37–61 (Margaret A. Gibson & John U. Ogbu eds., 1991).

290. *Grutter v. Bollinger*, 539 U.S. 306, 333, 338 (2003).

291. LEONG, *supra* note 284.

292. Kerry Anne Rockquemore & David Brunsma, *Socially Embedded Identities: Theories, Typologies, and Processes of Racial Identity Formation Among Black/White Biracials*, 43 SOCIOL. QUART. 335, 336 (2002).

293. *Id.*, at 338–40.

294. LEONG, *supra* note 284, at 7.

295. For example, *see* David Kaufman, Biracial Experiences in the United States, INTERRACE, Apr. 1994, 15, 19 (quoting a Multiracial college student as saying that ethnic identity and cultural awareness are very important, but that a single ethnic identity is not necessary: "Who are you if you are not the sum total of your physical, mental and environmental beings?").

296. JOHN STREGE, TIGER: A BIOGRAPHY OF TIGER WOODS (1997).

297. Dewayne Wickham, *Tiger Finally Takes a Public Stand-The Wrong One*, USA Today, May 16, 2000.

298. *Id.*

299. Melissa Herman, *Forced to Choose: Some Determinants of Racial Identification in Multi-Racial Adolescents*, 75 Child Dev. 730, 736 fig. 2 (2004).

300. David R. Harris & Jeremiah Joseph Sim, *Who is Multiracial? Assessing the Complexity of Lived Race*, 67 Am. Sociol. Rev. 614, 619–20 (2002).

301. Sandra S. Smith & Mignon R. Moore, *Intraracial Diversity and Relations Among African-Americans: Closeness Among Black Students at a Predominately White University*, 106 Am. J. Sociol. 1 (2000).

302. *See* David L. Brunsma & Kerry Ann Rockqemore, *What Does "Black" Mean? Exploring the Epistemological Stranglehold of Racial Categorization*, 28 Critical Soc. 101, 108–09 (2002). It was not clear from the study if all the students had one Black parent and one white parent or whether a few students had one Black parent and one that was neither Black nor white. The term "border identity" was proposed by Maria P. P. Root. *See, e.g.,* Maria P. P. Root, *The Multiracial Experience: Racial Borders as a Significant Frontier in Race Relations*, in The Multiracial Experience: Racial Borders as the New Frontier xiii (Maria P. P. Root ed., 1996).

303. *See, e.g.,* Sarah S.M. Townsend et al, *Being Mixed: Who Claims a Biracial Identity?*, 18 Cult. Divers. Ethn. Min. 91, 95 (2012) and Steven Hitlin, J. Scott Brown, and Glen H. Elder, Jr., *Racial Self-Categorization in Adolescence: Multiracial Development and Social Pathways*, 77 Child Dev. 1298, 1306 (2006).

304. Evelina Lou, Richard N. Lalonde, and Carlos Wilson, *Examining a Multidimensional Framework of Identity Across Different Biracial Groups*, 2 Asian Am. J. Psych. 79, 8107 (2011).

305. A 2006 study found that the younger people are the more likely they are to self-identify as multiracial. Steven Hitlin, J. Scott Brown, and Glen H. Elder, Jr., *Racial Self-Categorization in Adolescence: Multiracial Development and Social Pathways*, 77 Child Dev. 1298, 1306 (2006).

306. Linda Charmaraman & Jennifer M. Grossman, *Importance of Race and Ethnicity: An Exploration of Asian, Black, Latino and Multiracial Adolescent Identity*, 16 Cult. Divers. Ethn. Min. 144, 148 (2010).

307. *See* Angela R. Gillem, Laura Renee Cohn, and Cambria Throne, *Black Identity in Biracial Black/White People: A Comparison of Jacqueline Who Refuses to Be Exclusively Black and Adolphus Who Wishes He Were*, 7 Cult. Divers. Ethn. Min. 182, 183 (2001).

308. Christina Huffington, Single Motherhood Increases Dramatically for Certain Demographics, Census Bureau Reports, May 1, 2013, Huffingtonpost (May 1, 2013), *available at* http://www.huffingtonpost.com/2013/05/01/single-motherhood-increases-census-report_n_3195455.html (sixty-eight percent of black women had given birth in the past year were unmarried, compared to 11 percent of Asian women, 43 percent of Hispanics, and 26 percent of non-Hispanic whites.).

309. Toldson, *supra* note 71.

310. Brown, *supra* note 60, at 143, 149–51.

# Chapter Four

1. *See, for example,* Grace Kao and Marta Tienda, *Optimism and Achievement: The Educational Performance of Immigrant Youth*, 76 Soc. Sci. Quart. 1–19 (1995) (arguing that the academic success of children of immigrants is associated with immigrants' optimism) and Mary Waters, *Ethnic and Racial Identities of Second-Generation Black Immigrants in New York City*, in The New Second Generation, 171–96 (Alejandro Portes ed., 1996) (concluding that because the children of West Indians are more optimistic, they tend to identify in ethnic terms as opposed to racial).

2. The oppositional nature in the United States worked both ways. Professor Karst noted that in the South, which is the American ancestral home for the overwhelming majority of African Americans, to identify oneself as white meant, above all, to identify oneself as not black. *See* Kenneth L. Karst, Belonging to America 17 (1989). *See also* Amuzie Chimezie, *Black Bi-Culturality*, 9 W. J. Black Stud. 224 (1985) (defining and discussing black bi-culturality).

3. *See* Natasha Warikoo & Prudence Carter, *Cultural Explanations for Racial and Ethnic Stratification in Academic Achievement: A Call for a New and Improved Theory*, 79 Rev. of Educ. Res. 366, 370 (2009). There is a growing amount of literature that argues this is overemphasized. *See, e.g.,* James W. Ainsworth-Darnell & Douglas B. Downey, *Assessing the Oppositional Culture Explanation for Racial/Ethnic Differences in School Performance*, 63 Am. Sociol. Rev. 536, 536–53 (1998); Karolyn Tyson, William Darity & Domini R. Castellino, *It's Not a 'Black Thing': Understanding the Burden of Acting White and Other Dilemmas of High Achievement*, 70 Am. Sociol. Rev. 582, 582–605 (2005). *See also* Pamela R. Bennett & Amy Lutz, *How African American Is the Net Black Advantage? Differences in College Attendance Among Immigrant Blacks, Native Blacks, and Whites*, 80 Sociol. Educ. 70, 90 (2009).

4. *See, for example,* Pamela R. Bennett & Amy Lutz, *supra* note 3, at 79 (asserting that "much of the literature on immigration has made theoretical assumptions about the cultural propensities of African American students with respect to education without the kind of explicit empirical comparisons of their educational outcomes to those of immigrant blacks").

5. Immigration and Nationality Act, H.R. 2580, 89th Cong. (1965) (codified as amended in scattered sections of 8 U.S.C. 1151).

6. In 1960, the 125,000 foreign-born blacks made up about 0.7 percent of the black population. Campbell Gibson & Emily Lennon, U.S. Census bureau, Race and Hispanic Origin of the Population by Nativity: 1850 to 1990 (Mar. 9, 1999).

7. For 1970, 1980, and 1990 figures *see id.* For figures from 2000, *see* Jesse D. McKinnon & Claudette E. Bennett, *We the People: Blacks in the United States*, U.S. CENSUS BUREAU 7 fig.5 (2005). For 2005 figures, *see* Mary Mederios Kent, Immigration and America's Black Population 4 (2007).

8. For 2010 figures, *see* U. S. Census Bureau, The Black Alone or in Combination Population in the United Stats: 2010 tbl.4. *Nativity and Citizenship Status by Sex, for Black Alone or in Combination and White Alone, Not Hispanic: 2010* (2010). For 2012 figures, *see* U. S. Census Bureau, The Black Alone Population in the United Stats: 2012 tbl.7. *Nativity and Citizenship Status by Sex, for Black Alone and White Alone, Not Hispanic:* 2012.

9. About 60 percent of these children had a parent born in the Caribbean with about 40 percent having a black African born parent. Kent, *supra* note 7.

10. The figure drops to just 13 percent of black children if only non-Hispanic blacks are considered. *Id.* at 4.

11. *See*, Maria Sacchetti, *The Changing Face Of Citizenship* in the Boston Globe, March 25, 2014.

12. Kent, *supra* note 7, at 5.

13. *See* Randy Capps, Kristen McCabe, and Michael Fix, *Diverse Streams: Black African Migration to the United States* 3 (April 2012), published by the Migration Policy Institute.

14. For African-born immigrant percentage, *see id.* at 5 tbl 3. For Caribbean born immigrant percentage, *see* Kevin J. A. Thomas, *A Demographic Profile of Black Caribbean Migrants in the United States*, 3 tbl 1 (April 2012) published by the Migration Policy Institute.

15. For African-born immigrant percentage, *see*, Patrick L. Mason and Algernon Austin, Economic Policy Institute, The Low Wages of Black Immigrants: Wage Penalties for U.S.-Born and Foreign-Born Black Workers, 4, tbl 3. (February 28, 2011). For Caribbean born immigrant percentage, *see* Thomas, *supra* note 14 at 3 tbl 1.

16. Mason and Austin, *supra* note 15, at 4, tbl 3.

17. Kent, *supra* note 7, at 12.

18. Mason and Austin, *supra* note 15.

19. Kent, *supra* note 7, at 14 fig. 4

20. One of the ways that foreign-born blacks come to the United States is on student visas. The Guidance also requires educational institutions to report individuals on student visas under a separate category of foreign students. *See* C. Anthony Broh & Stephen D. Minicucci, Racial Identity and Government Classification: A Better Solution 15 (May 28, 2008). The average number of black Africans enrolled in higher education institutions who are also on student visas in the United States from 2001 to 2006 was approximately 33,100 per year. West Indians accounted for less than half of this number with an annual amount of 14,100. However, many of these students from Africa or the Caribbean were Asian or white. Thus, foreign-born blacks on student visas made up less than 50,000 individuals on college campuses. *See* Kent, *supra* note 7, at 9.

In contrast, there were over two and a half million blacks enrolled in college in 2007. *See* U.S. Census Bureau, *College Enrollment—Summary by Sex, Race, and Hispanic Origin: 2007*. Some of the statistics in this section regarding the number or percentage of Black Immigrants may include those foreign-born blacks on student visas.

21. Jeffrey S. Passel, *Demography of Immigrant Youth: Past, Present and Future*, in The Future of Children, 19, 30 (2011), *available at* http://futureofchildren.org/futureofchildren/publications/docs/21_01_FullJournal.pdf.

22. According to the 2007 census figures, of the 223,005,000 one race whites in the country, 17,412,000 were foreign-born, constituting 7.8 percent of the white population. *See* Grieco, *supra* note 13.

23. *Id.*

24. *A Solid Percentage of Black Students at U.S. Colleges and Universities Are Foreign Born*, 54 J. Blacks High. Educ. 22 (Jan. 2006).

25. *Id.*

26. *Id.*

27. *Id.*

28. *Id.*

29. Douglas S. Massey et al., *Black Immigrants and Black Natives Attending Selective Colleges and Universities in the United States*, 113 Am. J. Educ. 243, 248 (2006).

30. *See id.* at 245.

31. *Id.* at 248 tbl.1.

32. *Id.*
33. Ronald Roach, *Drawing Upon the Diaspora*, DIVERSE ISSUES IN HIGH. EDUC. 38, 40 (Aug. 25, 2005).
34. This was a nationally representative sample of eighth graders who were first surveyed in 1988. There were four follow-up surveys conducted in 1990, 1992, 1994, and 2000. For a discussion of the NELS 1988 survey see NATIONAL EDUCATIONAL LONGITUDINAL STUDY OF 1988. Bennett and Lutz in their research stopped at the 1994 data set. This set was two years after the students should have entered college. Pamela R. Bennett & Amy Lutz, *supra* note 3 at 75.
35. *Id.* at 79. Although the sample looked at a total of 8,552 students, there were only ninety-five immigrant blacks, 958 native blacks, and 7,499 whites. *Id.*
36. *Id.* at 70, 79.
37. Donald J. Hernandez, *Changing Demography and Circumstances for Young Black Children in African and Caribbean Immigrant Families* 3 (2012) published by the Migration Policy Institute. In addition, only Asian parents have a higher rate of enrolling their children in pre-kindergarten educational programs. *Id* at 1.
38. John C. Duncan, Jr. *Two "Wrongs" Do/Can Make A Right: Remembering Mathematics, Physics, & Various Legal Analogies (Two Negatives Make A Positive; Are Remedies Wrong?) The Law Has Made Him Equal, But Man Has Not*, 43 BRANDEIS L.J. 511, 517 n.18 (2005).
39. *See* JAMES WELDON JOHNSON, BLACK MANHATTAN 130 (1930).
40. *See* PHILIP KASINITZ, CARIBBEAN NEW YORK: BLACK IMMIGRANTS AND THE POLITICS OF RACE 91 (1992).
41. NATHAN GLAZER & PATRICK MOYNIHAN, BEYOND THE MELTING POT 35 (1963).
42. *See* Thomas Sowell, *Three Black Histories*, *in* AMERICAN ETHNIC GROUPS, 37, 41 (Thomas Sowell & Lynn D. Collins eds., 1978).
43. Abdi Kusow, *Africa: East*, *in* THE NEW AMERICANS: A GUIDE TO IMMIGRATION SINCE 1965, at 295, 299 (Mary C. Waters & Reed Ueda with Helen B. Marrow eds., 2007).
44. J. A. ARTHUR, INVISIBLE SOJOURNERS: AFRICAN IMMIGRANT DIASPORA IN THE UNITED STATES 20 (2000).
45. *See* Clarence Page, *Black Immigrants Collect Most Degrees But Affirmative Action is Losing Direction*, CHICAGO TRIBUNE, Mar. 18, 2007, §2, at 7.
46. For the graduation percentage over the age of twenty-five for blacks see Kurt J. Bauman & Nikki L. Graf, *Educational Attainment: 2000: Census 2000 Brief*, U.S CENSUS BUREAU, 5 tbl.2 (2003).
47. Kent, *supra* note 7, at 5.
48. *See id.* at 9, tbl. 4.
49. *Id.*
50. Hernandez, *supra* note 37.
51. Kusow, *supra* note 43. At least one researcher has found that while English speaking Caribbean immigrants in general do better economically than African Americans, the same cannot be said for Spanish speaking or French speaking West Indians. *See* Matthijs Kalmijn, *The Socioeconomic Assimilation of Caribbean American Blacks*, 74 SOC. FORCES 911, 917–23 (1996).
52. *Id.*
53. *Id.*
54. *See* U.S CENSUS BUREAU, *Table 85. Births to Teens and Unmarried Women, and Births with Low Birth Weight, by Race and Hispanic Origin: 1990 to 2005* (This percentage remained consistent from 1995 to 2004, ranging from 69.6 percent in 1995 to 68.2 percent in 2003.

This is in contrast to 30.5 percent in 2004 for whites. But the percentage of white babies born to single woman nearly doubled since the 1990 figure of only 16.7 percent).

55. See Kent, supra note 7, at 11.
56. Id.
57. Hernandez, supra note 37.
58. Mae M. Ngai, *The Architecture of Race in American Immigration Law: A Reexamination of the Immigration Act of 1924*, 86 J. OF AM. HIST., 67, 71 (1999).
59. 3 Stat. 489 (1819).
60. Roy Simon Bryce-Laporte, *Black Immigrants: The Experience of Invisibility and Inequality*, 3 J. OF BLACK STUD. 29, 33 (1972).
61. See *2003 Yearbook of Immigration Statistics*, OFFICE OF IMMIGRATION STATISTICS, DEPARTMENT OF HOMELAND SECURITY, 12–15 tbl.2 (2004).
62. A. Gordon, *The New Diaspora—African Immigration to the United States* 15 J. THIRD WORLD STUD. 79–103 (1998).
63. See, e.g., BENJAMIN QUARLES, THE NEGRO IN THE MAKING OF AMERICA 24 (1969).
64. CAPTAIN JOHN SMITH, THE GENERALL HISTORIE OF VIRGINIA, NEW ENGLAND, AND THE SUMMER ISLES, VOL. 1 246–47 (1907). This account can also be found printed in CIVIL RIGHTS AND AFRICAN AMERICANS 4 (Albert P. Blaustein & Robert L. Zangrando eds., Northwestern Univ. Press 1991) (1968).
65. This was the earliest date possible under the Constitution. "The Migration or Importation of such Persons as any of the States now existing shall think proper to admit, shall not be prohibited by the Congress prior to the Year one thousand eight hundred and eight, but a tax or duty may be imposed on such Importation, not exceeding ten dollars for each Person." See U.S. CONST. art. I, §9.
66. JOSEPH E. HOLLOWAY, *The Origins of African-American Culture* in AFRICANISM IN AMERICAN CULTURE 1 (1991).
67. Id.
68. MARY C. WATERS, BLACK IDENTITIES: WEST INDIAN IMMIGRANT DREAMS AND AMERICAN REALITIES 21 (1999).
69. For an article discussing the history of discrimination in American immigration policy towards Africans, see Andowah A. Newton, *Injecting Diversity Into U.S. Immigration Policy: The Diversity Visa Program and the Missing Discourse on its Impact on African Immigration to the United States*, 38 CORNELL INT'L L.J. 1049 (2005).
70. See IAN F. HANEY LOPEZ, WHITE BY LAW: THE LEGAL CONSTRUCTION OF RACE 42–46 (1996) (citing Naturalization Act, ch. 3, 1 Stat. 103 (1790)).
71. BUREAU OF THE CENSUS, *U.S. Dep't of Commerce, Ser. P-23, No. 80, The Social and Economic Status of the Black Population in the United States: An Historical View, 1790–1978*, at 254 (1979).
72. Id.
73. Id.
74. Id.
75. See LOPEZ, supra note 70, at 43–44. (citing Naturalization Act, ch. 255, §7, 16 Stat. 254 (1870)).
76. The Civil Rights Act of 1866 also declared that all persons born in the United States (including blacks) were citizens of the United States.
77. *Dred Scott v. Sandford*, 60 U.S. 393, 406 (1857).

78. *See* LOPEZ, *supra* note 70, at 46 (citing The United States Revenue Act, ch. 233, 43 Stat. 253 (1924)). Congress did not grant First Americans, for example, United States citizenship until 1924. It was not until 1952 that American naturalization law became race neutral. *Id.* at 41 (citing Immigration and Nationality Act, ch. 2, §311, 66 Stat. 239 (1952) (codified as amended at 8 U.S.C. §1422 (1998)).

79. MARILYN HALTER, BETWEEN RACE AND ETHNICITY: CAPE VERDEAN AMERICAN IMMIGRANTS, 1860–1965, 1 (1993).

80. COLM FOY, CAPE VERDE: POLITICS, ECONOMICS, AND SOCIETY 7–8 (1988).

81. HALTER, *supra* note 79, at 45.

82. *Id.* at 3.

83. *Id.* at 20.

84. *See id.* at 68–69.

85. WATERS, *supra* note 68, at 34.

86. *Id.* at 34. Other commentators have put the number at 140,000. *See* Florence L. Denmark, Khaya N. Eisenberg, Erica I. Heitner & Nicola A. Holder, *Immigration to the United States: The Dream and the Reality*, *in* MIGRATION: IMMIGRATION AND EMIGRATION IN INTERNATIONAL PERSPECTIVE 90 (Leonore Loeb Adler & Uwe P. Gielen eds., 2003).

87. Dawn Marshall, *Toward an Understanding of Caribbean Migration*, *in* U.S. IMMIGRATION AND REFUGEE POLICY: GLOBAL AND DOMESTIC ISSUES, 113–31 (Mary M. Kritz, ed., 1983).

88. NANCY FONER, IN A NEW LAND: A COMPARATIVE VIEW OF IMMIGRATION 44 (2005).

89. *Id.*

90. *Id.* at 44–46.

91. *See* 2003 Yearbook of Immigration Statistics, *supra* note 61.

92. *Irish and German Immigration from U.S. History Online Textbook*, U.S. HISTORY (2010), http://www.ushistory.org/us/25f.asp (last visited Mar. 30, 2014).

93. *Id.*

94. *See* 2003 Yearbook of Immigration Statistics, *supra* note 61.

95. *Id.*

96. *See* LOPEZ, *supra* note 70, at 37–38 (citing Chinese Exclusion Act, ch. 126, 22 Stat. 58 (1882); Act of July 9, 1884, ch. 220, 23 Stat. 115; Geary Act, ch. 60, 27 Stat. 25 (1892); Act of April 29, 1902, ch. 641, 32 Stat. 176; Act of April 27, 1904, ch. 1630, 33 Stat. 428).

97. *See* 2003 Yearbook of Immigration Statistics, *supra* note 61.

98. *See* Kevin R. Johnson, *Race, the Immigration Laws, and Domestic Race Relations: A "Magic Mirror" into the Heart of Darkness*, 73 IND. L.J. 1111, 1121 (1998).

99. 39 Stat. 874, 875 (1917). The 1917 Act also included a requirement that barred aliens over the age of sixteen who could not read English or some other dialect or language and who were incapable of reading. Ngai, *supra* note 58, at 80.

100. Lolita K. Buckner Inniss, *Tricky Magic: Blacks as Immigrants and the Paradox of Foreignness*, 40 DEPAUL L. REV. 85 (1999).

101. *See* U.S. IMMIGRATION AND NATURALIZATION LAWS AND ISSUES: A DOCUMENTARY HISTORY xxxi (Michael LeMay & Elliott Robert Barkan eds., 1999).

102. *See* 2003 Yearbook of Immigration Statistics, *supra* note 61.

103. *See* Michael J. Klarman, *Rethinking the Civil Rights and Civil Liberties Revolutions*, 82 VA. L. REV. 1, 49 (1996).

104. *Id.*

105. *See* MICHAEL W. APPLE, IDEOLOGY AND CURRICULUM 70 (1979).

106. Ellwood P. Cubberley, Changing Conceptions of Education 15 (1909).
107. *Id.*
108. *See, e.g.*, Bill Ong Hing, *Immigration Policies: Messages of Exclusion to African Americans*, 37 How. L.J. 237, 246 (1994).
109. H.R. Rep. No. 82–1365 (1952), *reprinted in* 1952 U.S.C.C.A.N. 1313 1667.
110. Ngai, *supra* note 58, at 67 fn 1 (1999).
111. *See* John Higham, Strangers in the Land: Patterns of American Nativism, 1860–1925, 311 (2005).
112. For a table of the allocation of the quotas, *see* Ngai, *supra* note 58, at 67, tbl. 74. The quotas for the North and Western Countries were Great Britain and Northern Ireland (65,721), Germany (25,957), Irish Free State (17,853), Sweden (3,314), Netherlands (3,153), France (3,086), Norway (2,377), Switzerland (1,701) Belgian (1,304), and Denmark (1,181).
113. According to immigration stats, less than 2000 Africans came to the U.S. between 1820 and 1890. *See 2003 Yearbook of Immigration Statistics*, *supra* note 61.
114. Ngai, *supra* note 61, at 73 (1999).
115. *See* Ira De Augustine Reid, The Negro Immigrant: His Background, Characteristics and Social Adjustments, 1899–1937 33 (1970).
116. Waters, *supra* note 68, at 35.
117. Florence L. Denmark, Khaya N. Eisenberg, Erica I. Heitner & Nicola A. Holder, *Immigration to the United States: The Dream and the Reality in* Migration: Immigration and Emigration in International Perspective 90 (Leonore Loeb Adler & Uwe P. Gielen eds., 2003).
118. *See* Richard A. Boswell, *Racism and U.S. Immigration Law: Prospects for Reform after "9/11,"* 7 J. Gender Race & Just. 315, 325 (2003). However, Congress did enact immigration reform measures that affected Mexican immigrants. *See* Kevin Brown and Tom I. Romero, II, *Social Reconstruction of Race & Ethnicity of the Nation's Law Students: A Request to the ABA, AALS, and LSAC for Changes in Reporting Requirements*, 2011 Mich. St. L. Rev. 1133, 1152–6 (2011).
119. *See* Campbell J. Gibson & Kay Jung, *Historical Census Statistics on the Foreign-Born Population of the United States: 1850–2000*, at tbl.1, U.S. Census Bureau, Working Paper Series No. 81 (2006).
120. *Id.*
121. Elizabeth M. Grieco, Yesenia D. Acosta, G. Patricia De La Cruz, Christine Gambino, Thomas Gryn, Luke J. Larsen, Edward N. Trevelyan, and Nathan P. Walter, *The Foreign Born Population in the United States: 2010 American Community Survey Report* 2, tbl. 1 (March 2012).
122. L. Cheng & P. Q. Yang, *Global Interaction, Global Inequality, and Migration of the Highly Trained to the United States*, 32 Int. Migr. Rev. 626, 628 (1998).
123. While it is illegal in France to take a census on race or religion, Solis, a marketing company, estimated that there are a little over 1,080,000 sub-Saharan blacks among France's 62,400,000 population. *See France's Crisis of National Identity*, The Independent (Nov. 25, 2009).
124. *See, e.g.*, Hing, *supra* note 111, at 237, 246.
125. Gordon, *supra* note 62, at 79–103.
126. Kent, *supra* note 7, at 8 tbl 2.
127. The five Commonwealth countries are Jamaica, Trinidad and Tobago, Nigeria, Guyana, and Ghana.
128. Ronald Fernandez, America Beyond Black and White 176 (2007).

129. *See* Ian R. G. Spencer, British Immigration Policy Since 1939: The Making of Multiracial Britain 3 (1997).
130. *See* Randall Hansen, Citizenship and Immigration in Post-War Britain 53 (2000).
131. *Id.* at 5.
132. *E.g.*, Kenneth Lunn, *The British State and Immigration, 1945–51: New Light on the Empire Windrush*, *in* The Politics of Marginality: Race, The Radical Right, and Minorities in Twentieth Century Britain 161, 165 (Tony Kushner & Kenneth Lunn eds., 1990).
133. Kevin C. Wilson, *And Stay Out! The Dangers Of Using Anti-Immigrant Sentiment As A Basis For Social Policy: America Should Take Heed Of Disturbing Lessons From Great Britain's Past*, 24 Ga. J. Int'l & Comp. L., 567, 568–76 (1995).
134. John Wrench & John Solomos, *The Politics and Processes of Racial Discrimination in Britain*, *in* Racism and Migration in Western Europe 157, 160–61 (John Wrench & John Solomos eds., 1993).
135. Hansen, *supra* note 130, at 80–84.
136. *See* Spencer, *supra* note 129, at 4.
137. Lunn, *supra* note 132, at 161, 168.
138. Hansen, *supra* note 130 at 18.
139. Foner, *supra* note 88, at 114.
140. Paul Foot, Immigration and Race in British Politics 129 (1965).
141. Hansen, *supra* note 130, at 80–81.
142. *Id.*
143. David Steel, No Entry: The Background and Implications of the Commonwealth Immigrants Act, 1968 32 (1969).
144. *See* Hansen, *supra* note 130, at 3.
145. Foot, *supra* note 140.
146. *See* Hansen, *supra* note 130, at 29.
147. A. Sivandon, *Race, Class, and the State: The Black Experience in Britain*, 27 Race Class 350–67 (1976).
148. Spencer, *supra* note 129, at 129.
149. *Id.*
150. Steel, *supra* note 143, at 52.
151. The United Kingdom also reserved a thousand of these vouchers for applicants from Malta. *See* Spencer, *supra* note 129, at 135–36.
152. Hansen, *supra* note 130, at 153–78.
153. A copy of the speech is available at http://www.telegraph.co.uk/comment/3643823/Enoch-Powells-Rivers-of-Blood-speech.html (last visited, Mar. 30, 2014).
154. Spencer, *supra* note 129, at 143.
155. *Id.* at 144.
156. *Id.* at 147.
157. Kent, *supra* note 7, at 8 tbl 2.
158. Phillip Kasnitz, *The Minority Within: The New Black Immigrant*, 10 New York Affairs 46 (1987).
159. *Id.* at 44, 46.
160. Waters, *supra* note 68, at 36.

161. I focus on sub-Saharan Africa because according to the United States Census Bureau, a white person is defined as "[a] person having origins in any of the original peoples of Europe, the Middle East, or North Africa". *See* OFFICE OF MGMT. & BUDGET, *Revisions to the Standards for the Classification of Federal Data on Race and Ethnicity* (1997).

162. Ghana (1957); Guinea (1958); Chad, Benin, Nigeria, Ivory Coast, Madagascar, Central African Republic, Mali, Niger, Senegal, Burkina Faso, Mauritania, Togo, Zaire, Somalia, Congo, Gabon, Cameroon (1960); Sierra Leone (1961), South Africa (under minority rule until 1995); Burundi, Rwanda, Uganda (1962); Kenya, Tanzania (1963); Malawi, Zambia (1964); Gambia (1965); Botswana, Lesotho (1966); Equatorial Guinea, Mauritius, Swaziland (1968); Guinea-Bissau (1969). *See* INDIGENOUS PEOPLE OF AFRICA AND AMERICA, http://ipoaa.com/african_independence.htm (last visited Mar. 30, 2014).

163. *See* Gordon, *supra* note 62.

164. NAOMI CHAZAN ET AL., POLITICS AND SOCIETY IN CONTEMPORARY AFRICA 314–15 (3rd ed. 1999).

165. *See* Gordon, *supra* note 62.

166. *Recovery from War's Trauma*, 34 AFRICA NEWS 6–7 (July 15, 1991).

167. Arthur Helton, *The Kindness of Strangers*, 39 AFRICA REPORT 33–35 (March/April, 1994).

168. WORLD BANK, WORLD DEVELOPMENT REPORT 65 (New York: Oxford University Press, 1995).

169. JOHN F. KENNEDY, A NATION OF IMMIGRANTS 68 (rev. ed. 1964).

170. ROGER DANIELS & OTIS L. GRAHAM, DEBATING AMERICAN IMMIGRATION, 1882–PRESENT 8 (2001).

171. Milton Vickerman, *The Center for Children, Families, and the Law Interdisciplinary Conference "Welcome to America: Immigration, Families, and the Law": Post-1965 Immigration and Assimilation: A Response to Randy Capps*, 14 VA. J. SOC. POL'Y & L. 206, 209 (2007).

172. DAVID M. REIMERS, OTHER IMMIGRANTS: THE GLOBAL ORIGINS OF THE AMERICAN PEOPLE 237 (2005).

173. Kent, *supra* note 7, at 6 box 2.

174. Immigration Reform and Control Act [IRCA], Pub. L. No. 99–603, 100 Stat. 3359 (1986) (codified in scattered sections of 8 U.S.C.).

175. The overwhelming majority, 87 percent, of the 1.7 million people who applied for general amnesty under this legalization provision were Mexican. *See* UNDOCUMENTED MIGRATION TO THE UNITED STATES: IRCA AND THE EXPERIENCE OF THE 1980S, at 184 (Frank D. Bean et al. eds., 1990).

176. Immigration Act of 1990, Pub. L. No. 101–649, § 131, 104 Stat. 4978 (1990); Immigration and Nationality Act (INA) §§ 201(a)(3), 201(e), 203(c), 8 U.S.C. §§ 1151(a)(3), 1151(e), 1153(c) (2000).

177. 8 U.S.C. § 1151(e). The statute actually provides for 55,000 visas. Beginning in FY 1999, 5000 of these visas were temporarily reallocated to adjustments under the Nicaraguan Adjustment and Central American Relief Act (NACARA). Pub. L. No. 105–100, § 203(d), 111 Stat. 2160 (1997).

178. *See* Newton, *supra* note 69, at 1053–54.

179. ROBERT J. NORRELL, THE HOUSE I LIVE IN: RACE IN THE AMERICAN CENTURY 333 (2005).

180. *Id.*

181. *See* Gibson & Jung, *supra* note 119.

182. Grieco et. al., *supra* note 121.
183. Kent, *supra* note 7, at 7 fig 3.
184. *Id.*
185. REIMERS, *supra* note 172, at 242.
186. Capps, *supra* note 13, at 7.
187. Kent, *supra* note 7, at 8 tbl 2.
188. *Id.* at 7.
189. *Id.*
190. Immigration Act, Pub. L. No. 101–649, § 131, 104 Stat. 4978 (1990); Immigration and Nationality Act (INA), §§ 201(a)(3), 201(e), 203(c), 8 U.S.C. §§ 1151(a)(3), 1151(e), 1153(c) (2000).
191. For a discussion of the history of the diversity visa program, see Newton, *supra* note 69.
192. Kent, *supra* note 7, at 6 box 2.
193. Capps, *supra note* 13, at 8.
194. *See, e.g.*, Kendall Thomas, Comments at Frontiers of Legal Thought Conference, Duke Law School (Jan. 26, 1990), *quoted in* Charles R. Lawrence III, *If He Hollers Let Him Go: Regulating Racist Speech on Campus*, 1990 Duke L. J. 431, *in* MARI J. MATSUDA, CHARLES R. LAWRENCE III, RICHARD DELGADO & KIMBERLÉ W. CRENSHAW, WORDS THAT WOUND 53, 61 (1993); *see also* D. Marvin Jones, *Darkness Made Visible: Law, Metaphor, and the Racial Self*, 82 GEO. L. J. 437 (1993) (arguing that racial categories are neither objective nor natural, but ideological and constructed. In these terms race is not so much a category but a practice: people are raced).
195. FONER, *supra* note 88, at 116.
196. Duncan, *supra* note 38.
197. *Grutter*, 539 U.S. 344, 338.
198. SAMUEL P. HUNTINGTON, AMERICAN POLITICS: THE PROMISE OF DISHARMONY 12 (1981).
199. ARTHUR SCHELSINGER JR., THE DISUNITING OF AMERICA 78 (1991).
200. THE DECLARATION OF INDEPENDENCE para. 2 (U.S. 1776).
201. *See* Abraham Lincoln, Gettysburg Address (Nov. 19, 1863).
202. *See, e.g.*, SAMUEL P. HUNTINGTON, *supra* note 198, at 23–24; ROBERT BELLAH ET AL., HABITS OF THE HEART: INDIVIDUALISM AND COMMITMENT IN AMERICAN LIFE 26 (1986); *see also* GUNNAR MYRDAL, AN AMERICAN DILEMMA: THE NEGRO PROBLEM AND MODERN DEMOCRACY 19 (1944).
203. Xue Lan Rong & Frank Brown, *The Effects of Immigrant Generation and Ethnicity on Educational Attainment Among Young African and Caribbean Blacks in the United States*, 71 HARV. EDUC. REV. 536, 548–51 (2001).
204. T. Alexander Aleinikoff & Rubén G. Rumbaut, *Terms Of Belonging: Are Models Of Membership Self-Fulfilling Prophecies?*, 13 GEO. IMMIGR. L.J. 1 (1998).
205. MALCOLM X, THE AUTOBIOGRAPHY OF MALCOLM X 201 (Ballantine Books 1992) (1965).
206. *See* Bennett & Lutz, *supra* note 3, at 70–100.
207. *See* Alejandro Portes and Rubén Rumbaut, *The Forging of a New America: Lessons for Theory and Policies*, *in* ETHNICITIES (Alejandro Portes and Rubén Rumbaut, 2001) and ALEJANDRO PORTES AND RUBÉN RUMBAUT, LEGACIES: THE STORY OF THE IMMIGRANT GENERATION (2001).

208. Bennett & Lutz, *supra* note 3, at 70, 72.

209. John U. Ogbu, *Immigrant and Involuntary Minorities in Comparative Perspectives*, in MINORITY STATUS AND SCHOOLING: A COMPARATIVE STUDY OF IMMIGRANT AND INVOLUNTARY MINORITIES 37–61 (Margaret A. Gibson & John Ogbu eds., 1991). Ogbu later adds a category for refugee minorities, who are primarily from Southeast Asia, who were forced to come to the United States as a result of political and or economic crises in their home countries. He notes that like voluntary immigrants, they have a "tourist attitude" and believe that to succeed in America they need to learn to speak and behave like white Americans, although they seek to maintain their separate cultural identity. *See* John Ogbu & H. D. Simmons, *Voluntary and Involuntary Minorities: A Cultural-Ecological Theory of School Performance with Some Implication for Education*, 29 ANTHROPOLOGY & EDUC. Q. 155–88 (1998).

210. Ogbu, *supra* note 209.

211. *See, e.g.*, G. Kao & M. Tienda, *Optimism and Achievement: The Educational Performance of Immigrant Youth*, 76 SOC. SCI. Q. 1–19 (1995).

212. *See, e.g.*, Claude Steele, *A Threat in the Air: How Stereotypes Shape Intellectual Identity and Performance*, 52 AM. PSYCHOLOGIST 613, 623 (1997).

213. *See* PAUL WACHTEL, RACE IN THE MIND OF AMERICA: BREAKING THE VICIOUS CIRCLE BETWEEN BLACKS AND WHITES 75 (1999). For a comparative discussion of the higher educational opportunities of African Americans in the United States and Dalits in India, see Kevin Brown & Vinay Sitipati, *Lessons Learned From Comparing The Application Of Constitutional Law And Federal Anti-Discrimination Law to African-Americans In The U.S. And Dalits In India In The Context Of Higher Education*, 24 HARV. BLACKLETTER L.J. 3 (2008).

214. PAUL WACHTEL, *supra* note 213, at 70.

215. *Id.*

216. *Id.*

217. *See id.*

218. *See* MICHAEL WEINER, THE ORIGINS OF THE KOREAN COMMUNITY IN JAPAN 1910–1923, 5 (1989).

219. African Americans retained more of their African heritage than people have appreciated. However, it is widely recognized that African American culture is a new culture influenced by African origins and shaped by American experiences. Eugene D. Genovese, *Blacks in the United States-From Slavery to the Present Crisis*, NEW REV. 3, 5 (1977).

220. MOLEFI ASANTE, THE AFROCENTRIC IDEA 99 (1998).

221. Professor Karst noted that in the South, which is the American ancestral home for the overwhelming majority of African Americans, to identify oneself as white meant, above all, to identify oneself as not black. *See* KARST, *supra* note 2, at 17.

222. *See, e.g.*, Malcolm Gladwell, *Black Like Them*, THE NEW YORKER, Apr. 29, 1996, at 74.

223. FONER, *supra* note 88, at 51.

224. FERNANDEZ, *supra* note 128, at 175.

225. *See* SAM MOYO, HUMAN DEVELOPMENT REPORT OFFICE, SOCIO-ECONOMIC DOMINANCE OF ETHNIC AND RACIAL GROUPS-THE AFRICAN EXPERIENCE (2004).

226. WATERS, *supra* note 68, at 29.

227. Colin Palmer, *The African Diaspora*, 30 BLACK SCHOLAR 56, 57 (2000).

228. One noted expert on West Indian immigration stated that "Jamaicans have historically eschewed rigid, American-style racial dichotomies in which people are classified as either 'Black' or 'white,' opting instead for a complex system in which a multiplicity of fac-

tors (e.g., ancestry, complexion, social standing, and education) determine 'race.' Consequently, on a day-to-day basis, Jamaicans hardly think about race—especially since all their role models (both social failures and the societies leaders) are Black." *See* Milton Vickerman, *Jamaica*, in THE NEW AMERICANS: A GUIDE TO IMMIGRATION SINCE 1965, at 485 (Mary C. Waters & Reed Ueda eds., with Helen B. Marrow 2007).

229. Byrce-Laporte, *supra* note 60, at 29, 39.

230. WATERS, *supra* note 68, at 144.

231. Jamaica (1962), Trinidad and Tobago (1962), Barbados (1966) and Guyana (1966).

232. WATERS, *supra* note 68, at 27.

233. *See* Matthijs Kalmijn, *supra* note 51, at 913–14.

234. WATERS, *supra* note 68, at 28.

235. *Id.* at 331.

236. *See generally* FROM DIFFERENT SHORES: PERSPECTIVES ON RACE AND ETHNICITY IN AMERICA (Ronald Takaki ed., 2d ed. 1994).

237. J. A. ARTHUR, *supra* note 44, at 128. Arthur conducted one of the first studies of African immigrants. He looked at 650 Africans over a three-year period that lived in four American cities—Charlotte (North Carolina), Washington, D.C., Atlanta, and Minneapolis-St. Paul.

238. *See generally* Devesh Kapur & John McHale, *Globalization at Work: Migration's New Payoff*, 139 FOREIGN POL'Y 48 (2003). In Jamaica, for example, migrants, who primarily live in the U.S., send an average of $640 per year back to families in Jamaica. This represents a substantial percentage of household income. *See* Alex Glennie and Laura Chappell, *Jamaica: From Diverse Beginning to Diaspora in the Developed World* (2010) (published by Migration Policy Institute).

239. *See* Kalmijn, *supra* note 51, at 911, 914–15.

240. FONER, *supra* note 88, at 123.

241. *See* Leonard M. Baynes, *Who is Black Enough for You? The Stories of One Black Man and His Family's Pursuit of The American Dream*, 11 GEO. IMMIGR. L.J. 97, 124 (1996).

242. WATERS, *supra* note 68, at 328.

243. Nancy Foner, *Then and Now or Then to Now: Immigration to New York in Contemporary and Historical Perspective*, 25 J. AM. ETHNIC. HIST. 33, 38–39 (2006). *See also*, FONER, *supra* note 88 and MILTON VICKERMAN, CROSSCURRENTS: WEST INDIAN IMMIGRANTS AND RACE (1999).

244. *See generally* DOUGLAS S. MASSEY, CAMILLE Z. CHARLES, GARVEY F. LUNDY & MARY J. FISCHER, THE SOURCE OF THE RIVER: THE SOCIAL ORIGINS OF FRESHMEN AT AMERICA'S SELECTIVE COLLEGES AND UNIVERSITIES 253 (2003). About 82 percent of black natives self-identified as "black, African American or Negro" compared to only 63 percent of first- and second-generation black immigrants. The immigrants were much more likely to use the "Other" category: 10 percent compared to 1.5 percent. A slightly larger percentage of immigrants identified themselves as mixed-race: 19 percent compared to 16 percent of native blacks.

245. This is in contrast to "[w]orking-class and poor families [from the West Indies who] live in neighborhoods and work in institutions in which their children come to see little difference between themselves and African-Americans." *Id.* at 330.

246. *Id.*

247. Waters, *supra* note 1.

248. Rong & Brown, *supra* note 203.

249. Rubén Rumbaut, *Children of Immigrants and Their Achievement: The Role of Family, Acculturation, Social Class, Gender, Ethnicity, and School Contexts*, 1, *available at* http://www.hks.harvard.edu/inequality/Seminar/Papers/Rumbaut2.pdf.

250. Sowell, *supra* note 42.

251. Rong & Brown, *supra* note 203.

252. Kalmijn, *supra* note 51, at 911, 928. His research also showed that Spanish-speaking and French speaking Caribbean immigrants fared worse than African Americans. However, second generation Spanish and French speaking Caribbean immigrants had caught up to African Americans. *Id.*

253. Sandy Baum & Stell M. Flores, *Higher Education and Children in Immigrant Families*, 21 THE FUTURE OF CHILDREN 171, 174 (2011).

254. *See* Rong & Brown, *supra* note 203, at 536, 548–51.

255. *See supra* note 6 and accompanying text.

256. *See* Milton Vickerman, *Jamaica in* THE NEW AMERICANS: A GUIDE TO IMMIGRATION SINCE 1965, 479 (Mary C. Waters & Reed Ueda eds., with Helen B. Marrow 2007).

257. Since this book is addressing the situation regarding the current group of blacks applying for admissions to selective higher education programs, the formulations of the definitions of Black Immigrants and Ascendant Blacks in this book are based upon that limitation. The definition of Ascendant Blacks includes third-generation descendants of foreign-born blacks. Whether the definition of Ascendant Blacks and Black Immigrants should be altered in the future to take account of succeeding generations is beyond the scope of the immediate issues this book addresses.

# Chapter Five

1. For a list of the over 500 institutions that accept the Common Application, see Common Application—Members, *available at* https://www.commonapp.org/Login#!PublicPages/AllMembers (last visited Mar. 30, 2014).

2. Common Application Fact Sheet *available at* https://www.commonapp.org/PDF/CommonApplicationFactSheet.pdf (last visited Mar. 30, 2014).

3. For a list of these institutions see the Universal College Application—College Membership, *available at* https://www.universalcollegeapp.com/member-colleges (last visited Mar. 30, 2014).

4. The Common Application: First Year Application Form for 2013–14.

5. *Id.*

6. Universal College Application form (2014), *available at* https://www.universalcollegeapp.com/documents/uca-first-year.pdf (last visited Mar. 30, 2014).

7. *Id.*

8. Department of Education, "Final Guidance, on Maintain, Collecting and Reporting Racial and Ethnic Data to the Department of Education," *Federal Register*, Vol.72, No. 202, at 59268, October 19, 2007. Henceforth, the "Final Guidance."

9. See *Gratz v. Bollinger*, 539 U.S. 244 (2003) (striking down a system that provided numerical points in the admissions process based on race and ethnicity because it failed to require admissions counselors to conduct the type of individualized consideration the Court's opinion in *Grutter* required when racial and ethnic classifications are used).

10. Final Guidance, *supra* note 8. *But see* C. Anthony Broh and Stephen D. Minicucci, Racial Identity and Government Classification: A Better Solution 4 (2008) (arguing that this assumption was not tested).

11. *Id* at 2.

12. *Id.* at 14.

13. According to the 2010 Census, for their racial category, 36.7 percent of those who indicated that they were Hispanic/Latino only checked Some Other Race and additional 53.0 percent selected only white. Karen Humes, Nicholas A. Jones, and Roberto Ramirez, *Overview of Race and Hispanic Origin: 2010*, 6 tbl 2 (2011). In contrast, 2.5 percent selected only the black racial box. *Id.* The 2.5 percent figure would be further reduced by those who have at least one foreign-born parent. Since over 37% of them were foreign-born in 2000, there will be a substantial reduction of the 2.5%. *See* Pew Research Center Publications, *U.S. Foreign Born Population: How Much Change from 2009 to 2010* (2012).

14. *Grutter v. Bollinger*, 539 U.S. 306, 334 (2003).

15. This was one of the points that Chief Justice Rehnquist stressed in his dissenting opinion in *Grutter*. *See id*, at 382–86 (Rehnquist, C.J., dissenting).

16. The mean SAT scores for blacks in 2013 were Critical Reading 431, Mathematics 429, and Writing 418; for Mexican Americans they were 449, 464, and 442, respectively; for Puerto Ricans they were 456, 453, and 445, respectively; for other Latinos they were 450, 462, and 443, respectively. *See* CollegeBoard, 2013 College-Bound Seniors: Total Group Profile Report 3 tbl.8 (2013).

17. Christine B. Hickman, *The Devil and the One Drop Rule: Racial Categories, African Americans, and the U.S. Census*, 95 MICH. L. REV. 1161, 1175 (1997).

18. I do not want to suggest that such a choice is ever freely made. For a black individual to pass as white—assuming their physical appearance would allow them to do so—still requires that they are willing to accept the huge costs in abandoning their former identity, the comfort of kin and familiar surroundings.

19. WALTER WHITE, A MAN CALLED WHITE 3 (1995). *See also* Paul Spickard, *The Power of Blackness: Mixed-Race Leaders and the Monoracial Ideal*, *in* RACIAL THINKING IN THE UNITED STATES 114–5 (Paul Spickard & G. Reginald Daniel eds. 2004).

20. The mean SAT scores for blacks in 2013 were Critical Reading 431, Mathematics 429, and Writing 418; for American Indians and Alaskan Natives they were 480, 486, and 461, respectively; for whites 527, 534, and 515, respectively; and for Asian Americans 521, 597, and 527, respectively. *See* CollegeBoard, *supra* note 17, at 3 tbl.8.

21. Of all multiracial combinations reported on the 2010 Census, the largest single group was black/white multiracials (20.4%), some other race/white (19.3%), white/Asian (18.0%); and white/American Indian and Alaskan Native (15.9%). Karen Humes, *supra* note 14, at 9 tbl 4.

# Bibliography

## Books

Anderson, M.J. & S.E. Feinberg, Who Counts: The Politics of Census-Taking (1999).

Apple, Michael W., Ideology and Curriculum (1979).

Aptheker, Herbert, American Negro Slave Revolts (1993).

Aptheker, Herbert, A Documentary History of the Negro People in the United States (1969).

Arsenault, Raymond, Freedom Riders: 1961 and the Struggle for Racial Justice (2006).

Arthur, J.A., Invisible Sojourners: African Immigrant Diaspora in the United States (2000).

Bachman, John, The Doctrine of the Unity of the Human Race Examined on the Principles of Science (1850).

Bachman, John, Selected Writings on Science, Race, and Religion (2011).

Banks, James A., Multiethnic Education: Theory and Practice (2d ed.) (1988).

Basler, Roy P., The Collected Works of Abraham Lincoln, Vol. VI (1953).

Bean, Frank D., et al., Undocumented Migration to the United States: IRCA and the Experience of the 1980s (1990).

Bell, Jeannine, Hate Thy Neighbor: Move-In Violence and the Persistence of Racial Segregation in American Housing (2013).

Bellah, Robert, et al., Habits of the Heart: Individualism and Commitment in American Life (1986).

Bennett, Jr., Lerone, Before the Mayflower: A History of Black America (1987).

Berlin, Ira, Many Thousands Gone: The First Two Centuries of Slavery in North America (1998).

Berlin, Ira, Slaves Without Masters: The Free Negro in the Antebellum South (1974).

Blackett, R.J.M., Building an Antislavery Wall: Black Americans in the Atlantic Abolitionist Movement 1830–1860 (1983).

Bowen, William & Derek Bok, The Shape of the River: Long-Term Consequences of Considering Race in College and University Admissions (1998).

Brameld, Educational Costs in Discrimination and National Welfare (1949).

Brown, Kevin, Race, Law & Education in the Post Desegregation Era: Four Perspectives on Desegregation and Resegregation (2005).

Bullock, Henry Allen, A History of Negro Education in the South: From 1619 to the Present (1967).

Bundles, A'Lelia, On Her Own Ground: The Life and Times of Madam C. J. Walker (2002).

Byrd, Charles Michael, The Bhagavad-Gita in Black and White: From Mulatto Pride to Krishna Consciousness (2007).

Calhoun, Arthur Wallace, A Social History of the American Family from Colonial Times to the Present (1945).

Carmines, Edward G., Issue Evolution: Race and the Transformation of American Politics (1990).

Carson, Clayborne, et al., Eyes on the Prize Civil Rights Reader (1997).

Cashin, Sheryll, Place, Not Race: A New View of Opportunity in America (2014).

Cashman, Sean Dennis, African-Americans and the Quest for Civil Rights (1991).

Chazan, Naomi, et al., Politics and Society in Contemporary Africa (1922).

CIVIL RIGHTS AND AFRICAN AMERICANS: A DOCUMENTARY HISTORY (Albert P. Blaustein & Robert L. Zangrando eds., 1968).

CLINTON, CATHERINE, HARRIET TUBMAN: THE ROAD TO FREEDOM (2004).

COTTROL, ROBERT J., THE LONG, LINGERING SHADOW: SLAVERY, RACE, AND LAW IN THE AMERICAN HEMISPHERE (2013).

CRONON, E. DAVID, & JOHN HOPE FRANKLIN, BLACK MOSES: THE STORY OF MARCUS GARVEY AND THE UNIVERSAL NEGRO IMPROVEMENT ASSOCIATION (1960).

CROSS, JR., WILLIAM, SHADES OF BLACK: DIVERSITY IN AFRICAN-AMERICAN IDENTITY (1990).

CRUSE, HAROLD, REBELLION OR REVOLUTION? (1968).

CUBBERLEY, ELLWOOD P., CHANGING CONCEPTIONS OF EDUCATION (1909).

DANIEL, G. REGINALD, MORE THAN BLACK?: MULTIRACIAL IDENTITY AND THE NEW RACIAL ORDER (2001).

DANIELS, ROGER & OTIS L. GRAHAM, DEBATING AMERICAN IMMIGRATION, 1882–PRESENT (2001).

DAVIS, DAVID BRION, THE PROBLEM OF SLAVERY IN THE AGE OF REVOLUTION 1770–1823 (1999).

DAVIS, F. JAMES, WHO IS BLACK: ONE NATION'S DEFINITION (1991).

DEGLER, CARL N., NEITHER BLACK NOR WHITE: SLAVERY AND RACE RELATIONS IN BRAZIL AND THE UNITED STATES (1971).

DE GOBINEAU, COUNT ARTHUR, THE MORAL AND INTELLECTUAL DIVERSITY OF RACES, WITH PARTICULAR REFERENCE TO THEIR RESPECTIVE INFLUENCE IN THE CIVIL AND POLITICAL HISTORY OF MANKIND (1856).

DELANEY, MARTIN, THE CONDITION, ELEVATION, EMIGRATION AND DESTINY OF THE COLORED PEOPLE OF THE UNITED STATES (1852).

DE TOCQUEVILLE, ALEXIS, DEMOCRACY IN AMERICA (1966).

DIXON, JR., THOMAS, THE LEOPARD'S SPOTS: A ROMANCE OF THE WHITE MAN'S BURDEN—1865–1900 (1902).

DORMAN, JAMES H. & ROBERT R. JONES, THE AFRO-AMERICAN EXPERIENCE: A CULTURAL HISTORY THROUGH EMANCIPATION (1974).

Drotning, Phillip T., Black Heroes In Our Nation's History: A Tribute To Those Who Helped Shape America (1969).

DuBois, W.E.B., Black Reconstruction in America 1860–1880 (1935).

Easton, Hosea, A Treatise on the Intellectual Character and Civil and Political Conditions of the Colored People of the United States and the Prejudice Exercised Toward Them (1837).

Edmonston, B. & C. Schultze, Modernizing the U.S. Census (1994).

Ernest, John, A Nation Within A Nation: Organizing African American Communities Before the Civil War (2011).

Fairclough, Adam, Better Day Coming: Blacks and Equality 1890 to 2000 (2001).

Feagin, Joe R., Racist America: Roots, Current Realities, and Future Reparations (2000).

Fernandez, Ronald, America Beyond Black and White: How Immigrants and Fusion are Helping us Overcome the Racial Divide (2008).

Ferrell, Claudine L., The Abolitionist Movement (2006).

Finkelman, Paul, The Law of Freedom and Bondage (1986).

Fischer, Roger A., The Segregation Struggle in Louisiana, 1862–77 (1974).

Fitzgerald, Michael W., The Union League Movement in the Deep South: Politics and Agricultural Change During Reconstruction (1989).

Foner, Eric, Reconstruction: America's Unfinished Revolution 1863–1877 (1988).

Foner, Nancy, In A New land: A Comparative View of Immigration (2005).

Foot, Paul, Immigration and Race in British Politics (1965).

Foy, Colm, Cape Verde: Politics, Economics, and Society (1988).

Frankel, Noralee, Break Those Chains at Last: African Americans 1860–1880 (1996).

Franklin, John Hope, & Alfred A. Moss, Jr., From Slavery to Freedom: A History of Negro Americans (6th ed. 1988).

Franklin, John Hope & Loren Schweninger, Runaway Slaves: Rebels on the Plantation (1999).

Frazier, E., The Negro in the United States (1949).

Freedman, John D'Emilio & Estelle B. Freedman, Intimate Matters: A History of Sexuality in America (1997).

Genovese, Eugene D., Roll, Jordan, Roll: The World the Slaves Made (1972).

Giddings, Paula J., Ida: A Sword Among Lions: Ida B. Wells and the Campaign Against Lynching (2008).

Glazer, Nathan & Patrick Moynihan, Beyond the Melting Pot: The Negroes, Puerto Ricans, Jews, Italians, and Irish in New York City (1963).

Goldenberg, David M., The Curse of Ham: Race and Slavery in Early Judaism, Christianity, and Islam (2003).

Gould, Benjamin Apthorp, Investigations in the Military and Anthropological Statistics of American Soldiers (1869).

Gould, Stephen Jay, The Mismeasure of Man (1982).

Grofman, Bernard, et al., Minority Representation and the Quest for Voting Equality (1992).

Gross, Ariela J., What Blood Won't Tell: A History of Race on Trial in America (2008).

Halberstam, David, The Children (1998).

Haller, Jr., John S., Outcasts From Evolution: Scientific Attitudes of Racial Inferiority, 1859–1900 (1971).

Halter, Marilyn, Between Race and Ethnicity: Cape Verdean American Immigrants, 1860–1965 (1993).

Hansen, Randall, Citizenship and Immigration in Post-War Britain (2000).

Harding, Vincent, There Is a River (1985).

Harlan, Louis R., Booker T. Washington: The Wizard of Tuskegee 1901–1915 (1983).

Harlow, V.T., A History of Barbados, 1625–1685 (1926).

HENING, WILLIAM WALLER, THE STATUTES AT LARGE; BEING A COLLECTION OF ALL THE LAWS OF VIRGINIA, FROM THE FIRST SESSION OF THE LEGISLATURE IN THE YEAR 1619, VOL. 3 (1823).

HENSTEIN, RICHARD & CHARLES MURRAY, THE BELL CURVE: INTELLIGENCE AND CLASS STRUCTURE IN AMERICAN LIFE (1994).

HERNANDEZ, TANYA KATERI, RACIAL SUBORDINATION IN LATIN AMERICA: THE ROLE OF THE STATE, CUSTOMARY LAW, AND THE NEW CIVIL RIGHTS RESPONSE (2013).

HIGHAM, JOHN, STRANGERS IN THE LAND: PATTERNS OF AMERICAN NATIVISM, 1860–1925 (2005).

HOERDER, DIRK, CULTURES IN CONTACT: WORLD MIGRATIONS IN THE SECOND MILLENNIUM (2002).

HOFFMAN, FREDERICK L., RACE TRAITS AND TENDENCIES OF THE AMERICAN NEGRO (1896).

HUNTINGTON, SAMUEL P., AMERICAN POLITICS: THE PROMISE OF DISHARMONY (1981).

HUTCHINSON, EDWARD P., LEGISLATIVE HISTORY OF AMERICAN IMMIGRATION POLICY, 1798–1965 (1981).

JAY, WILLIAM, THE LIFE OF JOHN JAY (1833).

JOHNSON, JAMES WELDON, BLACK MANHATTAN (1930).

KARENGA, MAULANA, INTRODUCTION TO BLACK STUDIES (2d ed. 1993).

KARST, KENNETH L., BELONGING TO AMERICA: EQUAL CITIZENSHIP AND THE CONSTITUTION (1989).

KELLEY, ROBIN D.G. & EARL LEWIS, TO MAKE OUR OWN WORLD ANEW (vol. 1, 2000).

KENNEDY, JOHN F., A NATION OF IMMIGRANTS (1964).

KENNEDY, RANDALL, FOR DISCRIMINATION: RACE, AFFIRMATIVE ACTION, AND THE LAW (2013).

KLUGER, RICHARD, SIMPLE JUSTICE: THE HISTORY OF *BROWN V. BOARD OF EDUCATION* AND BLACK AMERICA'S STRUGGLE FOR EQUALITY (1976).

KOGER, LARRY, BLACK SLAVEOWNERS: FREE BLACK SLAVE MASTERS IN SOUTH CAROLINA, 1790–1860 (1985).

Landers, Jane, Black Society in Spanish Florida (1999).

Landry, Bart, The New Black Middle Class (1987).

LeConte, Joseph, The Race Problem in the South (1892).

Lee, Jennifer & Frank D. Bean, The Diversity Paradox: Immigration and the Color Line in Twenty-First Century America (2010).

LeMay, Michael & Elliot Robert Barkan, U.S. Immigration and Naturalization Laws and Issues: A Documentary History (1999).

Levine, Michael L., African-Americans And Civil Rights: From 1619 To The Present (1996).

Lincoln, C. Eric, Race, Religion, and the Continuing American Dilemma (1999).

Litwack, Leon F., Been in the Storm So Long: The Aftermath of Slavery (1980).

Litwack, Leon, North of Slavery: The Negro in the Free States (1961).

Livingston, David, Adam's Ancestors: Race, Religion & the Politics of Human Origins (2008).

Loewen, James, Sundown Towns: A Hidden Dimension of American Racism (2005).

Lopez, Ian F. Haney, White by Law: The Legal Construction of Race (1996).

Marable, Manning, W.E.B. Du Bois: Black Radical Democrat (1986).

Margo, Robert A., Race and Schooling in the South 1880–1950: An Economic History (1990).

Marshall, Burke, Federalism and Civil Rights (1964).

Massey, Douglas S., et al., The Source of the River: The Social Origins of Freshman at America's Selective Colleges and Universities (2003).

McNealey, Earnestine Green, "The Pearls of Alpha Kappa Alpha: A History of America's First Black Sorority, Alpha Kappa Alpha Sorority, Incorporated" (2010).

McNeese, Tim, The Abolitionist Movement: Ending Slavery (2008).

McPherson, James M., Ordeal by Fire: The Civil War and Reconstruction (1982).

McPherson, James M., The Negro's Civil War: How American Blacks Felt & Acted During the War For the Union (1991).

McWhorter, John H., Losing the Race: Self-Sabotage in Black America (2000).

Mencke, John G., Mulattoes and Race Mixture: American Attitudes and Images, 1865–1918 (1979).

Moran, Rachel F., Interracial Intimacy: The Regulation of Race and Romance (2001).

Morgan, Edmund S., American Slavery, American Freedom: The Ordeal of Colonial Virginia (1975).

Morris, Richard B., The American Revolution Reconsidered (1967).

Moyo, Sam, Human Development Report Office, Socio-Economic Dominance of Ethnic and Racial Groups—The African Experience (2004).

Muhammed, Elijah, Message to the Black Man (1965).

Myrdal, G., An American Dilemma: The Negro Problem and Modern Democracy (1944).

Newby, Idus A., Jim Crow's Defense: Anti-Negro Thought in America, 1900–1930 (1965).

Nicholls, Michael L., Whispers of Rebellion: Narrating Gabriel's Conspiracy (2012).

Nieto, Sonia, Affirming Diversity: The Sociopolitical Context of Multicultural Education (1992).

Nobles, Melissa, Shades of Citizenship: Race and the Census in Modern Politics (2000).

Norrell, Robert J., The House I Live In: Race in the American Century (2005).

Nott, Josiah Clark, et al., Types of Mankind: Or, Ethnological Researches, Based Upon the Ancient Monuments, Paintings, Sculptures and Crania of Races, and Upon Their Natural, Geographical, Philological and Biblical History (1854).

Onwuachi-Willig, Angela, According to Our Hearts: Rhinelander v. Rhinelander and the Law of the Multiracial Family (2013).

Otto, David, Insiders' Guide to Shreveport (2010).

Pasco, Peggy, What Comes Naturally: Miscegenation Law and the Making of Race in America (2009).

Quarles, Benjamin, The Negro In The Making Of America (1969).

Rasmussen, Daniel, American Uprising: The Untold Story of America's Largest Slave Revolt (2011).

Ravitch, Diane, The Troubled Crusade: American Education 1945–1980 (1983).

Reid, Ira De Augustine, The Negro Immigrant: His Background, Characteristics and Social Adjustments, 1899–1937 (1970).

Reimers, David M., Other Immigrants: The Global Origins of the American People (2005).

Robertson, David M., The Buried Story of America's Largest Slave Rebellion and the Man Who Led It (2000).

Robinson, Cedric J., Forgeries of Memory and Meaning: Blacks and the Regimes of Race in American Theater and Film Before World War II (2007).

Robinson, Eugene, Disintegration: The Splintering of Black America (2010).

Rockquemore, Kerry Ann & David Brunsma, Beyond Black: Biracial Identity in America (2002).

Rodrigues, Junius P., The Louisiana Purchase: A Historical and Geographical Encyclopedia (2002).

Ross, Lawrence C., The Divine Nine: The History of African American Fraternities and Sororities (2001).

Sander, Richard & Stuart Taylor, Jr., Mismatch: How Affirmative Action Hurts Students It's Intended to Help, and Why Universities Won't Admit It (2012).

Schelsinger Jr., Arthur, The Disuniting of America: Reflections on a Multicultural Society (1991).

Schoulder, James, A Treatise on the Law of Domestic Relations: Embracing the Husband and Wife, Parent and Child, Guardian and Ward, Infancy, and Master and Servant (1870).

Schultz, Stanley K., The Culture Factory: Boston Public Schools, 1789–1860 (1973).

Schuman, Howard, Charlotte Steeh, Lawrence Bobo & Maria Krysan, Racial Attitudes in America: Trends and Interpretations (1997).

Segal, Ronald, The Black Diaspora: Five Centuries of the Black Experience Outside of Africa (1995).

Shaler, Nathaniel Southgate, The Neighbor: The Natural History of Human Contacts (1904).

Sickels, Robert, Race, Marriage and the Law (1972).

Smith, Adam, An Inquiry Into the Nature and Causes of the Wealth of Nations (1776).

Smith, Captain John, The Generall Historie of Virginia, New England, and the Summer Isles, Vol. 1 (1907).

Sollors, Werner, Interracialism: Black-White Intermarriage in American History, Literature, and Law (2000).

Spencer, Ian R. G., British Immigration Policy Since 1939: The Making of Multiracial Britain (1997).

Spencer, Jon Michael, The New Colored People: The Mixed-Race Movement in America (1997).

Spencer, Rainer, Reproducing Race: The Paradox of Generation Mix (2010).

Spencer, Rainer, Spurious Issues: Race and Multiracial Identity Politics in the United States 68 (1999).

Stampp, Kenneth M., The Peculiar Institution: Slavery In The Ante-Bellum South (1956).

Steel, David, No Entry: The Background and Implications of the Commonwealth Immigrants Act, 1968 (1969).

St. James, Warren D., NAACP: Triumphs of a Pressure Group 1909–1980 (1980).

Stonequist, E.V., The Marginal Man: A Study in Personality and Culture Conflict (1937).

Strege, John, Tiger: A Biography of Tiger Woods (1997).

Takaki, Ronald, From Different Shores: Perspectives on Race and Ethnicity in America (1994).

Taylor, Kimberly Hayes, Profiles: Black Abolitionists and Freedom Fighters (1996).

Thernstrom, Stephan, & Abigail Thernstrom, America in Black and White: One Nation, Indivisible (1997).

Tuck, Stephen, We Ain't What We Ought to Be: The Black Freedom Struggle From Emancipation to Obama (2010).

Tucker, William H., The Science and Politics of Racial Research (1994).

Tushnet, Mark, Making Civil Rights Law: Thurgood Marshall and the Supreme Court, 1936–1961 (1994).

Van Woodward, C., The Strange Career of Jim Crow (1974).

Vickerman, Milton, Crosscurrents: West Indian Immigrants and Race (1999).

Wachtel, Paul, Race in the Mind of America: Breaking the Vicious Circle Between Blacks and Whites (1999).

Wallenstein, Peter, Tell the Court I Love My Wife: Race, Marriage and Law—An American History (2002).

Wang Xi, The Trial of Democracy: Black Suffrage Northern Republicans, 1860–1910 (1997).

Waters, Mary C., Black Identities: West Indian Immigrant Dreams and American Realities (1999).

Watson, Elwood, There She is Miss America: The Politics of Sex, Beauty, and Race in America's Most Famous Pageant (2004).

Weiner, Michael, The Origins of the Korean Community in Japan 1910–1923 (1989).

Weiss, Nancy J., The National Urban League 1910–1940 (1974).

West, Cornel, Prophesy Deliverance! (1982).

White, Walter, A Man Called White (1995).

Williams, Kim M., Mark One or More: Civil Rights in Multiracial America (2006).

Williamson, Joel, New People: Miscegenation and Mulattoes in the United States 24 (1995).

Wilson, Ellen Gibson, The Loyal Blacks (1976).

Wood, Peter H., Black Majority: Negroes in Colonial South Carolina from 1670 Through the Stono Rebellion (1974).

Woodson, Carter G., The Education of the Negro Prior to 1861 (1919).

World Bank, World Development Report (1995).

X, Malcolm, The Autobiography of Malcolm X (1965).

Yanow, Dvora, Constructing "Race" and "Ethnicity" in America: Category-Making in Public Policy and Administration (2003).

Yeboah, Samuel, The Ideology of Racism: The Origin of Racism (1988).

Zinn, Howard, A People's History of the United States 1492 to Present (2003).

## Articles, Book Chapters, and Other Publications

*A Solid Percentage of Black Students at U.S. Colleges and Universities Are Foreign Born*, 54 J. Blacks Higher Educ. 22 (Jan. 2006).

Agency Information Collection Activities, *Notice of Submission for OMB Review; Final Comment Request to the Equal Employment Opportunity Commission*, 70 Fed. Reg. 71 (Nov. 28, 2005).

Ainsworth-Darnell, James W. & Douglas B. Downey, *Assessing the Oppositional Culture Explanation for Racial/Ethnic Differences in School Performance*, 63 Am. Sociological Rev. 536 (1998).

Aleinikoff, T. Alexander & Rubén G. Rumbaut, *Terms Of Belonging: Are Models Of Membership Self-Fulfilling Prophecies?*, 13 Geo. Immigr. L.J. 1 (1998).

Allen, Walter Recharde & Joseph O. Jewell, *A Backward Glance Forward: Past, Present and Future Perspectives on Historically Black Colleges and Universities*, 25 Rev. High. Educ. 241 (2002).

Alpert, Jonathon L., *The Origin of Slavery in the United States–The Maryland Precedent*, 14 Am. J. Legal Hist. 195 (1970).

Bair, Barbara, *Though Justice Sleeps: 1880–1900*, in To Make Our World Anew: A History of African Americans From 1880, Vol. II (2000).

Barnes, Mario L., Erwin Chemerinsky & Trina Jones, *Post-Race Equal Protection?*, 98 Geo. L.J. 967 (2010).

Baum, Sandy & Stell M. Flores, *Higher Education and Children in Immigrant Families*, 21 The Future of Children 171 (2011).

Baxter, Jedediah H., *Statistics, Medical and Anthropological, of the Provost-Marshal-General's Bureau: Derived From Records of the Examination for Military Service in the Armies of the United States During the Late War of the Rebellion of Over a Million Recruits, Drafted Men, Substitutes, and Enrolled Men* (Washington: Government Printing Office, 1875).

Baynes, Leonard M., *Who Is Black Enough for You: The Story of One Black Man and His Family's Pursuit of the American Dream*, 11 Geo. Immigr. L.J. 97 (1996).

Bell-Fialkoff, Andrew, *A Brief History of Ethnic Cleansing*, 72 Foreign Affairs 110 (1993).

Bennett, Pamela R. & Amy Lutz, *How African American Is the Net Black Advantage? Differences in College Attendance Among Immigrant Blacks, Native Blacks, and Whites*, 80 Sociology of Educ. 70 (2009).

Black, Charles L., *The Lawfulness of the Segregation Decisions*, 69 Yale L.J. 421 (1960).

Blaustein, Albert P. & Robert L. Zangrando, *An Act for Regulation Negro, Indian, and Mulatto Slaves Within This Province of New Jersey, Laws of New Jersey, C. ix, 1704*, reprinted in Civil Rights and African Americans (1991).

Bobo, Lawrence, Camille L. Zubrinsky, James H. Johnson, Jr., & Melvin L. Oliver, *Public Opinion Before and After the Spring of Discontent*, in The Los Angeles Riots: Lessons for the Urban Future (Mark Baldassare ed., 1995).

Bodenhorn, Howard, *The Mulatto Advantage: The Biological Consequences of Complexion in Rural Antebellum Virginia*, 21 J. Interdiscipl. Hist. 33 (2002).

Boswell, Richard A., *Racism and U.S. Immigration Law: Prospects for Reform after "9/11,"* 7 J. Gender Race & Just. 315 (2003).

Broh, C. Anthony and Stephen D. Minicucci, *Racial Identity and Government Classification: A Better Solution* (2008).

Brown, Kevin, *Change in Racial and Ethnic Classifications is Here: Proposal to Address Race and Ethnic Ancestry of Blacks for Affirmative Action Admissions Purposes*, 31 HAMLINE J. PUB. L. & POL'Y 143 (2009).

Brown, Kevin, *Now is the Appropriate Time for Selective Higher Education Programs to Collect Racial and Ethnic Data on its Black Applicants and Students*, 33 T. Marshall L. Rev. 287 (2009).

Brown, Kevin *Should Black Immigrants Be Favored Over Black Hispanics and Black Multiracials in the Admissions Processes of Selective Higher Education Programs?*, 54 How. L.J. 255 (2011).

Brown, Kevin & Jeannie Bell, *Demise of the Talented Tenth: Affirmative Action and the Increasing Underrepresentation of Ascendant Blacks at Selective Higher Educational Institutions*, 69 OHIO ST. L.J. 1227 (2008).

Brown, Kevin & Tom I. Romero, II, *The Social Reconstruction of Race & Ethnicity of the Nation's Law Students: A Request to the ABA, AALS and LSAC For Changes in New Reporting Requirement*, 2011 MICH. ST. L. REV. 1133 (2011).

Brown, Kevin & Vinay Sitipati, *Lessons Learned From Comparing The Application Of Constitutional Law And Federal Anti-Discrimination Law to African-Americans In The U.S. And Dalits In India In The Context Of Higher Education*, 24 HARV. BLACKLETTER L.J. 3 (2008).

Brunsma, David L. & Kerry Ann Rockquemore, *What Does "Black" Mean? Exploring the Epistemological Stranglehold of Racial Categorization*, 28 CRITICAL SOC. 101 (2002).

Bryce-Laporte, Roy Simon, *Black Immigrants: The Experience of Invisibility and Inequality*, 3 J. OF BLACK STUD. 29 (1972).

Bureau of the Census, U.S. Department of Commerce, 2000 PHC-T-8, *Race and Hispanic or Latino Origin by Age and Sex for the United States: 2000, Table 3. Black or African American Population, by Age and Sex for the United States: 2000.*

Bureau of the Census, U.S. Department of Commerce, *Historical Statistics of the United States: Colonial Times to 1970*, Part 1, Series A-195-209 (1975).

Bureau of the Census, U.S. Dep't of Commerce, Ser. P-23, No. 80, *The Social and Economic Status of the Black Population in the United States: An Historical View, 1790–1978* (1979).

Calhoun, Speech in the U. S. Senate, 1837, *in* Paul Finkleman, Defending Slavery: Proslavery Thought in the Old South: A Brief History with Documents (2003).

Campbell, Mary E., *Multiracial Groups and Educational Inequality: A Rainbow or a Divide?*, 56 Soc. Probl. 425 (2009).

Capps, Randy, Kristen McCabe, and Michael Fix, *Diverse Streams: Black African Migration to the United States* 3 tbl. 1 (2012), published by the Migration Policy Institute.

Carter, Robert L., *The Effects of Segregation and the Consequence of Desegregation: A Social Science* Statement, 37 Minn. L. Rev. 427 (1953).

Chapa, Jorge, *Hispanic/Latino Ethnicity and Identifiers*, Encyclopedia of the U.S. Census (Congressional Quarterly Press: Washington, DC, 2000).

Charmaraman, Linda & Jennifer M. Grossman, *Importance of Race and Ethnicity: An Exploration of Asian, Black, Latino and Multiracial Adolescent Identity*, 16 Cult. Divers. Ethn. Min. 144 (2010).

Chein, Isidor, *What Are the Psychological Effects of Segregation Under Conditions of Equal Facilities?*, 3 Int'l J. Opinion and Attitude Res. (1949).

Cheng. L., & P. Q. Yang, *Global Interaction, Global Inequality, and Migration of the Highly Trained to the United States,* 32 Int. Migr. Rev. 626 (1998).

Cheng, Simon & Seena Mostafavipour, *The Differences and Similarities between Biracial and Monoracial Couples: A Sociodemographic Sketch Based on the Census* 2000 (Jan. 2005).

Chenoweth, Karin, *African American College Presidents in Decline*, Diverse Issues in Higher Education (July 13, 2007).

Chimezie, Amuzie, *Black Bi-Culturality*, 9 W. J. Black Stud. 224 (1985).

Cho, Sumi, *Post Racialism*, 94 Iowa L. Rev. 1589 (2009).

Clark, K.B., *Effect of Prejudice and Discrimination on Personality Development* (Mid century White House Conference on Children and Youth, 1950).

College Board, *2000 College-Bound Seniors: Total Group Profile Report* (2000).

College Board, *2010 College-Bound Seniors: Total Group Profile Report* (2010).

College Board, *2013 College-Bound Seniors: Total Group Profile Report* (2013).

Committee on National Statistics, *National Research Council, Spotlight on Heterogeneity: The Federal Standards for Racial and Ethnic Classification* (1996).

Cook, Anthony E., *Beyond Critical Legal Studies: The Reconstructive Theology of Dr. Martin Luther King, Jr.*, 103 Harv. L. Rev. 985 (1990).

Dalessando, Susan P. et al., *LSAT Performance with Regional, Gender, and Racial/Ethnic Breakdowns: 2003–2004 Through 2009–2010 Testing Years* (2010).

Daniel, G. Reginald, *Black No More or More Than Black?: Multiracial Identity Politics and the Multiracial Movement, in* Racial Thinking in the United States (Paul Spickard & G. Reginald Daniel eds., 2004).

Davis, Angela J., *Prosecution and Race: The Power and Privilege of Discretion*, 67 Fordham L. Rev. 13 (1998).

Davis, Thomas M., *The Traditions of Puritan Typology, in* Typology and Early American Literature (Sacvan Bercovitch ed., 1972).

Davis, Timothy, *Racism in Athletics: Subtle Yet Persistent*, 21 U. Ark. L. Rev. 881 (1999).

Del Pinal, Jorge, Elizabeth Martin, Claudette Bennett & Art Cresce, *Overview of Results of New Race and Hispanic Origin Questions in Census 2000* (2007).

Delany, Martin R., *The Condition, Elevation, Emigration, and Destiny of the Colored People of the United States, in* Classical Black Nationalism: From the American Revolution to Marcus Garvey (Wilson Jeremiah Moses ed., 1996).

Delgado, Richard, *Words that Wound: A Tort Action for Racial Insults, Epithets and Name-Calling*, 17 Harv. C.R.-C.L. L. Rev. 133 (1982).

DeNavas-Walt, Carmen, Bernadette D. Proctor and Jessica C. Smith, *Income, Poverty, and Health Insurance Coverage in the United States: 2012 Current Population Reports* (Sept. 2013).

Denmark, Florence L., Khaya N. Eisenberg, Erica I. Heitner & Nicola A. Holder, *Immigration to the United States: The Dream and the Reality in* Migration: Immigration and Emigration in International Perspective (Leonore Loeb Adler & Uwe P. Gielen eds., 2003).

Department of Education, *"Final Guidance, on Maintaining, Collecting and Reporting Racial and Ethnic Data to the Department of Education," Federal Register*, Vol.72, No. 202, October 19, 2007.

Deutscher, Max & Isidor Chein, *The Psychological Effects of Enforced Segregation: A Survey of Social Science Opinion*, 26 J. Psychol. 259 (1948).

Directive No. 15 Race and Ethnic Standards for Federal Statistics and Administrative Reporting (as adopted on May 12, 1977).

DuBois, W.E.B., *Three Centuries of Discrimination*, THE CRISIS 54 (December 1947).

Dunbar, Paul Lawrence, *Hidden in Plain Sight: African American Secret Societies and Black Freemasonry*, 16 J. AFR. AM. STUD. 622 (2011).

Duncan, Jr., John C., *Two "Wrongs" Do/Can Make A Right: Remembering Mathematics, Physics, & Various Legal Analogies (Two Negatives Make A Positive; Are Remedies Wrong?) The Law Has Made Him Equal, But Man Has Not*, 43 BRANDEIS L.J. 511 (2005).

*The Effect of Higher Education on Interracial Marriage*, 16 J. BLACKS HIGHER EDUC. 55 (1997).

Eltis, David, *The U.S. Transatlantic Slave Trade, 1644–1867: An Assessment*, 54 CIVIL WAR HISTORY 347 (2008).

Executive Office of the President, Office of Management and Budget, *Tabulation Working Group of the Interagency Committee for the Review of Standards of Data on Race and Ethnicity*, "Provisional Guidance on the Implementation of the 1997 Standards for Federal Data on Race and Ethnicity." FEDERAL REGISTER, December 15, 2000.

Farley, Reynolds, *Identifying with Multiple Races: A Social Movement that Succeeded But Failed?*, in THE CHANGING TERRAIN OF RACE AND ETHNICITY (Maria Krysan & Amanda E. Lewis, ed., 2004).

Farrell, Jr., Walter C. & James H. Johnson, Jr., *Minority Political Participation in the New Millennium: The Demographics and the Voting Rights Act*, 79 N.C. L. REV. 1215 (2001).

Fears, Daryl, *In Diversity Push, Top Universities Enrolling More Black Immigrants*, THE WASHINGTON POST, Mar, 6, 2007.

Flagg, Barbara, *Was Blind, But Now I See: White Race Consciousness and the Requirement of Discriminatory Intent*, 91 MICH. L. REV. 953 (1993).

Foner, Nancy, *Then and Now or Then to Now: Immigration to New York in Contemporary and Historical Perspective*, 25 J. AM. ETHNIC. HIST. 33 (2006).

Force, Pierre, *The House on Bayou Road: Atlantic Creole Networks in the Eighteenth and Nineteenth Centuries*, 100 J. AM. HIST. 9 (2012).

*France's Crisis of National Identity*, THE INDEPENDENT (Nov. 25, 2009).

Fryer Jr., Ronald G., and Steven D. Fevitt, *Understanding the Black-White Test Score Gap in the First Two Years of School*, 86 REV. ECON. AND STATS. 447 (2004).

Fuentes-Rohwer, Luis, *Merit and Race*, NEW YORK TIMES OPINION PAGES, (Nov. 29, 2010).

Gay, Geneva, *Achieving Educational Equality Through Curriculum Desegregation*, 72 PHI DELTA KAPPAN 56 (1990).

Gellhorn, Ernest, *The Law Schools & the Negro*, 1968 DUKE L.J. 1069 (1968).

Genovese, Eugene D., *Blacks in the United States—From Slavery to the Present Crisis*, NEW REV. 3 (1977).

Gibson, Campbell, & Kay Jung, *Historical Census Statistics On Population Totals By Race, 1790 to 1990, and By Hispanic Origin, 1970 to 1990, For Large Cities And Other Urban Places In The United States* (2005).

Gibson, Campbell J. & Kay Jung, *Historical Census Statistics on the Foreign-Born Population of the United States: 1850–2000*, U.S. CENSUS BUREAU, WORKING PAPER SERIES NO. 81 (2006).

Gibson, Campbell J. & Emily Lennon, *Race and Hispanic Origin of the Population by Nativity: 1850 to 1990*, U.S. CENSUS BUREAU (Mar. 9, 1999).

Gilanshah, Bijan, *Multiracial Minorities: Erasing the Color Line*, 12 LAW & INEQ. 183 (1993).

Gillem, Angela R., Laura Renee Cohn, and Cambria Throne, *Black Identity in Biracial Black/White People: A Comparison of Jacqueline Who Refuses to Be Exclusively Black and Adolphus Who Wishes He Were*, 7 CULT. DIVERS. ETHN. MIN. 182 (2001).

Gladwell, Malcolm, *Black Like Them*, THE NEW YORKER, Apr. 29, 1996.

Golub, Mark, *Plessy as 'Passing': Judicial Responses to Ambiguously Raced Bodies in* Plessy v. Ferguson, 39 LAW & SOC'Y REV. 568 (2005).

Gordon, April, *The New Diaspora—African Immigration to the United States*, 15 J. THIRD WORLD STUD. 79 (1998).

Gordon, Craig, *Analysis: How Obama Won It*, NEWSDAY, Nov. 5, 2008.

Gordon, Lewis, *Thinking through Identities: Black Peoples, Race Labels, and Ethnic Consciousness, in* THE OTHER AFRICAN AMERICANS: CONTEMPORARY

African and Caribbean Immigrants in the United States (Yoku Shaw-Taylor & Steven A. Tuch eds., 2007).

Gotanda, Neil, *A Critique of "Our Constitution is Color-Blind,"* 44 Stan. L. Rev. 1 (1991).

Gould, Virginia M., *The Free Creoles of Color of the Antebellum Gulf Ports of Mobile and Pensacola: A Struggle for the Middle Ground*, in Creoles of Color in the Gulf South (James H. Dormon ed., 1996).

Greenberg, Jack, *Report On Roma Education Today: From Slavery To Segregation And Beyond*, 110 Colum. L. Rev. 919 (2010).

Greenberg, Kenneth S., *Introduction* to Nat Turner: A Slave Rebellion in History and Memory (Kenneth S. Greenberg ed., 2003).

Grieco, Elizabeth M., U.S. Census Bureau, *Race and Hispanic Origin of the Foreign-Born Population in the United States: 2007 American Community Survey Report*, 7 U.S. Census Bureau (Jan. 2010).

Grieco, Elizabeth M., Yesenia D. Acosta, G. Patricia De La Cruz, Christine Gambino, Thomas Gryn, Luke J. Larsen, Edward N. Trevelyan & Nathan P. Walter, *The Foreign Born Population in the United States: 2010 American Community Survey Report 2* (March 2012).

Gutiérrez, Ramón A., *Changing Ethnic and Class Boundaries in America's Hispanic Past*, in Social and Gender Boundaries in the United States (Sucheng Chan ed., 1989).

Guzmán, Betsy, U.S. Census Bureau, *The Hispanic Population, Census 2000 Brief* (2001).

Hall, Christine C. Ijima, *Please Choose One: Ethnic Identity Choices for Biracial Individuals*, in Racially Mixed People in America (Maria P. P. Root ed., 1992).

Hanger, Kimberly S., *Origins of New Orleans Free Creoles of Color*, in Creoles of Color in the Gulf South 4 (James H. Dormon ed., 1996).

Harris, David R. & Jeremiah Joseph Sim, *Who is Multiracial? Assessing the Complexity of Lived Race*, 67 Am. Sociol. Rev. 614 (2002).

Helton, Arthur, *The Kindness of Strangers*, 39 Africa Report 33 (March/April, 1994).

Hening, William W., The Statutes at Large: Being a Collection of All the Laws of Virginia, from the First Session of the Legislature in the Year 1619 (Act of 1680, ch. 10).

Herman, Melissa, *Forced to Choose: Some Determinants of Racial Identification in Multi-Racial Adolescents*, 75 Child Dev. 730 (2004).

Hernandez, Donald J., *Changing Demography and Circumstances for Young Black Children in African and Caribbean Immigrant Families* (2012).

Hernandez, Tanya Kateri, *Multiracial Discourse: Racial Classifications in an Era of Color-Blind Jurisprudence*, 57 MD. L. REV. 97 (1998).

Hickman, Christine, *The Devil and the One Drop Rule: Racial Categories, African Americans and the U.S. Census*, 95 MICH L. REV. 1162 (1996–7).

Higginbothan, Jr., A. Leon & Barbara Kopytoff, *Racial Purity and Interracial Sex in the Law of Colonial and Antebellum Virginia*, 77 GEO. L.J. 1967 (1989).

Hing, Bill Ong, *Immigration Policies: Messages of Exclusion to African Americans*, 37 HOW. L.J. 237 (1994).

Hitlin, Steven, J. Scott Brown, and Glen H. Elder, Jr., *Racial Self-Categorization in Adolescence: Multiracial Development and Social Pathways*, 77 CHILD DEV. 1298 (2006).

Hochschild, Jennifer & Traci Burch, Contingent Public Policies and Racial Hierarchy: Lessons from Immigration and Census Policies, *in* POLITICAL CONTINGENCY: STUDYING THE UNEXPECTED, THE ACCIDENTAL, AND THE UNFORESEEN (Ian Shapiro & Sonu Bedi eds., 2007).

Holloway, Joseph E., *The Origins of African-American Culture*, *in* AFRICANISM IN AMERICAN CULTURE (1991).

Hovenkamp, Herbert, *Social Science and Segregation Before* Brown, 34 Duke L.J. 624, (1985).

Humes, Karen, Nicholas A. Jones, & Roberto Ramirez, *Overview of Race and Hispanic Origin: 2010* (2011).

Hunt, Sanford B., *The Negro as a Soldier*, 7 ANTHROPOL. REV. 49 (January 1869).

Immigration and Nationality Act, H.R. 2580, 89th Cong. (1965).

Immigration Reform and Control Act [IRCA], Pub. L. No. 99-603, 100 Stat. 3359 (1986) (codified in scattered sections of 8 U.S.C.).

Immigration Act of 1990, Pub. L. No. 101-649, §131, 104 Stat. 4978 (1990); Immigration and Nationality Act (INA) §§ 201(a)(3), 201(e), 203(c), 8 U.S.C. §§ 1151(a)(3), 1151(e), 1153(c) (2000).

Inniss, Lolita K. Buckner, *Tricky Magic: Blacks as Immigrants and the Paradox of Foreignness*, 40 DePaul L. Rev. 85 (1999).

Jackson, Jennifer V. & Mary E. Cothran, *Black versus Black: The Relationships among African, African American, and African Caribbean Persons*, 33 J. of Black Stud. 576 (2003).

Johnson, Kevin R., *Race, the Immigration Laws, and Domestic Race Relations: A "Magic Mirror" into the Heart of Darkness*, 73 Ind. L.J. 1111 (1998).

Johnson, Lyndon B., *To Fulfill These Rights*, Commencement Address at Howard University (June 4, 1965).

Jones, D. Marvin, *Darkness Made Visible: Law, Metaphor, and the Racial Self*, 82 Geo. L. J. 437 (1993).

Jordan, Winthrop D., *American Chiaroscuro: The Status and Definition of Mulattoes in the British Colonies*, 19 William Mary Quart. 184 (1962).

Judis, John B., *It's A Wrap: The 2008 Campaign*, L. A. Times, Nov. 9, 2008.

Kairys, David, *Unconscious Racism*, 83 Temp. L. Rev. 857 (2011).

Kalmijn, Matthijs, *The Socioeconomic Assimilation of Caribbean American Blacks*, 74 Soc. Forces 911 (1996).

Kao, Grace & Marta Tienda, *Optimism and Achievement: The Educational Performance of Immigrant Youth*, 76 Soc. Sci. Quart. 1 (1995).

Kapur, Devesh & John McHale, *Globalization at Work: Migration's New Payoff*, 139 Foreign Pol'y 48 (2003).

Kasnitz, Phillip, *The Minority Within: The New Black Immigrant*, 10 New York Affairs 46 (1987).

Kennedy, Randall, *Martin Luther King's Constitution: A Legal History of the Montgomery Bus Boycott*, 98 Yale L.J. 999 (1989).

Kennedy, Randall, *McCleskey v. Kemp: Race, Capital Punishment, and the Supreme Court*, 101 Harv. L. Rev. 1388 (1988).

Kent, Mary Mederios, *Immigration and America's Black Population*, 62 Population Bull. 5 Box 1 (December 2007).

King, Sabrina Hope, *The Limited Presence of African-American Teachers*, 63 Rev. Educ. Res. 115 (1993).

Klarman, Michael J., *Rethinking the Civil Rights and Civil Liberties Revolutions*, 82 Va. L. Rev. 1 (1996).

Krieger, Nancy, *Shades of Difference: Theoretical Underpinnings of the Medical Controversy on Black/White Differences in the United States, 1830–1870* 17 Int. J. Health Serv. 259 (1987).

Kroll, Luisa and Dolan, Kerry A., *The Forbes 400: The Richest People in America, in* Forbes (Sept. 16, 2013).

Kujovich, Gil, *Equal Opportunity in Higher Education and the Black Public College: The Era of Separate But Equal*, 72 Minn. L. Rev. 29 (1987).

Kusow, Abdi, *Africa: East, in* The New Americans: A Guide to Immigration Since 1965 (Mary C. Waters & Reed Ueda with Helen B. Marrow eds., 2007).

Lawrence III, Charles, *The Id, the Ego, and Equal Protection: Reckoning with Unconscious Racism*, 39 Stan. L. Rev. 317 (1987).

LeConte, Joseph, "The Genesis of Sex," in *Popular Science Monthly* 16 (December 1879): 167; "The Effect of Mixture of Races on Human Progress," in *Berkeley Quarterly* 1 (April 1880): 89.

Lee, Sharon M., & Barry Edmonston, *New Marriages, New Families: U.S. Racial and Hispanic Intermarriage*, Population Bull., June 2005.

Leonard, Walter J., *The Development of the Black Bar*, 407 Annals of the Am. Aca. of Pol. and Soc. Sc., 140 (1973).

Leong, Nancy, *Multiracial Identity and Affirmative Action*, 12 Asian Pac. Am. L. J. 1 (2007).

Letter sent by the Consortium on Financing Higher Education written by Anthony Broh, Director of Research Policy, to Patrick J. Sherrill, U.S. Department of Education, dated September 22, 2006.

Lewis, Hope, *Lionheart Gals Facing the Dragon: The Human Rights of Inter/National Black Women in the United States*, 76 Or. L. Rev. 567 (1997).

Lockett, James D., *Abraham Lincoln and Colonization: An Episode that Ends in Tragedy at L'Ile a Vache, Haiti, 1863–4*, 21 J. Black Stud. 428 (1991).

Lou, Evelina, Richard N. Lalonde & Carlos Wilson, *Examining a Multidimensional Framework of Identity Across Different Biracial Groups*, 2 ASIAN AM. J. PSYCH. 79 (2011).

Lunn, Kenneth, *The British State and Immigration, 1945–51: New Light on the Empire Windrush*, in THE POLITICS OF MARGINALITY: RACE, THE RADICAL RIGHT, AND MINORITIES IN TWENTIETH CENTURY BRITAIN (Tony Kushner & Kenneth Lunn eds., 1990).

Marshall, Dawn, *Toward an Understanding of Caribbean Migration*, in U.S. IMMIGRATION AND REFUGEE POLICY: GLOBAL AND DOMESTIC ISSUES (Mary M. Kritz ed., 1983).

Massey, Douglas S., et al., *Black Immigrants and Black Natives Attending Selective Colleges and Universities in the United States*, 113 AM. J. EDUC. 243 (2006).

Massey, G. Estelle, *The National Association of Colored Graduate Nurses*, 33 Am. J. of Nurs., 534 (1933).

Matsuda, Mari, *Looking to the Bottom: Critical Legal Studies and Reparations*, 22 HARV. C.R.-C.L. L. REV. 323 (1987).

McKernan, Signe-Mary, Caroline Ratcliffe, Eugene Steuerle, and Sisi Zhang, *Less than Equal, Racial Disparities in Wealth Accumulation*, Urban Institute (2013).

McKinnon, Jesse D., & Claudette E. Bennett, *We the People: Blacks in the United States*, U.S. CENSUS BUREAU (2005).

Mezey, Naomi, *Erasure and Recognition: The Census, Race and the National Imagination*, 97 NW. U. L. REV. 1701 (2003).

Mills, Gary B., *Miscegenation and the Free Negro in Antebellum 'Anglo' Alabama: A Reexamination of Southern Race Relations*, 68 J. AM. HIST. 26 (JUNE 1981).

Moore, Kenya, *Crystle Stewart Crowned Miss USA*, THE DAILY VOICE: BLACK AMERICA'S DAILY NEWS SOURCE, April 12, 2008.

Morgan, Philip D., *British Encounters with Africans and African-Americans, circa 1600–1780*, in STRANGERS WITHIN THE REALM: CULTURAL MARGINS OF THE FIRST BRITISH EMPIRE 172 (Bernard Bailyn & Philip D. Morgan, eds., 1991).

Moses, Wilson Jeremiah, *Introduction* to CLASSICAL BLACK NATIONALISM: FROM THE AMERICAN REVOLUTION TO MARCUS GARVEY (Wilson Jeremiah Moses ed., 1996).

National Center for Education, *Historically Black Colleges and Universities, 1976 to 2001* (2004).

Nelson, Camille A., *Carriers of Globalization: Loss of Home and Self Within the African Diaspora*, 55 FLA. L. REV. 539 (2003).

Newman, Richard, *Good Communications Corrects Bad Manners: The Banneker-Jefferson Dialogue and the Project of White Uplift*, in CONTESTING SLAVERY: THE POLITICS OF BONDAGE AND FREEDOM IN THE NEW AMERICAN NATION (John Craig Hammond and Matthew Mason eds., 2011).

Newton, Andowah A., *Injecting Diversity Into U.S. Immigration Policy: The Diversity Visa Program and the Missing Discourse on its Impact on African Immigration to the United States*, 38 CORNELL INT'L L.J. 1049 (2005).

Noah, Barbara A., *A Prescription for Racial Equality in Medicine*, 40 CONN. L. REV. 675 (2008).

Nolan, Lawrence C., *The Meaning of* Loving: *Marriage, Due Process and Equal Protection (1967–1990) as Equality and Marriage, From* Loving *to* Zablocki, 41 How. L.J. 247 (1998).

Nott, Josiah Clark, *The Mulatto: A Hybrid: Probable Extermination of the Two Races If the Whites and Blacks are Allowed to Intermarry*, 29 BOSTON MED. SURG. J. 29 (1843).

Office for Civil Rights, U.S. Dep't of Educ., *Race-Neutral Alternatives in Postsecondary Education: Innovative Approaches to Diversity*, Feb. 2004.

Office of Management and Budget, *Revisions to the Standards for the Classification of Federal Data on Race and Ethnicity, Federal Register* Notice, October 30, 1997.

Ogbu, John U., *Immigrant and Involuntary Minorities in Comparative Perspectives*, in MINORITY STATUS AND SCHOOLING: A COMPARATIVE STUDY OF IMMIGRANT AND INVOLUNTARY MINORITIES 37 (Margaret A. Gibson & John U. Ogbu eds., 1991).

Ogbu, John & H. D. Simmons, *Voluntary and Involuntary Minorities: A Cultural-Ecological Theory of School Performance with Some Implication for Education*, 29 ANTHROPOLOGY & EDUC. Q. 155 (1998).

Onwuachi-Willig, Angela, *The Admission of Legacy Blacks*, 60 VAND. L. REV. 1141 (2007).

Page, Clarence, *Black Immigrants Collect Most Degrees But Affirmative Action is Losing Direction*, CHICAGO TRIBUNE, Mar. 18, 2007, §2.

Palmer, Colin, *The African Diaspora*, 30 BLACK SCHOLAR 56 (2000).

Panter, A.T., et al., *It Matters How and When You Ask: Self-Reported Race/ Ethnicity of Incoming Law Students*, 15 CULT. DIV. & ETHNIC MIN. PSYCH. 51 (2009).

Park, Robert, *Human Migration and the Marginal Man*, 33 AM. J. SOCIOL. 881 (1928).

Park, Robert, *Mentality of Racial Hybrids*, 36 AM. J. SOCIOL. 534 (1931).

Parks, Gregory S., & Jeffrey J. Rachlinski, *Implicit Bias, Election '08, and the Myth of a Post-Racial America*, 37 FLA. ST. U. L. REV. 659 (2010).

Passel, Jeffrey S., et al., Pew Research Center, *Marrying Out: One-in-Seven New U.S. Marriages is Interracial or Interethnic* 11–12 (2010).

Passel, Jeffrey S., *Demography of Immigrant Youth: Past, Present and Future*, in THE FUTURE OF CHILDREN 19, 30 (2011).

PEW RESEARCH CENTER PUBLICATIONS, *Almost All Millennials Accept Interracial Dating and Marriage* (2010).

PEW RESEARCH CENTER PUBLICATIONS, *U.S. Foreign Born Population: How Much Change from 2009 to 2010* (2012).

President, Executive Order, *"To Facilitate Coordination of Federal Education Programs, Executive Order 11185,"* CODE OF FEDERAL REGISTER, TITLE 3: THE PRESIDENT, 1964 AND 1965 COMPLIATION (1967).

Proposed Guidance on Maintaining, Collecting and Reporting Data on Race and Ethnicity to the U.S. Department of Education, 71 Fed. Reg. at 44866 (Aug. 7, 2006).

Pybus, Cassandra, *Jefferson's Faulty Math: The Question of Slave Defections in the American Revolution*, 62 WM. & MARY QUART. 243 (2005).

Rankin, David C., *The Impact of the Civil War on the Free Colored Community of New Orleans*, 11 PERSPECT. AM. HIST. 381 (1977–78).

Raymond, Daniel, *Race, Slavery, and Fertility*, reprinted in RACIAL THOUGHT IN AMERICA: FROM THE PURITANS TO ABRAHAM LINCOLN (Louis Ruchames ed., 1969).

*Recovery from War's Trauma*, 34 AFRICA NEWS 6 (July 15, 1991).

Riordan, Patrick, *Finding Freedom in Florida: Native Peoples, African Americans, and Colonists, 1670–1816*, 75 THE FLORIDA HIST. QUART. 24 (1996).

Roach, Ronald, *Drawing Upon the Diaspora*, DIVERSE ISSUES IN HIGHER EDUCATION (Aug. 25, 2005).

Robbin, Alice, *Classifying Racial and Ethnic Group Data in the United States: The Politics of Negotiation and Accommodation*, 27 J. GOV. INFORM. 129 (2000).

Robbin, Alice, *The Politics Of Representation In The US National Statistical System: Origins Of Minority Population Interest Group Participation*, 27 J. GOV. INFORM. 431 (2000).

Roberts, Sam, *Black Women See Fewer Black Men at the Altar*, N.Y. TIMES, June 4, 2010, at A12.

Rockquemore, Kerry Anne & David Brunsma, *Socially Embedded Identities: Theories, Typologies, and Processes of Racial Identity Formation Among Black/White Biracials*, 43 SOCIOL. QUART. 335 (2002).

Rong, Xue Lan & Frank Brown, *The Effects of Immigrant Generation and Ethnicity on Educational Attainment Among Young African and Caribbean Blacks in the United States*, 71 HARV. EDUC. REV. 536 (2001).

Root, Maria, *The Color of Love*, AM. PROSPECT, Apr. 8, 2002.

Root, Maria P. P., *Within, Between, and Beyond Race*, in RACIALLY MIXED PEOPLE IN AMERICA (Maria P. P. Root ed., 1991).

Roth, Wendy D., *The End of the One-Drop Rule? Labeling of Multiracial Children in Black Intermarriages*, 20 SOC. F. 35 (2005).

Rush, Benjamin, *Observations Intended to Favor a Supposition that the Black Color (as it is Called) of the Negroes is Derived from Leprosy*, reprinted in RACIAL THOUGHT IN AMERICA: FROM THE PURITANS TO ABRAHAM LINCOLN (Louis Ruchames ed., 1969).

Sack, Kevin, *After Decades, A Time to Reap*, N. Y. TIMES, Nov. 5, 2008.

Sadker, Myra, et al., *Gender and Educational Equality*, in MULTICULTURAL EDUCATION (James A. Banks & Cherry A.M. Banks eds., 1989).

Saragoza, Alex M., Concepcion R. Juarez, Abel Valenzuela Jr., & Oscar Gonzalez, *History And Public Policy: Title VII and the Use of the Hispanic Classification*, 5 LA RAZA L. J. 1 (1992).

Shaw-Taylor, Yoku, *The Intersection of Assimilation, Race, Presentation of Self and Transnationalism in America, in* THE OTHER AFRICAN AMERICANS (Yoku Shaw-Taylor & Steven A. Tuch eds., 2007).

Sivandon, A., *Race, Class, and the State: The Black Experience in Britain*, in RACE CLASS (1976).

Skiba, Russell J., Suzanne E. Eckes, & Kevin Brown, *African American Disproportionality In School Discipline: The Divide Between Best Evidence And Legal Remedy*, 54 N.Y.L. SCH. L. REV. 1071 (2009).

Smith, Sandra S. & Mignon R. Moore, *Intraracial Diversity and Relations Among African-Americans: Closeness Among Black Students at a Predominately White University*, 106 AM. J. SOCIOL. 1 (2000).

Snipp, C. Matthew, *Racial Measurement in the American Census: Past Practices and Implications for the Future*, 29 ANN. REV. SOC. 563 (2003).

Sowell, Thomas, *Three Black Histories, in* AMERICAN ETHNIC GROUPS (Thomas Sowell & Lynn D. Collins eds., 1978).

Spann, Girardeau A., *Disparate Impact*, 98 GEO. L.J. 1133 (2010).

Spickard, Paul, *The Power of Blackness: Mixed-Race Leaders and the Monoracial Ideal, in* RACIAL THINKING IN THE UNITED STATES (Paul Spickard & G. Reginald Daniel eds., 2004).

Steele, Claude, *A Threat in the Air: How Stereotypes Shape Intellectual Identity and Performance*, 52 AM. PSYCHOLOGIST 613 (1997).

Stonequist, Everett V., *The Problem of the Marginal Man*, 41 AM J. SOCIOL. 1 (1935).

Tafoya, Sonya M., Hans Johnson, & Laura E. Hill, *Who Chooses to Choose Two?, in* THE AMERICAN PEOPLE: 2000 CENSUS (Richard Farley & John Haaga eds., 2005).

Taylor, Paul, Wendy Wang, Kim Parker, Jeffrey S. Passel, Eileen Patten & Seth Motel, Pew Research Ctr., *The Rise of Intermarriage: Rates, Characteristics Vary by Race and Gender* 11 (2012).

Thernstrom, Stephen & Abigail Thernstrom, *We Have Overcome*, New Republic, Oct. 13, 1997.

Thomas, Kendall, Comments at Frontiers of Legal Thought Conference, Duke Law School (Jan. 26, 1990), *quoted in* Charles R. Lawrence III, *If He Hollers Let Him Go: Regulating Racist Speech on Campus*, 1990 DUKE L. J. 431, *in*

Mari J. Matsuda, Charles R. Lawrence III, Richard Delgado & Kimberlé W. Crenshaw, Words That Wound (1993).

Townsend, Sarah S.M., et al, *Being Mixed: Who Claims a Biracial Identity?*, 18 Cult. Divers. Ethn. Min. 91 (2012).

Turner, James, *Introduction, in* David Walker's Appeal to the Coloured Citizens of the World, But in Particular, and Very Expressly to Those of the United States of America (1993).

Tyson, Karolyn, William Darity & Domini R. Castellino, *It's Not a 'Black Thing': Understanding the Burden of Acting White and Other Dilemmas of High Achievement*, 70 Am. Sociological Rev. 582 (2005).

U.S. Bureau of Labor Statistics, *BLS Reports Report 1044 Labor Force Characteristics by Race and Ethnicity, 2012* (October 2013).

U.S. Census Bureau, *The American Community—Blacks: 2004* (2007).

U.S. Census Bureau, *America's Families and Living Arrangements* (2010).

U.S. Census Bureau, The Black Alone or in Combination Population in the United States: 2010 tbl.4. *Nativity and Citizenship Status by Sex, for Black Alone or in Combination and White Alone, Not Hispanic: 2010* (2010).

U.S. Census Bureau, *Race of Wife by Race of Husband: 1960, 1970, 1980, 1991, and 1992* (1998).

U.S. Census Bureau, *The Two or More Races Population: 2000, Census 2000 Brief* (November 2001).

U.S. Census Bureau, *2010 Census Shows America's Diversity* (March 24, 2011).

U.S. Commission on Civil Rights, Twenty Years After Brown: Equality of Educational Opportunity (1975).

Valentine, Curtis, *Rethinking the Achievement Gap: Lessons From the African Diaspora*, Washington Post, September 2, 2012.

Vickerman, Milton, The Center for Children, Families, and the Law Interdisciplinary Conference "Welcome to America: Immigration, Families, and the Law": *Post-1965 Immigration and Assimilation: A Response to Randy Capps*, 14 Va. J. Soc. Pol'y & L. 206 (2007).

Vickerman, Milton, *Jamaica, in* The New Americans: A Guide to Immigration Since 1965 (Mary C. Waters & Reed Ueda eds., with Helen B. Marrow, 2007).

Virginia Council, MINUTES OF THE COUNCIL AND GENERAL COURT OF COLONIAL VIRGINIA, 1622–1632, 1670–1676, WITH NOTES AND EXCERPTS FROM ORIGINAL COUNCIL AND GENERAL COURT RECORDS, INTO 1683, NOW LOST (H.R. McIlwaine ed., 1924).

Waldinger, Roger, *Immigration and Urban Change*, 15 ANN. REV. SOC. 211 (1989).

Wallman, Katherine K., Suzann Evinger & Susan Schechter, *Measuring Our Nation's Diversity: Developing a Common Language for Data on Race/Ethnicity*, 90 AM. J. PUBLIC HEALTH 1704 (2000).

Wallsten, Peter, *Election 2008: The Presidential Vote/News Analysis*, L. A. TIMES, Nov. 5, 2008.

Warikoo, Natasha & Prudence Carter, *Cultural Explanations for Racial and Ethnic Stratification in Academic Achievement: A Call for a New and Improved Theory*, 79 REV. OF EDUC. RES. 366 (2009).

Waters, Mary, *Ethnic and Racial Identities of Second-Generation Black Immigrants in New York City, in* THE NEW SECOND GENERATION (Alejandro Portes ed., 1996).

Watson, Elwood, *Miss America's Racial Milestones*, DIVERSE ISSUES IN HIGHER EDUCATION (Jan. 14, 2009).

White, Arthur O., *The Black Leadership Class and Education in Antebellum Boston*, 42 J. NEGRO EDUC. 504 (1973).

Wickham, Dewayne, *Tiger Finally Takes a Public Stand-The Wrong One*, USA TODAY, May 16, 2000.

Wiecek, William M., *The Origins of the Law of Slavery in British North America*, 17 CARDOZO L. REV. 1711 (1995).

Wildman, Stephanie M. & Adrienne D. Davis, *Language and Silence: Making Systems of Privilege Visible*, 35 SANTA CLARA L. REV. 881 (1995).

Wilkerson, Isabel, *Black-White Marriages Rise, but Couples Still Face Scorn*, N.Y. TIMES, Dec. 2, 1991.

Williams, Patricia J., *Spirit-Murdering the Messenger: The Discourse of Fingerpointing as the Law's Response to Racism*, 42 U. MIAMI L. REV. 127 (1987).

Wilson, Kevin C., *And Stay Out! The Dangers Of Using Anti-Immigrant Sentiment As a Basis For Social Policy: America Should Take Heed of Disturbing Lessons From Great Britain's Past*, 24 GA. J. INT'L & COMP. L., 567 (1995).

Wing, Adrien Katherine & Sylke Merchan, *Rape, Ethnicity, and Culture: Spirit Injury from Bosnia to Black America*, 25 COLUM. HUM. RTS. L. REV. 1 (1993).

Witmer, H., & R. Kotinsky, *Personality in the Making: The Fact-finding Report of the Midcentury White House Conference on Children and Youth* (1952).

Woods, Karen M., *"A Wicked and Mischievous Connection": The Origins of Indian-White Miscegenation Law*, 23 Legal Stud. F. 37 (1999).

Woodson, Carter G., *The Beginnings of Miscegenation of the Whites and Blacks*, 3 J. NEGRO. HIST. 335 (October 1918).

Wrench, John & John Solomos, *The Politics and Processes of Racial Discrimination in Britain*, *in* RACISM AND MIGRATION IN WESTERN EUROPE (John Wrench & John Solomos eds., 1993).

Wu, Frank H., *The Multiracial Classification Can Be Detrimental*, *in* INTERRACIAL AMERICA: OPPOSING VIEWPOINTS (Eleanor Stanford ed., 2006).

Xi, Wang, *Black Suffrage and the Redefinition of American Freedom 1860–1870*, 17 CARDOZO L. REV. 2153 (1995).

Zabel, William D., *Interracial Marriage and the Law*, Atlantic Monthly 216 (October 1965): 75–79.

*2003 Yearbook of Immigration Statistics*, Office of Immigration Statistics, Department of Homeland Security, 12–15 tbl.2 (2004).

## *Websites and Materials Available on the Internet*

Bauman, Kurt J. & Nikki L. Graf, *Educational Attainment: 2000: Census 2000 Brief*, U.S. CENSUS BUREAU, 5 tbl.2 (2003), *available at* http://www.census.gov/prod/2003pubs/c2kbr-24.pdf.

Carnevale, Anthony & Stephen J. Rose, *Socioeconomic Status, Race/Ethnicity, and Selective College Admissions* (2003), *available at* http://tcf.org/publications/pdfs/pb252/carnevale_rose.pdf.

*Censusscope, United States Multiracial Profile (2001)*, *available at* http://www.censusscope.org/us/print_chart_multi.html.

The Common Application for Undergraduate College Admission, *available at* https://www.commonapp.org/CommonApp/default.aspx.

Consortium on Financing Higher Education, *Home*, *available at* http://web.mit.edu/cofhe/.

DeLoggio Admissions Achievement Program, *Race and Ethnicity*, *available at* http://www.deloggio.com/diversty/race.html.

*EEO-1 Who Must File*, U.S. EQUAL EMP. OPPORTUNITY COMM'N, *available at* http://www.eeoc.gov/employers/eeo1survey/whomustfile.cfm.

Fowler, Joanne, *Caressa Cameron of Virginia Crowned Miss America*, PEOPLE (Jan. 31, 2010), *available at* http://www.people.com/people/article/0,,20340574,00.htm.

Huffington, Christina, Single Motherhood Increases Dramatically for Certain Demographics, Census Bureau Reports, May 1, 2013, *available at* http://www.huffingtonpost.com/2013/05/01/single-motherhood-increases-census-report_n_3195455.html.

Ifill, Sherrilyn A., *Summer of Our Discontent*, THE ROOT (August 19, 2013), *available at* http://mobile.theroot.com/articles/politics/2013/08/march_on_washington_at_50_the_summer_of_our_discontent.html.

*Irish and German Immigration from U.S. History Online Textbook*, U.S. HISTORY (2010), *available at* http://www.ushistory.org/us/25f.asp.

Kendle, John, *Players Boycott AFL All-Star Game*, Official History of Pro Football Hall of Fame (February 18, 2010), *available at* http://www.profootballhof.com/history/2010/2/18/players-boycott-afl-all-star-game/.

The Legal Advocate, *Wrap Up: National Bar Association 87th Annual Convention*, *available at* http://blog.nita.org/2012/08/01/wrap-up-national-bar-association-87th-annual-convention/.

Manning, Jennifer E., *Membership of the 113th Congress: A Profile 7* (from Congressional Research Service), *available at* https://www.fas.org/sgp/crs/misc/R42964.pdf.

MinorityNurse.com, *Eyes on the Prize*, *available at* http://www.minoritynurse.com/article/eyes-prize.

National Banker's Association, *History*, *available at* http://www.nationalbankers.org/history.asp.

National Bar Association, *Our History*, *available at* http://www.nationalbar.org/our_history.

National Dental Association, NDA History, *available at* http://ndaonline.org/about-nda/.

National Educational Longitudinal Study of 1988, *available at* http://nces.ed.gov/surveys/NELS88/.

National Medical Association, *History*, *available at* http://www.nmanet.org/index.php?option=com_content&view=article&id=3&Itemid=4.

National Newspaper Publishers Association, *NNPA History*, *available at* http://nnpa.org/about-us/nnpa-history/.

National Technical Association, Inc., *History*, *available at* http://www.ntaonline.org/aboutus/history.html.

Phi Eta Psi Fraternity, *available at* http://phietapsi1965.com/index.php/about-phi-eta-psi/founding-fathers/the-birth-of-phi-eta-psi-fraternity.

Reed, Holly E., and Catherine S. Andrzejewski, *The New Wave of African Immigrants in the United States*, *available at* http://paa2010.princeton.edu/download.aspx?submissionId=100606.

Rosenfield, Michael J., *CCF Briefing Paper: Interracial Marriage 40 years after Loving v. Virginia* (2007), *available at* http://maillists.uci.edu/mailman/public/dasa/2007-March/000633.html.

Rucker, W.C., Westmoreland Slave Plot (1687) (April 3, 2012) *in* ENCYCLOPEDIA VIRGINIA, *available at* http://www.EncyclopediaVirginia.org/Westmoreland_Slave_Plot_1687.

Rumbaut, Ruben, *Children of Immigrants and Their Achievement: The Role of Family, Acculturation, Social Class, Gender, Ethnicity, and School Contexts*, 1, *available at* http://www.hks.harvard.edu/inequality/Seminar/Papers/Rumbaut2.pdf.

Sigma Pi Phi Fraternity, *History of the Boulé*, *available at* https://www.sigmapiphi.org/home/history_of_the_boule/.

Toldson, Ivory, *Single Parents Aren't the Problem*, THE ROOT, July 3, 2013, *available at* http://www.theroot.com/views/single-parents-arent-problem.

University of Virginia, *The History of African-American Newspapers*, *available at* http://cti.itc.virginia.edu/~aas405a/newspaper.html.

U.S. Census Bureau, *History*, *available at* http://www.census.gov/history/www/through_the_decades/index_of_questions/1900_1.html.

U.S. Census Bureau, *America's Families and Living Arrangements: 2008, Tables C5; Nativity Status of Children Under 18 Years/1 and Presence of Parents by Race, and Hispanic Origin /2 for Selected Characteristics: 2008—Black alone* and *Tables C5. Nativity Status of Children Under 18 Years/1 and Presence of Parents by Race, and Hispanic Origin /2 for Selected Characteristics: 2008—Black alone or in combination with one or more other races*, available at http://www.census.gov/population/www/socdemo/hh-fam/cps2008.html.

U.S. Census Bureau, *College Enrollment—Summary by Sex, Race, and Hispanic Origin: 2007*, available at http://www.census.gov/compendia/statab/2010/tables/10s0274.pdf.

U.S. Census Bureau, *Hispanic Population of the United States, Hispanic Population in the United States 1970 to 2050* (2008), available at https://www.census.gov/population/hispanic/publications/hispanics_2006.html.

U.S. Census Bureau, *Historical Income Tables: People, Black CPS Population and Per Capita Income Table P-1B*, available at http://www.census.gov/hhes/www/income/data/historical/people/index.html.

U.S. Census Bureau, *Historical Income Tables: People, Hispanic of Any Race CPS Population and Per Capita Income Table P-1B*, available at http://www.census.gov/hhes/www/income/data/historical/people/index.html.

U.S. Census Bureau, *Table 3. Poverty Status of People, by Age, Race, and Hispanic Origin: 1959 to 2012*, available at http://www.census.gov/hhes/www/poverty/data/historical/people.html.

U.S. Census Bureau, *Table 85. Births to Teens and Unmarried Women, and Births with Low Birth Weight, by Race and Hispanic Origin: 1990 to 2005*, available at http://www.census.gov/compendia/statab/2008/tables/08s0085.pdf.

U.S. Equal Employment Opportunity Commission, *Final Revisions of the Employer Information Report (EEO-1)*, available at http://www.eeoc.gov/eeo1/.

# Index

A Place for Us, 180
Abbott, Robert S., 121
Abel, 84
Abolition, 28, 68, 70, 72–77, 97, 99, 103, 104–08, 114, 125, 165–66, 169, 171, 202–03, 271 n14, 286 nn186, 187, 194
Abraham, 84
Ad Hoc Committee on Racial and Ethnic Definitions, 45–46, 267 n58
Adam and Eve, 167
Adams, Henry, 120
*Adarand Constructors, Inc. v. Pena*, 91, 276 n105, 277 nn109, 120
Adult Black Immigrants, 217–19, 223–29, 231
Africa, 4, 6, 12, 14–15, 22, 28, 31, 36, 45, 47, 49, 53, 66–67, 70, 73, 75, 97–98, 101, 104–05, 120, 140, 142, 178, 184, 194–97, 199–201, 203–04, 206–09, 211, 213–16, 225–26, 228, 237, 252, 256 nn18–19, 22, 258 nn48, 50, 259 n51, 263 n103, 264 n109, 265 n3, 267 n60, 270 n152, 279 n157, 294 n93, 303 n9, 304 nn13–15, 20, 305 nn37, 43–44, 306 nn62, 69, 308 n113, 310 nn161–62, 164, 166–67, 311 n203, 312 nn219, 225, 227, 313 n237; *see also* African Immigration and Black Immigrants
African Immigration, 194, 196–97, 208, 209, 213–16, 303, 306, 308, 312; *see also* Africa and Black Immigrants
African Methodist Episcopal Church (AME), 116, 119, 120
African Methodist Episcopal Zion Church, 116, 119
Agassiz, Louis, 167, 173
Akaka, Daniel, 53
Alabama, 79, 112, 118, 130, 163–64, 167, 169–70, 175, 178–79, 197, 275 n89, 283 n275, 296 nn142, 148, 154, 297 nn190, 192, 299 n242
Alaska(n) Native, 20, 26, 34, 45–47, 53–55, 61, 236, 238, 245, 264 nn108, 117, 270 n148, 315 nn20–21
*Alexander v. Choate*, 277 n118
*Alexander v. Sandoval*, 276 n105, 277 n118

351

Ali, Muhammad, 130
Alienkoff, Alexander, 220
Allen, Richard, 104, 116
Alpha Kappa Alpha Sorority, 123, 285 n314
Alpha Phi Alpha Fraternity, 123
American Association for the Advancement of Science, 173
American Association of Medical Colleges, 26, 264 n117
American Baptist Home Mission Society, 119
American Colonization Society, 75, 104
American Football League, 130
American Geographical and Statistical Society, 40
American Indian, 20, 26, 34, 40, 45–47, 49, 51, 53–55, 61, 85, 150, 152, 236, 238, 264 nn108, 117, 270 n147, 299 n247, 315 n20; *see also* Native American
American Nurses Association, 123
American Missionary Association, 119
American Society of Free Persons of Color, 104
American Statistical Association, 39
*Amsterdam News*, 121
Anglo Alabama, 164
Antimiscegenation statute, 145–46, 148, 156–58, 160, 162, 166, 169–70, 177–80, 190, 297 n190; *see also* Mulattoes
Aptheker, Herbert, 99, 279 n154, 282 n260
Arkansas, 112, 175, 197, 283
Asante, Molefi, 224, 312 n220
Ascendant Blacks: admissions forms, 21–24, 232–39, 248; attendance at selective higher education programs, 9–10, 16, 150–53, 197–98; definition, 5; experiences of engaging in struggle against racism, 12–14; experiences of racism, 12–14; Final Guidance impact on admissions of, 20–22, 33–35, 58–64, 234; goals of Proposal, 24–25, 32, 233, 240–41, 248; Harvard, 7–8, 151, 259 n53; impact of elimination from selective higher education programs increases in U.S. population, 10–17; impact of Proposal on admissions prospects, 247–49; Supplemental statement, 22–25, 32, 238–39, 247–48; *see also* Blacks and Black Hispanics
Asian, 9, 11, 14, 20, 26, 34, 45–47, 49, 53–55, 57, 61, 63, 85, 93–94, 134, 144, 150, 152–53, 185, 200–01, 205, 210–11, 214, 236, 238, 245, 259 n58, 264 nn108, 117, 270 n148, 277 nn125–26, 289 n22, 291 n44, 292 n57, 302 n306, 308, 304 n20, 305 n37, 315 n20
Association of MultiEthnic Americans, 180, 300 n267
Attucks, Crispus, 22
Avery College, 117

Bachman, John, 167, 296 nn159–60
Bacon's Rebellion, 71, 99–100
Baker, Josephine, 22
Baldus, David, 135
Baldus Study, 135–37
Baldwin, James, 158
Baltimore, Lord, 159

Banks, James, 89, 275 n96
Banneker, Benjamin, 104, 280 nn189, 191
Barbados, 161–62, 272 n16, 313 n231
Baynes, Leonard, 229, 261, 313 n241
Bell, Derrick, 256
Bennet, Pamela R., 8, 198, 260 n62, 278 n142, 279 n144, 303 nn3–4, 305 n34, 311 n206, 312 n208
Berea College, 174
*Berea College v. Commonwealth*, 200 n222
*Berea College v. Kentucky*, 174, 298 n221, 299 n222
Bethel Church, 104, 116
*Beyond the Melting Pot*, 199, 305 n41
Bibb, Henry, 105
Bible, 67
Binet, Alfred, 86
Birmingham, 210
Black, Charles, 81, 273 n54
Black Church, 114–16, 120, 122
Black Codes, 76–77, 81, 111
Black Community, 4–5, 12–13, 22–23, 25–26, 28–30, 67, 89, 96–98, 102–04, 107, 111, 114–15, 117–18, 123–25, 127, 131–34, 137, 139–40, 168, 176, 189, 220, 231, 234, 244, 251, 285 n319
Black Consciousness Movement, 186, 252
Black Hispanics: admissions forms, 20–21, 34, 232–39; definition, 20, 34, 50, 233; Final Guidance impact on admissions of, 20–21, 33–35, 56, 58–62, 64, 234; impact of Proposal on admissions prospects, 240–43, 248; inability to differentiate from Ascendant Blacks, 34, 60, 242; LSAT scores, 152; population, 54–55; Supplemental statement, 22–25, 238–41
Black Immigrants: admissions forms, 32, 233–39, 248; attendance at selective higher education programs, 7–10, 21, 31, 193–95, 197–99, 216–17, 232–33, 251, 258 n49, 260 nn60, 62, 261 n79, 265 n3, 279 n142, 291 n45; contribution to struggle in U.S. against racial oppression, 22, 204–05; cultural differences from Ascendant Blacks, 31, 193–94, 216–32, 246–47, 260 n67; definition, 5, 20–21, 35, 197, 217, 234, 248–49; education, 8, 31, 197–99, 216, 258 n48, 260 n60; experiences of engaging in struggle against racism, 12–13, 15, 31, 193–95, 200–01, 217–32, 246–49; experiences of racism, 9, 12–16, 31, 193–95, 204, 217–32, 246–49; family characteristics, 9, 14, 30, 194, 196, 199, 201, 204; family income, 9, 194, 196, 199, 201; Final Guidance impact on admissions of, 35, 56, 62–64, 234–35, 246–47; Harvard, 7–8, 151, 259 n53; history of immigration, 31, 194, 200, 202–06, 208–16; inability to differentiate from Ascendant Blacks, 4, 7, 21–22, 35, 56, 62–63, 195, 234–35, 237–38, 246–49; in-

creases in U.S. population, 5–6, 9, 17, 31, 195–200, 231, 303 n6; parental education, 194, 196, 199–201; parental cultural influence, 15, 217, 228–32, 260 n67; poverty rates, 201; Supplemental statement, 22–25, 234, 238–41, 246–48; U.K. immigration law changes, 205, 208–12; *see also* Africa, African Immigration, Caribbean Immigrants, and foreign-born Blacks

Black Multiracial: admissions forms, 20–21, 33–34, 233–39 ; attendance at selective higher education programs, 7–10, 150–53, 251; contribution to struggle in U.S. against racial oppression, 22, 240; cultural differences from Ascendant Blacks, 9, 13, 30, 180–90; definition, 4, 50–52, 142–43, 233; differentiation from single-race blacks, 39–40, 142, 145–47, 177, 180–84; education, 150–53; experiences of engaging in struggle against racism, 9, 12–15, 185–90; experiences of racism, 9, 12–15, 185–90; family characteristics, 9, 153–55 ; family income, 9, 30, 153, 155; Final Guidance impact on admissions of, 13, 20–21, 33–35, 58–62, 64, 234; Harvard, 7–8, 151, 259 n53; impact of immigration on self-identification, 142, 184; impact of Proposal on admissions prospects, 242–46, 248–49; inability to differentiate from Ascendant Blacks, 4–5, 7–8, 33–34, 37, 40–41, 145–46; increases in U.S. population, 6, 144, 150; LSAT scores, 152; parental education, 6, 153–54; pass as white, 4, 177, 184; poverty rates, 155; self-identification, 13–14, 141–42, 146–47, 180–84; supplemental statement, 22–25, 32, 238–39, 242–46 ; *see also* antimiscegenation statutes, Black Hispanics, Blacks with Two or More Races, Mulattoes, and Miscegenation

Black Nationalist, 120, 131, 205
Black Panther Party, 131
Black Power, 131, 174, 286 n360
Black voters, 43, 79–80, 112, 127, 130
Blackmun, Justice, 90
Blacks: admissions forms, 20–21, 33–34, 233–39; attendance at selective higher education programs, 3, 7–10, 150–53, 193–95, 197–99, 216–17, 232, 233, 251, 258 n49, 260 nn60, 62, 261 n79, 265 n3, 279 n142, 291 n45; definition, 4, 44–48 , 52–53; education, 94, 118–20, 137–39, 150–53, 197–99, 216; experiences of engaging in struggle against racism, 97–139, 185–90; experiences of racism, 66–96, 185–90; family characteristics, 9, 93–94, 153–55, 194, 196, 199–201; family income, 93, 153, 155, 194, 196, 201; family wealth, 94; Final Guidance impact on admissions of, 13, 20–21, 33–35, 56, 58–62, 64, 234–35, 246–47; Harvard,

7–8, 151, 259 n53; impact of proposal on admissions prospects, 241–49; incarceration rates, 94; life expectancy, 94; LSAT scores, 152; parental education, 153–54, 184, 200–01; population 3–4, 54–55; poverty rates, 93–94, 155, 201; supplemental statement, 22–25, 32, 238–39, 241–49; *see also* Black Codes, Black Community, Black Consciousness Movement, Black Church, Black Hispanics, Black Multiracials, Black Nationalist, Black Panther Party, Black Power, Black voters, Blacks with Two or More Races, and Single Race Blacks

Blacks with Two or More Races: admissions forms, 22–24, 34, 232–39; definition, 20, 34, 233; Final Guidance impact on admissions of, 20–22, 33–35, 58–62, 234; impact of Proposal on admissions prospects, 243–46; supplemental statement, 22–25, 32, 238–39, 243–46; *see also* Black Multiracials

Blanche, Bruce, 113
Blood fractions, 159, 165, 175
Bloody Sunday, 130
Blumenbach, Johann, 85
Boas, Franz, 86
Bok, Derek, 3, 151, 255 n1
Bonaparte, Napoleon, 163
Boring, E.G., 86
Boston, 102, 116–117, 122, 167, 204, 258 n40, 282 nn256, 259, 304 n11

Bowen, William G., 3, 16, 151, 255 nn1, 3, 262 n87
Brain size, 85, 171–72, 298 n198
Britain, 102, 107, 124, 163, 205, 207, 209–12, 308 n112, 309 nn129–30, 132–34, 147; *see also* England and United Kingdom
British Immigration restrictions, 208–12
British Nationality Act of 1948, 209
British North America, 28, 99–100, 156, 161, 263 n103, 279 n159, 296 n158
Broca, Paul, 85
Broh, C. Anthony, 242, 258 n48, 259 nn56, 58, 265 nn4, 8, 270 n132, 291 n44, 304 n20, 315 n10
Brotherhood of Sleeping Car Porters, 126, 285 n319
*Brown v. Board of Education*, 29, 69, 83, 87–89, 95, 98, 128, 146, 178, 186, 272 n19, 274 nn65, 75, 275 nn86–88, 90, 93, 285 n344, 298 n219, 299 n241; *see also* desegregation, Desegregation Era, segregation, and Segregation Era,
Brown, Frank, 230, 311 n203
Brown, H. Rapp, 131
Brown, William Wells, 105
Bryant, Kobe, 18, 262 n94
*Buchanan v. Warley*, 125
Bunche, Ralph, 126
Burakumin, 223
Burns, Ursula, 18, 133
Butler, Benjamin F., 76, 109
Butler University, 123
Byrd, Charles Michael, 182, 301 n281

Cain, 84–85, 115
Cain, Howard, 18
Calhoun, John C., 39, 73, 272 n26
Camper, Pieter, 85
Canada, 103, 121, 200, 207, 209
Cape Verde, 52, 63, 203–04, 279 n152, 307 nn79, 80
Carlos, John, 130
Carmichael, Stokley, 22, 131, 286 n360
Caribbean Immigrants, 22, 31, 63, 184, 196–97, 201, 204–05, 207–08, 212, 215–16, 225–26, 228–30, 237, 256 n19, 261 n79, 264 n109, 303 n9, 304 nn13, 15, 20, 305 nn37, 40, 51, 307 n87, 311 n203, 314 n252; *see also* Black Immigrants and foreign-born blacks
Carolina Colony, 99–100, 103, 144, 156, 160–62, 295 n116
Census Bureau, 4, 9, 37–38, 40–44, 46–48, 50, 53–54, 58, 146, 148, 154, 176, 178, 181, 183, 197, 230, 238, 255 nn6, 10, 256 nn13, 16, 257 nn29, 33, 258 nn37, 48, 265 n13, 266 nn27, 42, 267 n49, 269 n103, 272 nn22–23, 47, 277 n126, 278 nn128–29, 132, 288 n2
Central High School, 89
Charles III, King, 163
Charleston, 29, 101–02, 111, 113, 145, 156, 161–62, 167
Chesapeake Bay, 66, 158
Cheyney State Training School, 117, 283 n262
*Chicago Defender*, 121
Chicano, 42, 45; *see also* Hispanic/Latino

China, 45, 47, 53, 236
Chinese, 40–41, 170, 187, 205
Chinese Exclusion Act, 205, 307 n96
Chisholm, Shirley, 22
Christian Methodist Episcopal Church (CME), 116, 119
Church of God in Christ, 116
Churchill, Winston, 210
*City of Richmond v. J.A. Croson Co.*, 91, 276 n105, 277 nn111–12, 115, 119
Civil Rights Act of 1866, 77–78, 111, 166, 169–70, 273 n45, 297 nn182, 190, 306 n76
Civil Rights Act of 1875, 78, 81, 273 n45, 297 n182
Civil Rights Act of 1964, 44, 88–89, 130, 186, 252, 276 nn103, 105, 277 n118
*Civil Rights Cases*, 81, 274 n56
Civil Rights Division of the Department of Justice, 126, 180
Civil War, 29, 69, 70, 72, 74, 76, 78, 82, 85, 97, 103, 107, 108, 111, 113–14, 117, 129, 145, 156, 165–66, 169, 171–73, 202–04, 213, 271 n4, 280 n179, 281 nn213, 217, 283 n275, 296 n142
*The Clansman*, 141
Classical immigration theory, 220
Clay, Henry, 75
*Clay v. U.S.*, 286 n359
Clinton, Sir Henry, 103
Coale, Ansley, 40
Coalition Statement, 182, 300 n277
*Code Noir*, 163, 295 n129
Cohabitation, 5, 6, 147, 149–50, 189, 240
College Board, 26, 154–55, 292 nn61, 62, 293 n64

INDEX 357

Colorado, 42, 78
Colored Creole, 163, 164, 295 nn128, 130, 296 n148
Colored Press Association, 122
Common Application, 235–38, 265 n3, 314 nn1, 2, 3
Commonwealth, 209, 211, 308 n127, 309 n143
Commonwealth Act, 211, 309
Commonwealth Act of 1962, 211
Commonwealth Immigrants Act in 1968, 211
*Commonwealth v. Jennison*, 73
Compromise of 1877, 79, 113
Confederate states, 77–79, 88, 97, 109, 112–13, 117, 169, 252, 283 n275
Congo, 66, 256 n18, 310 n162
Congress, 27, 31, 36, 38–39, 44, 69, 73, 77–79, 81–83, 89, 104–05, 108–09, 111–13, 118, 120, 126, 130, 132, 166, 168–69, 194, 202–03, 205–07, 209, 214–16, 252, 262 n97, 265 n12, 273 n44, 287 n372, 297 n190, 306 n65, 307 n78, 308 n118
Congress of Racial Equality, 129, 131, 219
Congressional Black Caucus, 181
Connecticut, 73, 106, 156
Consortium on Financing Higher Education (COFHE), 8, 151, 259 n57, 291 n43
Constitutional Convention, 71–72, 112, 203
Cornell University, 123, 259 n57, 291 n43
Cornish, S.E., 121
Cornwallis, Lord, 103
Cosby, Bill, 18, 133, 262 n92

*The Crisis*, 125, 271 n9
Critical mass, 10–11, 24, 32, 193, 231, 233–34, 241, 244–45, 247
Crummell, Alexander, 105
Cuba (ns), 26, 42–43, 45, 47, 50, 207, 214, 236, 264 n117, 265 n7
Cubberley, Ellwood, 206, 308 n106
Cuffee, Paul, 105
Cult of Victimology, 96, 260 n67, 271 n8, 301 n289
*Cumming v. Richmond County Board of Education*, 81, 274 n61

Dalits, 13, 223, 312 n213
Davis Bend, 113
Davis, Hugh, 157, 293 n78
Davis, Jefferson, 113
Davis, John, 126, 280, 285 n331
Death penalty, 135–37
Declaration of Independence, 71–72, 85, 104, 111, 160, 219, 311 n200
*DeFunis v. Odegaard*, 128, 139, 286 n347, 288 n396
De Gobineau, Count Arthur, 169, 297 n179
De jure segregation, 81, 87, 89, 90, 128, 276 n102; *see also* Desegregation Era, school desegregation, Segregation, and Segregation Era
Delany, Martin, 96, 105, 131, 279 n148, 280 n197
Delta Sigma Theta Sorority, 123
Democratic Party, 79–80, 112
Denmark, 75, 308 n112
Department of Education (DOE), 13, 20, 28, 33–36, 55–56, 58–63, 142, 146, 148, 151, 158, 182, 197, 233–34, 242, 246,

248, 259 n58, 261 n81, 265 n2, 269 n107, 278 n131, 291 n44, 312 n8
Department of Labor, 46
Desegregation, 69, 83, 88, 90, 127, 148; *see also De jure segregation*, Desegregation Era, School desegregation, Segregation, and Segregation Era
Desegregation Era, 29, 68, 83–91, 97, 98, 127–33, 275, 296; *see also De jure segregation*, School desegregation, Segregation, and Segregation Era
Deslondes, Charles, 101
Detroit, 102, 116, 187
*Detroit Tribune*, 121
Diallo, Amadou, 217
Directive 15, 27, 36, 43, 46–49, 51–53, 180, 183, 267, 300
*Disintegration: The Splintering of Black America*, 17, 262 n89, 287 n371
District of Columbia, 78, 103, 104, 121, 170, 179, 235, 283 n275
*Diverse Issues of Higher Education*, 8, 259 n53, 262, nn95, 96, 291 n40, 305 n33
Diversity Visa Program, 214, 216, 306 n69, 311 n191
Dixon, Thomas F., 141, 288 n1
Double-positive consideration, 32, 240, 247, 249
Douglas, Justice, 128, 139, 286 n347, 288 n396
Douglass, Frederick, 22, 105–06, 109, 116, 281 n203
*Dred Scott*, 72, 81, 203, 272 n21, 306 n77

DuBois, W. E. B., 66, 76, 107, 118, 124–25, 271 n9, 273 n42, 281 n207
Dunmore, Lord, 102

Easton, Hosea, 117, 282 n259
*Ebony* Magazine, 18, 121, 262 n93, 263 n100
Educational Testing Service, 8, 198
EEO-1 Report, 56–58, 269 n112
Eisenhower, 89
Elementary and Secondary Education Act, 88
*Ellis v. State*, 297 n190
Emancipation, 73–75, 110, 161, 272 n25, 279 n149; *see also* abolition
Emancipation Proclamation, 75, 110
Emigration, 75, 98, 104, 105, 114, 120–21, 208, 212, 279 n148, 280 n197, 307 n86, 308 n117
Enforcement Act of April 20, 1871, 78, 273 n45, 297 n182
Enforcement Act of February 28, 1871, 78, 273 n45, 297 n182
Enforcement Act of May 31, 1870, 78, 273 n45, 297 n182
England, 68, 70, 71, 75, 100, 156, 158, 164, 209, 220; *see also* Britain and United Kingdom
English colonies, 68, 71, 75, 99–101, 144, 156–59, 161–62, 202
English language, 105, 154, 162, 169, 209, 215, 220, 225–26, 229–30, 255 n7, 293 n64, 295 n129, 305 n51, 307 n99
*E Pluribus Unum*, 66
Equal Employment Opportunity Commission (EEOC), 28, 36, 46, 56–59, 180, 182, 229 n112

Equal protection clause, 80–81, 92–93, 126, 132, 135–36, 169–70, 263 n104, 276 nn103, 105, 287 nn374, 380, 294 n86
Ethiopia, 4, 197, 206–07, 209, 216
Europe, 12, 70, 72, 75, 84–85, 109, 121, 174, 202, 208–09, 212–13, 224, 237, 310
European colonies, 4, 29, 75, 99, 162, 207, 212–13, 221, 257 n22
European Community, 211
European Economic Community, 211
European immigration, 42, 45, 47, 52–53, 120, 164, 200, 204–06, 208, 212–13, 218, 220–21, 237, 310 n161
European immigration restrictions, 208–09, 213
Executive Order 11185, 45, 267 n57
Executive Order 8802, 126, 285 n338
Executive Order 9981, 127

Fair Employment Practice Committee, 126
Fair Housing Act, 44, 89
Family income: black, 17, 93–95, 134, 277 nn125, 126; Black Multiracials, 9, 144, 148, 155; foreign-born blacks, 9, 194, 196, 199, 201, 230; Native Blacks, 9, 194, 196, 199, 201, 230; Single-Race Blacks, 9, 148, 155
Federal Interagency Committee on Education, 45, 49, 50, 52, 267 n58, 268 n94,
FICE Subcommittee on Minority Education, 45

Fifteenth Amendment, 78–80, 112, 113
Filipino, 51, 63, 170
Final Guidance, 13, 20–22, 27–28, 31, 33–36, 55, 56, 58–64, 142, 144, 146, 151, 233–48, 259 n58, 261 nn81–82, 264 n108, 265 nn2, 6, 7, 267 n55, 269 n106, 270 nn131–33, 150, 153, 291 n44, 314 n8, 315 n10
First Confiscation Act, 109
First Morrill Act, 118
First Reconstruction Act of 1867, 112
Fischer, Claude, 223
Fisher, Abigail, 138
*Fisher v. Texas*, 7, 138, 142, 185, 258 nn41, 47, 276 nn99–100
Flint, Michigan, 123
Florida, 79, 81, 101, 112, 118, 164, 169, 179, 197, 279 nn165, 166, 283 n275
Foreign-Born Blacks: causes of U.S. immigration, 202, 209–12, 213–16; concern about those in country of origin, 15; contribution to struggle in U.S. against racial oppression, 240, 247; countries of origin, 22, 196–97, 209, 215–16, 264 n109; cultural differences from native blacks, 194–95, 199, 201, 216–28; cultural differences of children from native blacks, 228–32; definition, 256 n15; education, 197, 198, 200–01, 258 n48, 304 nn20–21; embraced by native blacks, 31; family characteristics, 9, 15, 194, 197–201; immi-

360  INDEX

gration into Britain, 209–12; impact of McCarran-Walter Act, 209, 212; increases in U.S. population, 4–6, 17, 193, 195–96, 199, 231, 240, 256 n16, 303 n6; more likely to have children, 6, 196; prominent U.S. blacks, 22; understanding of racism, 15, 200, 221–28, 304 n15; where reside in U.S., 197, 204; *see also* Africa, African immigration, Black Immigrants, and Caribbean immigrants
Forman, James, 96
Fort Erie, 124
Fort Mose, 100
Fort Sumter, 108
Forten, James, 104
Founding Fathers, 71
Fourteenth Amendment, 77–78, 81, 111–12, 166, 169–70, 179, 180, 203
France, 12, 75, 145, 163–64, 169, 208–09, 212, 225–26, 305 n51, 308 nn112, 314 n252
Free blacks, 38–39, 68, 70, 73–75, 97, 100–05, 108, 115, 145, 160–64, 168, 203, 272 n28, 295 n124, 296 nn143, 145
Free mulattoes, 145, 158–64, 168, 295 nn124, 128, 296 nn142–43, 148
Freedman's Aid Society of the Methodist Episcopal Church, 119
Freedmen's Bureau, 113
*Freedom Journal*, 121, 284 n285
Freedom riders, 129, 286 n354
*Freeman v. Pitts*, 88
French and Indian War, 163–64

Fryer, Roland, 95, 278 n141, 279 n145
Fugitive Slave Law, 103, 105

*Gaines v. Canada*, 275 n85, 286 n345
Gallup Poll, 5, 148
Garrison, William Lloyd, 106, 125
Garvey, Marcus, 22, 114, 120, 280 n195, 283 n280, 285 n319
Gates, Henry Louis, 7, 151
*Gayle v. Browder*, 129, 275 n89, 286 n350
Genesis, 84, 167, 274 n69, 296 n155
Genovese, Eugene, 99, 279 nn153, 156, 282 n248, 312 n219
Georgia, 71, 79, 92, 103, 112–13, 135, 137, 175, 181–82, 283 n275
Ghana, 4, 197, 209, 213, 216, 256 nn18, 22, 257 n22, 308 n127, 310 n162
Gingrich, Newt, 182
Glazer, Nathan, 199, 305 n41
Gliddon, G.R., 40, 169, 173
Globalization, 6, 208, 261 n79, 262 n86, 313 n238
GMAT, 61
Goddard, H. H., 86
Gonzalez, Henry, 42, 267 n46
Gotanda, Neil, 135, 287 n381, 288 n1
Gould, Benjamin, 172, 298 n204
Graham, Gordon, 181
Graham, Susan, 181, 182
Grandfather Clauses, 80, 125, 285 n331
Grant, Ulysses, 112
*Gratz v. Bollinger*, 264 n111, 314 n9
GRE, 61
Great Depression, 126, 205, 207

Great Migration, 120
*Green v. County School Board*, 89, 275 nn90, 94, 276 n104, 285
*Green v. State*, 297 n190
Griffith, D. W., 141
*Griggs v. Duke Power*, 276 n103
*Grimes v. Sobol*, 287 n383
*Grutter v. Bollinger*, 7, 10–11, 28, 60, 65, 139, 147, 233, 258 n43, 259 n52, 261 n70, 264 n111, 270 nn146–47, 271 n2, 288 n395, 289 n10, 301 n290, 311 n197, 314 n9, 315 n14
*Guardians Association v. Civil Service Commission of New York City*, 276 n105, 277 n118
Guiner, Lani, 7, 151
*Guinn v. United States*, 125, 273 n52, 285 n331
Guyana, 209, 212, 215, 225, 308 n127, 313 n231

Haiti, 75, 101, 107, 121, 163, 197, 207, 209, 212, 215–17, 225–26, 272 n36
Hall, Prince, 22, 117, 282 n260, 283 n261
Halter, Mary, 204, 307 nn79, 81
Ham, 84–85, 115, 274 n68
Hannibal Guard, 108
Harding, Vincent, 101–02, 272 n17, 279 nn150, 167, 169, 280 nn178, 192, 281 n231, 282 n236, 286 n352,
Hart Cellar Act, 6, 31, 194, 202, 207, 212, 214–15
Harvard, 7–8, 86, 151, 167, 173, 259 nn53, 57, 291 n43
Hayes-Tilden Compromise of 1877, 113

Health, Education, and Welfare, 45, 46, 276 n103
Henry, Patrick, 75
Herman, Melissa, 153, 187, 302 n299
Hernandez, Tanya, 137, 264 n115, 288 n391
Hernstein, Richard, 95
Hickman, Christine, 244, 266 n24, 294 n82, 300 n276, 315 n17
Hispanic/Latino: admissions forms, 20, 34, 235–37; definition, 20, 44–48, 49–50, 265 n7; education, 94, 278 n132; EEOC treatment, 57–58; family income, 277 nn125–26; Final Guidance impact on admissions of, 34–35, 58–62, 64, 151, 239, 248; impact of Proposal on admissions prospects, 235, 238–43, 248; inability to differentiate Black Hispanics from other Hispanic/Latinos, 34, 146, 182–83, 185, 233, 259 n58; increases in U.S. population, 54–55, 255 n6, 257 n33, 266 n42, 267 n49; life expectancy, 94; poverty rate, 93–94, 278 n129; recognized only by race, not ethnicity, 3, 151; reporting of separate racial groups by standardized testing agencies, 26; SAT scores, 61, 243, 264 n116; separate racial identities of Hispanic/Latinos not reported to federal government, 20, 34, 57, 59, 146, 182–83, 233, 259 n58; unemployment rate, 93; U.S. Census treatment, 36–38, 41–43, 256 n13, 266

n43, 268 n84, 290 n36; 1970 undercount, 44; *see also* Black Hispanics
Historically Black Colleges and Universities (HBCU), 3, 119, 283 nn272, 274
Hoffman, Connie, 178–79
Hoffman, Frederick, 173, 298 n213
Holistic evaluation, 23–24, 32, 240–41
*Holmes v. Atlanta*, 275 n89
Hoover, Herbert, 125
House of Representatives, 18, 37–38, 75, 77–78, 82, 105, 113, 132–33, 182, 282 n260, 286 n356
Housing and Urban Development, 46
Hovenkamp, Herbert, 174, 274 nn75, 80, 298 n219, 299 n225
Howard, General Oliver, 113
Howard University, 90, 119, 123, 126, 276 n98
Howard University College of Medicine, 3
Humphrey, Richard, 117
Hunt, Stanford, 85, 171–73, 274 n79, 298 n199

I.Q., 86, 222
I.Q. Tests, 86
Ifill, Sherrilyn, 134, 287 n377
Illinois, 74, 124, 127, 169, 182, 197
Immigration: African, 17, 196–97, 200–03, 208–09, 213–16; Asian, 142, 178; avoiding slavery, 74; Caribbean, 196–97, 200–02, 204, 207–10, 212, 215–16; China, 205; increases, 31, 62–63, 142, 184, 200, 205–08, 212–15, 220; Final Guidance not motivated by immigration, 35, 64; Immigration and Naturalization Service, 44; Immigration Act of 1924, 202, 204, 206–07, 306 n58; Immigration Act of 1990, 214, 216, 310 n176; Immigration and Nationality Act Amendments of October 20, 1976, 214; Immigration Reform and Control Act, 214, 215, 310 n174; impact on determining a person's race, 142, 146, 178, 184, 190; Japan, 205; Latin America, 142, 178; Mexico, 41, 207; Middle East, 142, 178, 184; New Orleans, 163; North Africa, 142, 178, 184, 202; Philippines, 205–204; pull factors, 207; push factors, 207; Southern and Eastern Europe, 205–07; West Indies, 161; Western Hemisphere, 204, 207–08, 212, 214–15; *see also* Adult Black Immigrants, Black Immigrants, Chinese Exclusion Acts, classical immigration theory, Diversity Visas, Hart-Cellar Act, Next-Generation Black Immigrants, Refugee Act of March 17, 1980, and segmented immigration theory.
Immigration Act of 1971, 211
Independent Village Guard, 102
Indiana, 74, 170, 175, 182, 197, 297 n188
Indiana University, 8, 123, 151, 259 n59, 291 n46
Indianapolis, 116

*Indianapolis Recorder*, 121
Interagency Committee, 45, 49–50, 52, 267 n58, 268 n94
*Interracial Voice*, 182
Involuntary immigrants, 221–23, 260 n67, 301 n289, 312 n209
Iota Phi Theta Fraternity, 123
Irish Nell, 159
Ivy League, 3, 8, 198

Jackson, Jesse, 58, 181
*Jackson v. Alabama*, 299 n242
Jamaica, 120, 197, 209, 212, 215, 225–26, 231, 251, 261 n79, 262 n86, 308 n127, 312 n228, 313 nn231, 238, 314 n256; *see also* Black Immigrants, Caribbean immigrants, and foreign-born blacks
James, LeBron, 18, 262 n94
Jamestown, 19, 156, 157, 263 n103
Japhet, 84
Jarrett, Valerie, 133
Jarvis, Dr. Edward, 39
Jay, John, 73, 272 n27
Jefferson, Thomas, 75, 103–04, 280 nn183, 189, 191
Jeremy, 101
Jews, 111, 203
Jim Crow, 40, 272 n33, 278 n133, 297 n180
Johnson, Andrew, 111, 113
Johnson, James Weldon, 22, 199, 305 n39
Johnson, John H., 121
Johnson, Lyndon, 27, 36, 44–45, 77, 89–90, 130–31, 133, 276 n98, 305
Johnson, Magic, 18, 262 n92

Johnson, Robert, 17, 133, 262 n92
Joint Center for Political and Economic Studies, 182
Joint Committee on Reconstruction, 77
Jones, Absalom, 104, 116
Jordan, Barbara, 79
Jordan, Michael, 18, 133, 262

Kalmijn, Matthis, 230, 305 n51, 313 nn233, 239, 314 n252
Kappa Alpha Psi Fraternity, 123, 285
Karst, Kenneth, 224, 279 n143, 303 n2
Kennedy, Justice Anthony, 18–19, 39, 92, 214, 263 n102, 277 nn114, 116, 310
Kennedy, John F., 89, 214, 310 n169
Kennedy, Joseph C. G., 39
Kennedy, Randall, 137, 260 n69, 271 n1, 286 n348, 288 nn384, 392
Kentucky, 75, 109, 125, 174, 175, 197, 283 n275, 298 n221, 299 n222
Kenya, 16, 25, 197, 211, 216, 256 n18, 258 n48, 310 n162
*Keyes v. School District No. 1*, 276 nn102, 105
King Jr., Martin Luther, 129–32, 282 n249, 286 n348
*Kinney v. Commonwealth*, 297 n188
Korean minority, 12, 223, 312 n218

Lamarck, Jean Baptiste, 175
Latin Alabama, 164
*Lau v. Nichols*, 276 n103
Law School Admissions Council, 26, 152, 245, 264 n115, 292 n50, 301 n288, 308 n118

Lawrence, Charles, 134–35, 261 n316, 263 n103, 271 n10, 287 n380, 311 n194
Lawyer's Committee on Civil Rights under the Law, 182
League for Nonviolent Civil Disobedience to the Draft, 127
LeConte, Joseph, 173, 298 nn210–11
Lempert, Richard, 10–11
Leong, Nancy, 186, 266 n36, 301 nn284, 291, 294
*The Leopard's Spots*, 141, 288 n1
Leviticus, 84
Levitt, Steven, 95, 279 n145
Liberia, 4, 75, 105, 197, 206–07, 216
Lincoln, Abraham, 75–76, 79–80, 97, 109–11, 124–26, 171, 219, 272 n35–36, 281 n216, 296 n160, 311 n201
Lincoln University, 117
Linnaeus, Carolus, 85
Little Rock, 89
London, 171, 210, 271 n12
Louima, Abner, 217
Louis XV, King, 163
Louisiana, 79–80, 101, 112, 117–18, 130, 163–64, 168–69, 175, 197, 263 n99, 283 n275, 295 n132
Loving, Richard and Mildred 179, 308, 311
*Loving v. Commonwealth*, 300 n256
*Loving v. Virginia*, 5, 30, 146, 177, 179, 181, 257 nn24, 26, 288 n4, 289 nn9, 15, 294 n86, 299 nn235, 40, 47, 300 nn256–57
LSAT, 26, 61, 138–39, 152–53, 185, 245, 263 n107, 270 n149, 288 n3, 292 nn52–53, 57

Lutz, Amy, 8, 198, 260 n62, 278 n142, 279 n144, 303 nn3–4, 305 n34, 311 n206, 312 n208
Lynching, 82, 121–22, 124, 126–27, 175, 285 n318

Maine, 74, 197
Malcolm X, 22, 131, 220, 311 n205
Malone, A. E., 122
Maori, 223
March against fear, 131
March on Washington, 129, 286 n355
Marginal Man Thesis, 176, 181, 299 nn230–31,
Marshall, John, 75
Maryland, 71, 75, 109, 156, 158–60, 175, 181, 197, 283 n275, 286 n345, 294 n88
Maryland antimiscegenation law, 158–60
Massachusetts, 6, 18, 73–74, 106, 117, 124, 156, 160, 162, 196–97, 204, 258 n40, 282 n282
Massachusetts antimiscegenation law, 160
Massey, Douglas S., 151, 259 n54, 260 n60, 291 n39, 304 n29, 313 n244
Matsuda, Mari, 67, 261 n80, 271 nn10–11, 311 n194
*Mayor & City Council of Baltimore v. Dawson*, 275 n89
MCAT, 26, 61, 264 n117
McCarran-Walter Act, 207, 209, 212
McCleskey, Warren, 135–37
*McCleskey v Kemp*, 135–37, 288 nn385, 389–90
McLaughlin, Dewey, 178–79
*McLaughlin v. State*, 299 n244

*McLaurin v. Oklahoma State Regents*, 275 n85, 286 n345
McWhorter, James, 96, 260 n67, 271 n8, 278 n139, 279 n146, 287 n378, 301 n289,
Meharry Medical College, 3
Menendez, Francisco, 100
Meredith, James, 131
*Metro Broad. v. FCC*, 277 n114
Mexican Americans standardized test scores, 26, 243, 264 nn116–17, 270 n148, 315 n16
Mexican American Legal Defense and Education Fund (MALDEF), 57, 60
Mexico, 26, 37, 40–43, 45, 47, 50, 57, 207, 236, 265 n7, 266 n37, 308 n118, 315 n175
Mfume, Kwesi, 181
Miami, 197, 204
Middle East, 45, 47, 49, 52–53, 63, 142, 178, 184, 237, 310 n161
Migration Policy Institute, 200, 262 n86, 264 n109, 304 n13, 305 n37, 313 n238
Millennials, 5, 149, 257 n27, 289 n16
*Miller v. Johnson*, 91, 277 n113
*Milliken v. Bradley*, 276 n102
Mills, Gary, 164, 296 nn143, 146
Minicucci, Stephen D., 242, 258 n48, 259 n58, 265 n4, 270 n132, 291 n44, 304 n20, 315 n10
Miscegenation, 30, 43, 143–45, 156–61, 164–67, 171–73, 175, 177, 289, 293, 294, 296, 297
Miss America, 18, 133, 262 n96
Miss USA, 18, 133, 262 n96

Mississippi, 76, 79, 81, 110, 112–13, 118–19, 130–31, 169, 175, 197, 273 n49, 283 n275
Mississippi River, 163
Missouri, 109, 175, 197, 283 n275
Mobile, 29, 145, 156, 161, 164, 167, 296 n148
Monogenesists, 167
Monroe, James, 101
Montgomery, 129–30, 275 n89, 286 n348
Montgomery, Colonel James, 104
Montgomery Improvement Association, 129
Morgan, Edmund, 157, 272 n15, 279 n159, 281 n206, 293 n79, 294 nn81, 98
Morgan State University, 123
Morton, Samuel, 85, 167, 169, 171–72
Moynihan, Patrick, 199, 305 n41
Mulatto: brain weight, 171–72; buffer class, 156–57, 161–64; census category, 37, 40, 145, 160, 168; Charleston, 161–62; children of wealthy whites, 145, 156, 161–62; concern of miscegenation, 29, 159–60, 166–69, 171–77, 293 n75, 294 n108, 296 n163; definition, 159–60, 165, 294 n99; distinguished from blacks, 144, 145, 156, 161–64, 166–69, 171–75, 293 n77; dominated free black communities, 161, 163–64, 168; Mobile, 164; New Orleans, 163–64; physical differences from blacks, 171–75; psychological issues, 176–77, 301 n281; same as blacks, 100, 145, 157, 159–62, 298 n197; *see*

*also* Black Multiracials and Blacks with Two Races
Multiracial Movement, 30, 146, 177–78, 180–82, 244, 300 n276
Multiracial solidarity march, 182
Munzel, Erica, 11
Murray, Charles, 95, 278 n140
Muslim Moors, 70

NAACP Legal Defense and Education Fund (LDF), 80, 87, 125–28, 131, 134, 274 n84
*Naim v. Naim*, 299 n243
Nation of Islam, 131–32
National Afro-American Council, 122
National Asian Pacific American Legal Consortium, 57
National Association for the Advancement of Colored People (NAACP), 80, 87, 124–28, 181–82, 199, 244, 274 n84, 285 nn319, 326, 331
National Association of Colored Graduate Nurses, 123, 284 n304
National Association of Colored Women, 122
National Banker's Association, 113, 284 n311
The National Baptist Convention, 116
National Bar Association, 123, 284 nn307, 309
National Center on Education Statistics, 94
National Coalition for an Accurate Count of Asians and Pacific Islanders, 53
National Dental Association, 123, 284 n301

National Education Longitudinal Study, 198
National Household Education Surveys' Parent and Family Involvement Survey, 155
National Medical Association, 123, 284 n300
National Negro Business League, 122
National Negro Congress, 126
National Newspaper Publishers Association, 123, 284 n312
National Technical Association, 123, 284 n310
National Urban League, 122, 182, 284 n296
Native Americans, 23, 37–38, 53, 85, 94, 164, 166, 170, 187, 259 n58, 262 n96, 288 n3, 291 n44
Native Hawaiian, 20, 26, 34, 49, 51, 53–55, 170, 237–38, 264 nn108, 117
Naturalization Act of 1790, 203
Nebraska, 78, 175
Negro Plot of 1687, 100
*The Negro as a Soldier*, 171, 274 n79, 298 n199
Netherlands, 75, 308 n112
Nettles, Dr. Michael T., 8, 198
New Bedford, 102, 204
New Bedford Independent Blues, 102
New England, 74, 156, 263 n103, 271 n13, 306 n64
New Hampshire, 73–74, 156
New Jersey, 73–74, 116, 160, 197, 294 n108
New Mexico, 42, 169
New Orleans, 29, 101, 111, 117, 129–30, 145, 156, 161, 163–64, 275 n89, 295 n128, 296 n142

*New Orleans City Park Improvement Ass'n v. Detieg*, 275 n89
New York, 18, 73, 100, 102, 121, 160, 177, 197, 199, 204–05, 212, 217, 230, 256 n21, 259 n51, 276 n105, 279 n163, 280 n182, 281 n203, 289 n5, 303 n1, 305 n40, 309 n158, 310 n168, 312 n222, 313 n243
Newton, Huey, 131
Next Generation Black Immigrants, 217, 228–31
Niagara Movement, 124–25
Nigeria, 197, 209, 213, 216, 221, 225, 251, 256 n18, 260 n67, 301 n289, 308 n127, 310 n162
Nixon, 42, 43, 132
Nixon Administration, 43, 132
Noah, 84
North Africa, 45, 47, 49, 53, 70, 142, 178, 184, 310 n161
North Carolina, 71, 79, 112, 117–19, 125, 129, 156, 160, 175, 283 n275, 313 n237
Northwest Ordinance, 73, 272
Nott, Josiah C., 40, 167–69, 173, 296 n163, 297 n178
Notting Hill, 210
Nottingham, 210

Obama, President Barack, 16, 18, 22, 25, 133, 251, 263 n101, 279 n149
O'Connor, Justice Sandra Day, 7, 10–12, 28, 65, 91, 139, 143, 147, 193, 217, 277 n112
Office of Federal Contract Compliance Programs (OFCCP), 56–58
Office of Management and Budget (OMB), 27, 36, 46, 48–53, 56, 58, 180, 182, 246, 267 n71, 268 n76, 94, 269 n111, 300 nn261, 277
Ogbu, John, 221–22, 226, 260 n67, 301 n289, 312 nn209–10
Omega Psi Phi Fraternity, 123
One-drop rule, 4–5, 13, 25, 30, 37, 40, 51, 61–62, 141–43, 145–47, 165–66, 171, 175–78, 181, 183–84, 187, 190, 242, 244–45, 249, 265 n1, 266 n24, 268 n75, 288 n1, 290 n24, 293 n78, 294 n82, 300 n276, 315 n17
One question format, 47, 60, 242
O'Neal, Stanley, 18, 133
Onwuachi-Willig, Angela, 177, 256 n21, 259 n51, 299 n239
Oppositional cultural theory, 95
Oregon, 74
Oriental Jews, 223
Osborne, Sir Cyril, 210
Other category, 22, 46, 50, 53–55, 58–59, 180, 181, 268 n84, 313 n244, 315 n13
Other Pacific Islander, 20, 26, 34, 53–55, 237–38, 264 nn108, 117

*Pace v. Alabama*, 166, 170, 179, 296 n154, 297 n192
Paddington, 210
Pakistani, 63
*Palmer v. Thompson*, 276 n103
*Parents Involved in Community Schools v. Seattle School District No. 1*, 18, 92, 263 n102, 277 nn116, 123
Park, Robert, 166, 176, 299 nn230, 232
Parker, John J., 125
Parks, Rosa, 129

Parsons, Richard, 18
Pascoe, Peggy, 171
Patrick, Deval, 18, 263 nn98–99
Patterson, David, 18, 263 n99
*Pearson v. Murray*, 286 n345
Pennsylvania, 7–8, 73, 85, 102, 117, 145, 160, 198, 259 n57, 291 n43
*Personnel Administrator of Mass. v. Feeney*, 288 n389
Pew Research Center, 5, 149–50, 257 n257, 289 n16, 290 n29, 315 n13
Phi Beta Sigma Fraternity, Incorporated, 123
Phi Eta Psi, 123, 285 n316
Philadelphia Plan, 132
Pinchback, P. B. S., 22, 263 n99
*Pittsburgh Courier*, 121
*Plessy v. Ferguson*, 81, 274 n58, 295 n127
Plymouth Rock, 220
Poitier, Sidney, 22
Polygenesists, 167
Portes, Alejandro, 220, 289 n5, 303 n1, 311 n207
Post-Racial/Colorblind Era, 18, 29, 70, 90–98, 132–39, 251–52, 278 nn133, 138, 287 nn374, 376
Powell, Colin, 22
Powell, Enoch, 211, 309 n153
Powell, Justice Lewis, 16, 91, 136
President's Committee on Civil Rights, 126, 285 n341
Prison population, 94
The Progressive Baptist Convention, 116
Project RACE, 180–82
Proposal, 19–20, 23, 25, 31, 233–49, 260 n65, 292 n60

Proposed Guidance, 56, 58–59, 269 nn107, 130
Prosser, Gabriel, 101, 279 n169
Provost Marshal General's Bureau, 173, 298 n206
PSAT, 154
Public Law 94-311 (1976), 44
Puerto Rico, 26, 43, 45, 47, 50, 61, 236, 243, 264 nn116–17, 265 n7, 270 n148, 292 n57, 315 n16
Pulaski, Charles, 135

Quadroon balls, 164

Race and Ethnic Standards for Federal Statistics and Administrative Reporting, 27, 36, 46, 267 n66
*Race, Slavery, and Fertility*, 74, 272 n35
Racial Integrity Act, 179–80, 299 n247
Racially ambiguous blacks, 142, 178, 184, 190
Rainbow PUSH, 57
Rainey, Joseph, 113
Randolph, A. Phillip, 126–27, 285
Raymond, Daniel, 74, 272
Reconstruction, 29, 77, 80, 82, 97, 108, 112–14, 120, 166, 169, 171, 273 nn42–43, 281 n213, 282 n234, 295 n134
Reconstruction Amendments, 78, 166, 169
Redman, Charles Lenox, 105
Refugee Act of March 17, 1980, 214
*Regents of University of California v. Bakke*, 16, 90–91, 255, 262 n87, 276 nn101, 106
Remond, Sarah Parker, 105

Republican Party, 43, 78, 80, 110–12, 273 n48, 281 n230
Resistance, 13, 29, 81, 88, 96–99, 102–07, 117, 121, 218, 224
Revels, Hiram, 113
Revisions to the Standards for the Classification of Federal Data on Race and Ethnicity (1997) Revisions, 27–28, 36, 48–53, 55, 57–58, 61, 63, 141–42, 146, 182–84, 267 n71, 268 nn79, 82, 269 n97, 270 n152
Revolutionary War, 68, 70, 73, 101, 103, 162
Reynolds, Grant, 127
Rhode Island, 73–74, 108, 156, 197, 204
Rice, Susan, 133
Richmond County Board of Education, 81
The Rights of All, 121, 124, 130, 195, 210, 273, 306
Ringgold, Samuel, 105
Robinson, Eugene, 17, 133, 262 n89, 287 n371
Rolfe, John, 70, 263 n103, 271 n12
Rong, Xue Lan, 230, 311 n203, 313 n248, 314 nn251, 254
Root, Maria, 51, 268 n93, 289 n14, 299 n233, 302 n302
Rumbaut, Rubén, 220, 311 nn204, 207, 314 n249
Rush, Benjamin, 85, 274
Russwurm, John B., 121

Salem Female Anti-Slavery Society, 106
Sandys, Sir Edwin, 70, 271 n12

SAT, 26, 61, 138, 154–55, 243, 245, 264 n116, 270 n148, 292 nn61, 62, 293 n63, 315 nn16, 20
School desegregation, 18, 88–91, 119, 128–30, 275 nn86, 95, 96, 276 n102, 296 n162; *see also De jure segregation*, Desegregation, Desegregation Era, and segregation
*Schuette v. Coalition to Defend Affirmative Action; Schuette*, 7, 142, 185, 258 n42
Scientific Revolution, 85
Seale, Bobby, 131
Second Confiscation Act, 109
Second Morrill Act, 119
Segmented immigration theory, 220
Segregation, 5, 14, 27, 29, 36, 43, 67–69, 80–84, 87–90, 97–98, 108, 114, 117–19, 121–29, 135, 145, 171, 174, 178, 186, 231, 240, 252, 273 n53, 274 nn62, 75, 275 nn86, 89, 276 nn102, 105, 283 n257, 286 nn345, 354, 287 n370, 295 n141, 298 nn198, 219; *see also De jure segregation*, Desegregation, Desegregation Era, School segregation, and Segregation Era
Segregation Era, 29, 98, 114, 122–24, 127; *see also De jure segregation*, Desegregation, Desegregation Era, School desegregation, and Segregation Era
Senegal River, 66
Seven Years War, 163
Seward, William Henry, 75
Shaler, Nathanial, 173–74, 298 n216

*Shape of the River*, 3, 151, 255 n1
*Shaw v. Reno*, 277 n112
*Shelley v. Kraemer*, 126, 275 n85, 285 n334
Shem, 84
Sherman, General William Tecumseh, 113
Shields, Dennis, 11
Shultz, George, 132
Sigma Gamma Rho Sorority, 123
Sigma Pi Phi, 123, 284 n313
Single Race Blacks, 5, 9, 13, 29, 141–42, 144–45, 149, 152–54, 178, 184–85, 187, 244, 289 n24, 293 nn68, 69, 70; *see also* Blacks
Singleton, Benjamin, 120
*Sipuel v. Oklahoma State Board of Regents*, 275 n85, 286 n345
*Slaughterhouse Cases*, 111, 170, 281 n228
Slavery Abolition Act, 103, 107
Smalls, Robert, 22
Smallwood, Thomas, 103
Smith, Adam, 106, 281 n204
Smith, Tommy, 130
*Smith v. Allwright*, 125, 273 n53, 285 n333
Social Darwinism, 86
Society of Anthropology, 85
Some Other Race (SOR), 50, 53–5, 58, 150, 268 n84, 290 n36, 315 nn13, 21
South Africa, 14, 209, 214, 256 n18, 261 n84, 310 n162
South Carolina, 39, 71, 79, 99–101, 103–04, 108, 112–13, 117–19, 144, 156, 160–62, 169, 197, 263 n98, 283 n275, 287 n373, 295 nn115, 116, 124
Southampton County, 102, 165

*Southern Horrors*, 124
Southern Strategy, 43
Sowell, Thomas, 199, 230, 305 n42, 314 n250
Spain, 42, 100, 163, 212, 236
Spanish, 37, 42–5, 47, 49, 50, 100, 145, 160, 163–64, 202, 255 n7, 265 n7, 279 n165, 305 n51, 314 n252
Special Field Order No. 15, 113
Spirit murdering, 19, 263 n105
Spitzer, Elliot, 18, 263 n99
Springarn, Arthur, 125
Springfield, Illinois, 124
Stampp, Kenneth, 102, 280 n177, 281 n207
*State v. Gibson*, 170, 297 n188–89
St. George Methodist Church, 116
St. Thomas African Episcopal Church, 116
Steward, Barbara, 105
Stonequist, Everett, 166, 176, 299 nn231, 234
Stono Rebellion, 100, 295 n116
Student Nonviolent Coordinating Committee (SNCC), 129, 131
Sub-Sahara Africa, 4, 68, 70, 84, 213, 216, 225–26, 308 n123, 310 n161
Superintendent of the Census, 39
Supplemental statement, 23–25, 32, 234–35, 238–45, 247–49
Supreme Court, 5, 7, 10–11, 24, 26–27, 29, 30, 36, 44–45, 60, 65, 69–70, 73–75, 80–81, 83–84, 87–95, 98, 111, 118, 125–26, 128–30, 132–33, 135–39, 142, 145–46, 166, 170, 174–75, 177–81, 185–86, 193, 203, 233–34, 255 n2, 258 n45,

264 n111, 267 n60, 274 n84, 275 n90, 276 n103, 277 nn112, 118, 285 nn331, 332, 286 n345, 288 n384, 289 n12, 297 n190, 314 n9
*Swann v. Charlotte-Mecklenburg Board of Education*, 89, 276 n104
*Sweatt v. Painter*, 275 n85, 286 n345

Tabulation Working Group, 52, 268 n94
Takaki, Ronald, 227, 313 n236
Taney, Chief Justice Roger, 72
Tennessee, 78, 129, 175, 283 n275
Terman, Lewis, 86
Terrell, Mary Church, 122
Texas, 42, 80, 119, 130, 169, 175, 197, 283 n275
Thatcher, Margaret, 219
Thirteenth Amendment, 76, 77, 81
Thomas, Justice, 91, 258 n45, 276 n99, 277 n110
Thompson, Don, 18
Three fifths, 37–38
Tillman, Ben, 79
Title IV of the Higher Education Act, 33
*To Secure These Rights*, 127, 285 n341
Torrey, Charles T., 103
Tower of Babel, 166
TransAfrica movement, 195
Transatlantic Slave Trade, 4, 71, 104, 107, 195, 202, 204, 225, 251, 257 n22, 271 n4
Transcendents, 17, 133
Treaty of Fontainebleau, 163
Trinidad and Tobago, 197, 209, 212, 215, 225, 308 n127, 313 n231

Trotter, Monroe, 125
Truman, Harry S., 126–27, 177
Truth, Sojourner, 105, 116
Tubman, Harriet, 103–04, 116, 280 n188
Turner, Bishop Henry McNeal, 22, 120
Turner, Nat, 102, 165, 280 n175
Tuskegee Institute, 118
Two or more races, 20, 34–35, 52, 54–62, 64, 147, 151, 182–83, 185, 233–35, 239, 241, 243–48, 259 nn59, 269 n109, 291 nn44, 46
Two parent homes, 155, 196, 252
Two question format, 34, 47, 50, 57–58, 242
*Types of Mankind*, 40, 169, 297 n178

U.S. Bureau of Justice, 94, 278 n134
Unconscious racism, 19, 128, 134–35, 137, 263 n104, 277 n124, 287 nn368, 380
Underground Railroad, 103
Underrepresented racial minority, 11–12, 14, 23–24, 28, 65–66, 137–39, 193, 232, 241, 244–45, 247–48
Unemployment, 93, 214
Union Army, 97, 103, 109–11, 113
Union Leagues, 112
United Kingdom, 208–09, 219, 309 n151; *see also* Britain and England
United States Census
    1790, 36–38, 63, 203, 255 nn6, 10, 265 nn3–14, 272 nn22–23, 288 n2, 289 n17, 295 n124, 306 n71
    1810, 38

1820, 38
1830, 39, 164
1840, 37–39, 168, 265 n14
1850, 37, 39–40, 145, 168, 256 n16, 258 n35, 296, 303 n6, 308 n19
1860, 40, 164
1890, 40, 206
1900, 37, 40, 266 n27
1910, 40
1920, 37, 39–40, 145
1930, 4, 37–38, 40–42, 146, 176, 266 nn37, 39
1940, 40, 42, 266 n40
1950, 41–42, 183
1960, 3, 4, 37, 41–42, 141, 146, 177, 183–84, 193, 196, 231, 255 n10, 256 n13, 289 n18, 303 n6
1970, 27, 36, 37–38, 40–41, 43–44, 183, 202, 255 n6, 256 n13, 265 n13, 267 n49, 272 n23, 278 n132, 288 n2, 289 n18, 303 n7
1980, 146, 149, 183, 257 n29, 289 n18, 290 n29, 303 n7
1990, 49, 52, 149, 154, 181, 183, 230, 255 n6, 256 n16, 258 n35, 265 n13, 272 n23, 288 n2, 292 n58, 295 n115, 303 nn6–7, 305 n54
2000, 13, 28, 30, 36, 48, 50–51, 53, 54, 57–60, 146, 148–51, 178, 180–82, 208 n119, 200–01, 215, 244, 258 n48, 260 n64, 266 nn42–43, 268 nn84, 94–95, 269 n103, 270 n143, 290 nn29, 36, 291 n41, 292 nn49, 58, 303 n7, 305 n46
2010, 6, 48, 50, 53, 55, 148, 150, 185, 196, 257 nn29, 32, 268 n86, 278 nn132, 134, 290 nn29–30, 32, 291 n38, 303 n8, 315, 13, 21
United States Constitution, 35, 37–38, 67, 72, 76–78, 80–81, 91–92, 126, 166, 219, 286 n348, 287 n381, 288 n1, 306 n65
United States Sanitary Commission, 171–73
*United Steelworkers of America v. Weber*, 276 n104
Universal College Application, 235–38, 265 n3, 314 nn3, 6
Universal Negro Improvement Association, 120, 283 n280
University of Michigan Law School, 7, 10, 11
University of Mississippi, 131
University of Pennsylvania, 7, 8, 198, 259 n57, 291 n43
Upshur, Abel, 39, 266 n19
*U.S. v. Bhagat Singh Thind*, 267 n60
Utah, 175, 197

Vermont, 73, 74, 106, 197
Vesey, Denmark, 101–02, 162
Veto, 77
*Village of Arlington Heights v. Metro. Hous. Dev. Corp.*, 276 n105, 277 n118
Virginia, 19, 70–71, 75, 79, 99–103, 109, 112, 119, 130, 157–161, 165, 168, 175, 178–80, 262 n96, 263 nn99, 103, 271 nn12–13, 272 nn15, 24, 279 nn160–61, 283 n275, 284 n288, 293 n77,

294 n95, 297 n188, 299 n247, 306 n64
Virginia antimiscegenation laws, 158
Virginia Colony, 70–71, 102, 156, 159–60, 263 n103
Virginia General Assembly, 157
Voting Rights Act, 44, 89, 92, 130, 186, 252

Waihee, John, 53
Walker, David, 105, 115, 165, 281 n199
Walker, Madame C. J., 122, 284 n290
Walters, Bishop Alexander, 125
Warren, Chief Justice Earl, 87, 128, 180
Washington, Booker T., 22, 118, 122, 175, 283 n269
Washington Society of Colored Dentists, 123
*Washington v. Davis*, 132, 133, 276 n105, 277 n118
Waters, Mary C., 226, 229, 230, 289 n5, 303 n1, 305, n43, 306 n68, 307 n85, 308 n116, 309 n160, 312 n226, 313 nn228, 230, 232, 234, 242, 247, 314 n256
*Wealth of Nations*, 106, 281 n204
Webster, Daniel, 75
Weinberger, Caspar, 45
Wells, Ida B., 124–25, 285 n319
*West Chester & P. R. Co. v. Miles*, 289 n7
West Virginia, 197, 283 n275
White abolitionists, 75, 105, 106
White, George, 79
White privilege, 4, 9, 19, 154, 181, 300 n276

White, Steve & Ruth Bryant, 180, 182
White, Walter, 22, 125, 126, 244, 315 n19
Wilberforce University, 117
Williams, Kim, 180, 257 n23, 268 nn88–89, 270 n144, 289 n11, 300 nn261–62, 266, 269, 301 nn279, 281
*Williams v. Mississippi*, 80, 273 n51
Winfrey, Oprah, 17, 133, 262 nn91–92, 94
Women's Political Council, 129
Woods, Tiger, 18, 187, 262 nn92, 94, 301 n296
Woodson, Carter G., 144, 283 n261, 289 n6, 294 nn90, 94, 96, 295 n129
Woodworth, George, 135
World War I, 69, 83, 86, 120, 122, 176, 204
World War II, 80, 83, 86, 208, 209, 213, 223, 298 n203
*Wygant v. Jackson Board of Education*, 277 n121

Yerkes, R. M., 86
Youman, Edward, 174
Young, Andrew, 79

Zeta Phi Beta Sorority, Incorporated, 123

1866 Civil Rights Act, 77, 78, 111, 166, 169, 170, 273 n45, 297 nn182, 190, 306 n76
1964 Civil Rights Act, 44, 88–89, 130, 186, 252, 276 nn103, 105, 277 n118

1965 Voting Rights Act, 44, 89, 130, 186, 252
1968 Fair Housing Act, 44, 89
1968 Mexico City Olympics, 131
1990 Immigration Act, 214, 216, 310 n176, 311 n190
1997 Revisions, 27, 28, 36, 48–50, 52–53, 55, 57–58, 61, 63, 141–42, 146, 182–84, 267 n71, 268 nn79, 82, 269 n97, 270 n152, 310 n161

WITHDRAWN

JAN 2 1 2016